❦ Moving Europeans

Interdisciplinary Studies in History

Harvey J. Graff,
GENERAL EDITOR

Moving Europeans

Migration in Western Europe since 1650

Leslie Page Moch

INDIANA UNIVERSITY PRESS
Bloomington & Indianapolis

The paper used in this publication meets the minimum requirements of American National Standard for Information Sciences—Permanence of Paper for Printed Library Materials, ANSI Z39.48-1984.

⊗™

Manufactured in the United States of America

Library of Congress Cataloging-in-Publication Data

Moch, Leslie Page.
    Moving Europeans : migration in Western Europe since 1650 / Leslie Page Moch.
       p. cm. — (Interdisciplinary studies in history)
    Includes bibliographical references and index.
    ISBN 0-253-33859-X (alk. paper)
    1. Europe—Emigration and immigration—History. I. Title.
II. Series.
JV7590.M63   1992   92-6678
304.8'094—dc20

1 2 3 4 5 96 95 94 93 92

For my parents,
Walter Howard Page
and
Genevieve Schroeder Page

❦ C O N T E N T S

Acknowledgments   *xi*

1. Putting Migration into History   1

Explaining Migration Patterns   6
Region, State, and City   9
Individuals, Social Relations, and Migration Systems   13
Definitions and Data   18

2. Migration in Preindustrial Europe   22

The Character of the Age   23
The Politics of Migration: War, Empire, and
Intolerance   26
Migration in the Preindustrial Countryside   30
    Family, Service, and Marriage   30
    Inheritance and Landholding   36
Portrait of a Migration System   40
Movement to the Preindustrial City   43
Conclusion   58

3. Migration in the Age of Early Industry   60

The Character of the Age: Politics, Population,
and Landholding   63
"Hybrid Societies" and the Family Economy   68
Early Industry and Migration   70
The Expansion of Temporary Migration   76
Portrait of a Migration System   83
Vagrancy, Crime, and Illegitimacy:

The Marginal Migrant   88
Migration to Eighteenth-Century Towns and Cities   93
Conclusion   99

**4. Migration in an Age of Urbanization
and Industrialization   103**

The Character of the Age: War, Peace, and
Migration   105
Rural Europe   108
  Population and Landholding in the Nineteenth
  Century   108
  The Disintegration of Rural Livelihoods   111
  Changing Patterns of Circular Migration   120
  The Example of East Elbia   123
Migration and Urbanization   126
  Migrants and the Urban Economy   131
  Crime and Illegitimacy: The Marginal Migrant   143
Migration to the Americas   147
  Patterns of Transatlantic Migration   147
  A Global Labor Force   149
  The Process of Transatlantic Migration   153
Conclusion   158

5. Migration in the Twentieth Century   161

Migration among European Nations, 1914–1945   164
Population, Migration, and Urbanization after 1914   170
Foreign Labor in Postwar Europe   174
From Migrant Labor to EEC Partners:
The Portuguese in France   184
From Migrant Labor to Ethnic Minority: The Turks
in Germany   185
Conclusion   189

  Notes   193
  Bibliography   235
  Index   251

Maps

1:1 Regions and Cities Emphasized in Text   3
2:1 Western Europe in 1650   24
3:1 Western Europe in 1750   63
3:2 Rural Industry in Eighteenth-Century Europe   71
3:3 Temporary Migration Systems in Western Europe, ca. 1800   77
4:1 Western Europe, 1871–1914   110
4:2 European Cities of 100,000 or More in 1800 and 1900   126

Tables

2:1 Incidence of Migration in Southern and Midland England,
    1660–1730   31
3:1 Estimated Population Growth in Northwestern Europe,
    1750–1800   65
4:1 Estimated Population Growth in Western Europe, 1800–1910   109
5:1 Foreigners Residing in Selected European Countries by
    Country of Citizenship and Labor Force Participation,
    Early 1960s, Early 1970s, and 1981   178

Acknowledgments

This study of migration in western Europe presents and interprets patterns of human mobility since 1650. I take the long view to create a general framework for understanding migration. This perspective allows me to delineate the shape and direction of changes in human mobility, but it necessitates that I do so at the expense of describing the myriad regional variations that affected patterns of mobility, such as the variety of agricultural routines, inheritance practices, and local economies. History interweaves change with continuity; this study highlights shifts in the migration routines of European men and women, while recognizing that some practices, such as short-distance moves at the time of marriage, persisted from one period to another.

Moving Europeans relates the story of European migration for a general audience, while examining the connections between human mobility and historical change. It also may serve as a sounding board for the findings and theories of advanced students and migration scholars.

I am delighted to acknowledge the debts incurred in the creation of this book. The interpretation of migration history is my own, but I have leaned heavily on the writings of other scholars, employing case studies to illustrate and enliven this study. I am grateful to the authors whose books and articles made this general interpretive history possible. A summer stipend from the National Endowment for the Humanities, a summer faculty fellowship from the Rackham School of Graduate Studies at the University of Michigan, a semester's research leave from the University of Michigan—Flint, and a research project award from the Graduate School of the University of Texas at Arlington supported the writing of this study.

Colleagues provided thought-provoking feedback at meetings of the Social Science History Association. I would also like to thank those who heard me out and exchanged ideas at the social history seminar at Southern Methodist University, meetings of the conference on the European fertility decline, the seminar on international migration at M. I. T.'s Center for International Studies, faculty colloquia at the University of Michigan—Flint, department seminars at Michigan State University's history department, the women's studies seminar at the University of Arizona, the emigration colloquium in Le Châble, Switzerland, and the migration symposium in Bremerhaven, Germany.

Because scholarship is best done in community, I am particularly grateful to the supportive and inquisitive network of historians in Michigan that consistently offers stimulating conversation. The community of scholars extends from San Diego to New York City and from Maine to Texas as well. Several historians from this far-flung network took valuable time from their own work to comment on previous versions of this manuscript. Harvey Graff encouraged me to undertake this project and has been a faithful friend throughout. Rachel Fuchs and Anne Meyering had the fortitude to read and the kindness to critique the entire draft manuscript. Scholars of German migration Steve Hochstadt and James Jackson, Jr., made insightful and challenging suggestions based on their thorough knowledge of German migration patterns. Charles Tilly gave me invaluable friendly encouragement, then broad insights that cast a new light on the manuscript. Colleagues Robert Heywood and Theodosia Robertson each offered the perspective of a general reader as well as comments from their respective areas of expertise. Nora Faires made astute conceptual and editorial suggestions. I am immeasurably grateful to these readers. I hasten to add that the shortcomings of this study rest with none of them, but rather with me.

Although colleagues provide the community so crucial to scholarship, writing is a solitary act that inevitably impinges upon one's household. I would like to thank Michael Moch and our daughter Sarah Page Moch for their kind support and patience. Perhaps life would be more tidy without their gentle yet persistent diversions, but it would also be rather narrow.

My most fundamental debt remains to my beloved parents, Genevieve Schroeder Page and Walter Howard Page. In deepest gratitude I dedicate this book to them.

❦ Moving
Europeans

CHAPTER

1

Putting Migration into History

The young men of Pradelles knew from an early age that they would leave home. The thin soil and long winters in their village—nestled high on the south slope of France's central highlands—could not support even its 220 souls year-round. After planting, many of the men from about age 16 upwards traveled to the Mediterranean plain to labor in the vineyards and fields while the women and elders of the village took on their labors. When upland harvests began, the men returned with a gold piece or two toward their family's tax debts, their sisters' dowries, or a plot of land. They knew about the dangers of the road—especially terrifying when the village men were in possession of their pay or had to travel alone. One of the older migrants from Pradelles had perished by the road from hunger and exposure on his way home. A more fortunate single man had come into property with richer soil and a better climate when he married the daughter of a lowlands peasant who had no sons. So it was with mixed emotions that the families of Pradelles sent their men on this grueling annual adventure.[1]

The men of Pradelles do not fit a common understanding of the eighteenth-century peasant life, because they left home. Yet leaving home was as much a part of life in this village as were the fields of home. Some peasants in this region expected to quit their area for a season in the 1730s, others were certain to leave home for good. A surprisingly large proportion left the village of their birth. Our image of a sedentary Europe, then, is seriously flawed. People were on the move; and where and why they traveled tells us a good bit about the past and about the pressures and processes that produced the world with which we are familiar. Human movement is connected to every level of life in western Europe—from the intimacy of family decisions about how cash will be earned to the global scale, where it reflects Europe's place in the world economy. Migration, in short, connects the changes in European history with the lives of men and women in the past.

Our understanding of history alters dramatically with the realization that its actors were not sedentary. Village life is more lively when we realize that the rural community was constantly renewed by new people from the region who bought land, rented farms, married, and hired on as farmhands. Simultaneously, villagers of all ages, but especially young men and women, were likely to depart for a season or for a lifetime. Our view of the building and growth of the cities of Europe and of the rise of the modern state takes on a new cast when we realize that country folk and people from small towns built the expanding cities of the eighteenth and nineteenth centuries. Some went home when their job was completed, but others returned annually for more work in the construction trades, and still others took up long-term residence in the city. As the modern state grew, bureaucracy expanded, employing great numbers of office workers, postal clerks, schoolteachers, railroad workers, and municipal laborers. In the nineteenth century, these people rarely followed in the footsteps of their parents; rather, the sons and daughters of rural and small-town workers sought jobs that were more secure than those of their parents. This view is neither as Whiggish nor as benign as it may seem, for not everyone who left home was a success. Moreover, poverty, insecurity, and misfortune themselves sent people on the road. Stability was a privilege.

Three centuries ago, western Europe was a sparsely populated rural society in which the vast majority of men and women inhabited small villages and hamlets. In order to produce sufficient food, most folk had to be engaged in agricultural production of one kind or another. The distribution of people over the landscape has changed fundamentally since the seventeenth century; namely, Europe is now more heavily populated and its people are spaced less evenly than in early modern times. The population is concentrated in large cities and in conurbations such as the Paris region, greater London, and the urban centers that run from the Ruhr through the Netherlands. A relatively small fraction of the people of Europe currently provides food for the rest.

This book analyzes the migrations of western Europeans during these three centuries of change; it does so in terms of four periods that fit in a general way with economic change. The first of these extends from c. 1650 to c. 1750, which I will call the "preindustrial" period; this falls between the devastations of the Thirty Years' War in Germany and the beginning of the intense population increase and proliferation of rural industry that was to mark the eighteenth century. Peasant ownership was an important pattern of landholding, population growth was generally insignificant, most rural production was for local consumption, and there was relatively little capital outside the great cities. Yet movement was a normal part of rural routines as young people sought work in agriculture, harvest teams moved across the countryside, and people moved to marry or acquire land; cities could not maintain their numbers without the intrepid newcomers who streamed through their gates.

To describe the migration itineraries in this period, I focus especially

Map 1:1 Regions and Cities Emphasized in Text

on the rural English midlands, Artois in northern France, Tuscany, and parishes just south of Stockholm. I draw on the German cities of western and central Europe, London, and Amsterdam and sketch the migration systems linking German Westphalia to the western Netherlands. (See Map 1:1.)

The intensification of rural industrial production and the increase in population introduce the second period, c. 1750 to c. 1815. Rural industry is the focus of this period, concentrating in the eighteenth century. A prolonged population increase particularly characterized regions where rural industry employed adult males and their families. Dependence on wage work and population expansion together increased the proportion of landless workers in the countryside, so the rural proletariat grew more than the peasantry. The countryside was alive with movement as men and women found work in booming industrial villages and small towns that could retain and support increased numbers; however, those countrysides that lacked manufacturing simply could not support so many villagers, so they put many people on the road. As a result, workers in seasonal and temporary migration systems, like the men of Pradelles, expanded their numbers.[2]

The analysis of this period's migration routines emphasizes rural industrial villages in Normandy, the English midlands, today's Belgium, and the Vienna highlands. Bordeaux in southwestern France and the industrial towns of Norman Rouen and Belgian Verviers provide the focus for urban areas. In addition, I portray a migration system that connected the men of the French highlands with the realm of Spain.

The third age is the premier age of urbanization, characterized by new and larger cities and coinciding with the period c. 1815 to c. 1914, roughly the nineteenth century. Migration shifted with the growth of machine production that centralized industry and the accompanying increase in commerce and urban services. Although the machine age has drawn attention to the city where capital and the demand for labor concentrated, patterns of rural production are a key to the shift in nineteenth-century migration patterns. Rural areas deindustrialized, collapsing in the face of competition from less expensive machine-produced goods. At the same time, the continuing population boom and expansion of capitalist agriculture created a larger rural proletariat and made agricultural work more seasonal with short-term tasks.[3] This combination was devastating to rural livelihoods. These changes in nineteenth-century demography and labor demands created an urbanized labor force and the urban world that is familiar to us today. However, the transition from rural population growth and economic decline on one hand to increased urban labor demands on the other was not a smooth one. Insecurity kept people on the road and many European workers vacillated between countryside and city. In addition, crises at home brought Europeans into the global labor market in greater numbers than in any time in history. Portuguese, Scandinavians, British, Italians, Poles, and Germans, especially, found work in North and South America.[4]

When describing the migration changes in this period, I focus especially on the deindustrializing countrysides of Normandy and Languedoc as well as the prosperous agrarian areas of Prussia and northern France. I emphasize the growing cities of French Roubaix, German Duisburg, and Cologne. In addition, I single out the links between Polish territories in the Austro-Hungarian Empire and eastern Prussia and western Germany and the United States.

The fourth period in migration patterns began when the outbreak of World War I abruptly stopped international migrations. The final period, c. 1914 to the present, began with a "thirty years' war" that depressed human movements, a period of economic and demographic stagnation during which state policy discouraged migration across national borders. With the war of 1914, countries had little desire for men of other nations on their soil and needed their own citizens at hand to serve as soldiers. Ten years later, migration from Europe to the western hemisphere was severely restricted as the United States adopted restrictive migration quotas. On the other hand, wars and forced displacements caused more movement on the Continent between 1919 and 1949 in absolute numbers than any other time in history.

In the postwar age, a string of conurbations came to dominate the cities in western Europe and urbanism pervaded the Continent. The countryside became less agricultural and more the site of leisure activities than before; like many cities, it now emphasized its service and touristic functions at the expense of its productive ones. Demographic stagnation and economic expansion made the Continent hungry for workers in the boom years of the 1960s and 1970s. There was still an impulse to leave a fast-growing rural population for work in the European city, but the new urbanites were not from the European countryside, where birthrates are low, but from the less developed areas of the Mediterranean basin and from former European colonies. The history of migration in Europe will help explain the nature of recent migration between places like Turkey and Germany, or Portugal and France; it will also clarify differences between past experience and the present.

In describing the international migrations of the twentieth century, I emphasize the movement of foreign nationals into France and Germany. In the case of France, first Belgians and Italians, then Portuguese and North Africans are important. In the case of Germany, first the Poles, then wartime-forced laborers, and then postwar Turks and Eastern Europeans are emphasized.

This plethora of migrations raises a series of questions about the relocation of people throughout history. Who was likely to move? When people moved in past centuries, where did they go? Why did they move? What impact did their movements have on society? How has the frequency, range, and permanence of movement been altered over the years? Aside from the *patterns* of movement, what can we know about the *process* of movement in the past? How did people decide to leave home and where to go? What bearing did their familial and social relationships have on migrations?

In the past decade, it has become clear that people have long moved in a variety of ways. Harvest workers have gathered crops at the culmination of the agricultural cycle; others have moved to countryside or city to earn cash for a period of a few years. Some rural people have always moved to the city, just as city dwellers have moved to other urban areas. Europeans long have departed their continent for other parts of the globe and more recently have attracted African and Asian neighbors. In short, there have always existed seasonal, temporary, rural-rural, rural-urban, and urban-urban migration, alongside emigration from and immigration to Europe. Migrations are not a signal of the modern age but rather "continuous phenomena which are embedded in the social and economic framework of human organization," and as a consequence, they are part and parcel of the history of Europe.[5] But the movement of people has varied extensively over the centuries, and the balance among kinds of migration has changed over time. This book seeks to explain why European migrations have changed, and how.

Change in European migration patterns has been both geographically uneven and temporally discontinuous. The large-scale changes in rural work, land ownership, and urbanization, for example, affected Britain and the low countries long before they came to the eastern territories of Germany or central France. Moreover, great port cities and their hinterland were in the forefront of the economic and social changes that reshaped migration itineraries. The differences in development that moved from west to east and distinguished port city from provincial capital produced a variety of migration patterns at any given time. Temporally, continuity and change in migration patterns interplayed to produce changes in mobility patterns, on one hand, simultaneous with enduring migration traditions, on the other. As a consequence, alongside new patterns of movement to new destinations, there existed familiar, long-standing migration itineraries.

EXPLAINING MIGRATION PATTERNS

To investigate such a sweeping issue as migration over a period of three centuries requires analysis at several levels, for only a multilayered perspective can get at the economic, demographic, and social aspects of change in human mobility. In general, I view the evolution of migration in terms of the fundamental structures of European economic life: landholding, employment, demographic patterns, and the deployment of capital. I also consider individual traits that affected the likelihood of moving, such as life cycle, class, and gender. Because mobility has significant social aspects, the context of family, village, and migration system is important as well. On the most general level, European mobility exists in a world-system in which Europe exploited human and natural resources beginning in the sixteenth century, acted as an exporter of labor to a world labor market in the nineteenth century, and then imported labor in the twentieth century.

The global and local levels of this study are complementary. Within large-scale economic frameworks that circumscribed the limits of the possible, European men and women chose to move, or not to move, in the context of their own village, family, and belief systems. If we focus on the macroeconomic level alone, we lose the actors who are essential to this drama, dismissing their agendas and denying the factor of human agency. If we focus on the personal alone, we miss the opportunity to connect migration with historical change. But when we see both the broader economy and the personal context of migration, our understanding of the process is profoundly enhanced.

In this volume, I argue that changes in migration patterns since the seventeenth century originate in large-scale changes in landholding patterns, employment demands, demographic patterns, and the location of capital. In a model of historical change, these structural variables are the scaffolding of migration patterns. I begin with the countryside, where the vast majority of Europeans resided in the seventeenth and eighteenth centuries. Among the structural factors that immediately affected the ability of rural people to survive was land ownership.

Land ownership bound free peasants to their property. Ironically, the ownership of land periodically expelled some rural people (like the peasants of Pradelles) to earn cash to buy more parcels of land and, increasingly, to pay taxes on their possessions. During the eighteenth and nineteenth centuries, many peasants became rural proletarians by losing their landholdings. For some this was a quick transition brought on by selling out to a large landowner and renting a cottage; for others, becoming a proletarian was a long and gradual loss of acreage. By either route, those who became proletarians lost an essential tie with the land; these men and women were those most likely to be part of the mobile masses of modern Europe.[6] Proletarian status is often associated with urban, industrial settings, but it is also a key to the history of rural life and mobility. As Charles Tilly observed, "over the whole history of capitalism, indeed, agriculture and rural industry have provided the main sites for proletarianization."[7]

The amount and type of work available in the countryside also shaped people's ability to support themselves at home. In the seventeenth century, rural areas largely produced their own clothing and tools; the production of these goods supported village artisans and kept villagers spinning, weaving, carving wooden shoes, and producing tools in winter months. Then from the close of this century and increasingly through the next, rural industry expanded dramatically; in some regions production for distant markets far outstripped production of goods to meet local needs. Consequently, many more rural folk could earn cash at home than before. Where rural industry blossomed, a greater population—an increasingly proletarian one—could be supported at home. However, the market for rural handcrafted products collapsed when massive factory production arose in the nineteenth century; its demise foreclosed the livelihoods of many rural people.

Third, rural population patterns determined just how crowded the countryside was. In the seventeenth century, the European marriage pattern held: marriage was late and far from universal, limiting fertility.[8] High mortality, exacerbated by periodic crises of disease and famine, helped to create a sparsely populated continent. But in the eighteenth century, the disappearance of the Black Plague and reduction in famines lessened mortality. In addition, as rural industry expanded in the countryside, villages swelled with in-migrants in some regions; large families increased because people were more likely to marry and to do so at a younger age, and fewer children died. In this way, rural population patterns acted in concert with rural employment to create a full countryside by 1850.

Rural landholding patterns, employment, and demographic trends all reflect the distribution of capital. In the seventeenth century, European capital was relatively scarce and diffused, outside of the important world trade centers such as Amsterdam and London. With the growth of rural industry, capital flowed to the European countryside where it was distributed in the form of raw materials and paid to village workers, penny by penny. With the rise of trade and factory production between 1790 and 1940, European capital shifted from a dispersed and agriculturally based mode to a concentrated and urban pattern. It is the shift and focus of capital that had the power, in the end, to arrest the vacillation of rural people between agriculture and urban work, pulling them into full-time, year-round jobs in mines, mills, offices, and workshops.

What role do cities play in this story? On the face of it, the city is the long-term gainer, ultimately housing the lion's share of the European population. The starring role of urban areas is based on their growing demand for labor. They became increasingly the locus of innovation for capital— the site of commercial undertakings, node for rural production, site of burgeoning textile mills, then locus of the iron and steel mills that dominated heavy industry by the late nineteenth century. Capital cities like London, Amsterdam, and Paris long required the bureaucrats, functionaries, and services that came to be needed only in the nineteenth century in more remote administrative locations.

Ironically, the role of migration in city growth declined by the time of the triumph of urbanization in the twentieth century. In the early modern period, cities had very high death rates and too few births; as a consequence, only by attracting migrants could cities grow. Crowds of young people who came to the city maintained urban populations by their sheer numbers—because many young men and women neither married nor bore children, but departed the city or died without having done so. Although many newcomers married and bore children in the city, this was not the rule.[9] But gradually, cities became healthier places, less dependent on newcomers to maintain or increase their populations. As sanitary water and sewage systems were installed in the later nineteenth century, urban areas became healthy even for infants and children.

REGION, STATE, AND CITY

This book focuses on the commonalities of migration patterns in western Europe. The general rhythms and patterns of migration responded similarly to the economic and social forces that have transformed city and countryside since 1650: the growth of capital cities, proliferation of rural industry, long-term population growth, creation of factory industry and the industrial town, and the burgeoning of the service conurbation. Yet trends and patterns of mobility clearly varied considerably from region to region; for example, local, circular migration characterized some seventeenth-century regions, while long-distance chain migrations systems joined other regions to distant locations—and each was affected differently by the impulse of rural industry and the population increases of the eighteenth century. Allowing for such differences, this book will emphasize the factors that produced changes in the dominant patterns of human movement since 1650. It will focus on western Europe, because, since the seventeenth century, most of the people of western Europe have been free to move. By contrast, the rural people of central Europe were bound more tightly to their lord's domain by the "second serfdom" of the sixteenth century and were less free to relocate until the nineteenth century.[10] Consequently, I concentrate on territories west of the Elbe River to the north and the Adriatic sea to the south, emphasizing first France, Germany, Belgium, the Netherlands, and England, then Italy, Scandinavia, and Iberia. In addition, I include migration systems from eastern Europe and the Mediterranean basin that entered western Europe in the nineteenth and twentieth centuries.

The region constitutes the primary unit of discussion. It is best suited to the study of migration because the vast majority of human movement occurred within regions, and regions varied enormously one from the other. Most important, the region is the best level at which to discern economic and demographic change. For example, it was areas in the Rhineland, Flanders, Saxony, and Normandy that developed a great need for cottage workers in the late seventeenth and eighteenth centuries, not the whole of France or the German states. It was the Rhine-Ruhr zone that created a need for urban industrial, service, and construction workers at the end of the nineteenth century, drawing people from other regions where employment was on the wane. A regional perspective enables us to see shifts in migration systems that supplied these growing cities. Until the recent past, regions were distinct in demographic as well as in economic terms.[11]

The European state, in its multiple forms, played fundamental roles in migration.[12] States have long articulated policies toward moving peoples, rejecting some and welcoming others; early examples include the *reconquista* of Spain that expelled Jews and Moors in the late fifteenth century and the Dutch policies that provided relief from taxes and citizenship fees as incentives to French Protestants in the seventeenth century.[13] Migration policies have been most important in the twentieth century: movement from southern and eastern Europe was stifled when the United States curtailed migration in 1924; on the Continent, states have excluded or controlled ethnic groups like the Poles in German states before World War I or the Germans in Poland after World War II. The postwar policies of the Western European countries toward workers from Italy, Spain, Portugal, North Africa, Greece, and Turkey have shaped migration systems—albeit without controlling them. The opening of borders among European Economic Community countries effectively creates a single European labor force. The recent opening of Eastern Europe released a flood of migrants into the west whose movements had been repressed since the end of World War II.

Internal state politics also influenced migration patterns early on by shaping agrarian regimes and, as a consequence, patterns of mobility as well. In England, powerful landowners consolidated holdings at the expense of small peasant proprietors without constraint from the crown beginning in the seventeenth century.[14] Here, early capital investment in the countryside increased agricultural productivity at the expense of peasant smallholders, producing a larger proportion of rural proletarians than on the Continent. Consequently, the English were exempt from both the subsistence crises that continued to plague the Continent and from the constraints on property ownership placed on marriage and childbearing. The English population increased more than any other in the eighteenth century; its villages and towns came to rely on emigration to the new worlds and migration to the cities and towns. By contrast, the strategy of the French absolutist state was to extract maximum tax revenues from the peasantry; this inhibited the consolidation of landholdings and thereby prolonged the existence of smallholders. As a consequence, the landowning rural classes were relatively robust in eighteenth- and nineteenth-century France, and probably more geographically stable than the English (although given to temporary migration to earn money). This landholding peasant population had an incentive to control births and, with a relatively small population increase, was less likely to emigrate to the Americas than other Europeans.[15]

Resource-hungry states set off movements as they sought to extract money and cannon fodder from their people. For centuries, landholders sought work away from their home villages in order to pay their taxes and dues; this was particularly true in France, where a centralized national state demanded heavy tax revenues. In the nineteenth century, many Europeans claimed to have sought a home in the Americas especially because they could avoid high taxes; after all, taxation of colonies was a primary issue in the American War of Independence. Army service moved large contingents of young men from their home, sometimes to distant shores. Before 1700 these were most likely to have been mercenaries like the famous Swiss warriors down from mountain villages. Subsequently, conscription and pay increasingly drew young nationals to their state armies. The conscripted were legion: some 600,000 men in Napoleon's multinational Grand Army entered Russia in 1812, and by 1900, over 6 percent of French and German men aged 20 to 44 were serving in their armed forces.[16] Likewise, dodging conscription inspired many a departure for a few months or for the dangerous years of their twenties. For young men coming of age during the Napoleonic wars or around 1848 in the German states, conscription was an important inspiration to decamp.[17] Strategically timed migrations should be added to the "weapons of the weak."[18]

State colonial and mercantile policies affected migration in each period of this study. Early on, the Spanish empire fueled the European economy with its specie and drew workers to the wealthy cities of Antwerp in the Spanish Netherlands and Seville in Spain. In the sixteenth and seventeenth centuries, as the countries of western Europe emerged as a dominant core in a world system, "for the first time the world began to be one migratory network dominated by a single group of technologically advanced and culturally similar states."[19] In the seventeenth and eighteenth centuries, the Dutch and British empires drew off thousands of people through their ports, creating a far-reaching demand for labor in their capital cities. Abroad, Europeans set off labor movements of native peoples in Asia and the Americas and engendered an enormous forced movement of enslaved Africans.[20] In the short period between 1876 and 1915, as a half-dozen states "distributed or redistributed" about a quarter of the world's land surfaces, the colonial holdings of Belgium, Britain, France, Germany, Italy, and the Netherlands expanded to unprecedented degrees.[21] These colonies literally came home to roost, particularly in the largest imperial power of Britain, as colonials of European and native descent moved into Western Europe in the decades after World War II.

Migrations permeate the wars, political oppression, and religious persecutions of the European past. The emigration of Puritans from England, the Thirty Years' War, and Louis XIV's persecution of Protestants all produced massive movements of men and women who sought safe havens during the seventeenth century. The French Revolution and Napoleonic wars may have moved fewer people than the events of the seventeenth century, but these conflicts irrevocably disrupted existing patterns of movement. In the late nineteenth century, Czarist pogroms reversed the movements of Jews to the east that had come in the wake of the post-plague persecutions of the Middle Ages, and Jews fled to western Europe and North America. In the twentieth century, the tenets of the Versailles treaty and the repercussions of World War II caused unprecedented population movements.

This study will put these dislocations in the context of a broader history of migration. It will emphasize the systems of mobility that existed in times of peace, the relatively quotidian and invisible movements, rather than the forced movement of peoples dislocated by war and persecution; the persecuted have been studied masterfully by others.[22] I nonetheless recognize that state power is intimately linked with human movement, for "what we in blithe retrospect call 'state formation' included the setting of ruthless tax farmers against poor peasants and artisans . . . the loosing of brutal soldiers on a hapless civilian population, the conscription of young men who were their parents' main hope for comfort in old age . . . and the imposition of religious conformity in the name of public order and morality."[23]

More benign, but extremely important to the mobility of Europe's men, was state expenditure on public works. The princely tradition of construction recruited workers for Versailles and Leningrad in the seventeenth and eighteenth centuries, for example. Infrastructure construction accelerated in Britain, then on the continent, in the nineteenth century. Armies of foreign and native-born navvies crossed the countrysides and dug into cities to provide canals, roads, railroad systems, new public buildings, piped water, and sewage systems. The improved transportation infrastructure in turn facilitated the movement of women and children over great distances.

The role of migration in the history of the European city provides an important subplot to this work. In the seventeenth century, the growth of cities was substantial—particularly the large capital and commercial cities. After 1750, rural populations expanded, and while many rural people took to the road and ultimately lived in cities, burgeoning rural industries provided a living for unprecedented numbers of people in the countryside. With the nineteenth century came massive urbanization and the growth, once again, of the great old cities and of the highly visible new industrial towns. This resulted in the cities of our day and our thoroughly urbanized world, one in which the rural population pressure that pushes people away from home and into the city is no longer that of northwestern Europe, but the population growth of North Africa, southern Europe, and the eastern Mediterranean.

The victory of the city is neither complete nor simple. Although it seems to have pulled masses of people from the countryside to permanent urban lives, the history of labor demands, urban geography, and demography all indicate that migration to the city was complex, entailing far more than a one-time rural-urban move for most people. There was a great volume of seasonal movement between city and countryside caused by the power of agricultural work to draw urban dwellers out to harvest and by the seasonal nature of many urban jobs, from construction work to early textile mill employment. Rural and small-town people worked in cities for a few years as, for example, domestic servants, water carriers, or construction workers. Temporary movement is vastly underrated.[24] Moreover, for the multitudes of historical actors who moved—often routinely—between country and city, the rural-urban dichotomy is more a statistical chimera than a reality. Others, even once settled in the city, continued to grow their own vegetables and take food, family gatherings, and leisure in rural homeplaces.

As cities outgrew their old boundaries, which were in many cases defined by medieval walls, *extra muros* sprawls appeared that were both rural and urban in nature. These areas, which were not statistically or administratively part of most towns, grew even faster than the core city. They contained great numbers of people who, like those within the city walls, could work in town and trade in urban markets; but, like country folk, they could also cultivate gardens, avoid city taxes, and live closer to the open air. These settlements outside city walls, gradually incorporated into cities, tell us a great deal about urban work and people's accommodation to it. Demographically, they are part of the city, but a neglected part; this neglect helps to explain why rural and urban environments have been mistaken for separate worlds.[25]

In the sections of this history that focus on cities, I will emphasize urban areas that exemplify urbanization of their times. For the early modern period, I will focus on London and Amsterdam, great capital and trading cities. In the next chapter, eighteenth-century Rouen will be featured for its symbiotic relationship with its rural industrial hinterland. Duisberg and Roubaix—a steel town and a textile manufacture that burst with industrial might—are key examples in the urban sections of the chapter on nineteenth-century industrialization.

INDIVIDUALS, SOCIAL RELATIONS, AND MIGRATION SYSTEMS

Changes in rural landholding, employment, demographics, and capital holdings acted together over the long run to crowd the countryside, then to dispel rural populations to cities and towns. These structural factors explain the most general kinds of migration patterns. They do not, however, explain what made some people move while others stayed in place— for these explanations we must turn to individual Europeans and their social networks. Migration is a selective process. The young, single, and childless historically have been most likely to take to the road. These include young men ready for apprenticeships, terms as farmhands, or simply trying their luck in the city; they include young women who worked in the kitchen of the farm or urban middle-class family—or, later, the factory, and then the office or schoolroom. The children of landless laborers in early modern Europe knew from a very early age that they would have to find a living outside their parents' home. Likewise, prolific peasant families could rarely support all their children. In either case, moving was part of coming to maturity in many rural families.[26] Moreover, migration was embedded in familial patterns of work, authority, and money-earning, for families designated who should depart. It was family strategies that moved some children and retained others at home, deciding individual destinies in the interests of the group.[27] For example, which men of Pradelles would join the local team of migrants in the spring was decided by their family. Families with the least money and property could not retain their children and the poorest among them disbanded altogether.[28]

Occupation and social status linked migrants with particular contacts and attracted them to distinct destinations. Most rural laborers like the men of Pradelles traveled to other rural areas and worked within agricultural itineraries. The men of Pradelles knew agricultural work, because they were tied into the information available from the people of their village. Had Pradelles been near coalfields, they might have worked in the mines before spring planting began. The elite of the region—nobles, officials, and wealthy landowners who moved in loftier circles—were likely to move longer distances and to have distinct destinations. They may have traveled to the lowlands, but they might visit the sovereign court of the city, not the fields that surrounded it. Like the bureaucrats of a later day, they would be more likely to see Berlin, London, or Paris. The poor were the bulk of migrants on the roads of Europe, for their livelihoods were least secure.

Of all individual characteristics that influence the migration experience, gender is perhaps the most fundamental but least systematically explored.[29] Studies of female migrants appeared in the 1980s and are especially well established among studies of today's migrants to North America and Europe.[30] However, gender has rarely been seriously analyzed among historical migrants.[31] This study will investigate explicitly the migrations of both men and women, because just as most other activities in historical Europe were gendered, women's movements were different from men's. At the same time, men's and women's mobility is inextricably linked.[32] Their productive and reproductive roles shaped the migration of European women.

The labor force long has assigned different tasks to men and women; as a consequence, the chances for men and women to earn their bread sometimes led them down different roads. While the men from the village of Pradelles left for the lowlands in harvest teams, most wives stayed at home, shouldering extraordinary responsibilities for livestock, farm management, and community administration. If young women left the village, it would be to work in another family, to marry, or to join a convent.[33] As rural economies changed, men and women sometimes left a given area at different times because the earnings for men declined at a different time than for women. For example, the collapse of rural industries in the nineteenth century affected female spinners earlier than it affected male weavers.[34] Coalmining towns rarely offered the single village woman the chance to earn her way, although they may have promised a good living to her brother. While her brother went into the mines, the village girl was more likely to strike out for a more bourgeois town that would offer her a place as domestic servant. This process created coalmining towns that were predominantly male and administrative towns that were predominantly female. Single migrant women responded to the demand for urban domestic servants, especially when they moved without their families.[35] Those who traveled in the company of their families—and who therefore did not need the housing that domestic service provided—were more likely to be factory workers in the nineteenth and twentieth centuries. The work of married migrant women, from the wives of metalworkers in the Ruhr valley to southern Italian women in the United States, responded to the demand for female domestic labor, whether or not they also worked for cash.[36]

Women's capacity for reproduction distinguishes their migration in ways that have not yet been fully researched. In rural societies, women moved at marriage, whether to join their husband's family or to found a new household. Unwanted pregnancies that could not result in marriage provided an impetus for departure from home for some women. Single women usually moved under the protection and supervision of family members or lived in familial situations; among them are the urban live-in domestic servants and the mill workers who lived in rural dormitories supervised by nuns. Men, by contrast, lived in commercial lodgings or slept outdoors; although they often traveled and worked with compatriots, young men did not live and work in such supervised surroundings. Protective arrangements reflect in part efforts to protect women from pregnancy. For single migrant women, childbirth was a vivid manifestation of their social vulnerability.[37] For both the people at home and at destination, including state policymakers, women's capacities for reproduction signaled that when they joined a migration system, male migrants were more likely to stay at destination and form an immigrant community through chain migration. For this reason, nations of the Americas and Europe restricted with special care the entry of women and families whom they wanted to exclude as permanent immigrants. For example, the entry of Polish workers in the eastern provinces of nineteenth-century Germany was regulated to prevent family settlement.

Demographic characteristics such as age, marital status, and gender help us to understand why certain kinds of people left home in the past, but in order to explain why men and women left particular villages, and how they chose their specific destination, we must see migrants in their social context. Each migrant had a "personal information field"—a body of information about moving and destinations particular to each person.[38] Migration information was shared by kin, friends, and acquaintances who often chose the same destination and helped each other find work. These networks solve a central problem by explaining why migrants did not act like perfectly rational decision-making atoms, why they possessed incomplete knowledge about the options open to them, and why they concentrated on particular destinations and occupations. The idea of the personal information field moves *human relations* to the center stage of migration studies: historically, people have been the most effective conduits of information about migration possibilities. In a compelling case study of the role of social networks in the decision to emigrate from Europe, Sune Åkerman emphasizes "the multiplier effects that were released as a consequence of interpersonal relations."[39] Information passed on about a particular location created migration streams between one's home area and destination.

Because they were generated by webs of relationships, migration streams constituted one building block of what we might call regional cultures. As kin and acquaintances moved from village to village, from market town to provincial center, they established contacts among people who spoke a similar language and shared such cultural habits as cuisine, religious practice, and fertility patterns. Migration linked villagers and townspeople who were part of the same "regional network of economic opportunities and constraints, a system of shared knowledge and ramifying kinship networks."[40] As a result, migration was far more than a purely economic phenomenon that merely reflected changes in the labor force. It was a manifestation of family systems, social connections, and regional solidarities.

This history adopts a *systemic* perspective. Migration itself is conceived as a socially constructed, self-perpetuating system that includes home and destination—a responsive system that expands, contracts, and changes according to circumstance.[41] One such system is the seasonal practice of working lowland harvests shared by the men of the village of Pradelles. This migration system expanded women's village responsibilities and gave a particular annual rhythm to conceptions; as village population and lowland agriculture both expanded in the eighteenth century, more villagers depended on harvest work to get by. Local systems of migration animated rural dwellers within a valley or a region in seventeenth-century Europe, while large cities such as Amsterdam and London stimulated far-reaching systems of movement that included people in western Germany and northern England.

This study categorizes migration systems into four groups according to the distance of the move and the definitiveness of the break with home, following the historical scheme of Charles Tilly.[42] The first of these was *local migration*, systems that moved people within their home market; this was a marriage market, a land or a labor market. It may have extended over a long distance, but it did not remove people from home contacts. Local migrants include peasants who purchased land and moved to a nearby village and women who married in a nearby parish. *Circular migration* returned people home after a specified interval within each particular system. The annual harvest work in the lowlands by the men of Pradelles was a system of circular migration. In the nineteenth century, Italians working the Argentine grain harvest were circular migrants who covered a considerably greater distance. Systems of *chain migration* involved social arrangements with people already at destination, who characteristically helped newcomers to find jobs and housing. These systems operated like a transmission belt that brings newcomers from one area to a particular location. Chain migrants included urban domestics who came to the city to join a compatriot and then stayed on and construction workers who settled in the city after a few summers of urban work. Finally, systems of *career migration* were distinct because the needs and geography of the hiring institution rather than village contacts or family needs determined the timing and destination of moves. In early modern Europe, people who moved within such systems were likely to be church personnel, but with the bureaucratization of the state in the nineteenth century, the majority were white-collar functionaries. Both the mother superior and the schoolteacher, the cardinal and the judge, were career migrants.

Other kinds of migration are peripheral to this book. The *colonizing migrations* that settled much of Australia, the Americas, and eastern Russia do not play a large role here. The *coerced migrations* of refugees and displaced persons do not take center stage in this study until the twentieth century. The coolie trade is part of the history of the Americas, but less important to Europe. On the other hand, European interests in the production of sugar, coffee, and cotton in the Americas generated the trade in enslaved Africans that was a protracted and massive coerced migration. Relatively few Europeans were engaged in slaveholding enterprises, so that many more Africans than Europeans crossed the Atlantic between 1600 and 1840; only after 1840 did Europeans begin to consistently outnumber Africans.[43]

The free migrations that dominate the history of European mobility before 1914 were local, circular, chain, and career movements. These kinds of migration overlap, and many individuals changed from one system to another over time. Systems rose and fell with the economic fortunes of the destination. In some cases, circular migration systems from countryside to city became chain migration systems that eventually depleted rural populations. We will see the migration systems from villages like Pradelles become systems of chain migration that sent an increasing proportion of young men and women to settle permanently in the lowlands. This typology of migration systems is especially useful for a long-term historical study, particularly because a shift in importance among types of migration systems has occurred over the past three centuries: the local migration systems and circular migration that dominated movement in seventeenth-century Europe gave way in the nineteenth and twentieth centuries to chain migration systems and the proliferation of career migration.

DEFINITIONS AND DATA

Writing this history requires a pioneering spirit. There is neither a simple and universally accepted definition of migration nor a single body of data that measures it. Thus it is quite different from the much neater demographic processes—birth, marriage, and death—for which we have histories. Indeed, Jan de Vries showed considerable restraint when he observed that "unlike fertility, mortality, and marriages . . . migration is a more unruly phenomenon which no single historical or contemporary source records in a comprehensive fashion."[44] Here I will give this "unruly phenomenon" wide berth, defining it as a change in residence beyond a municipal boundary, be it a village or town. For the purposes of this history, then, migration includes moves from one village to another as well as from one side of the Atlantic to another. Temporally, migrations include moves that last only a season as well as permanent relocations. The latitude of this definition is designed to capture the nuances of historical change.

Measurement and data offer more intractable problems. The systematic study of migration began a little over a century ago with Arthur Ravenstein's analysis of the British census of 1881, which he expanded with an analysis of censuses from the low countries, Scandinavia, the German Empire, France, Iberia, central Europe, and the Balkans.[45] Subsequent studies of mobility have relied heavily on censuses, parish lists, birth and death records, registers of specific urban groups such as citizens (Bürgerbucher) and apprentices, and occasional government inquiries. The most famous inquiry surveyed temporary migration for the whole of the French Empire in 1811.[46] Such sources yield excellent information on some aspects of migration—that they often list occupation enables the researcher to understand the origins of various segments of the labor force; that they list birthplace enables the researcher to investigate the geographical draw of a village or town.

From these sources, migration researchers have formulated certain fundamental "rules" of migration: Migration is a function of distance—the longer the distance, the fewer the migrants; migrants move in stages—from village to town, from town to city; for each stream of migrants, there is a counterstream back to origin; people in urban areas are less likely to migrate than those in rural areas; women constitute the majority of short-distance migrants; and economic motives dominate the decision to migrate. Demographers, sociologists, economists, and historians have refined and refuted these observations, improving our understanding of the selectivity and volume of movement.[47]

But parish lists, occupational lists, and census data are limiting. They force the scholar to infer movement from static data; thus, they yield little information about the actual volume of movement, return migration, or repeated moves. As a consequence, these sources give the impression that historical actors moved infrequently and that they stayed at their destination. Ravenstein initiated theories about migration streams and counterstreams, but until recently historians did not produce data that directly measure movement within migration chains and circulatory systems.

Historians now are exploring two kinds of sources that allow a direct measure of migration in Europe. The first source is migration statistics from Germany (*Meldewesen*), gathered annually at the local level from individual records of in-migration and out-migration by gender and marital status. These data, reexplored and used to measure gross migration in the nineteenth century by American scholars James Jackson, Jr., and Steve Hochstadt, reveal massive movements into and out of German cities.[48]

The second set of data originates in population registers, long maintained in Sweden and introduced to western European countries such as Belgium, Italy, and Holland after 1840. Population registers monitored individuals over time; as a consequence, they allow us to see migration in the context of the life cycle, to observe the frequency of individual moves, and to discern specific migrant streams and mobile subpopulations.[49] The registers of Belgium and of Italy have been analyzed by American scholars George Alter, Dennis Hogan, and David Kertzer to discern the movement of people into and out of the textile town of Verviers, Belgium, and the rural outpost of Bologna, Italy, called Casalecchio. Alter, Hogan, and Kertzer have used life-table methods to measure the likelihood of migration by gender and age. In both locations, migrants were not likely to stay long and (aside from the native-born women of Verviers) everyone was likely to move—primarily within a regional system.[50]

These rich records of human mobility inform us about a limited period of time. The German migration statistics began with Napoleonic rule over the Rhineland at the opening of the nineteenth century; they were adopted by the Prussian district of Düsseldorf after the Napoleonic wars and were extended to Berlin in 1838. After 1866, it seems that statistics were gathered primarily for cities of over 50,000 alone. Most population registers are limited to a part of the nineteenth century, introduced in Belgium in the 1840s and in Italy in the 1860s. Three separate registers from Verviers cover the period from 1849 to 1880; the period of the Casalecchio study extends from 1861 to 1921.[51]

The population registers that have been most exploited for migration researchers can address changes in migration patterns only during the nineteenth century after 1840. As registers are investigated for the period after 1919, they may be able to tell us about shifts in migration after World

War I, but such work has only begun.[52] The population registers can enrich enormously our understanding of the migrations that occurred during an era that generated a great volume of movement and enormous contemporary concern—the era of urbanization and the growth of factory industry in the late nineteenth century. Just as important, the registers can induce migration researchers to ask better questions of the extant data about other periods. However, no single source can, alone, serve to support or deny a historical theory of migration over the long term.

Despite formidable source problems, researchers have managed to draw on extant sources—parish records, censuses, migration statistics, and population registers—to discern the volume, direction, and timing of movement. Four notable instances will serve here as exemplary cases. David Souden used data from family reconstitution projects for seventeenth- and eighteenth-century English parishes to analyze local migration fields. Steve Hochstadt used a plethora of urban citizenship registers (*Bürgerbucher*) from seventeenth- and eighteenth-century Germany to discern and calculate substantial rates of preindustrial mobility. Jan Lucassen has amassed a wide variety of sources to augment the French Imperial survey of temporary migration in order to trace the rise and demise of migration systems supplying labor to the Netherlands from the seventeenth to the twentieth centuries. Finally, using a backward population projection technique, Myron Gutmann traced trends in human movement over a two-century period in and around Verviers, Belgium, in the seventeenth and eighteenth centuries.[53]

Such excellent, nuanced case studies as these are a primary reason that an attempt can now be made to interpret migration patterns in Europe since the seventeenth century. A critical mass of exciting new work gives hint to the shape of migration trends. Also, Jan de Vries and Charles Tilly, in sketching out general approaches to the history of the European population, urban and proletarian respectively, have suggested the complex, but key, role that human migrations have played in producing an urban proletariat where there was once a peasantry.[54] Moreover, population reconstructions of preindustrial peoples, effected by Jan de Vries for the European city and by Myron Gutmann for the Verviers region, suggest a role for migration that is subtle, changeable, and important.[55] Finally, studies of industrialization and deindustrialization emphasize movements of capital and workers, replacing a long-standing emphasis on technological innovation. This shift has brought the history of industrialization closer to that of human mobility by clarifying a history of production that is geographically flexible as well as reversible: in many regions, industries have folded, leaving working men and women to scramble for declining resources or move to find employment.[56]

These works suggest that a rethinking of human mobility is at the heart of the current writing of European history. Migration is a missing piece in the standard understanding not only of the preindustrial world but of the nature of historical change as well. By writing this history of migration, I hope to bring the patterns of mobility into our thinking about preindustrial life, rural industry, the industrial revolution, and urbanization. Migration is present in every level of historical study. It should enliven the historical study of the family, that most intimate of social groups. On the village and regional levels, migration constitutes a part of the "social glue" of subcultures and responds to economic and social change. State politics themselves both inspired and inhibited migration. Finally, European mobility responds not only to familial and local demands but also to those of the world economy.

This book interprets migration patterns and processes in historical Europe and the points of discontinuity in human mobility. It outlines the changes in rural employment, demographics, and landholding patterns and the shifts in capital deployment to reveal a countryside that filled, then expelled much of its population with the collapse of rural industry and long-lived agricultural systems. The central story is that of human movement, comprising primarily local and seasonal migration in the seventeenth century that subsequently shifted, then dramatically expanded by the end of the nineteenth century. Migration brought a different experience to men and women, to the propertied and the proletariat, and those differences are themselves an important part of this history. I seek not only to interpret the history of migration but also to probe the substantial blank spots in our understanding of human mobility.

CHAPTER

2

Migration in Preindustrial Europe

Joseph Mayett left his parents' Buckingham cottage northwest of London in 1795 at age 12, when his father, a farm laborer, hired him out to be "in service." The young man ate, slept, and resided with his masters since service was paid in room, board, and a wage. Mayett departed the next September; local custom dictated that farm servants then present themselves at the Michaelmas fair to be hired out for the coming year's employment. Both Mayett and his parents tacitly expected him to be a farm servant, to be hired by the year, and to move annually. Neither party anticipated that he would again live at home, and he did not, except for one very short period when he was forced to take work as a farm laborer and find shelter with his parents. Mayett took 11 positions as a farmhand in eight years, sometimes returning to a former master, and never once living more than 23 kilometers from his parents' cottage. He followed a pattern established in Buckingham county since the sixteenth century. Mayett's departure from home, his annual moves, and his work as a farm servant all make him quite typical of men and women in early modern Europe—particularly typical among rural young people from families of modest means.[1]

Leaving home as Joseph Mayett did was an integral part of European life in the seventeenth century. Studies of nearly every village, town, and city reveal that the face of Europe was bustling with movement long before the industrial revolution. Indeed, the image of a sedentary Europe may be most inaccurate for the preindustrial period. Jan de Vries's simulation of urban growth in early modern Europe suggests that there was more migration in the seventeenth century than there would be in the eighteenth and early nineteenth centuries; he postulates that the important "net flows of rural-urban migration . . . were part of a larger, probably much larger, stream of gross rural-urban migration. This in turn was embedded in a yet more general migration phenomenon continually redistributing population among villages and market towns."[2] Similarly, "the most striking and fundamental finding" from Peter Clark's wide-ranging study of migration in southern England, 1660–1730, was that mobility was the norm. Seven thousand biographies of court witnesses show a pattern of ubiquitous movement: about 65 percent of men and women departed their home parish.[3] (See Table 2:1.)

Pervasive mobility flies in the face of stereotypes about premodern life and, more seriously, historians' assertions that the most populous of European nations, France, was fundamentally sedentary between the sixteenth and nineteenth centuries, anchored by its people's visceral attachment to the soil.[4] This chapter describes and analyzes the wide range of migration experiences in preindustrial Europe, elaborating the factors that made some people more mobile than others.

I define preindustrial Europe as the age before people labored in large-scale production for outside markets in the countryside *or* in the city, before patterns of work and residence were altered by the proliferation of rural industry *or* the development of machine production.[5] Migration in the period before large-scale rural industry is difficult to pin down because there are very few acute sources or studies that address mobility. One must make careful inferences from local and regional studies for this age that lacks migration statistics, population registers, or census data. However, local studies have the advantage of providing vivid portraits of migration patterns in particular settings. It is essential to comprehend migration *before* the proliferation of rural industry in order to understand the changes wrought by its spread. Since rural industry and its crucial urban components were expanding rapidly in Britain and parts of the Continent by 1660, and elsewhere during the eighteenth century, this chapter will focus on the 1650–1750 period, emphasizing the seventeenth century for some regions and the early eighteenth century for others.

This chapter opens with a brief portrait of the age and a sketch of its migrations that were compelled by war, empire, and intolerance. It then shifts to the more subtle movements of ordinary men and women in the preindustrial countryside and city. I include a sketch of what may have been the largest system of labor migration of the seventeenth century: the annual movement of Westphalian men to work in the fields of Holland. (See Map 2:1.)

THE CHARACTER OF THE AGE

This period followed an era of expansion marked by overseas trade and exploitation during which silver and gold from the New World had filled the coffers of Imperial Spain. The previous century had also been one of intolerance and religious conflict that had bred religious wars in France (1562–1593) and the Revolt of the Netherlands against Spain (1572–1581), which made possible the rise and commercial expansion of the United Netherlands and, finally, Spain's recognition of Dutch independence in 1648. The Thirty Years' War intermittently bled and starved German terri-

Map 2:1 Western Europe in 1650

tories from 1615 to 1648. England, too, was divided by religious quarrels, the emigration of dissenters, and finally by civil war from 1642 to 1660.

The 1650–1750 period was also one of economic stagnation.[6] Regions differed very markedly from one another, and only very large capital cities and ports on the Atlantic were likely to grow; the cities of Mediterranean Europe and textile cities of northern Europe were devastated by murderous plagues, economic crises, and chronic unemployment. In this period, London, Paris, and Amsterdam came to dominate the continent while the great cities of Italy stagnated; Venice, Naples, and Milan lost population after 1600. Small and medium-sized cities actually declined.[7] In terms of long-term economic cycles, Paul Hohenberg and Lynn Lees have indicated that the period between 1650 and 1750 was one during which cities suffered, while simultaneously production was beginning to take hold in the countryside. Thus, a gradual turnaround—a shift in the location of economic productivity—was embedded in this era of stagnation.[8]

The population of western Europe slumped as well, partly because the preindustrial demographic regime was a deadly one. In the countryside, high rates of marital fertility were offset by low marriage rates, late marriage, and high rates of infant and child mortality. Periodically, massive mortality crises brought on by illness and hunger would destroy the meager increases in rural populations. Demographic crises proliferated on the continent in the late seventeenth century when "the 'times were out of joint' as the saying went," and repeatedly wet summers and bad harvests reduced crops in 1674–1679, 1681, and 1684. The winter of 1693–1694 brought a great famine that devastated much of northern Europe. The majority of people were short of food; at least one-tenth of the French died in a space of a few months, and less than half the usual number of children was born. The "great winter" of 1709–1710 froze crops and subsequently starved thousands of people.[9] Urban and rural disasters were one and the same in this age when a bad harvest immediately translated to a rise in the price of grain and quick drop in urban employment; city records show that in times of high grain prices, new apprentices were not taken on and weavers had no orders.[10]

This was an essentially rural world. The vast majority of men and women lived in villages or very small towns.[11] Only one European in nine lived in a town of 5,000 or more, and towns of 20,000 to 30,000 were considered large. This was particularly true in the north, which had fewer urban areas than Italy or Iberia. Indeed, when the English town of Norwich reached 30,000 in 1700, it was counted as the largest city in England, London aside. There was only a handful of very large cities; in 1650, Paris, London, and Amsterdam figured at about 450,000, 400,000, and 175,000 respectively; Italy had five cities of over 100,000 (Venice, Milan, Rome, Naples, and Palermo); and both Madrid and Lisbon numbered about 130,000. Although southern cities declined and northern cities prospered, most people lived and worked in the countryside throughout this period.[12]

Migration in this age is of interest precisely because population growth was slow and urbanization a negligible factor. A prolonged population boom would not begin until about 1750; before this time, Europe was marked neither by the rural overpopulation that pushed people from the countryside nor by the plethora of growing cities that is said to have pulled them to urban areas later in history. In the year 1650, England, France, Germany, and the remainder of western Europe were much less populated than they would be at the end of the eighteenth century after fifty years of demographic expansion. In short, the preindustrial world lacked the massive pressures that would accompany migration in the eighteenth and nineteenth centuries.

This describes what is often called the traditional world. Rural areas were relatively self-sufficient; as yet, few countrysides had begun to produce for faraway markets, and goods imported from abroad rarely found their way to rural areas. Tools and clothing were produced in the same area in which they were used. Villages were not simply agricultural communities, but they included craft artisans and service people like innkeepers in addition to producers of grain and livestock; in concrete terms this meant that villages included a smithy who shod animals and forged tools, a shoemaker, and perhaps a weaver and a seamstress. We infer from the autarky of preindustrial Europe that country people lived out their lives in their natal village, "in earshot of the same parish bell."[13]

Landholding patterns reinforced this impression, because the landholding peasantry, the least mobile sector of the population, was near its peak in many parts of Europe during the seventeenth century. By this time, rural dwellers in England, France, the low countries, and western Germany had gradually been released from the constraints of serfdom on mobility and property ownership. After the bubonic plague swept Europe in the fourteenth century, the resulting labor shortage enabled common people in many areas to replace feudal labor obligations with payments, to acquire land, and to obtain freedom of movement in the fifteenth and sixteenth centuries. By contrast, the social, legal, and political position of the rural people in central and eastern Europe deteriorated in the sixteenth and early seventeenth centuries; their feudal obligations expanded at the expense of their freedom to move as estate agriculture grew in Poland and the eastern German provinces.[14]

THE POLITICS OF MIGRATION: WAR, EMPIRE, AND INTOLERANCE

The kind of movement we often associate with this "traditional" world is the extraordinary displacements caused by the overseas expansion and religious turmoil that transformed the early sixteenth century. On one level, this impression is correct: the politics of war and intolerance motivated more migration in this period than they would at any time before the twentieth century. The best-known and most dramatic of movements were those of refugees from religious persecution and religious wars that reverberated through Europe during and after the Protestant and Catholic Reformations. The religious wars in France (1559–1598) and the Revolt of the Netherlands (1566–1587) ended the sixteenth century with the flight of Protestants. The wars that divided France destroyed rural areas and devastated cities like Lyon, where half the population was ousted by bouts of the plague and war. Silk production and commerce collapsed; hundreds of houses sat empty. Huguenots from the north of France found refuge outside their hostile homeland in Alsace, where John Calvin had founded the first reformed parish in Strasbourg in 1538.[15] The Dutch revolt again Spanish rule of the Netherlands and the subsequent invasion of the southern Netherlands by the French drove Dutch Protestants north to the United Provinces of the Netherlands, east into cities such as Frankfurt, and across the channel to England.

Sixteenth- and seventeenth-century persecution sought to obliterate Judaism in western Europe.[16] After a long period of coexistence with Christians on the Continent, Jews were forced to convert or be expelled from many areas between 1420 and 1520. The greatest shock to the Sephardic community was the expulsion of unbaptized Jews from Spain in 1492—a heterogeneous community that probably numbered at least 200,000; among the some 100,000 who departed, the largest group went to Portugal, from which unbaptized Jews were banned in 1497. Before 1512, Geneva, southern France, southern Italy, and numerous German and Austrian cities and provinces expelled Jews.[17] In the conflicts of the sixteenth-century Reformation and Thirty Years' War, Jews were mistreated or driven out of Protestant provinces and more likely to be protected in archdioceses and bishoprics. The persecution and removal of Sephardic Jews from western Europe shifted European Jewry's center of gravity from west to the east of the Continent.[18] The largest Jewish community in the world developed in Poland and Lithuania, where Ashkenazi refugees from Germany, Bohemia, and Hungary had played a major role in expanding the Jewish population from about 30,000 in 1500 to perhaps 150,000 in 1575.[19]

In both the conflict-ridden Netherlands and war-torn Germany, however, religious and ethnic upheaval also bred toleration—not always as a policy, but as an unintended result of neglect of religious affiliation. As a consequence, Jews began to return to the west as the sixteenth century drew to a close. The community in the Free City of Frankfurt grew from 150 in 1500 to 3,000 out of a total population of 20,000 in 1613. Culturally, the most significant development was the settlement of 200 to 300 Portuguese in Amsterdam by 1600—Jewish *conversos* or New Christians who moved in the maritime trade routes that brought Mediterranean and especially southern Iberian products like silk and olive oil to the ports of France, England, the Netherlands, and northern Germany. During the seventeenth century, a community developed in Amsterdam where the so-called New Christians could explore the faith of their ancestors. Ashkenazim came from Germany and Sephardim came from Iberia to expand the number of practicing Jews in the city to 4,000 by 1700; this "Dutch Jerusalem" became the largest Jewish community west of Poland or the Balkans.[20]

Christian refugees and religious dissidents also continued to relocate in the face of seventeenth-century strife and intolerance. The highest rate of net emigration in British history came in the wake of English conflict as Protestants took to the new world in the 1630s—and continued to do so after the civil war, fall of Cromwell, and restoration of the monarchy in 1660.[21] French Huguenots joined a vast immigration into Alsace, which welcomed Protestants until it became part of Catholic France in 1681. Then, Louis XIV rescinded the remains of tolerance for Huguenots in 1685, setting off an exodus of 140,000 to 160,000 in the next five years. About a third of these French Protestants found a place in England, another third in the Netherlands, and the rest in Swiss and German centers like Geneva and Frankfurt. Because the Huguenots included many artisans and prosperous people, many of them were welcomed, if not recruited, to new locations. The intolerance that depleted the southern Netherlands and France of wealthy and skilled citizens transferred immeasurable assets of human talent and fed the success of England and the Dutch Republic.[22]

War hammered at the people of northern Europe, particularly in the first half of the seventeenth century. The Thirty Years' War (1618–1648) proved to be the worst catastrophe since the Black Death; so devastated were German territories that an estimated average of 33 percent of the urban populations and 40 percent of the rural populations perished—either murdered or dead from hunger, typhus, dysentery, the plague, or syphilis. Although the destruction was uneven, devastating some cities and regions while allowing others merely to stagnate, the Holy Roman Empire lost 7 to 8 million people. The Fronde, the French revolt against the crown, brought destruction to the Ile-de-France around Paris and a more profound and widespread crisis throughout the kingdom of France in the 1640s and 1650s. After Louis XIV ascended to the French throne in 1661, his aggression plagued the Dutch Republic, Spanish Netherlands, and western German territories during the War of Devolution (1667–1668), invasion of the United Netherlands (1670–1679), war with the League of Augsburg (1689–1697), and War of the Spanish Succession (1702–1713). Although destruction never matched that of the Thirty Years' War, armed conflict continued to bring death, misery, and dislocation.[23]

Overseas imperial ambitions of the seventeenth century also inspired migration by providing work for people far from their homes. For example, the Spanish invasion of the new world drained off ambitious young men in the army, clergy, and administration. This void of manpower was exacerbated by the toll taken on the commercial community and the manual labor force when Spanish religious zeal and nationalism, in the form of the *reconquista*, worked to expel both the Moors and the Jews in 1492. Rich in gold and silver, a wealthy Spain could support foreign laborers who earned three times what they could earn at home. Spain's need for manpower was filled by Frenchmen from the Pyrenees, the southwest plain, and the Auvergne beginning in the sixteenth century. A massive migration of workers in systems of temporary circular and even chain migration furnished the kingdom with its manual laborers and small traders. On his voyage into Spain in 1655, Antoine de Brunel saw French everywhere, working as water carriers, masons, carpenters, and manual laborers. Some came for a harvest season or for a few years, others married and remained, and most participants in this massive movement were poor like the water carriers of Madrid. Spain and France were at war during de Brunel's visit; nonetheless, he estimated that over 40,000 French then resided in Madrid alone, and 200,000 in all of Spain—many of whom hid their origins to protect themselves from political and economic reprisals.[24] This massive migration would change in character and function in the coming centuries, then eventually cease; but in the seventeenth century, French labor supported the Spanish Empire.

The Spanish center of trade was not in the Spanish port of Seville, but north in Antwerp, then under Spanish rule. This city's economy collapsed in 1580 during wars between Protestant and Catholic, Dutch and Spanish/French forces. Subsequently Amsterdam rose as the commercial and financial capital of the seventeenth century, the star city of the new United Provinces, the Dutch Republic. Burghers from the south, international traders, and highly skilled artisans joined the city's elite. Many had fled the intolerance exhibited by the Spanish and French in the southern Netherlands. That is why 44 percent of Amsterdam's new burghers came from defeated Antwerp in the 1580s. Among the new arrivals came descendants of Jews who had fled Spain in the 1490s. The trickle of Huguenots became a flood after 1685 when Louis XIV revoked religious tolerance and 50,000 to 60,000 found refuge in the Netherlands.[25] These relatively skilled and educated people enriched the expanding city. The elite city council was open to newcomers of wealth; indeed council policy granted to the most valuable among immigrants free citizenship and tax exemptions to sweeten the pot.[26] The victorious and prosperous Republic altered the economic fortunes and the labor force of northern Europe.

The Dutch Republic required those without money or skills—sailors, laborers, maidservants, and journeymen—as well as burghers. During the expansion between 1600 and 1650 when Amsterdam grew from about 60,000 to 175,000, two-thirds of the city's brides and grooms were born elsewhere. These men and women came to Amsterdam primarily from the rural Netherlands, but a large proportion came from abroad. Nearly 60 percent of its sailors and seamen were foreigners, a fifth were city natives, and another fifth were from within the Republic of Holland. Among foreign sailors, the largest number were Germans, followed by Norwegians.[27] The German *Hollandsgänger* participated in a vast system of seasonal, circular migration that provided labor to build and maintain an empire that required seasonal work in brickmaking, peddling, hawking, canal construction, agriculture, and dock work. By 1700, an estimated 15,000 German workers crossed the Zuiderzee to Amsterdam every year

TABLE 2:1

Incidence of Migration in Southern and Midland England, 1660–1730

	Stationary (or intratown move)	Total migrants	Intra-county move	Extra-county move	Unspecified move
Males					
Rural	31.3%	69.0%	45.7%	15.2%	8.1%
Urban	42.7%	55.3%	31.5%	19.5%	4.3%
Overall	36.5%	63.2%	38.5%	17.4%	7.2%
Females					
Rural	23.7%	76.3%	55.3%	16.0%	5.0%
Urban	42.2%	57.9%	37.5%	17.8%	2.6%
Overall	32.9%	67.1%	46.4%	16.9%	2.6%

Note: Figures are from biographical data on 7,047 witnesses in diocesan courts. Percentages are weighted means of county percent-ages for Gloucestershire, Kent, Norfolk, Oxfordshire, Suffolk, West Midlands, Wiltshire, and Dorset.
SOURCE: Calculated from Peter Clark, "Migration in England during the Late Seventeenth and Early Eighteenth Centuries," *Past and Present* 83 (1979), 64–67.

for seasonal work in Holland.[28] I describe this migration system in detail below.

Systems of long-distance migration like those of Germans working in the Netherlands and of French laboring in Spain were not marginal phenomena to the nations and economies of the seventeenth century. Upon visiting Spain in 1607, the Baron de Sancy asked how the Spanish could work the land without the French, if the French did not come to help and to marry and settle. Who would harvest if more troops of French did not come? And who would serve the Spanish in the fields and cities if these same French did not?[29] In their numbers, the need for their labor, the financial returns at home, and the impact of their absence on family and society at home, the movement of these men was central, not marginal, to preindustrial Europe. Long-distance migration systems supplied labor to the few prosperous regions in an age of widespread economic stagnation.

MIGRATION IN THE PREINDUSTRIAL COUNTRYSIDE

Family, Service, and Marriage

The migrations caused by war and religious intolerance have not dispelled the stereotype of a rooted, traditional society, a European countryside where the "immobile village" was the norm. The countryside was bustling with movement; this was frequently local movement, but it nonetheless took people away from their home parish. Evidence from across southern England indicates that between 1660 and 1730, a clear majority of rural men (69%) and rural women (76%) left their parish of birth, although relatively few men (15%) or women (16%) left their home county.[30] (See Table 2:1.)

The four kinds of migration systems described in the introduction all were present in preindustrial Europe. In addition to considerable local mobility, circular migration moved a growing number of harvest workers and temporary urban workers from their home village, then back home again. Visible chain migration systems began to develop from the largest of circular systems, as some men and women remained at their destination, had families there, and provided a base for newcomer compatriots. Career migration—movement by the logic of the employing organization—was for church and government officials who were much smaller in number than they would be in the nineteenth and twentieth centuries.

Moving about was an integral part of preindustrial rural routine, central to the rhythm of seasons, the life cycle, and family life and tied to patterns of family life, labor, and land ownership. Gender marked migration behavior, just as it framed almost all aspects of work and social life in early modern Europe. Men and women were much more likely to move at some life cycle stages than at others. As á social practice, migration was embedded in the dynamics of decisions, family formation, and inheritance. Larger forces affected migration decisions as well. Property ownership: members of landowning peasant families sometimes migrated for short-term work in order to earn cash or moved to new landholdings, but rural laborers who had little or no land were much more likely to decamp to a new village. Deployment of capital and labor demand: the distribution of capital created the demand for workers in specific regions of town and country. Demographics: most fundamentally, population trends produced a shortage of people in some places and overcrowding in others. This section focuses on two primary determinants of rural mobility in this age, the family and the land.

Local migration was an integral part of rural folkways, permeating systems of family and marriage. Men and women in northwestern Europe married at relatively late ages and had high rates of celibacy: generally speaking, men married in their late twenties and women in their mid-twenties. Ten percent, and up to 20 percent in some areas, of men and women remained unmarried for life. By contrast, marriage was nearly universal in Asia and women married young.[31] European late marriage and high mortality kept the number of children down. In Britain, northern France, the Netherlands, Belgium, Austria, and western Germany—much of Europe north of the Loire River—the nuclear family of parents and children was the norm. On the other hand, large extended families, stem families, and polynuclear families were more common in parts of central and eastern Europe, Italy, and southern France. Generally speaking, household composition in western Europe varied dramatically according to the family life cycle.[32] And European households contained more than related people; indeed, there was no word for family in French or German before the seventeenth or eighteenth centuries to distinguish kin from the larger household of helpers. Rather, such words as *Haus, demesne, feu*, and *oustan* described the household in a less privatized age. In English, the word family did not distinguish related people from servants and apprentices.[33]

European family systems had clear implications for geographical mobility.[34] The high proportion of single people produced a large contingent that could move easily from one household to another. The majority who eventually wed had a period of at least eight years when they could move for work and training. This was especially true for aspiring craftsmen whose families could afford an apprenticeship and for the children of cottagers and landless workers. This was a labor-intensive age. Feeding a household, running a farm, and, more specifically, transforming raw wool into cloth, milk into cheese, or grain into bread required many hours and the work of many people. The array of helpers and servants who were part of productive households performed the bulk of this work.[35]

Despite this need for labor, many rural families could spare at least some of their adolescent members. Some men and women had to leave because they had to be trained, and those from poor families had to be fed as well. Consequently, a large proportion of rural single people destined for agricultural vocations moved out of their parental household. Departure constituted a routine part of rural lives—part and parcel of a system of training, employment, and economic support. Young people's high rates of mobility account for the lion's share of the "striking . . . degree of individual mobility" that characterized peasant societies in the seventeenth century.[36]

Most mobile young people worked as rural servants like Joseph Mayett, whose story opened this chapter—what Americans call farmhands, the French *valets de ferme*, the Germans *Gesinde*, and the English servants in husbandry. Rural service was widespread in western Europe—Germany, Scandinavia, France, and England—where labor was free to move. Young workers lived away from home and customarily changed employers annually, moving from farm to farm and village to village. According to Ann Kussmaul, they supplied over a third of hired agricultural labor in early modern England. But servants are elusive; because the majority of them moved annually, the servant in one farm account book, census, or tax list rarely appeared in the next one. Because servants worked in this occupation prior to marriage, they were not listed as servants in marriage registers. Had they owned property, they would appear on tax rolls; had they been unhealthy, they might have left wills; had they been literate, they might have bequeathed letters or diaries.[37] But farm servants appear only in the occasional parish list or investigation of their status as unemployed poor in England, where the Settlement Law of 1662 regulated former rural servants' right to claim residence and, thus, charity in a parish.

Nonetheless, farm servants clearly figure large in preindustrial England and the Continent. From the Scottish border to London and south, the English put their children out to work. In the 63 available English parish listings, dating from 1574 to 1821, servants accounted for about 60 percent of the male and female population aged 15 to 24. Lists from the parishes on the Danish island of Moen drawn up in 1645 show that the majority of rural households had a servant. Although probably less ubiquitous in early modern France than in England, servants lived in prosperous French peasant households, such as those in the Limousin where seven or eight people worked landholdings of 25 to 50 acres.[38] In northern French Artois, young servants were more likely to enter and exit the village than any other group; 70 percent of single men aged 20 to 24 moved in any given year. Like most rural servants, these were hired on one-year contracts.[39]

Children entered service when their physical strength and families permitted them to do so. Although some children in western Europe entered service by the age of 10, most servants began their career in their mid-teens. For example, all children aged 14 and younger in the village of

Ealing, Middlesex, lived at home with parents in 1599; however, 80 percent of the boys and nearly 30 percent of the girls aged 15 to 19 lived and worked with other families—those of yeomen, husbandmen, farmers, and laborers. A century later, northern English children left home in the Westmorland parish of Kirkby, Lonsdale, in their early to mid-teens. And on the Danish island of Moen, few children went out to service before their mid-teens in 1645.[40]

Gender determined the duties of young farm servants. Women milked cows, cared for the small barnyard animals, and prepared food; men handled the draught animals and sheep and performed the heavy labor of plowing and carting. In most regions, everyone worked the harvest. Parish lists reveal that nearly as many women as men worked as farm servants. The proportion was very close for Danish villages, and in extant English parish lists, 1574–1821, the ratio of male to female farm servants was 121:100.[41]

Many rural people, then, spent their youth in work, training, and movement. Yearly migrations made sense to both masters and servants. From the master's viewpoint, whether foul-mouthed, incompetent, drunken, ill, or pregnant, servants could be undesirable. In England, the Settlement Laws of 1662 may have made masters particularly willing to release their servants, since those who left the parish became ineligible for poor relief.[42] Servants, for their part, would wish to leave a farm that was too isolated or ruled by a master and mistress who were stingy with food, vicious, or overly familiar. Whatever the current place, the next one could promise better wages and a better position. As a consequence, some two-thirds of servants moved annually. Eventually, most would marry. Farm servants departed to take another job, marry, or to quit service. In any case, some two-thirds of servants moved annually; like Joseph Mayett, they were likely to be gone from the parish in a year.[43]

In terms of mobility, what was the significance of farm service? By today's standards, servants did not go far; consequently, this local or regional migration is sometimes dismissed as micro-mobility or a sort of percolation that is distinct from meaningful migration.[44] It is true that the movement of young people like Joseph Mayett did not change the overall geographical distribution of population significantly, nor were their lives part of a sea change marking a transformation of the rural labor force. Yet although servants did not go far, their departure from home was an important life course transition, signaling the end of their childhood and dependence on parents. Moreover, rural service was important to the agricultural labor force because it trained people like Mayett in agricultural tasks while giving them the chance to develop their skills and reputation. At the same time, service introduced young men and women to the larger pool of potential mates and taught them the limitations of their abilities and personality (which in Mayett's case included a fiery temper). They experienced the attitudes, personalities, and peculiarities of others. Mayett, for example, never moved far, but his service exposed him to a remarkable variety of people and lifeways. Between ages 12 and 19, this Methodist boy lived in a Catholic household with a drunk who beat him, in a house of "scholars" who taught him to read, and in another where he learned to rob pear trees. Along the way, he began to keep company with women. Leaving home proved a broadening experience in this small world where one angry employer threatened to "blast his character so that he could not get another place within five miles."[45] Consequently, although the distance covered by rural servants may not have been great, the institution of rural service nonetheless had enormous import. It showed young men and women the world in which they would spend their lives, trained them to work in it, and introduced them to its characters and potential marriage partners.

Servants were primarily poor young men and women, from landless and nearly landless families like the Mayetts—simply because their parents had no land for them to work. Indeed, turn-of-the-century Danish scholar E. P. Mackeprang calculated that while 38 percent of landed farmers' children were servants (at ages 15 to 19) on the island of Moen in 1645, 91 percent of the landless laborers' children were so employed. Usually, they served the wealthier and landed members of society in a system by which the poor literally leased their children's labor to families that were better off.[46] Yet service was an integral part of training young people at every level of agricultural society. While children of land-poor and proletarian families learned the farming skills that would make them able agricultural laborers, some of the sons and daughters of farmers and of wealthier peasants went into service as well. They trained in farm operations, saving money to stock farms and to marry.

Their parents' reasons for sending them out are not entirely understood, but clearly economic need was not the only motive. It was probably seen as best that children be trained by outsiders and that servants be hired in their stead. For the farmer, this took some of the training of his children off his hands and freed him to hire whomever he wished. Of the midlands of England, one observer remarked that large landowning farmers sent their sons into farm service "as PUPILS, with superior farmers, at some distance from their father's residence."[47]

Marriage migration, like farm service, was built into the western European family. Throughout the Continent, an incest taboo prevented men and women from marrying members of their own family and only in extraordinary cases were first cousins, for example, allowed to wed.[48] This fundamental principle of European family life meant that men and women often had to find a partner outside their hamlet or village. In addition, village social norms dictated that men and women marry someone of similar standing; landless laborers married each other, or married into a smallholding family, and middling peasants married one another; but a wealthy peasant could no more marry a day-laborer than could a member of the gentry. For this reason as well, partners had to be found for many men and women outside their hamlet. All other kinds of movement aside, then, men and women often moved to marry and set up a new household. Typically, husband and wife moved into a new household in the husband's parish. Where the stem family prevailed, such as in southwestern France and Tuscany, wives moved into their husband's household. In peasant households lacking a son, the new groom would enter as son-in-law and eventual master of the holding. Much marriage migration was quite local; most village brides married someone from a nearby hamlet in the same village or a nearby parish. In the densely settled Beauvaisis in northern France studied by Pierre Goubert, almost 90 percent of brides and grooms came from the same parish, although many were from different hamlets.[49] In many of the seventeenth-century parishes whose marriage records have been studied, brides and grooms found their partners in their home parish—or within about a 10-kilometer radius.[50]

The local nature of marriage migration has gone far to promote the stereotype that preindustrial society was fundamentally sedentary. Although rural marriage markets did not usually stretch far beyond neighboring parishes, the records of rural marriage provide a very incomplete view of mobility. This is because marriage registers, like the parish registers of birth or burial, reveal nothing about people who depart from their home village temporarily or permanently. Parish registers cannot ascertain several kinds of migrations that were important in the 1650–1750 period: those of families who procured land in a nearby parish and moved with their children; those of single people who left—whether they relocated in a nearby village, town, or city; those temporary departures of seasonal migrants who returned to their home parish. A most dramatic example of the way in which marriage records distort migration experience is the records from a village in the Marche in central France. Village records show that 68 percent of brides were born in the parish, another 26 percent less than 10 kilometers away. Yet, although 94 percent of the brides were from nearby, the experience of village men in this period was much less narrow than it may appear, because the village sent masons to Paris to work in summer construction.[51] In such a case, the geographically limited marriage market does not reflect a narrow field of experience; rather, the arena in which men found work was much larger than the region in which they found wives. Men traveled in long-distance circular migration systems, women in localized marriage markets. So although marriage records tell us a good bit about marriage markets, they omit a great deal about rural people's migration experience.

Inheritance and Landholding

A rich variety of inheritance practices also influenced property holding and thereby shaped patterns of leaving home. Impartible inheritance, which kept family property intact, typified southern France and Britain. The heir was the eldest son in rigid systems of primogeniture, but in many regions parents designated which child would inherit. Elsewhere, rural property was divided among the heirs, or one heir would head the household in the next generation and his siblings would be paid off—brothers in cash and sisters with a dowry.[52]

Inheritance systems and family forms gave some children a privileged position from the first years of their lives and condemned others to celibacy or departure.[53] This was particularly true in systems of primogeniture, where all children, except the eldest son, knew that they did not have a secure position in their family of origin. While the fortunes of the inheriting son could advance him in the world, those of younger siblings might have been quite reduced.[54] Whether the heir was designated by parents or established at birth, those who did not inherit the family land could either go away to seek their fortune or stay and take on the status of a helper. In regions where nuclear households and small farms were the norm (northern France, Britain, the low countries, or much of western Germany), sons and daughters would have to leave their parents' home in order to marry and have a family. Inheritance systems varied, but most of them paid off the children who did not receive the land, then dispersed them in order to keep the holding intact. Only systems of extended and multiple families like the French *frérèches* and Italian sharecropper families could retain all family members in the household, working together.[55]

Landowning families sought to preserve the patrimony. It cannot be overemphasized that the passing on of land was driven by "the fear of extinction, *which is more the fear for the household than for individuals.*"[56] Preserving the landholding intact meant avoiding a division of land among children, even where inheritance was legally partible. This is why non-inheritors were bought off, encouraged to leave, or allowed to stay if they did not marry. Paradoxically, the strategies undertaken by families to preserve landholdings of a workable size promoted individualized destinies for the offspring. Some children would, "over a period of years, partially or completely disappear from the family structure."[57]

Landowning peasant families were doubtless more rooted than their more cottager or laborer counterparts, because a family's attachment to the patrimony was elemental. "Adequate land was shelter from want. As for the holding, it was the standard of the village hierarchy."[58] Young people from peasant families were less likely than proletarians to move from the time they were young, because they could more likely work the land of their family, rather than become a farm servant. French scholars use a "sedentary model" to describe their population before 1750 partly because a greater proportion of French were peasant proprietors at this time than were the English (more of whom were dispossessed by enclosure and whose economy included more nonagricultural workers).[59]

Nonetheless, not all peasant families remained in one location. We will never know why the family of infant Martin Guerre walked out of the French Basque country, where they owned a farm and fields, to the village of Artigat at the foot of the Pyrenees in the 1520s, but we can speculate that the opportunity to establish a farm in a friendlier climate could move an entire household (which included, in this case, the Guerre brothers and the wife and child of the elder brother).[60] Alan Macfarlane's investigation of rural parishes in northern England contradicts the image of the sedentary peasant. Land was significant, but it appears that particular landholdings were not. After searching through wills and legal cases, Macfarlane concluded that precious little sentiment bound family to farm; "it is symbolic," he remarked, "that the farms were hardly ever called after families, but after natural features: [such as] Foulstone, Greenside. . . . " He found, for example, that in the two generations after 1642, fewer than half the original 28 families of Lupton township remained.[61] Clearly, some landowning peasants did move as they bought and sold fields. It is likely that land ownership goes a long way toward accounting for the sedentary model of society to which the French subscribe, in contrast to the mobile model for southern England. Yet sources play an important mediating role in this particular contrast, because the sedentary model is grounded in early modern rural marriage records, which cast a very fine net over village property owners but underrepresent more mobile sectors of the population. By contrast, legal records of northern England and church court records of southern England capture a more varied population as well as a less land-bound economy.[62]

Studies that focus specifically on the link between landholding and family migration show that cottager, laborer, and sharecropper families were more likely to move than peasants—and to move as a unit. In early modern Sweden, the households of tenant farmers in the manor-dominated parishes near Stockholm were much more likely to relocate than those in peasant or mixed-economy communities. In fact, different mobility rates were the primary demographic trait that distinguished those households (rather than fertility or family composition, for example). People born in the seventeenth century who worked as tenant farmers were likely to move around; two-thirds to three-quarters of them died outside their village and parish of birth. By contrast, two-thirds to three-fourths of people in villages where land ownership was common died in their parish of birth. David Gaunt concludes that "real stability" in the sense of remaining in one's village of birth was not a general feature of early modern Swedish society; rather, this was characteristic only of males in areas where peasant ownership was common. Permanent settlement was a luxury reserved primarily for landowners.

Because they were so mobile, agricultural workers were not known by fellow workers even after they were married and had children; obituaries were short and included such comments as "no one here a relative, so no one could tell of her past," and "about her life before coming here no one knows."[63] In such societies, the obituary of laborers like Brita Ersdotter had to be pieced together: As a young woman, Brita Ersdotter was likely to have moved frequently because most moves in any manor parish were those of single servants. Upon marriage in the early years of the eighteenth century, Ersdotter lived seven years with her husband at his parents' home; subsequently, the couple worked in four parishes. After her husband's death, she remained two years where he had died, then as an aging widow found a place in three other parishes in the Stockholm region before her death in 1757.[64]

Sharecropping moved family units too, as dissatisfaction with work and strained relations between estate managers and laborers put families in search of a new position. Emmanuel Todd's comparison of agricultural laborers on large farms in northern France with sharecroppers in Tuscany shows a remarkable contrast in patterns of movement. Sharecroppers (*mezzadri*), who lived in complex families and owed half their crops to the landowners, moved frequently and moved together as a group; males relocated along with their families at all ages, and women moved with marriage and for service work. Young male sharecroppers did not leave home to work as farmhands in other families; rather, they remained with their fathers and moved along with the large family group. By contrast, the conjugal families of French agricultural laborers who owned their own house, garden, and sometimes a bit of arable land had a very different pattern of mobility: migration as an adolescent rural servant was common, but household mobility was not. Sharecropping produced family solidarity, household moves, and complex households, whereas the system of agricultural labor and small plot ownership "permitted, or imposed, an early rupture between family and individual."[65]

Between service and marriage, women may have been especially likely to leave their home village. Indeed, of the over 7,000 English biographies surveyed for the period between 1660 and 1730, rural women were most likely to leave home. Over three-quarters of them, as opposed to less than 70 percent of the rural men, moved during their lifetime.[66] Of the 23 girls baptized between 1660 and 1669 in the Westmorland parish of Kirkby, Lonsdale, none remained in this parish of 2,500 in the year 1695.[67] In systems of local migration in peasant societies, then, women may have been on the whole more likely to leave home than men—at least before widespread rural textile production made girls who spun or made lace more valuable to their families and kept them at home.

In the uncrowded countryside of the seventeenth century, migration was due less to large-scale changes such as rural overpopulation or the widespread shift of capital and employment to urban areas than it was to be in future years. Movement was due more to structures of village and individual life such as property-holding, gender, service, and marriage. If one desired, or was forced, to leave home, local traditions provided the itineraries and the destination. In many areas, this meant a village in the same market system, a market town, or the regional capital city. In the case of Germans in Westphalia, local information signaled the Netherlands; in the south of France, it pointed to Spain. Witness the story of Martin Guerre, a sixteenth-century peasant whose story has been told in film and in print.[68]

Martin Guerre was an unhappy young man. As the first-born son in a prosperous peasant family, he would eventually be head of a comfortable household, were it not for a combination of circumstances that spoiled this promising situation and prompted his departure. Martin's parents and his Uncle Pierre had come to his village of Artigat beneath the foothills of the French Pyrenees when he was two years old; in Artigat, no other boy was named Martin because it was the name for an ass in the local patois. The teasing he received as a boy followed him into his marriage, because when no children came for years after his wedding it was clear to the entire village that Martin suffered from impotence. He was thought to have been bewitched. The eventual birth of his son, after the spell preventing conception was broken, did little to give Martin a man's place in the village. He was still young, having married at 14 and fathered a child at 17. Moreover, after the marriage he remained under the roof of his father, as did all young husbands in the region, and under the thumb of his volatile Uncle Pierre as well. There was no way to change his life in the village of Artigat, so Martin chose to disappear. Like thousands of young French men since the beginning of the sixteenth century, he went to Spain. There, also like many others, he initially found work as a servant.[69]

PORTRAIT OF A MIGRATION SYSTEM

The most visible of migrations in the 1650–1750 period were those in which people moved and worked together. In this agricultural age, collective movements of harvest workers were most notable and most crucial to annual rhythms of agricultural production. These circular migrations were particularly massive to the "bread baskets" of wheatlands near the great cities such as London and Paris. Between 1660 and 1700, harvest teams organized from the north of England, descending on East Anglia for the harvest that fed London. Grain harvesters from La Perche west of Paris labored on the large farms of the Ile-de-France. Smaller groups from the villages like Pradelles in the southern highlands of France, described at the opening of chapter 1, harvested wheat and gathered grapes on the Mediterranean plain. Both massive and small-scale systems of seasonal, circular migration animated western Europe; they gave labor to needy cities and harvests while simultaneously feeding and maintaining hungry rustics.[70]

Here I focus on one migration system that dramatically demonstrates the traits of a circular migration system for temporary work. Such systems are characterized by a significant difference between money-earning possibilities in the home area and destination, cash-hungry migrants, and a need for short-term labor at destination. The migrants themselves experienced a collective journey, a specific labor routine, and considerable deprivation away from home. Likewise, home routine adjusted to migrants' absences. Finally, short-term labor migrants were usually ill-perceived by their hosts. All of these traits ring true in the system that joined the Westphalian *Hollandsgänger* to the Dutch province of Holland in the seventeenth and eighteenth centuries.

This system was part of a broad movement of workers who came to work in the Netherlands, originating in an arc that reached from French Calais in the south up to the German states on the North Sea. Germans especially provided the Dutch with servants, sailors, flax workers, strong arms for land reclamation, peat digging, harvests, brickmaking, construction, and the digging of roots from the dye plant madder. Migration began in the seventeenth century when "*Hollandsgänger*" from Westphalia in the northwestern German territories began to travel to the Netherlands for seasonal rural work cutting hay, cutting peat, digging madder, and harvesting grain.[71] On one hand, the Netherlands had a sophisticated, specialized, and capital-intensive economy with a sizable need for short-term workers. On the other hand, there were men in nearby Westphalia who were unable to live from their small landholdings alone, who could perform the tasks the Dutch required, who were willing to leave home, and whose lives were structured so that their absence could be tolerated. The self-perpetuating exchange of labor and capital between the regions found its roots in the complementarity of these two areas.

In 1650, the specialized Dutch economy produced cheese for the international marketplace, which in turn fueled capital-intensive dairy farming.[72] Farmers raised dairy cattle exclusively for the production of cheese and butter in the meadowlands of Holland and Friesland. The enterprise of gathering milk and producing cheese and butter kept an army of farm workers occupied year-round. The cattle grazed in the summer but were fed hay in the winter, and this crucial feed had to be cut and gathered within a period of about six weeks in June and July. Local people were unable to carry out the crucial task of making hay, so migrants were brought in. Migrants also performed other tasks, but the first and most timely task of the temporary worker was cutting hay.[73]

Relative to wages in Westphalia, those in Holland were high—and "relative" was the important consideration for the worker trekking abroad. Early nineteenth-century data suggest that the Westphalian smallholder could earn a third of family annual income during three months of work in the hayfields and peat bogs of Holland. Moreover, the Westphalian could be absent from home from about May 25 to July 25 and still sow his own fields before departure and reap the harvest upon return; the hay crop was small enough to be cut and gathered by women and children. Westphalians had small landholdings because their population increased much more than other areas in the seventeenth century. The region suffered less severe losses in the Thirty Years' War than had German territories to the south and east; and once the war ended, population grew rapidly—by 40 percent in the last half of the century in Lippe, for example. This increased population lived on smaller landholdings. In Osnabrück, for example, plots worked by tenant farmers and cottagers increased by 56 percent, while the number of full-sized farms decreased between 1670 and 1718. An increasing number of Westphalians subsisted on holdings far too small to support a family. (Most migrants probably lived on a mere two to five acres when about 12 acres were required to live off the land.[74]) By the 1670s, rural linen production had begun to expand in Westphalia. This industry became important for many weaver families, but for spinners and part-time weavers it could not furnish more than a small by-income. These nearly landless families required subsidies from seasonal migration.[75]

The earliest record of the migration system that developed between these complementary areas is a 1608 Osnabrück document attesting to workers migrating to "Friesland and to other places outside this bishopric." Other early seventeenth-century records from parts of Westphalia, including Lippe and Münster, testify to an increasing number of *Hollandsgänger*, who doubtless numbered 1,000 from Osnabrück alone by 1660. The spring peat cutters and summer hay mowers contributed to a migration system that Jan Lucassen ascertains to have grown quickly in the 1630s and again in the 1680s. By 1730, at least 15,000, if not 25,000, migrant workers traveled annually in a broad "North Sea system" to the province of Holland.[76] The entire North Sea system probably peaked with about 30,000 workers before the wars of the French Revolutionary era began in 1792. After the Napoleonic wars, Westphalians would find brighter fortunes elsewhere, first in the United States, then in the prosperous German Rhine-Ruhr industrial zone.[77]

For the Westphalian migrant, the trip began by meeting up with others. In a satirical Dutch farce of 1685, Westphalian Hans replies to the question "How did you get here . . . ?" with

> There were ten of us,
> Farm lads all, at an inn, and we
> really got loaded . . .
> We set off for Holland.[78]

Migrants met at particular locations that became regular meeting places like the "Frisian Oaks" (*Frieseneiche*) on the northern route to Friesland and a mammoth boulder (the *Breite Stein*) en route to the Zuiderzee by a central track. By the time those bound for Holland reached the shores of the Zuiderzee, they numbered in the hundreds, so ferry captains vied furiously for their business on the crossing to Amsterdam. In June of 1728, the 13 regularly scheduled voyages from the port town of Hesselt to Amsterdam were augmented by 23 extra voyages for migrant hay cutters (and 12 others for cattle, which reveals a bit about shipboard conditions!). The uncomfortable one-day crossing brought Westphalians nearer their goal. Grass mower Slenderhinke described the ferry trip in a 1712 farce:

> And I went in a ship across wide water, the Zuiderzee, a vast, wide lake, mad white caps that could not be calmed; and my stomach began to growl. I spoke to the skipper and said, you thief, the gallows is too good for you. . . . [After being sick] I fell asleep until morning and saw then for the first time this great Haspeldam, this Amstelholland. That cheered me up. Then I thought, Hinke, you're going to make a lot of money.[79]

Upon arrival in the great city of Amsterdam, workers stayed in cheap lodgings that catered to them in a neighborhood called the German Exchange (*Moffenbeurs*) before departing to the south to dredge peat or to the north to cut hay. This trip remained unchanged for 200 years until trains and steam ferries hastened the journey.[80]

Hay mowers worked vast grasslands where each herd of 50 cows required nearly 50 acres of meadowland. They cut in teams of two from before dawn until evening, "Westphalian heroes who wield the scythe as a spear, / Grass knights, intrepidly swinging their arms."[81] The mowers preceded hay makers, who turned the grass, then gathered it in. These were sometimes women, and sources suggest that some teams included both men and women who worked as hay mowers and hay makers, respectively. After haying, some migrants went south to Brabant or north to Friesland for a second harvest. They returned home by St. Jacob's day, July 25.[82]

This trip required purposeful deprivation and self-exploitation.[83] Migrants walked long distances, carried heavy tools and supplies, and endured a dangerous return trip when they carried cash. They brought their own food and slept in tents or by the road. All of these behaviors were designed to maximize their profits from this trip whose explicit purpose was to earn cash. Indeed, for this reason, some carried along a bolt of Westphalian linen in the eighteenth century to sell without yielding profit to a middleman.[84] Group travel and purposeful deprivation designed to maximize earnings forecast the routines of the short-term migrants who would proliferate throughout Europe in the second half of the eighteenth century. We will meet them in the next chapter.

MOVEMENT TO THE PREINDUSTRIAL CITY

Migrants were part of life in every urban area of preindustrial Europe; they came to large and small towns, to trading and manufacturing cities, and they joined every level of society. The citizenship lists of towns and cities from Danzig and Berlin, south to Marseille, and west to near Cornwall show that the "respectable" portion of society commanded at least a regional draw; there were intimate connections between urban and rural elites, and among the elite of various towns.[85] The origins of urban citizens, or *Bürgers*, are the best recorded. German records from before 1800 show that about half of the urban citizens were migrants.

Together with their families, urban citizens accounted for about half the population of most towns—and the other, less prosperous half was more mobile. For example, in Frankfurt am Main, about half the citizens were migrants in 1700, but about two-thirds of the noncitizens were migrants; the figures for nearby Würzburg in 1675 were 57 percent and 74 percent respectively. Thirty-nine percent of the *bourgeois* of the Norman city of Caen were migrants in 1660, yet most migrants were less prosperous "*petites gens.*" Marriage records, which track a relatively sedentary sector of any population, show that from 1670 to 1749, 44 to 52 percent of the grooms who settled in town after marriage were migrants to the northern French city of Rouen. Those who do not appear in its marriage records—single household servants, apprentices, and journeymen—were more likely to be from out of town. Steve Hochstadt has estimated the mobility of German *Bürgers* at a minimum annual rate of .02 to .08, and of all urban dwellers an annual rate of .10 or more for many communities—that is, he calculates that 10 percent of urban populations moved in or out of the city annually.[86]

The city, then, was a node of movement in the preindustrial world. It must serve as the final resting place for the stereotypical view of sessile preindustrial life. This section discusses the demographic and labor needs of urban areas and general migration patterns to cities. It then focuses on the fortunes and migrants of smaller, typical cities before turning to the great cities of London and Amsterdam.

Unfortunately, we can never know how many people actually moved into and out of the early modern city. Similarly, we cannot know what proportion of city people were migrants, where they came from, how long they were in town, or how likely they were to stay on, marry, or bear children. Indeed, for this era, less is known about people in the city than in the countryside. In the absence of the census or population registers, much must be inferred from case studies.[87] We can only be certain that net figures of city growth (even when balanced against urban population deficits) come nowhere near to measuring migration because they do not include the servant women who went back home or to another town, journeymen who moved on, apprentices who found work elsewhere, or day-laborers who returned to the countryside.

The constant presence of migrants in preindustrial cities resonates with the fundamental demographic finding that most preindustrial cities produced more deaths than births. Few towns could maintain their numbers without an influx of migrants.[88] For this reason, migration to the city in early modern Europe was more crucial to populating the city than it would be in the centuries to come. Generally speaking, smaller towns were less deadly than larger ones, yet infant mortality was universally high in urban areas, and towns were subject to intense bouts of mortality from the bubonic plague and other epidemics of communicable disease. These scourges struck with particular force in poor urban parishes. As a consequence of its size, social structure, and sanitation, seventeenth-century London accounted for about one death in eight of all of England, although only one in thirteen English resided there.[89] Urban natural decrease became most important in the seventeenth century in northern Europe, particularly due to the depredations and repercussions of the Thirty Years' War, the Fronde in France, and Louis XIV's wars in the low countries and western Germany. The plague reverberated through the cities of western Europe. Unfortunately, the difficulties of the Swabian city of Nördlingen were not unusual. About 100 kilometers northwest of Munich, this city was in demographic decline from the beginning of the Thirty Years' War; at least one-sixth of its population perished in the plague in the waning months of 1634. Despite a surge of marriages, remarriages, and births in the subsequent year, the population continued to fall. Between 1627 and 1640, the number of citizen households dropped by about half, from 1,600 to 800. At the end of the war, Nördlingen began to recover, but its people then suffered from the disastrous hunger years (1693–1694, 1709) and were hit by the opening campaigns of the War of Spanish Succession. In 1700, the population of Nördlingen was about 6,000 and there were about 1,200 citizen households in the city, considerably fewer than a century previously when there had been 1,700 households.[90] The four horsemen of the apocalypse—war, strife, famine, and death—took their toll on the early modern city.

The demographic complement to urban mortality was the sparse rural population. Jan de Vries's systemic analysis of the populations of preindustrial Europe reveals that migration to cities and towns had a greater impact on rural populations than it would have on a more populous countryside in later years.[91] This is because high infant and child mortality meant that many couples could only replace themselves, if even that. In the Beauvaisis in northwestern France, for example, only half the children survived to age 20.[92] Of those who survived, the ones who left home for domestic service, moved to a nearby village, or decamped to an urban area were far from negligible. De Vries calculates that an average of about 3 percent of rural-born young people definitively relocated in the city and that about 6 to 10 percent "eventually got a taste of city life." These permanent departures were, in the late seventeenth century, the bulk of rural young people who could be spared by family and village.[93]

Aside from episodes of strife and war, not many cities could sustain their numbers; thus urban migrants were most important at this time in history. Because data on city people is so spotty, their role is far from clear. Allan Sharlin asserted that migrants were a sort of demographic underclass because as apprentices and servants they did not marry and because their poverty subjected them to high mortality conditions in cities like Frankfurt.[94] Migrants probably did marry later than native-born townspeople, on the average, and thus perhaps bore fewer children.[95] On the other hand, death struck infants and young children hardest of any urban group, so that mortality of the very young—probably not migrant mortality—was responsible for the natural decrease of urban populations.[96] Moreover, although apprentices and single servants often were newcomers, migrants also were well represented among more elite members of urban society, who did marry and bear children in the city. Finally, scholars like A. M. van de Woude ascertain that migrants were a positive demographic force in urban populations because they tended to arrive at or near the age of marriage and childbearing.[97] On balance, migrants probably contributed more than they subtracted from city populations.

Urban natural deficit is a demographic fact, but migration is a social phenomenon. Migrants entered the gates of cities not to fill in for deceased children but to seek a livelihood or pursue a career. The early modern town was much more than a deathtrap to the migrant, who acted as "the linchpin of the urban economy."[98] This was a labor-intensive age for urban tasks just as for rural tasks. The town needed vast numbers of people, some of whom by necessity would be newcomers.

For example, a London bakery in the seventeenth century absorbed the labor of some 13 people, including two maidservants, two apprentices, and two or three journeymen, as well as the master baker, his wife, and their children. A Parisian printer's workshop in the late 1730s gave something of a livelihood to two starving apprentices and a host of insecurely employed journeymen, all enthusiastic participants in "the great cat massacre" because the enterprise sumptuously fed and clothed the master, his wife, their daughters, and, not the least, the mistress's favorite cats.[99] These apprentices and journeymen very likely were newcomers to the city; so, too, were untold numbers of migrant women who served in urban institutions—waiting on households, performing menial tasks in workshops, and praying behind convent walls.

Indeed, women were the majority in most western European cities. For example, the French city of Lille in 1686 enumerated only 79 men for every 100 women in a census that counted valets and maidservants as adults. By the same criteria, there were 74 men per 100 women in Zurich in 1671 and 79 men for every 100 women in Venice in 1655. Sex ratios (the number of men per 100 women) increased to the east because Russian, Asian, and Indian cities were primarily male. West of the Elbe, a few cities, like the Prussian military center of early modern Berlin and the papal city of Rome, also housed more men than women.[100] Generally, cities have become more female as time has passed and this trend continues to the present day. The implications of this fact for migration are very important. Yet, unfortunately, if there is little systematic data on men in the city, there is even less on women. In the 1650–1750 period, they do not appear in citizens registers or apprenticeship records; in the absence of the census, even the ubiquitous serving girl is invisible. And marriage records, so valued as a source of information on migrants to French cities, systematically undercount migrant women, who by tradition married in their home parish, if they did not remain in the sizable ranks of single people.

Despite gaps in our knowledge about urban migrants, researchers have elucidated several geographic and social patterns of migration that apply to most towns. Urban areas were served primarily by what Jean-Pierre Poussou calls a "demographic basin," or primary fund of nearby villages and towns. The volume of newcomers to urban areas from demographic basins suggests that we see city walls not as a barriers but rather as semipermeable membranes through which nearby populations flowed. In times of expansion, demographic basins became more extensive. From the immediate region came a wide range of newcomers, from humble servants and apprentices to the children of local elites who sought to rise in society.[101] Peter Clark and Paul Slack include this flow of intra-regional migration in their category of "betterment migration" because the servants, apprentices, and hopeful young landholders all aspired to social and economic improvement. The masses of young women are poorly documented, but the apprentices moving into towns are better known; typical among them are the aspiring weavers from the Norfolk villages who came to the provincial textile capital of Norwich for training.[102] Some of this fairly local migration was among towns and small provincial cities through which traveled skilled workers like weavers and printer's journeymen in search of work, small-town lawyers in search of a better position, and servants in search of a more sophisticated domestic position. For example, most of the town-born migrants in Peter Clark's study of southern English migration, 1660–1730, traveled within their own county (57% of male and 62% of female migrants).[103] Most migration, then, was regional.

Certain kinds of people traveled farther afield: the very poor, the very wealthy, and refugees. Prominent among long-distance travelers were vagrants and beggars, the distressed people of Europe who were driven far from home by hunger. Typically, these "subsistence migrants," to use Clark and Slack's term, traveled farther than "betterment migrants." Over half of the vagrants and beggars in the East Anglia city of Norwich, for example, came from beyond the Norfolk borders, from not only other counties within a 150-kilometer radius but also from farther afield: London, Middlesex, Scotland, and Ireland. Some cities put vagabonds out at the city gates, and the rare detailed record gives us a glimpse of their identities. Of the nine people who were expelled from the city of Amiens in northern France on February 28, 1644, one was a man of 82 who had been begging for four years, no longer able to earn his living as a slate worker; another was a boy of 12 who had been caught at stealing the iron circles from buckets at a communal well (which he doubtless planned to sell in order to buy bread). The children who were sent on their way were too weak to work, "parasites at the family table," abandoned, or orphaned. The adults were those who had not managed to recoup between bad years, to buy back their pawned clothing, or to find steady work.[104]

Although they were never systematically counted, vagrants figured large in the consciousness of authorities, country folk, and charities. Sent back out on the road, vagrants and beggars met suspicion in villages and farms. For the destitute, cities—particularly the great cities like London and Paris—held out much more hope of work or charity than the village. The unemployed crowded into poor urban neighborhoods and "squatted in suburban slums" that lay around every city.[105] The numbers of poor who traveled long distances in order to work for, beg, or steal their food seem to have subsided in Britain after the 1660s; local conditions and charity improved, and the poor laws and settlement acts acted as an *ex post facto* system of control, sending home the unsuccessful. The fate of the poor would be quite different on the Continent, where they were subject to a curious mixture of incarceration and freedom in the years to come.[106]

Refugees such as the Jews and Protestants discussed earlier in this chapter were also long-distance migrants to the early modern city, especially in England, Holland, western Germany, and Switzerland. Those in Norwich give us an example of the role foreign refugees played in an urban society in this period. In the sixteenth century, Norwich housed families of Protestant Walloons who fled the Spanish in the southern Netherlands. Then in the 1680s, Huguenot weavers were invited to Norwich by a descendant of those Protestants, wool manufacturer Onias Philippo. The Huguenots were greeted by a municipal riot on the part of local weavers who feared the newcomers would undercut pay rates. Nonetheless, some 100 to 200 Huguenots settled in, just as had Onias Philippo's Protestant Walloon family a century earlier.[107]

Third among long-distance travelers were professionals, gentry, university students, and some members of the bourgeoisie. In southern England, those who traveled the farthest were urban-born professionals— lawyers, physicians, and clergy who moved an average of over 90 kilometers. Large cities such as Paris and London—and provincial capitals like Norwich and Rouen—had the greatest draw for highly educated people who worked in urban courts, government offices, and churches. Moreover, these migrants and their families delighted in the fine artisanal creations, the fabric and fashions, and music and entertainments that urbane surroundings supported. They also possessed the money to spend on housing, interior decoration, personal luxuries, and entertainment, which in turn supported a plethora of urban livelihoods.

In this period, both in England and on the Continent, city architecture

and building materials were upgraded and wooden housing was pro-
scribed in many locations to prevent fires like the blaze that decimated
London in 1666. Princes and their governments ordered public squares
and streets constructed in the baroque style. In Louis XIV's France, for
example, construction projects transformed much of Paris, fortified border
cities, and created Versailles.[108]

When English physician Martin Lister visited Paris in 1698 after a long
absence, he reported that

> It may very well be, that Paris is in a manner a new City within this forty
> Years. 'Tis certain since this King came to the Crown, 'tis so much al-
> tered for the better, that 'tis quite another thing . . . the greatest part of
> the City has been lately rebuilt. In this Age certainly most of the great
> Hotels are built, or re-edified; in like manner the Convents, the Bridges
> and Churches, the Gates of the City; and the great alteration of the
> Streets, the Keyes upon the River, the Pavements; all these have had
> great Additions, or are quite new.[109]

These improvements had a most dramatic and direct impact on migration, because they required great teams of seasonal construction workers
in addition to the laborers and artisans of the city. In fact, the very notable
annual migration of stone masons from the Haute-Marche in central
France to Paris dates from the mid-seventeenth-century mandate that
Paris be built from stone; by 1694, 6,000 masons from that small highland
region worked in the capital city during the construction season.[110] Not
only did large cities such as London, Paris, and Amsterdam attract working newcomers from afar; but the new cities of early modern Europe—the
spas, dockyards, and government creations such as Versailles—did so as
well.[111]

In all kinds of cities, the turnover among urban dwellers was high.
Many migrant apprentices and rural-born servants came for a temporary
stay, and in addition, people passed through smaller towns to larger ones.
Although contemporary accounts refer to the arrivals and departures of
citizens and servants, the precise volume of this turnover is impossible to
measure, and it is not even picked up by the most sophisticated analyses
of urban populations.[112]

Unusual documentation gives some idea of this turnover. A complete
census of Würzburg in 1701 indicates that the city was turbulent with the
coming and going of young, single people and of families. The clear majority of adults in Würzburg (74% of the men and 57% of the women) had
been born elsewhere, and although migrants were 69 percent of the male
household heads, they constituted 89 percent of male non-kin household
members—apprentices, journeymen, and servants—who were the most
likely to migrate again. Natives of the city also departed; an age breakdown of the native-born population indicates that over a third of young

men born in Würzburg left the city between ages 15 and 24 and nearly as many women left in their twenties, perhaps to marry. Peter Clark's survey of migration in southern England reveals that city-born people were less mobile than village folk; nonetheless, the majority of them (55% of men and 58% of women) moved at least out of their home parish. More urban dwellers moved at least 60 kilometers from home and more left their home county (20% of men and 18% of women)—probably because they relocated in another urban area rather than a neighboring village.[113] (See Table 2:1.)

Difficult times caused much of this turnover in the 1650–1750 period. For example, religious conflict, economic hardship, and high death rates all worked to reduce the population of Rouen in northern France by both mortality and emigration; nonetheless, in some of its worst times (1680–1700) over 7,000 migrants, net, moved to the city. The actual number of newcomers was doubtless several times that. In fact, close study of the families of Rouen led Jean-Pierre Bardet to conclude that the city was a passageway, a "sieve," to use his metaphor, that only retained a small proportion of newcomers.[114]

Men and women who came to and left the early modern city moved in systems of circular, chain, and career migration. Most of the young women who worked as serving girls, for example, probably planned to return to their village or small town.[115] The same was true of rural men who came to the city for the winter to do odd jobs and the construction workers who moved with teams from home for summer work. In some cases, a few of these circulating migrants, such as Germans in Amsterdam or upland masons in Paris, stayed in the city and opened an inn or flophouse for their compatriots, initiating a system of chain migration. Men like the lawyer moving from small-town to urban practice or court and the cleric in the cathedral chapter came to the city by the logic of career migration, dictated by the structure of the legal profession or church. Many beggars and vagrants moved in groups and in seasonal patterns, returning home in good weather or favorable times.[116]

The common patterns of migration to early modern cities appear to be relatively high turnover, intense local migration, long-distance movements of the very poor and elites, and circular and career movement. But neither all cities nor all regions were alike; profoundly different economies and historical circumstances created a wide range of migration patterns. Cities that grew the most and had the greatest geographical draw combined the functions of a government capital in this age of state consolidation with those of world trade and empire. Two in particular, London and Amsterdam (with 400,000 and 175,000 people respectively in 1650), came to primary importance in a world system of commerce and exploitation. Some cities grew because they were new state or commercial creations, such as St. Petersburg and Versailles. Others, like the English center of Norwich, attracted newcomers by dint of their local industries and functions as provincial capitals. Most cities, however, were less fortunate. In this age of war, demographic stagnation, and decline of urban fortunes, it is instructive to contrast Norwich with the French provincial capital of Amiens and the smaller town of Beauvais.

Norwich was a center of wool production that grew to house 30,000 people by 1700, to be the second largest city in the realm, after London. Penelope Corfield has calculated that about 400 newcomers, net, moved to Norwich each year in the 1670s and 1680s. Although its primary contacts were with London and with its port of Yarmouth, about 30 kilometers to the east, vagrants came from near and far, apprentices came primarily from within Norfolk county, and a community of Huguenots settled in as well. The lively and diverse life of Norwich supported not only master weavers, journeymen, apprentices, spinsters and finishers of raw wool and fabric but also the commercial and social life of a regional trade center and a multitude of services "ranging from sin to repentance."[117] The city thrived in this time of peace and relative prosperity.

The French city of Amiens also had a population of about 30,000 in 1700. Amiens, however, was only one of the *"bonnes villes de la France;"* there were six cities of greater size, including Paris, by far the largest city on the Continent with 510,000 people.[118] Amiens was the provincial capital of Picardy, cathedral city, and, like Norwich, a wool-producing town with markets throughout France and abroad. Located on the navigable Somme River about 60 kilometers from the English channel, it had access to international commerce. Essentially, Amiens drew people from the surrounding province of Picardy, "sons [and daughters] of peasants, artisans, and shopkeepers come to try their adventure," joining compatriots as bakers, shoemakers, or domestics. Like Norwich, Amiens drew apprentices from the region; it too attracted skilled workers from other textile centers (like the 48 weavers who arrived from Lille in the 1660s). Merchants, masters, and journeymen who were registered as members of the bourgeoisie came from farther afield in northern France, "weaving of their thousand individual destinies," in the words of Pierre Deyon, "the cultural and economic unity of the country north of the Loire."[119] In addition to all the functions of Norwich, Amiens supported ecclesiastics associated with its important gothic cathedral.

Amiens did not grow as rapidly as Norwich because the 1650–1750 period was neither so peaceful nor prosperous for the people of Picardy as it was for the English. The crises of 1693–1694 struck Amiens with full force: an agricultural catastrophe followed by hunger, starvation, and epidemics of typhoid and smallpox made for two long years of high prices and unemployment. So catastrophic was this disaster that mortality was twice as high as it would be in 1710—a year when the harvest was virtually nil in many locations and in which many people of the Continent once again perished from disease because they were so weakened by hunger. In addition, monies were siphoned off to the state at a great rate to pay for the last wars of Louis XIV.[120] Consequently, although Norwich and Amiens were about the same size, both were textile cities, and the patterns of migration to them seem similar, the political economies in which they were embedded meant that their fates were very different in the 1650–1750 period.

Beauvais, Amiens's smaller neighbor to the south, was probably more typical of European towns and of urban fortunes in this period than either Norwich or Amiens. This city better illuminates regular relations between town and country. Somewhat smaller, its population remained at about 13,000 from 1680 to 1730. Beauvais was also more isolated. Unlike Amiens, it did not import grain from Danzig or cheese from Holland; the sea was two hard days away by road. Although primitive, the roads were nonetheless full of people from all social stations. The poor were quick to come and go in times of trouble; beggars, women with a pack en route to market, and men with bolts of cloth on their shoulders traveled on foot. Donkeys carried market packs, mules traveled with loads of pottery and fish. Those fortunate enough to travel on horseback were wealthy farmers and gentlemen.[121]

This textile town was close to rural life. A town list of 1696 shows that the over half the residents were employed by the manufacture and marketing of wool and linen. Another third of the population worked at urban trades like bread production and shoemaking; one family in five was supported by an officer or a member of the bourgeoisie. Beauvais supported the bishop and his staff, 17 churches, and 10 religious houses, all within the one square kilometer enclosed by its walls. However, a tenth of its residents had rural occupations: agricultural laborers, vineyard keepers, coopers, and smithies. This serves as a reminder that the preindustrial town was one in which agricultural and urban occupations lived cheek by jowl.[122]

Country folk came to work in the city. To work as a wool comber for the widow Restaut, one peasant walked eight kilometers a day; two weavers from the same village worked for Robert Gimart. Even in the depressed period before the eighteenth century, over 1,000 villagers were employed in the city, some 250 as combers, 640 as weavers, and 227 as cloth finishers who worked as teaselers and cloth shearers. Later, a quarter of the town's apprentice combers and one-seventh of its weavers would come from a broad ring of villages around Beauvais.[123]

In the low-pressure demographic regime of Beauvais, the people were more sedentary at the end of the seventeenth century than they would be later, to judge from marriage records; only perhaps 10 percent of marriage partners were born outside the urban parishes surveyed. In 1700, nearly all marriage partners came from within a 20 kilometer radius.[124] These low mobility figures systematically underrepresent the movement of Beauvasiens because they do not catch temporary migrants, church personnel, or families; they even miss the marriages of urban servant women who wed in their home parish. Nonetheless, these figures are low even for marriage records, suggesting a relatively sedentary population.

Low mobility probably reflects the fact that Beauvais suffered bad times between about 1660 and 1730. The city declined after 1650, depleted by the Fronde, the wars of the kingdom, and by the dearth of markets for its fine, thick wools in a depressed economy. In this sense, its troubles were emblematic of the late seventeenth century. Underpinning these weaknesses was the fragile and death-ridden demographic system intimately tied to food supply and industrial output; when grain prices rose in times of shortage, cloth orders were short, and looms stood still. The wool-combers of Beauvais complained of hunger, numbering their fellows who had left to work the fields or to beg their bread.[125]

Developing rural industry offers another clue to the sedentary Beauvaisiens. In the late seventeenth and eighteenth centuries agriculturalists in Europe increasingly worked in rural manufacturing to earn a living without leaving the countryside. The Beauvaisiens had little reason to move into their troubled regional capital, but there are indications that they had cause to remain in their home village where industrial production may have been expanding. It is clear that rural women already were spinning for the wool manufacturers of the city in the seventeenth century, and late-century complaints about the low rates of village weavers suggest that there were enough rural weavers to aggravate the city. By 1708, 7,900 looms dotted the plain between Beauvais and Amiens, 60 kilometers to the north.[126] The stagnating urban economy, the demographic disasters of the time, and the possibility of work in the countryside all help to explain the low mobility of the Beauvaisiens. They foreshadow the more prosperous countryside that would develop during the eighteenth century.

At the other end of the urban spectrum from Beauvais were the most attractive cities of the age—the capital and port cities that were preeminent in urban growth between 1600 and 1750.[127] The capitals and ports of Atlantic trade thrived above all in the mercantilist and centralizing policies of the seventeenth- and early eighteenth-century states that expanded government and trade. In terms of their attraction for newcomers, the quintessential cities of the age were Amsterdam and London, both of which depended on a vast influx of migrants. Significantly, their draw for Europeans also reflects their global power.

As center of the dynamic Dutch Republic, Amsterdam combined the functions of both the central place and gateway in an international imperial network. It dominated a national hierarchy of towns and cities as economic, cultural, and political center, while simultaneously serving as a port for colonial trade.[128] The city provided the heart of the Republic that successfully challenged Spanish domination of the Netherlands and the ambitions of Louis XIV. With the collapse of Antwerp at the hands of the French and Spanish in the 1580s, highly skilled artisanal production shifted north to Amsterdam. Its merchants reached northeast into the Baltic Sea region to sustain a grain trade that yielded enormous profit, particularly in times of famine, when Europe would pay high prices for relief. The centerpiece of its wealth, however, was the East India Company. Chartered in 1602, the company had powers of trade from the Cape of Good Hope east to the Straits of Magellan; it was empowered to make treaties with local rulers, to administer, to defend, and to make war on Spain and Portugal. Its great success was extracting gold from the East Indies in the form of colonial trade.[129]

Dutch success transformed Amsterdam. From a population of 30,000 in 1550, it expanded to 100,000 in 70 years and to 175,000 by 1650. By the turn of the eighteenth century, the city housed 200,000. Construction throughout the seventeenth century converted the 450-acre town into a graceful half-moon of canals, new dwellings, and commercial buildings that stretched over 1,800 acres.[130] Amsterdam was a far cry from a troubled provincial manufacturing town like Beauvais, which was contained in a single square kilometer. The fall of Antwerp sent an initial flood of migrants to Amsterdam, visible in the high proportion of burghers from Antwerp in the 1550s (44%) and from the Spanish Netherlands into the 1590s (39%).[131] The subsequent growth of the city was fed by the Dutch hinterland of the United Provinces, and by thousands of foreigners. In fact, international migration played a unique role in the history of the Dutch Republic. Tens of thousands of people from Flanders to the south immigrated between 1580 and 1620; subsequently, the greatest numbers of men and women immigrated from German territories and Scandanavia (especially the south Norwegian coast). Although it is impossible to know how many people came to the Republic or to Amsterdam, gross immigration clearly numbered in the hundreds of thousands. One-third of Amsterdam's seventeenth-century marriage partners and one-fourth of its eighteenth-century marriage partners (183,000 in all) were foreign immigrants. In the 1650s, Germans were predominant among the seamen and sailors who married in the city—numbering nearly as many as the Amsterdammers (1,086 German and 1,192 Amsterdammer seamen married between 1651 and 1665). By the late 1680s, over a quarter of the burghers of Amsterdam were Germans. The vast size of migration systems with Germany was reflected by the fact that over 28,000 German men married in seventeenth- and eighteenth-century Amsterdam. Perhaps more telling, in terms of systems of chain migration between German areas and Amsterdam, over 19,000 German women married there, many of whom began their life in the city as domestic servants.[132]

The overall number of people attracted to the city exceeds even the astounding figures of city growth. Those net figures of expansion from 100,000 to 200,000 between 1620 and 1700 mask an incalculable flow of servants, sailors, and other temporary workers who subsequently departed Amsterdam. This is true of any city, even ones like Beauvais that

did not grow in this period. Yet for ports such as Amsterdam, the phenomenon of "seaborne mortality" or "maritime drain" was also at work:
the number of migrants in Amsterdam was very much larger than figures
of net growth because, among the young men who came to the city, thousands went to sea, never to return. An estimated 700,000 of the million
people who left the Republic under the aegis of the Dutch East India Company died at sea or died abroad at a colonial post. In the early eighteenth
century, when about 3,000 perished per year, a quarter of the fatalities
were men from outside the Dutch Republic, such as the German sailors.
Even more Dutch men were lost, creating a demographic deficit filled by
thousands of immigrants who go uncounted in net migration figures.[133]

The same is true for London, as the stepping-off point for thousands
of sailors, colonials, and indentured servants in the seventeenth century.
Over 1,000 indentured servants per year departed in the 1680s; it is rea-
sonable to assume that a minimum of 3,000 people left London annually,
never to return.[134] An estimated three-quarters of the servants were part
of the massive migration that fueled London growth in the seventeenth
and eighteenth centuries. Like Amsterdam, London grew fivefold between 1550 and 1650 (from 80,000 to 400,0000) and, also like the Dutch
capital, it more than doubled in the seventeenth century. Between 1550
and 1750, 1 million people are estimated to have moved to London; a net
gain of 8,000 per year in the second half of this period pushed the city to
575,000. This net growth masks those who left London for the colonies or
died at sea and others who came to London but left again. If the gross
movement of migrants into London were only 50 percent greater than the
city's net gain (an outlandishly conservative figure), mobility was still re-
markably high; such a figure suggests that nearly one-sixth of the population of England had some experience of London life by the end of the
seventeenth century. Biographies from a Shropshire village some 190 kilometers to the northeast confirm this estimate; here one family in six had
a member who had lived in London.

Long traditions linked London to East Anglia and the north from
whence aspiring Londoners had come since the fourteenth century. Of the
some 20,000 apprentices in London in 1650, about 85 percent were migrants; they came not only from the home counties, but about 8,000 came
from the midlands and the north of England as well. Steve Rappaport's
observation of the city in 1550, "London served as a vocational training
centre for young men throughout England," applies equally well to the
city a century later.[135]

The draw of this city profoundly affected the people of the surrounding regions. The immediate hinterland was a wellspring; for example, the
1599 parish lists from nearby Ealing in Middlesex show that the number
of daughters living at home declined by 75 percent between the group
aged 10 to 14 and those aged 15 to 19; most of the elder group were
probably in service in London.[136] More fundamentally, the attraction of

London for the women of southeastern England seems to have influenced the population composition of nearby counties in the long term. David Souden's analysis of eighteenth-century parish register abstracts suggests that the emigration of women from the southeastern counties "bit deeply into the population" of London's hinterland to the extent that the sex ratios of those counties were altered. They had an overabundance of men. The reverse was true in the western counties, where there were many opportunities for women in dairy work as well as traditions of seafaring and emigration for men.[137]

Women were crucial among new Londoners. They outnumbered men, giving the city a sex ratio of 87 in 1695 (87 men per 100 women).[138] Urban areas in general, and London in particular, needed women in great numbers to produce yarn and thread, to launder clothing, to shop, to sell and prepare food, to bear and raise children, to sew clothing and serve beer—in short, to carry out particular service, productive, and reproductive tasks that maintain urban life. These functions shaped their urban fortunes. Most women came to London to work. Migrant women who lived with kin could earn their keep in London as a seamstress or knitter. For those who had no kin in the city, or whose kin could not take them in, domestic service offered the best work because it gave room, board, and the potential for quasi-familial relations, although it had the disadvantage of being a clearly subordinate position.[139] Some women came to bear a child in secret. In this era, Jane Crooke left Oxford for London, for example, sent to the great city by her lover until she could be discreetly delivered of their child.[140] For others, marriage was a goal.

A portrait of the migrant woman in London in the early seventeenth century emerges from marriage license applications. Young women typically entered the city in their late teens, at about the same age as apprentices. Many had lost their father just before they left for the city, which suggests that this death hastened or even precipitated their departure. Vivien Brodsky Elliot's analysis of the records suggests that there were two distinct subgroups of migrant women in London: one consisted of women who lived with kin in the city, and the other of the 35 percent who worked as servants. The young women servants had dramatically fewer resources at their disposal. Their fathers were more likely to be deceased by the time they married (74%) than the fathers of other migrants (64%). Although many of the servants had a relative in London, it was usually a brother, whose youth and apprentice or journeyman status perhaps prevented him from housing his sister. Migrant women who worked as servants were from lower-status families than those who lived with kin; servants were the daughters of laborers, husbandmen, common craftsmen, and yeomen. By contrast, a third of the migrants who lived with kin were from gentry families. Over one-fifth of the migrant women lived with a relative—a married sister, brother, aunt, or uncle (in that order).[141]

For migrant women, two marriage tracks operated in London. Those who lived with kin "almost invariably" married men of higher status than their fathers and they married relatively early (at 23.7 years, on average). Many of them had been sent to the city to marry; the records often stated explicitly that the migrant woman living with kin had been "sent up to London by her father for that purpose." By contrast, migrant servants tended to marry down, into the ranks of sailors and craftsmen, and to marry about three years later than migrant women who resided with kin (at age 26.5). They also married men close to themselves in age. Both migrant groups are distinct from London-born women, who married at a younger age (20.5 years on average) and married higher-status men substantially older than themselves (four to eight years older); most of these marriages were doubtless negotiated by London families.[142] These patterns testify to the effectiveness of family protection and sponsorship in the marriage market and to servant women's lack of clout.

But Elliot perceives another side to this coin as well; migrant women's courtships were freer from parental constraints, and their marriages were more egalitarian than those of native-born urban women. Marriage records suggest that the social lives of young newcomers centered at work, implying that a most common ground for meeting spouses in seventeenth-century London was the households in which young men and women cohabited as servants and apprentices. This would make Margaret Lawe typical: her courtship with William Fellowe began in the Greene household, where she worked as a servant and he as a scrivener's apprentice; they married in the summer of 1604, when she was 28 and his apprenticeship was completed.[143]

As people streamed into London after 1550, the emblematic tale of Dick Whittington appeared in English folklore.[144] A poor orphan from the country, Whittington found work in a merchant's kitchen after nearly perishing from hunger and an injury suffered in the streets of the city. Once employed, he nearly quit London, so miserable was his life made by the cruel cook during the day and by the rats that would scamper over his face at night. On the point of leaving the city, he was dissuaded by the bells of Bow church that he heard to ring out "turn around, Dick Whittington, thrice Lord Mayor of London." Dick took courage; he faced his daytime tormentor fortified by the kindness of the merchant's daughter and defeated his nocturnal enemies with the aid of a cat he managed to acquire. Whittington's fortune was made when his cat was sold by the merchant's men for a princely sum when they were shipwrecked on the lands of a potentate overrun by rats. He achieved instant wealth, married the merchant's daughter, was sheriff, and finally, as the bells foretold, served three terms as Lord Mayor of London. Significantly, foreign trade made Whittington's fortune, just as it did that of many a Londoner. As successful outsider, he was in good company, because 90 percent of London's greater merchants and three-quarters of its mayors came from outside London in the sixteenth and early seventeenth centuries.[145]

Whittington's success story was apocryphal, and the real Richard Whittington neither was from humble origins nor married his master's daughter.[146] The possibilities for the poor orphan boy, and for even a young apprentice, were modest. Many, such as Francis Haires, aged 16, "his father and mother and all friends dead and he a miserable wandering boy," though like the fabled Whittington, would move on from London; in the 1680s, 1,000 per year went off to the colonies as indentured servants.[147] A realistic definition of success in London was offered by one John Browne in 1631. Browne had worked some 110 kilometers north in Leicester, unable to make a living at dressing hemp. In London, however, he declared, "I am a freeman of the city and of the company of merchant tailors," and self-employed.[148] Such success and security was about as much as one could hope for, particularly because there were so many migrants less successful than John Browne and cities less prosperous than London in this age of war and religious intolerance.

CONCLUSION

We amend our rather cozy vision of preindustrial life. "Everyone had his or her circle of affection," wrote Peter Laslett of "the world we have lost." Yet this was by no means true for all Europeans in the preindustrial age. For many, it was not true that "time was when the whole of life went forward in the family, in a circle of loved, familiar faces."[149] It may be more accurate to write that everyone *sought* a circle of affection. Those with land and fortunes could more easily remain with family and could more easily find a place. For the landless, inhabitants of war-torn lands, young people, and orphans, and particularly the women in each of these groups, home was to be found or created.

Certain traits of the migration process that endure into the next centuries are visible in the preindustrial world sketched out in this chapter. Migration was a social process mediated by family interests and embedded in the world of kin and village contacts. Those who took to the road operated within a known world of opportunities and practices provided by the social body. Within this framework the individual traits of gender, life-cycle stage, and (among landowners) birth order helped to pinpoint who would move and where and why.

The economic and social composition of preindustrial Europe included a large proportion of peasants and artisans—people who may have moved as young farm or domestic servants and may have moved to marry, but who, if married, tended to settle and remain with their landholding or workshop. If adult males left home, they were likely to depart for a temporary cash-earning trip. This overwhelmingly rural and largely peasant configuration meant that much mobility would be local movement of servants and marriage partners or circular, seasonal migration.

Some sectors of the preindustrial economy needed a massive impulse of labor and attracted many migrants. In the countryside, these were the capital-rich large farms like the wheat fields on the outskirts of Paris that fed the Continent's most populous city and the dairy farms of Holland that met an international demand for Dutch cheese; such areas encouraged the development of systems of circular, seasonal migration. The early modern city also had a great demand—not simply for servants, apprentices, and laborers who came to every sort of town for a temporary stay, but also for new people in its bourgeoisie, mercantile class and professional groups who would become long-term residents. The largest and most successful of cities drew newcomers from a widespread hinterland, some of whom entered the world economy as wholesale merchants and others of whom left European shores as lowly sailors or indentured servants.

Migrants in the preindustrial world moved in systems of local, circular, chain, and career migration. In the 1650–1750 period, local movement was a key element of the life cycle for rural people. In a few specific regions, such as in Westphalia or the French highlands, circular, seasonal migration took men away from home for seasonal work; near most towns, temporary migration for a few years to work as a domestic servant was part of young women's lives. In some cases, chain migration systems began to retain circular migrants at their destination as Germans settled in Amsterdam and French settled in Spain. Career migration was the pattern of a rather elite few, such as the highly placed men and women of the church, court officials, and government agents. The significance of the balance among these kinds of migration lies in the fact that most rural movement was probably local or circular. Although many Europeans moved, most stayed within their province and the distribution of population did not change dramatically.

The balance among the various kinds of migration, as well as the propensity to migrate, would shift in the later eighteenth century with changes in the forces underlying preindustrial migration patterns. Both circular and chain migration would become more important in some regions, and migration would slow altogether in others. This happened as demographic patterns altered and the population began to grow. Chances for cash-earning in rural areas increased with the impulse of merchant capital into the countryside and the expansion of rural industry. And population expansion and rural manufacture combined to reduce peasant holdings and reduce land ownership after about 1750.

CHAPTER

3

Migration in the Age of Early Industry

The tax collectors in the rugged highlands of central France could extract nothing from Antoine Salez in 1739. Salez had left to work in Spain, his wife explained, because he could pay neither his debts nor his taxes. The desperation of peasants like Salez and the frustration of state agents would only increase as the eighteenth century went on, because a growing population pressed on limited land and few other sources of revenue existed around Aurillac in the central highlands. As a consequence, some Aurillaçois went to Spain, to Paris, and to the port city of Bordeaux; still others left for the season to work as sawyers or to harvest crops on the Mediterranean littoral and to work as tinkers as far north as the Netherlands. What the mountains had to offer was the strong arms of their men. Women and children accompanied harvest teams to glean and to beg only in very bad years; they usually journeyed within their region, working as farm servants or domestics in the little towns of the uplands, if they left home at all.[1] Between 1750 and the 1789 Revolution, long-standing systems of temporary, circular migration expanded under pressure from population increase and the need for capital.

By contrast, families were quite sedentary some 500 kilometers to the north in the Pays de Caux near Rouen. There, merchants' porters delivered warps for weavers and raw cotton for spinners to villages like Auffay, about 35 kilometers from the city. Thus, when Marie and widower Jean Hebert married in 1762, the bride brought a spinning wheel as part of her dowry. She would make weekly trips with other women of the village to sell her thread at a market town 10 kilometers away. Father and son wove together and worked as laborers on the rich commercial farmlands around Auffay. This was not a peasant family but a proletarian family, almost entirely dependent on the cash they were all able to earn. Auffay grew as the century passed, partly because outsiders came and stayed. It also expanded because during most of the eighteenth century, the men and women of Auffay remained at home—all year round and all of their lives: women spun year-round, men wove in the winter, and everyone worked the harvest in the fall.[2] Those who did move in the Pays de Caux generally went in the direction of Rouen, toward the belt of villages on the outskirts of the city that became virtual industrial suburbs. City and countryside were a unit; and the entire area depended on the vagaries of the international textile market.[3] In this region, the proliferation of manufacturing in the village setting enabled rural people to earn necessary cash without leaving home.

The proletarians of Auffay and the landowning peasants of the Aurillaçois represent two exemplary experiences of eighteenth-century Europeans. They offer contrasting mobility scenarios in the extremes of increased migration born of pressures on areas with a chronic lack of resources, on one hand, and a more sedentary regime underwritten by rural industry, on the other. The eighteenth century is a conundrum in terms of human mobility, precisely because two very different general patterns emerged. This chapter explores and explains migration paths that were marked with particular clarity after about 1750—a turning point in the economic, demographic, and social history of Europe.

This chapter must be considered against the backdrop constructed by the previous chapter, because most patterns of preindustrial migration persisted through the 1750–1820 period. Systems of seasonal migration thrived. Rural service continued to be the means by which young people became trained in agricultural work and earned their keep, and for the majority of young people this vocation demanded annual moves. At marriage, brides continued to relocate in their husband's parish. Some marriage markets expanded after 1750; more young people married outside the parish, and others found spouses farther afield. Some peasant families moved, but it was still more likely that proletarian families left their parish. Evidence from eighteenth-century cities indicates that about half the *burghers* continued to be newcomers, a third to half of urban marriage partners were migrants, and a substantial turnover in city population persisted. None of these patterns was new.

What was new in eighteenth-century Europe that altered migration patterns was a substantial increase both in population and in rural employment outside agriculture. Population and labor force change were the fundamental engines of change in human mobility. In the eighteenth century, these developments contained migration in rural industrial areas and increased circular and chain migration in areas with little industry.

In addition to population and labor force changes, shifts in the deployment of capital and landownership helped to shape migration patterns. The proliferation of rural industry reflects the spread of capital into the countryside. Villagers experienced this "offensive of capitalism" by working for the cash doled out—penny by penny—by merchants. Landholding patterns changed as a reduced proportion of rural families were able to own adequate holdings to support themselves. Urban demography changed as well, as some cities became less deadly; the urban labor force came to include a larger proportion of laborers compared to the proportion of master artisans. Moreover, many cities concentrated on commercial transactions and specific production tasks that finished and marketed products fabricated in the countryside.

A keystone of the chapter is early industry, or protoindustry: the expansion of manufacturing that began outside the factory in the seventeenth century and became crucially important in the eighteenth. This massive production for export markets is central to economic change, both the spread of rural production and the building of the eighteenth-century city.[4] Town and country together acted as units of production because goods were produced in villages, then finished, processed, and marketed in towns. Villagers of the region, for example, manufactured the Nottingham hosiery and Lyon silk that were named for these urban finishing and marketing centers.[5] Such systems of manufacture brought workers even in remote villages into international markets; their livelihoods came to depend on the vagaries of taste for particular fashions (such as printed silk and cotton blends), needs for particular products (like the large nails used by Dutch shipbuilders in their heyday), peace among nations, and protective trade agreements. Scholarship on early industry published in the 1970s and 1980s is of incalculable value to this study of migration and more generally to understanding early modern Europe. It highlights the importance of rural production before the factory age and elucidates the connections between production and population. More important for the purposes of this book, this research yields detailed information about population patterns in an apparently sedentary age.

This chapter explores the connections among migration, the increased population, and the economic changes wrought by the eighteenth century. It focuses on a variety of regions, some where rural industry abounded and others with relatively little manufacture. Because changes that affected migration occurred unevenly from one region to another, this chapter skips through time as well as space. Population growth and rural industry were more intense, and earlier, for example, in the English midlands and low countries than in the highlands of Swiss Glaris and Zurich. Consequently, I emphasize the 70 years following 1750 but also include material from earlier times where it is appropriate.

After an examination of the migration itineraries produced by early industry and by a lack of resources in the face of a growing population, the chapter turns to a portrait of the exemplary migration system that linked the French highlands with Spain. It then analyzes the increase of impoverished migrants in the period after 1750. Finally, it focuses on the urbanward movement most characteristic of this age—movement into and around towns that were nodes of production and marketing in early industry. First, however, I sketch the character of the age in terms of international politics, population, and landholding.

Map 3:1 Western Europe in 1750

THE CHARACTER OF THE AGE: POLITICS, POPULATION, AND LANDHOLDING

Western Europe remained essentially rural in this period. In 1750, the countries of the north and west had an estimated 160 cities of 10,000 or more people, bringing the urban population to about 7 percent of the total. By 1800, there were 240 cities of 10,000, but because many of these were relatively small and the rural population grew substantially also, the proportion of urban dwellers remained small. Over nine Europeans in 10 lived in villages or small towns into the nineteenth century.[6]

And most of these people lived in peace. After the bloody War of Spanish Succession was settled in 1713, the people of eighteenth-century Europe gained relief from the political, economic, and demographic upheavals that had been so devastating in the seventeenth century. European forces fought most of their battles in faraway North America, where France and Britain struggled for hegemony in the Seven Years' War (1756–1763), and England contested the independence of some of its colonies (1775–1783). The War of Austrian Succession (1740–1748) and the continental portion of the Seven Years' War were fought partly in the low countries and northern France, but they took their toll primarily in Silesia, which was the object of struggle between the Prussian and Austrian crowns. The great continental famines waned, particularly after the 1730s; the wars of politics and religion that devastated vast areas during the seventeenth century subsided until the very end of the eighteenth. This respite from warfare and the accompanying diseases and crop devastations underwrote an era of expansion that lasted until the wars of the French Republic and Napoleonic Empire that began in 1792.

Some of this expansion took the form of foreign settlement. Many Germans were recruited to settle the plains of southeastern Europe that were opened by the defeat of the Turks in the seventeenth century. At least 60,000 German colonists arrived in Hungary between 1748 and 1786, followed by 180,000 private settlers. From 1763 to 1800, about 37,000 Germans settled in Russia's Volga districts and near the Black Sea. Encouraged by Frederick the Great, some 300,000 Germans moved east to colonize Prussian territories.[7]

The Americas also attracted newcomers. At least 125,000 Germans entered North America in the eighteenth century, primarily through Philadelphia. After a surge of emigration in the seventeenth century, both British and French settlement abated in the eighteenth. But the settlement of the Seven Years' War in 1763 consolidated British control of North America and precipitated an unprecedented surge of transatlantic migration. Understandably, the French ceased massive movement to North America after defeat, and British settlement soared. Between 1760 and 1775, more than 125,000 newcomers arrived in British North America from the British Isles (55,000 Protestant Irish, 40,000 Scots, and 30,000 English). In addition to smaller groups of Swiss, 84,500 enslaved Africans arrived and 12,000 Germans debarked in Philadelphia. In a short fifteen years, then, over 221,500 newcomers arrived, reflecting the military and mercantile triumphs of Britain.[8]

As important as those settlers became to North America and to the plains of eastern Europe, their absence did not cause fundamental stresses because there were plenty of people left at home. This was an age of population increase. After the crises that marked the decades of the 1690s,

TABLE 3.1
**Estimated Population Growth in Northwestern
Europe, 1750–1800
(in millions)**

	c. 1750	c. 1800
Norway	0.7	0.9
Sweden	1.8	2.3
Finland	0.5	1.0
Denmark	0.7	0.9
Germany	18.4	24.5
Netherlands	1.9	2.1
Belgium	2.2	2.8
Switzerland	1.4	1.7
France	24.5	29.0
Scotland	1.3	1.6
Wales	0.3	0.6
England	5.8	8.7
Ireland	2.4	5.2

Note: The figures for Germany are for the 1914 boundaries less Alsace and Lorraine. The figures for other countries are for the borders of 1850.
SOURCE: Michael Anderson, *Population Change in North-Western Europe, 1750–1850* (London: Macmillan, 1988), 23.

1700s, and 1730s, the European population expanded rapidly, rising from 81 million in 1700 to 123 million a century later. In the "long eighteenth century" that stretched from 1680 to 1820, the population of western Europe grew by 62 percent, with most of the growth occurring after 1740. The German population expanded by 51 percent, the French by 39 percent, the Spanish by 64 percent, the Italian by 53 percent, the English by an astounding 133 percent.[9] From the 1750s to the 1790s, population growth was especially rapid in Ireland (at 1.7% per annum) and England (where the growth rate increased from .5% to 1%), but in most of Europe it grew at a rate of about .5 percent per year. Although this growth rate would be outstripped in the nineteenth century, it accrued enormous increases in the number of Europeans. For example, between 1750 and 1800, the number of Germans increased by 33 percent (from 18.4 to 24.5 million) and the number of English increased by 50 percent (from 5.8 to 8.7 million).[10] (See Table 3:1.)

Two fundamental changes underlay this demographic expansion: a decrease in mortality and an increase in fertility that accompanied earlier and more widespread marriage. Exactly how each operated continues to be debated. It is certainly true that the mechanics of demographic expansion varied from place to place. A widespread drop in catastrophic mortality crises allowed more people to survive. Neither city nor countryside suffered from disease as it had before 1715. With a few notable exceptions, such as the terrible plague mortality spreading to southern France from the Mediterranean port city of Marseille in 1720, the bubonic plague nearly disappeared. On the Continent, relief from the hunger that rendered people susceptible to disease, killing children and cutting marriages short, seems to have been most responsible for population expansion.[11] This was particularly true in the years of good harvest between 1740 and 1786.

Changed patterns of marriage and childbearing produced more children. Particularly in England, a greater proportion of people married, and married younger. The age at marriage fell from an estimated 26 to 23 among English women in the 1680–1820 period, and the proportion who remained single fell by half, from 15 percent to 7.5 percent.[12] This pattern also occurred in some of the rural industrial areas of Flanders and Switzerland. More years of marriage extended women's time of childbearing, producing more children. The "prolifick power" of earlier marriage has been accepted as the mainspring of population increase in many regions of early industry.[13] Yet not all workers in rural industry married early; rather, a high age of marriage remained an important part of family culture in some regions, particularly where rural industry did not yield long-term income increases for men.[14]

Both in areas with dense rural industry and those without, a trend to proletarianization accompanied population increase. Proletarians were the men and women who supported themselves by wage labor rather than by their own shops or agricultural property. The increase in the proportion of proletarians and concomitant decrease in proportion of peasants between 1650 and 1800 signaled a major change in European rural populations. A marked decline from the high-water mark of the peasantry occurred from England east to Saxony and from Scandinavia to southern France. In rural Europe, the eighteenth century saw an increase in peasants whose landholdings were too marginal to support families without supplemental wage work and in *de facto* proletarians, cotters, and renters who did not own any land to speak of.[15]

Statistics from the Kingdom of Saxony, in a rare source that distinguished the number of people by class, show the disproportional increase of proletarians.[16] The rural population of Saxony more than doubled in the two centuries between 1550 and 1750; the urban population—which included the cities of Dresden and Leipzig—increased by even more. With population increase and urbanization came a sharp rise in the ranks of rural landless and urban dependent workers: gardeners and cotters, constituting 7 percent of the rural population in 1550, made up 48 percent in 1750, while dependent workers increased from 16 to 45 percent of urban dwellers. Over the course of these two centuries, nearly half of Saxon society had become proletarian.

This remarkable change in European society reverberated across Europe. For example, in the Leicestershire village of Wigston Magna, peasants held 40 percent of the land in 1765 and large-scale capitalist farms held the rest. With enclosure three years later and a shift from farming to livestock pasturage, the number of resident peasant landholders was reduced by a third as they sold out or rented out their land. By 1831, the peasant economy had totally disappeared. In France, where peasant ownership was much stronger, Albert Soboul estimated that 40 percent of the rural population was semi-proletarian or proletarian by 1790. There was a visible minority of proletarians even in peasant strongholds like rural Brittany (20–25%) and the mountain parishes of the Pyrenees (30–40%). Surveying urban areas, Catharina Lis and Hugo Soly concluded that the proletariat expanded just as much in cities; Strasbourg was typical, where the proportion of wage laborers rose from 29 percent in 1699 to 45 percent in 1784.[17]

Two forces expanded the proportion of proletarians in the European countryside: downward social mobility and population increase.[18] Debt made proletarians of peasants, as families lost fields when they were unable to gather the cash to repay their creditors. Enclosure movements in the west and the expansion of estate agriculture in the east also closed families out of meaningful property ownership. Finally, many children from peasant families who were not the designated heir lost their landed status if they were unable to purchase land or marry into another landholding family.

Proletarianization was tied to the increase in population in two ways. The land could not absorb the increased number of peasants, so more children meant the division of landholdings—sometimes into holdings too small to be viable. This applied especially in areas where families divided land among all children such as the west and southwest German territories. In regions where the inheritor bought out siblings and family lands were not divided up, the expanded peasant population put more children on the road. More important, perhaps, proletarian families produced more children than landholding ones, and they did not respond to hard times by having fewer children.[19] "As the population grew, most of the growth occurred at the bottom of the social scale," concluded Myron Gutmann of his study of a mixed population of farmers and rural industrial workers.[20]

More widespread marriage, earlier marriage, higher marital fertility, and lower infant mortality all worked together to produce more children in propertyless families.

Rural industry, proletarianization, and population expansion were mutually linked.[21] One of the keys to proletarianization was the growth of rural industry, which changed family and reproductive patterns to increase the numbers of cottage workers. Likewise, proletarianization offered a key to migration in this period. People who did not own land were the most mobile; they could most easily depart as young people to seek their fortunes as servants, rural manufacturing workers, agricultural laborers, or urban wage workers. Proletarian families could, and did, take to the road in search of a village where they could find work.

As a result of population increase and proletarianization, the eighteenth century produced a new kind of hardship for the mass of Europeans, which translated differently through the political systems of England and France. In England a unique relationship among landlord, tenant, and laborers increased agricultural productivity at the expense of the peasantry; enclosures were untrammeled after the mid-seventeenth century and agricultural productivity soared. In France, by contrast, the peasantry remained in place, and the landholding nobility was held in check by an absolutist regime that extracted the maximum of taxes from the peasantry. The nobility was relatively powerless against absolutism in France, but it did have the power to fleece peasants and sharecroppers with increased feudal dues. Thus, taxes and fees pressed the rural people of France while dependence on wage labor pressed those of England.[22] In both instances, there was a squeeze on the people of Europe that impoverished the inhabitants of a crowded land.[23] Mountains spilled over with people, cities grew, and the plains became full. The implications for migration are tremendous: this time of economic expansion and release from the old demographic regime divided more sharply those who could earn a living at home from those who could not.

"HYBRID SOCIETIES" AND THE
FAMILY ECONOMY

With the expansion of rural industry in eighteenth-century Europe, what Myron Gutmann calls "hybrid societies" developed. Early industry completely dominated only a few regions, like the linen-working county Armagh in Ulster, Ireland, but in most regions agricultural work continued to be important. Small-scale production for local markets continued to be ubiquitous as well; every good-sized village had its shoemaker and smithy. As a result, villagers combined rural manufacturing with other money-earning activities, including labor migration. For example, with the expansion of linen production in Rhineland territories, poor Westphalian families drew both on home linen production and on men's seasonal migration to Holland. In the same highlands that sent Antoine Salez (whose story opened this chapter) to Spain, women earned a bit of cash by lacemaking, ribbon weaving, and putting pins into papers with their children—pins fashioned by men of the same mountains.[24] These upland industries, however, were neither as vigorous nor as dense as those in the lowlands; rather, they were fragile and ill-remunerated, depending as they did on meager capital, poor communications, and merchants who were themselves little more than peddlers. Thus for the woman who stayed at home in the Velay, while the men of the village went to the lowlands to harvest or work in the great cities of provincial France, rural industry brought in little, but badly needed, cash.

The concept of the family economy provides a powerful prism through which to view the balance between rural production and migration.[25] Peasant and proletarian families alike saw themselves as units of production and consumption (among other things) that deployed the labor of their members in the best interests of the group—which in the case of wealthy peasants was the maintenance and increase of family properties and for the proletarian poor the survival of the family intact.[26] In "the cottage economy," a family member might migrate with a harvest team, become a farm servant elsewhere, or stay at home to spin or work the fields; this is because families were flexible—not devoted to manufacture or to agriculture but rather attempting to do as well as possible under the given circumstances. The poor exploited themselves and their children, getting by on an "economy of makeshifts."[27] People used every expedient they knew of in order to survive until the next harvest, the next bout of taxation, tithes, and dues. In some areas, those opportunities were at hand in the form of cash-earning employment that could be done at home. But in others, one had to leave to get by—or combine a bit of lacemaking with gleaning, begging, and working away from home.

The adults in the household decided who remained at home, taking into account gender, birth order, strength, and age. The tasks of rural industries, like nearly all tasks, were assigned either to men or to women and children. As a consequence, the family's men or women could work in cottage industry, while the remaining family members concentrated on agricultural work or seasonal migration. For example, the women of Auffay in Normandy spun thread while the men worked the fields; those in the mountains of Velay filled papers of pins while the men trekked to the lowlands.

More women than men doubtless worked in rural industries. In textiles, numerically the most important employer, women and children usually worked as spinners, while men most often worked as handloom weavers; and the work of six to 10 spinners was required to supply each weaver. In addition, lacemaking employed thousands of workers, most of them women and children. By contrast, nailmaking and other rural met-alworking—generally work for men—employed fewer workers.

Consequently, in the hybrid societies of the eighteenth century, the family deployed its members in various sectors of mixed economies. All family members were not necessarily engaged in rural production, nor did they always work together, or even remain at home. This was especially true when women and children were the ones engaged in very low-paid rural production as lacemakers or spinners. They required supplementary work from other family members. Detailed information on the English countryside allows a village-level view of family labor assignments. In eighteenth-century Bedfordshire, for example, about 45 miles northwest of London, girls began making pillow-lace before the age of 10 and con-tinued doing so into their teens or turned to the spinning of linen or jersey. Their brothers, however, left home to go into agricultural service. Likewise, in the Bedfordshire village of Cardington in 1782, 78 percent of the boys and 29 percent of the girls aged 15 to 19 were out in service; the girls remaining at home worked at needlework or spinning. Twenty-five miles to the southwest, Joseph Mayett, the rural servant whose story opened chapter 2, helped at home with lacemaking in the 1790s for three years before he went into farm service at age 12.[28]

EARLY INDUSTRY AND MIGRATION

Rural manufacture for distant markets expanded to unprecedented peaks in this era, as villages filled the orders of urban merchants for such prod-ucts as thread, cloth, nails, and tools. Although no complete survey of rural production exists, it is possible to sketch out the regions of primary concentration. In England, some of the largest rural employers were wool manufacturers concentrated in West Riding, Yorkshire, where production multiplied eightfold in the eighteenth century. A similar expansion at-tracted a quarter of the population of Ulster in Ireland—some 200,000 peo-ple—into linen production by 1800. On the Continent, linen doubtless employed the most workers. In the Netherlands, it was concentrated in the Overijssel Province. In Westphalia, linen production flourished in Osnabrück, the Teuteberg Forest, and Lippe; in Minden-Ravensberg 70 percent of the population depended on linen production by 1800. Manu-facture expanded enormously in the lower Rhineland as well between 1750 and 1800. Farther to the east, rural people in Saxony, Silesia, Bohe-mia, and lower Austria spun flax and wove linen. In the west, the densely populated and rich plain of Flanders was the center of linen manufacture. Linen production on the French Flemish plain (the present-day *département* of the Nord) tripled from 1746 to 1788 and employed three out of four villagers. Likewise, the success of the cotton-linen blend called *siamoise* in the *généralité* of Rouen expanded the number of fabric workers from about

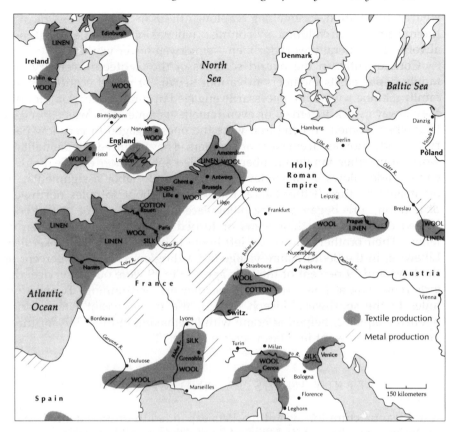

MAP 3:2 Rural Industry in Eighteenth-Century Europe

Source: McKay, John P., Hill, Bennett D., and John Buckler, *History of Western Society*, Fourth Edition. Copyright 1991 by Houghton Mifflin Company. Used with permission.

57,000 to over 188,000 in 50 years—nearly one-third the population of up-per Normandy worked in textiles by 1782. There were about eight spin-ners to one weaver. Wool was important on the Continent as well; between 1700 and 1790, production increased over 140 percent in Lan-guedoc and over 125 percent in Champagne, where 30,000 weavers pro-duced woolen fabric. In the Forez and Lyonnais surrounding Lyon, 100,000 workers prepared silk for urban weavers. Cotton was a rural prod-uct in Alsace (where 25,000 cotton spinners worked in the 1780s) and northern and eastern Switzerland. Some manufacturers employed a great many men and women despite the fact that their workers lived in villages; indeed, more rural workers came to depend on a single employer than would enter one factory later in history. For example, merchant-entrepre-neur Bernard Scheibler employed over 6,000 rural spinners and weavers in the region just north of Liège.[29] (See Map 3:2.)

In early industry, production headquarters were usually located in a town, where bookkeeping, the finishing of goods, and marketing occurred; but the vast majority of production processes, and employees, were in the countryside. Figures for the Austrian Schwechat cotton firm provide an example. In 1752 Schwechat employed four bookkeepers and agents in Vienna; four office employees and 408 workers in bleaching and printing fabric worked at company headquarters just south of Vienna. In lower Austria 39 employees distributed raw materials and 436 wove and 5,655 spun cotton.[30] The Schwechat firm gives an idea of the area covered by rural production, the vast number of people employed, and the high ratio of spinners per weaver (7.7 in this case). Of the million people in lower Austria in 1790, over 182,000 worked in the textile industry alone—about one in 13 adult men and one in three women and girls. Here, as elsewhere, when industry thrived, it expanded rapidly: where there were 20,000 textile workers in 1762, there were over 180,000 in 1790.[31]

Rural manufacturing was not ubiquitous, but it was crucial to eighteenth-century economic growth. Industrial expansion and the enormous, widespread rural labor force underwrote industrial output. Moreover, this burgeoning output measured very nearly equally throughout western Europe in 1750—an international pattern of output very different from that which would come with machine industry, pushing England into the forefront. Paul Bairoch's calculations of the per-capita levels of industrial output for about 1750 (as a percentage of British production in 1900) estimate that Britain, Belgium, and France had about the same levels of production, only slightly ahead of Germany and Italy and a little farther ahead than Switzerland.[32]

Rural industry had a distinct and complex impact on European mobility. Early industry enabled people to earn necessary money while remaining in the countryside and working outside agriculture. It also produced manufacturing villages that attracted and retained newcomers. At the same time, early industry reduced the geographic and economic divisions between town and country. Foremost, rural manufacturing enabled country people to find work in a village setting. It thrived because it matched chronic rural underemployment to urban merchant capital. For those whose age and gender fit the tasks at hand, there was no need for the kind of seasonal migration undertaken by the men of Westphalia or the central highlands of France. Indeed, Jan Lucassen estimates that only the very poorest among Westphalian linen weavers was forced to work seasonally in Holland.[33] Because rural industry made seasonal migration unnecessary by substituting the cash-earning function of temporary mobility, the province of Ulster in Ireland, the lowlands of northern France, the Netherlands, the Rhineland, and present-day Belgium, where rural industry was especially vigorous, were areas without widespread currents of circular migration.

Ironically, migration allowed the establishment of rural industry because the freedom to settle is at the core of its proliferation. Production flourished where people were free to reside where they chose and where legal systems and landholding patterns made it possible to divide holdings, build new cottages, and occupy a variety of buildings. For example, industry thrived in English freeholding villages where manors did not restrict settlement, while it never took root in villages where there were community restrictions on the subdivision of farms or settlement of newcomers.[34] Where feudalism restricted free movement, rural industry thrived only in regions like Silesia, where it was incorporated into the feudal obligations of the serf.[35] In the Austrian Waldviertel, where Schwechat cotton workers lived, law restricted settlement, the division of landholdings, and the construction of new cottages. As a consequence, legal space for the expansion of a full-time manufacturing cottager class did not exist. Production depended on men's off-season weaving and the spinning of their wives and daughters; consequently, fewer than 440 men wove for the Schwechat firm—and did so only part of the year.[36] Lutz Berkner concluded that laws on migration and settlement put a ceiling on Austrian rural production precisely because they restricted those most likely to work in early industry: the landless, those with insecure tenure, gardeners, and poor cottagers.[37]

Manufacturing villages in western Europe tended to attract and retain people more than other kinds of settlements. In some cases, rural industry actually decreased mobility. For example, emigration from the eastern Swiss canton of Glaris dropped by half with the development of its cotton production. Peter Clark speculates that growing industrial employment in villages helped to slow subsistence migration in eighteenth-century England.[38] Manufacturing villages were most attractive early in their industrial history, when they were establishing a labor force whose prolific marriages would supply needed workers later on. In a fascinating comparison of mobility among 16 English villages, David Souden found that industrial villages had high levels of inward movement and relative permanency. From the end of the seventeenth century, the advent of rural industry brought a great wave of immigrants. Subsequent generations of villagers were likely to stay in their home settlement throughout their lifetime. By contrast, married people often departed villages that lacked manufacturing employment. Likewise, the industrial villages of the Düsseldorf district of Prussia had lower rates of migration than the region's factory towns or agricultural villages in the 1820s.[39] These general findings are borne out by close studies of industrial villages in the English midlands, Normandy, and present-day Belgium.

Shepshed, the most industrial village in the English midlands in the eighteenth century, lived from the stocking trade; its people used knitting machines to produce woolen hose. The village experienced rapid growth in the eighteenth century, expanding from about 600 to 700 people in the seventeenth century to about 3,000 in 1812. In contrast to nonmanufacturing villages nearby, Shepshed's population increase relied on a drop in the age of marriage—and high fertility—that came with the proliferation of employment in the stocking industry. But many of the mothers and fathers in Shepshed initially had been attracted to the village as single people. Marriage records show that 70 percent of the adults in the parish married in Shepshed rather than elsewhere in the early and full-scale industrial periods (1680–1809). The number of weddings boomed after rural industry took off in about 1749 and the majority of nuptials joined a Shepshed native with an outsider. Most newcomers to Shepshed hailed from nearby, from the industrial villages of the region; in most cases they were already proletarians. The village industry attracted outsiders, then retained them—for during the industrial period, over half the families had married children living in town. This pattern of attraction and retention for Shepshed contrasted with its preindustrial times, the subsequent industrial involution, and with the trends in pastoral villages.[40]

The history of the Ing family in Shepshed demonstrates the potential of early industry to support rural people. Framework knitter William Ing arrived in Shepshed from the south and established residency before his 1754 marriage to Mary Coulson, daughter of a village slater whose family had been in Shepshed for over a century. The couple remained in the village and produced 13 children, of whom two sons and two daughters married in the village; in time they had six married grandsons in the village, all of whom appear to have worked as knitters. Although the fate of William and Mary's seven remaining children is unknown, the continued presence of the couple, their children, and their grandchildren is testimony to their ability to live from hosiery production.[41]

The industrial village of Auffay on the populous northern French plain of the Pays de Caux likewise expanded early with rural manufacturing. The most spectacular growth occurred in the "golden age of spinning," when cotton spinning employed most village women (1751–1786), and Auffay quickly grew by 65 percent, from about 656 to 1,080 people. During the heyday of spinning, high birth rates, low death rates, and immigration expanded the population. The number of households in Auffay increased from 164 to 270 between 1750 and 1789, a 65 percent increase in 39 years. Where did these new households come from? Many came from Auffay itself, because most women married in this village where females had earning power; the village's celibacy rate was only a little over 2 percent compared to the national figure of about 8 percent. In addition, some single men and women, moving independently of their families, were attracted to Auffay (9% of the grooms and 7% of the brides). Doubtless, families came to the village as well, settling into the small dwellings available for the expanding village.[42] Like William Ing and Mary Coulson of Shepshed, Marie and Jean Hebert of Auffay (whose story was the second of the two that opened this chapter) could make their living from industry and remain in one village for their married lives, even though they were essentially proletarians.

Research on the industrial villages around Verviers, Belgium, demonstrates the role of migration in the industrial countryside. The six villages formed a "hybrid society," more typical of western Europe, not populated primarily by textile workers but embracing landowning peasants, day-laborers, traditional craftsmen, and other industrial workers (nailmakers, in this case) as well. In the vicinity of Verviers, a high age of marriage and high fertility accounted for much population growth. Using a backward projection technique to trace demographic patterns, Myron Gutmann found that mobility was important to the villages. Strong net in-migration fed their growth, particularly in the early period between 1675 and 1720 when the quantities of industrial work were expanding and village economies were growing proportionally more than urban production. Newcomers came from more remote villages in the region where the conversion of grain-producing farms to dairy farms created a large pool of underemployed people.[43] Between 1675 and 1695, the annual net migration rate into the three industrial villages of Thimister, Ensival, and Soiron was between .068 and .066. These figures mean that in a village of 1,000 people, however many servants, young people, and families came and went, net, during the course of one year, 66 to 68 new people remained at the year's end. It is easy to see how significant these numbers were to village life. People who moved into Ensival joined a commune where textiles thrived; it would become a center for weavers and skilled cloth processors (teaselers and shearmen) typical of rural, proletarian industrial workers over the course of the eighteenth century. Soiron was poorer; its industry employed nailmakers and spinners, who were the most poorly remunerated of rural workers. Thimister remained more agricultural than these last two villages; its industrial workers were weavers, then spinners. Each of the villages offered industrial work to newcomers, particularly when it first began to expand.[44]

Supported by supplemental income in manufacturing regions, expanding numbers of European villagers survived over the course of the eighteenth century. However, the rural industrial workers existed squarely in the market system. As producers of goods in national or international markets, rural spinners, weavers, or nailmakers were terribly vulnerable to slumps in demand, however remote or obscure their home village. As the proportion of rural-dwellers dependent on industry increased in the eighteenth century, the proportion of those who could be completely undermined by an industrial crisis expanded as well. The proliferation of rural industry has been correctly labeled the "offensive of capitalism" for the way in which it welded the welfare of hundreds of thousands of rural Europeans to distant markets, fluctuations in international trade relations, and the politics of war. This fact was brought home to families of northern France when the commercial treaty allowing British textile goods into France was signed in 1786 and thousands were immediately thrown into "one of the most severe periods of dearth, unemployment, and hardship"

of the century.[45] Many others would follow in their footsteps in the coming century. We will follow the fate of these rural workers in the next
chapter.

THE EXPANSION OF TEMPORARY MIGRATION

At the same time that population expanded in industrial areas, regions
without strong manufacturing grew as well, albeit less dramatically. In
these areas, population increases were fundamental to the creation of new
migration systems and the expansion of extant systems of circular and
chain migration. Patterns of movement did not fundamentally change so
much as they became more important as migration increased. Seasonal
and temporary migration became a more crucial part of the annual rhythm
of village life and of individuals' life cycles in the Pyrenees, the Alps, the
central highlands of France, the province of Connaught in western Ireland, the area around Liège in Belgium, and northwestern Germany.
Mountain people had particularly strong traditions of seasonal migration
embedded in alpine climates, practices of livestock grazing, and trading
needs. From the Pyrenees, mountaineers would descend to work in Spain,
the growing city of Bordeaux, or the rich lowlands of western Languedoc.
Savoyards would come out of the Alps in the fall to take odd jobs in the
city, to work as chimney sweeps, and to tutor. The central highlands of
France annually sent an army of men to Spain, to the cities and plains of
southern France, to Paris, and even to the northern reaches of the realm.[46]
However, upland populations were not the only ones in circular migration
systems. Lowland rural people who paid increased rents for diminishing
plots of land took to the road in search of work as harvesters or petty
artisans. Among these were Germans who swept into the Netherlands to
work the harvest and cut peat.

During the 1750–1800 period seasonal migration and circular migration
systems expanded in western Europe. To the north, laborers moved from
central Sweden to the eastern Swedish coast, from southern Sweden to
the Danish island of Sjaelland, and from the North Sea coast to Schleswig-
Holstein. Inland and to the south, movements from southern Lorraine to
Alsace increased. In the southwest, seasonal migration increased from the
central highlands of France toward the winegrowing plain of Bordeaux.
Several hundred to a few thousand workers moved in these, and other,
systems.[47] In addition, seven massive systems engaged at least 20,000 people by 1800, the vast majority of whom were men.[48] Seasonal migration
grew to such proportions between 1750 and 1815 that it seriously dis-
turbed army recruiting efforts and thereby inspired government inquiry.
Consequently, the major source for these migrations is a Napoleonic inquiry between 1808 and 1813 designed to trace the manpower of the

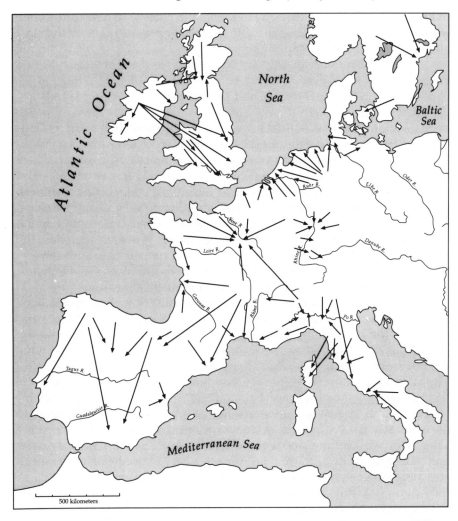

MAP 3:3 Temporary Migration Systems in Western Europe, ca. 1800
Source: Jan Lucassen, *Migrant Labour in Europe 1600–1900.*

French Empire; the inquiry was distributed to officials in today's France, Belgium, Luxembourg, Netherlands, westernmost Germany, and parts of Italy and Switzerland. When the survey was made, temporary migrations were actually at an ebb, because they had been disrupted by the Napoleonic wars and the economic chaos that accompanied them; it is therefore most appropriate to survey these major migration systems at their peak, near the end of the eighteenth century.[49] In northern Europe, major mobility systems included migrants to the Paris basin, Holland and surrounding provinces, and eastern England; in the south, large systems took migrants to central Italy, the Po Valley, the Mediterranean coast of France, and central Spain. (See Map 3:3.)

The greatest number of workers in northwestern Europe came to the Paris basin to work every year in response to the double attraction of harvest work in the Ile-de-France and employment in Paris. At least 60,000 French were involved. In the city, many worked as water carriers, petty traders, laborers, and construction workers; in the fields that surrounded the city, they worked as harvesters or vineyard laborers. The largest group of migrants came from the central highlands of France; others came from the Alps and the west of France.[50]

The North Sea system that targeted Holland was the next most important numerically; it probably included 27,000 men in 1750 and perhaps 30,000 around 1790. The greatest migration streams came from German territories to the east of the Netherlands, but many also came from Belgium and French provinces to the south. Like the seventeenth-century migrants described in chapter 2, some worked as sailors or servants, others as agricultural laborers, and still others as dike workers.[51]

In a third north European system, some 20,000 workers traveled to work in London, the home counties, and East Anglia. Like those who worked in the Paris basin, they were divided among those who worked in the city as construction workers, peddlers, or laborers and those who worked in the countryside with teams that harvested grain and cut hay. The majority were from western Ireland, and many of the rest were from the Scottish highlands and northern Wales.[52]

The largest system of temporary migration was south of the Alps; it drew at least 100,000 people to Corsica, Rome, and Italy's central plain. Those who worked on Corsica and the plain were primarily grain harvest and vineyard workers; those who went to Rome worked as navvies, construction workers, tradesmen, and service workers. For the most part, they came from the mountainous Abruzzi and the Apennines as well as from Umbria, north of Rome.[53]

The Po Valley engaged at least 50,000 people in its fields and in the cities of Turin and Milan. The majority of agricultural laborers came to work in the rice fields, and urban workers found work in the trade and service sectors and in construction. These migrants came from the Alps and northern Appennines.[54]

Meanwhile, Madrid and Castile drew workers both from Spain and France. The 25,000 grain harvesting teams and public works navvies from Galicia in northwest Spain who traveled to Castile in the 1760s numbered 40,000 in 1775 and about 60,000 at the end of the century. They were joined by French workers from the Pyrenees and the Auvergne, migrants examined in detail below.[55]

Finally, the coastal plain of the Mediterranean, stretching from Catalonia through southern Languedoc to Provence, attracted some 35,000 laborers. People descended from the Pyrenees, the central highlands, and the Alps. Most worked as agricultural laborers, harvesting grain and working the grape harvest, but some found short-term work in Barcelona and Marseille.[56]

These seven systems of migration were key phenomena in the workings of the eighteenth-century economy and the overall history of European mobility. Larger and better-documented than earlier migrations, they forecast later temporary systems in their social organization. It is possible to see in eighteenth-century mobility the changes both in the home conditions that augmented those migrations and in the work of migrants, the impact of their departure, and the ultimate impact of temporary migration.

Because a regional examination sheds light on the workings of this process, I have chosen to highlight the systems of temporary migration from a quintessential "reservoir of men," the central highlands of France. The experience of this region exemplified the increase of population and temporary migration wrought by the eighteenth century. For nearly 50 years, the number of people in this sparsely populated region increased by a half percent annually, so that between 1740 and 1774, the highlands came to support 30 percent more people and there were a great many more mouths to feed.[57] Simultaneously, landholdings were reduced in size as they were divided among family members; for example, a group of villages in the Auvergne that had 490 holdings of less than 2.2 acres (one hectare) in the first part of the eighteenth century had 870 of these "microfundia" by the 1790s.[58] It was impossible to produce enough grain, chestnuts, and turnips on these holdings for the increased population. The lack of food was exacerbated by the need to bring in cash, for taxation had made a barter economy impossible in the mountains since the seventeenth century. The convergence of difficulties for French montagnards set their region apart from the lowlands, which were a "theater of innovation for capitalism" where some salaries were on the rise, grain was relatively plentiful, and employment a possibility. Thus, temporary migration became a more widespread cash-earning strategy for the upland poor. Unable to export their products, mountain villages exported their people.[59] The eastern highlands alone, the Auvergne, sent some 12,000 men to the lowland provinces of France and to Spain at the end of the 1760s.[60]

Migrants specialized in certain occupations. Auvergnats' jobs were those that required brute strength, for their specialties were work as sawyers and navvies; sawyers converted trees to boards for construction and carpentry before the labor-saving advent of the sawmill; navvies' work consisted of digging ditches, excavation, preparation of uncultivated soil, clearing forests, draining swamps, building river and canal dikes, and cutting networks for drainage. Other jobs such as cleaning chimneys (which was reserved for boys) required smaller bodies and less strength but considerable fortitude. A few migrants displayed picturesque mountain specialties; these were the ones with a wolf, whistling marmot, or bear to show. Many were peddlers, with all their cash reserves or borrowed capital tied up in a heavy pack.[61] Auvergnats tended to migrate in the winter, while men from the Limousin, in the western part of the central highlands, left home for fair-weather construction work. They long had specialized as masons in Bordeaux, Lyon, and Paris; with construction projects in Paris, Bordeaux, Lyon, Versailles, and smaller cities, the "swallows" of the Limousin honed and expanded this specialization. Masons from the Haute-Marche in the Limousin working annually in Paris numbered about 6,000 in 1698, 15,000 by 1769, and 20,000 by 1790.[62]

Wives usually stayed at home to care for the animals, the children, and the landholding. Only in very bad years did some wives go along, gleaning after harvest teams and begging their bread.[63] The movements of single women, though, are underexplored: What is one to make of the fact that villages like Mauriac—a gathering of 548 souls in the rugged highlands of the Auvergne—included few adolescent men *or women* in 1756?[64] The paucity of boys is attributed to out-migration, because Mauriac was in an area that sent sawyers, navvies, and some knife-sharpeners to the lowlands of southwestern France. But this is male work. It is feasible that kin and fellow villagers found places for young women as domestic and farm servants in the nearby highland burgs or in the farms and villages of nearby lowlands. Young women may also have worked in the silk mills of the Cévennes mountains and the Lyonnais to the south and east designed to house young women and supervised by nuns. They may have been among the "veritable avalanche" of young servant girls from the central highlands in the city of Lyon.[65] Other young women doubtless became servants in the upland city of Clermont-Ferrand, which housed about 18,000 people. These possibilities remain conjectural, because there is no detailed study as yet of the movements of upland single women during the old regime.

Much of women's temporary migration remains invisible to the historical record and government inquiry because women were more likely than men to move in domestic, privately sponsored, small-scale arrangements. They earned less than men and they were not required to join a militia or an army; consequently, tracing young women was not of interest to the state. By contrast, the late eighteenth-century conscription lottery was rescheduled for summer months in French mountain parishes from which young men were absent in winter, and the authorities kept track of their movements, creating maps showing the areas that sent men out for the express purpose of exacting taxes from the returnees.[66] Migrant men were also more visible than migrant women because men so often traveled with a work team of harvesters, masons, hemp workers, sawyers, or navvies. They lived together, whether they slept by the roadside, in a harvesters' tent, or in an urban flophouse.[67] Tinkers, knife-grinders, and peddlers worked alone, but they tended to come from the same villages and to venture forth together. Migrant teams included an entire hierarchy of workers in many cases, from young helpers to the seasoned "boss" who negotiated jobs and provided leadership and discipline.

Kin and village groups constituted specific migration streams. For example, certain villages of the Auvergne sent out a high proportion of their men for a period of months and even years. Groups from villages or mountain valleys shared a destination. Men from around the town of Aurillac worked in Spain; those from the region surrounding them went to southwestern France; 60 kilometers to the north, men traveled to northern France. Other parishes—some only a few kilometers away, with the same poverty and the same basic economy—did not yet join or develop migration streams. People from the eastern edges of the province took the road heading for Lyon and the Rhone valley of eastern France.[68] Village-specific practices of migration, and non-migration, indicate the degree to which mobility was a socially mediated phenomenon, shaped by local practice. Migration traditions and solidarities were perpetuated by the fact that it was risky to head for an unknown destination.

Temporary migrants traveled together for company and guidance, but also for safety, staying together at a trusted inn and sleeping in barns along the way. A lone woman on the road risked rape; a lone man risked assault. To travel alone exposed the migrant to the hostilities of passersby; returning migrants were a temptation for thieves because they carried their precious earnings with them. In addition, the lone traveler had no companion to watch for his welfare. This is what killed Antoine Tronche of Peyrusse, an upland villager about age 50 who spent winters touring the lowlands as a peddler. Tronche's wife had expected him at Easter time, but he had not arrived. Having nearly arrived home in unseasonably cold rain, Tronche had perished of exposure on the commons of a nearby village during an April night in 1775. Migrants also needed each other at destination, where life could be equally hazardous. Accidents were rife at the work sites for sawyers and navvies, where men risked drowning, falls, felled trees, and exposure, in addition to disease. Wounds, illness, and accident brought hunger in their wake when they prevented pay. Without family to care for them, some laboring migrants entered the hospitals of the lowlands, where records of their deaths offer a mournful reminder of their vulnerability.[69]

With luck, these peasants returned from their labors with a few coins in their pockets. The migrants of central France did three things with their money: they bought land, got out of debt, and paid their taxes.[70] Land purchases were part of a veritable "Brownian movement" of transactions that exchanged tiny parcels of land; to maintain and enlarge holdings were the goals of the migrant peasant family. These were people plagued by debt, however, so when they arrived home, they first had to repay myriad creditors: the local church, noble, or commune that had supported their needy family in their absence; the merchant to whom they had paid a premium for grain in the expensive period of food shortage (the *soudure*); the merchant from whom they had borrowed their pack of goods to sell on the road; their brothers, whose share of the inheritance had to be paid in cash over a period of years; their sisters, whose dowry was their obligation as well.[71] The hierarchy of mountain villages was a web of debt that linked migrant to merchant and large landholder.[72]

Temporary departures from the Auvergne fostered permanent emigration. The growing provincial cities and prosperous lowlands sorely tested fondness for home country, particularly in the case of young single men who would not inherit a landholding. Parents justifiably feared that their sons would never return. The provincial capital of Clermont-Ferrand, with its population of some 18,000, could not absorb appreciable numbers of villagers. Rather, the wool- and silk-producing areas of the Cévennes mountains and southern Languedoc toward the Mediterranean littoral, the basin that cradled Bordeaux and Toulouse, the rich valley of the Loire, and the booming Lyon area, to say nothing of Paris, all beckoned. And young men heeded the call. One village that sent men out to work in the construction trades reported in 1788 that every year it lost about 18—one tenth of them. The Auvergnat village of Landogne reported that before 1750, only eight to 10 boys had left per year—and those to work as rural servants—but by 1788, 111 men and boys left to work in Lyon and other cities. A village in the eastern highlands reported that most of its young men returned after their yearly trip, but that 50 families had left for the lowlands in the last 20 years. Some had gone to the industrial areas of the north. As the writer Legrand d'Aussy traveled through the countryside south of Clermont in 1787 and 1788, he found half-deserted hamlets, houses in ruins, traces of a countryside recently abandoned. Forty young people had just departed one village for Champagne and Picardy to the north.[73] Generally, upland systems of circular migration left a residue of settlers in the lowlands that began to shade into systems of chain migration. For example, some Limousin masons who worked lowland cities came to prefer this urban work to the less remunerative agricultural labor at home; subsequently, the men who stayed on in Paris or Bordeaux paved the way for the exodus that would come in the nineteenth century.[74]

Migration systems like those of the Auvergne promoted the proletarianization of migrants and their families. Ironically, because circular migration systems brought in financial supports, they provided a series of intermediate stops between full-scale peasant ownership and inadequate landholdings and ultimately decreased reliance on the land. As Charles Tilly observed, "temporary expedients imperceptibly became a proletarian life."[75] Moreover, systems of circular migration took people out of communities in which they had solidarities and rights—professional networks, family, landholdings, and a place in the village council—and removed them to communities in which they had fewer solidarities or rights. Although they may have been working and living with compatriots, montagnard migrants were vulnerable in the lowlands. Outside of their home community, they were more subject to intimidation and ill health.

PORTRAIT OF A MIGRATION SYSTEM

Migration systems affected home societies, those who departed, and destination societies as well. Yet historians rarely find evidence of the impact of migration streams. Fortunately, the tireless research of Abel Poitrineau has yielded a portrait of the migration system joining the central highlands of France to Spain. By the eighteenth century, this mature system of long-distance circular migration was sufficiently documented to demonstrate the workings of a system that moved only adult males but affected the workings of an entire society. In this way, it is archetypical not only of eighteenth-century migration systems but of some temporary systems into the present day.

Some 200 kilometers north of the Mediterranean Sea lay a group of French parishes that for centuries had sent men across the Pyrenees to Spain. (See Map 3:3.) Among the migrant "Spaniards," as they were called by compatriots, was Antoine Salez, whose story opened this chapter. The migration system that developed between his homeland and Spain was as developed as the Westphalian system described in chapter 2. Since the Middle Ages, Spain had been the "land of gold, of dreams, of escape" for men of the French highlands.[76] Pilgrims to Saint James of Compostella (now Santiago in the northwestern corner of the Iberian peninsula) had found employment to pay for their trip. The combination of the 1492 *reconquista* that depopulated Spain of the Moorish workers and the triumphs in the New World that filled its coffers brought migration to a peak in the seventeenth century; masses of French laborers "went to seek their piece of America beyond the Pyrenees."[77]

During the eighteenth century, this migration subsided somewhat as French men found work closer to home, because more opportunities for seasonal work had arisen on the French Mediterranean plain and in the vast fields around Bordeaux, and there was greater hope for work in French ports and regional capitals of rural industry. Spanish workers began to replace the French, due to Spain's eighteenth-century demographic recovery and the end of legal restrictions on seasonal and temporary relocation in 1761. Finally, the difference between Spanish and French earnings diminished (perhaps from threefold to twofold).[78]

Clearly, however, the tradition of emigration to Spain endured the changed conditions of the eighteenth century because the money to be made in Spain continued to work on the collective imagination in some French parishes. Englishman Henry Swinburne noted some 12,000 French in the port city of Cadiz in the year 1775, and a French government report from the Revolutionary period estimated at 80,000 the French nationals who lived in Spain in 1789. Nonetheless, it is impossible to know exactly how many French were migrants from the central highland villages in the Aurillac in the eighteenth century.[79] Generally speaking, three kinds of French migrants worked in eighteenth-century Spain: young single men, whose first trip of several years would acquaint them with the language and customs of the country; members of the great commercial houses of Castile, who worked with important capital, stock, and efficient divisions of labor; and a residue of poor and unskilled migrants without support or capital who continued the earlier tradition, the "rear guard of the hordes of destitute who went, four or five generations earlier, to seek subsistence in the times of great famines, troubles, or endemic poverty."[80] The second-ary sector—which ranged from itinerant peddling to participation in the great companies of colonial commerce—played a larger role than before among migrants from France, who served as merchants and as inn and tavern keepers. Consequently, the French migrant in Spain was less likely to be an unskilled worker like the young Martin Guerre, who had worked as a lackey in the sixteenth century, or the harvest workers of the seven-teenth century; in their stead, a relatively elite migrant became important in the eighteenth century.

French and Spanish records indicate that specific local systems made up the eighteenth-century movement between France and Spain: an in-ventory of the French in the Atlantic port city of Cadiz in 1777 shows that they came from some 18 villages not more than 20 miles from each other; notaries' minute-books from the French highlands show migrants in the province of Valencia on the Mediterranean coast from some 17 villages not more than 18 miles apart. Probably about one-fifth of the men from cer-tain highland villages and towns were away in Spain at any one time, and those who were absent were the most productive men between about 18 and 50 years of age. In 1774, a subdelegate calculated the proportion of men over 14 who were absent from the region around Aurillac as 22 to 24 percent for some villages, 47 percent for another. The records of nine up-land notaries show pockets of French in southern Spain (in Cadiz, Seville, Cordoba, and around Grenada), in and around Madrid, and scattered in the northern provinces of Catalonia and Aragon.[81]

The most formally organized migration streams established family commercial companies in the second half of the eighteenth century. For example, members of the Société Chinchon (which had headquarters in the town of this name just south of Madrid) hailed exclusively from the southern Auvergne. Indeed, the 102 known members of the company all hailed from about 20 parishes in the area north of the town of Aurillac.[82] At its peak, the Société had about 200 members and a capital worth of a million and a half pounds; it dealt in linens, wools, and haberdashery items like pins, buttons, needles, and ribbons. The Auvergnats sold their wares as peddlers in the countryside and at fairs, as well as in the company's stores located in 25 Spanish towns.

Strict rules governed admission to the Société Chinchon, the conduct of its members, and movement between France and Spain—rules designed to maintain a system of temporary migration and to send money home. Those who joined were forbidden either to marry or to establish their household in Spain. New members (sponsored by their father or father-in-law), who had to be at least 16 years of age, paid an entry fee of 4,000 pounds, then served an apprenticeship of three years in Spain. They were subsequently quarter-members of the Société who served another four years in Spain before their first return home. This first "rest period" of two years was often the time when the family arranged the man's marriage. Each subsequent two-year period of "active service," broken by two-year rest periods, gained the migrant another eighth share. After five trips of two years each, which involved a 20-year stretch of working in Spain, then at home in France, the migrant had a full share in the company, which would pay, in good years, 2,000 pounds. At this point, sons and sons-in-law would enter the company. Participants in the Société Chinchon and like companies could amass considerable landholdings at home, provide their daughters with honorable dowries, set up their male offspring, and leave a good inheritance.

Like most migration systems, those between France and Spain left a residue of people who never returned home—young men who remained bachelors and returned home less frequently or who married in Spain and stayed there. For the upland French, it was relatively easy to come to feel at home in Spain, a country equally as fervently Christian as central France, where the migrant's occitan dialect was not a very far cry from Catalan or Castillian. A 1797 report on the status of French in Spain estimates that half of the 80,000 French were married, the vast majority of them to Spanish women.[83]

This was a system that moved males almost exclusively, partly because the trip to Spain was long, difficult, and dangerous. Travelers passed over high mountain passes, endured bad and sometimes dangerous food, risked theft, and exposed themselves to illness. Some neophytes could afford a guide who would guarantee arrival and furnish food for the journey, knowing the safest route, inns, and cabarets en route. Twenty-five to 30 days were required for the trip on horseback, much longer for the trek on foot. Funds promised in wills and marriage contracts underwrote this costly journey. For example, at marriage the groom might promise to take his new brother-in-law along to Spain. Knowing they risked death, migrants deposited wills before departure that opened with the words "On the point of leaving for the realm of Spain. . . . "[84] Epidemics, travel, and accidents took their toll. Hospital records from Barcelona and Madrid testify to the presence of French, like the Hospital Saint-Louis in Madrid that received 519 Frenchmen between 1721 and 1739. Abel Poitrineau compares the migrant to Spain to a bird on a wire, whose health, liberty, money, and even life were at risk.[85]

The absence of men in the prime of life deeply affected life in the highlands. Beginning in adolescence, men departed, leaving behind a truncated labor force and skewed gender balance. Because many died or did not return, their departures meant that many women never married. While some elder daughters stayed at home, others found work as spinners, lacemakers, or servants in nearby towns. Many found a spiritual and social home in lay orders of the Catholic church, such as those of Saint-François, Saint Cominique, Mont-Carmel, and especially Sainte Agnès. Abel Poitrineau explained that by becoming *menettes* (the local name for the women of the lay order of Saint Agnès), adult and elderly single women received the benefits of a residence and social support that "permitted them to better withstand their situation in a world hard on single women, while preparing their salvation and giving themselves to pious and useful works." These women were a substantial minority in Aurillac. Between 1763 and 1774, over half the wills received by the notary Geneste in Aurillac were women's wills, of which nearly one in five came from devout spinsters who belonged to lay orders.[86]

In this environment, settling a marriage with a "Spaniard" was a triumph for the household—the *oustau* that anchored the family and provided a fixed point to which the migrant could return, a refuge where the family line would hopefully be perpetuated. In fact, "Spaniards" were often recruited to a bride's family, marrying "in house" as the saying went; 64 percent of migrants' marriage contracts in the Upper Auvergne (1761–1790) negotiated the groom's entry into his wife's household.[87] Marriage contracts fixed the sum that these relatively wealthy grooms, with good earning prospects, paid their in-laws to compensate for the expenses of their departure: the upkeep of their wife and future children and wages and food for a servant (*valet de ferme*) who would replace their labor power. Those left behind lived in a stem family, or some sort of collective household, for mutual aid and protection. For example, when newlywed Robert Gelly departed the village of Tarrieu in October of 1735, he left behind his wife, aging parents-in-law, an aunt, and two young brothers-in-law, in addition to his own relatives; no children were born as yet. He had drawn up a lease (in the name of his father-in-law) to his own brother Pierre, for the domain of his in-laws, one goat, four cows, 11 sheep, and a pig to assure the feeding of the Couderc household for four years. He promised to pay his brother 100 pounds for each year Pierre fed and cared for his family. Such supple systems of social security ensured that their wives, children, in-laws, and other kin could survive their absence.[88]

The departure of married "Spaniards" endowed their wives with unusual responsibilities. In the home, they were more exclusively in charge of training both female and male children; outside the home, they were more actively involved in the management of farmlands. Husbands gave wives the power of attorney to manage and dispose of property and to manage succession until their children were grown should they die abroad. And although it was completely illegal, "Spaniards' " wives performed public duties while authorities turned a blind eye. For example, the wife of Antoine Martres fulfilled his function as village consul by collecting the most important tax of the realm, the *taille*; Martres was caught for neglecting his legal charge in 1742 only because his wife inopportunely died in his absence. Wives even paid the onerous *corvée royale*, maintaining the royal roads and repairing or even constructing bridges.[89]

The absence of adult men caused painful and delicate problems for migrants' families. They were less able than others to defend themselves and their interests against chicanery, violence, threats, and village intrigues. Marriage relations were difficult. Many women's families negotiated a very early marriage for their daughter (even at the age of 14 or 17) to a much older "Spaniard," because they were interested in the profits and prestige such an alliance bestowed.[90] Marriages that were largely lived separately caused problems for the spouses, yet infidelity and marital unhappiness were by and large an "iceberg deeply immersed in the waters of family respectability."[91] Only occasionally were cases between spouses brought to court or was the paternity of a child denied by its legal father, although migrants' descendants testify that there were "undesirable" children, offspring silently brought into the family. Perhaps the most palpable sign of difficulties was the number of men who took advantage of the trip across the Pyrenees to break all ties with family, village, and province. Whether they died or simply found a new life, they left a legion of *de facto* widows who could not remake their lives. Thus Françoise Moussieu, a day laborer who had heard nothing from her husband in 10 years, sought court authorization to arrange the marriage of her daughter with a family counsel; only her husband had the legal right to do so, but she had no idea whether or not he was alive. When divorce was legalized by revolutionary legislation in 1793, women who had not seen their husbands for 20 years came forward to regularize their status.[92]

The purpose and the payoff of this dangerous and painful migration was to earn the cash that would support and expand rural holdings. "Spaniards" built proud family traditions, like that of nineteenth-century writer Arsène Vermenouze, who boasted that "from my maternal and paternal great-grandparents . . . we have all been in my family those Auvergnats that are still called 'Spaniards' here. We all followed the great stream . . . that pushed a good part of the districts of Aurillac and several cantons of Mauriac from the mountains."[93] The records of central France suggest that working in Spain was indeed profitable in the eighteenth century. Communes that sent men to Spain were wealthier than sedentary villages or villages that sent men to the French lowlands. In France, this meant that those villages paid more taxes than the others. The state was hostile to a migration system that made men unavailable for military call-up, and the wealthy of the region were likewise hostile to a system that raised the price of local agricultural labor. Yet only the hostility of the

Spanish themselves could deter the men of France's highlands. Spanish indifference to "*gavachos*" turned to political animosity with the 1789 Revolution, when the French in the city of Cadiz were called to either take an oath of loyalty to Spain or to depart.[94] Animosity was transformed into hatred by the invasion of Spain by Napoleon in 1808; the Spanish response to Napoleon virtually obliterated this migration system when Iberia had a second *reconquista*, this time to expel the French, successor to the indispensable Moor.[95]

VAGRANCY, CRIME, AND ILLEGITIMACY: THE MARGINAL MIGRANT

After 1750, the squeeze on population and provisions expanded the number of people who had to leave home in search of work and food, forcing many people to take to the road who had no routine migration itinerary to follow. Even lowland areas with relatively little tradition of chain migration systems put the poor on the road. For example, in 1745, a royal *intendant* observed that the people of lower Normandy rarely left the region to seek their fortune; indeed, traditions of seasonal migration were relatively weak in this region. The following quarter-century increased the normal population by 30 percent, bringing a generation to maturity that was forced on the road in search of work. From the lowland farm area (the *bocage*), men left for harvest work, while others worked as peddlers, masons, coppersmiths, and knife-grinders in Paris or Rouen every winter. The 1770 *intendant's* reported considerable mobility while the people complained of the necessity of migration to find work.[96] Likewise, the usual avenues of movement and work for upland sawyers and peddlers were stretched to the limit. With hunger and poverty, those without skills or a work plan increasingly joined migration streams. Subsistence migration increased.[97]

Even those with a work plan met with misfortune and, lacking protective labor solidarities or group help, turned to vagrancy and begging to get by. Those who were crushed by the experience of migration usually lacked the social solidarity of harvest workers and masons; they became part of the "floating population" that roamed the countryside of the late eighteenth century, filled the outskirts of the great cities, and peopled the workhouses, prisons, and hospitals. Many crossed the thin line that distinguished poverty from indigence and harvest worker between jobs from professional beggar or permanent vagrant. Maturin Besne exemplified the migrant who fell through the cracks. Besne took to the road from the Alps as a young peddler; his downward spiral began with the theft of his peddler's pack. He joined the army only to earn his bread after the theft of his pack. Besne ended his days in a port city charity hospital in western France in the fall of 1783 as a captured army deserter.[98]

The ill and lonely Maturin Besne was among the vagrants and beggars who flooded the highways of western Europe as the numbers of poor increased after 1750.[99] The aged, women, and children begged on the steps of churches and the side of roads. Charity bureaus and public hospitals for the aged, infirm, and orphans, as well as religious charities, were inundated by the poor and hungry.[100] The "grimmest evidence" of immiseration is the record numbers of infants abandoned at foundling homes in the great cities of London and Paris as well as in small provincial centers. The *Hôpital des Enfants-Trouvés* of Paris, for example, took in over 5,000 infants annually after 1760—25 times as many as a century earlier.[101]

The line between migration and vagabondage was crossed, time and again, by thousands of Europeans. In response, governments accelerated the "Great Confinement" begun in the seventeenth century; poorhouses and workhouses proliferated in England as expenses of poor relief rose by 60 percent between 1760 and 1784. Institutions like the *Arbeitshäus* of Berlin housed hundreds of inmates who suffered dismal conditions. The French royal workhouses (*dépôts de mendicité*) were given new lease in 1767 to incarcerate beggars. In the following year, over 10,000 persons were arrested for beggary and vagrancy; this figure rose to over 12,000 in 1770; all in all, over 230,000 people were detained in France between 1768 and 1790.[102] Those from areas like France's central highlands had the greatest resources on which to draw under these circumstances: knowledge of the road and possible work sites, contacts in the lowlands and abroad. Nonetheless, they too increasingly were forced to resort to begging just as did the lowland poor. The indigence of those on the road who resorted to begging, either for complete lack of work or because their usual work was unavailable, overwhelmed charitable and incarcerating institutions.

The children of the poor, the most blameless victims of the century, crowded orphanages and were occasionally retrieved in better times.[103] The parents of those abandoned infants and children were in some cases married couples, who continued to travel in their search for work. Husband and wife Mathurien Gallié and Louise Fouqueray, for example—he a blacksmith's helper, she a spinner—traveled a circuit in the Loire Valley, Brittany, Normandy, and Versailles from soon after their 1769 marriage until 1782. They had been "arrested in the street, a man and wife unknown," because they had "appeared suspect." Routine investigation revealed that Gallié and Fouqueray were not childless, as they had claimed; the couple had several children, two of whom had been left at the charity hospital of the town of Le Mans.[104]

As the arrest of Mathurien Gallié and Louise Fouqueray suggests, the able-bodied stranger drew suspicion. It was healthy men in particular who aroused fear of petty theft and the agressive begging that bordered on extortion. Most young men who were arrested were those whose chances of a steady living had been nipped in the bud by the death of their parents and a lack of skills. Typical of these was René Françoise, son of landless laborers who had made a meager living between day-laboring and fishing. His parents had both died by the time he was seven, then François had wandered Normandy for 15 years before his arrest in 1776 at age 22, peddling dressmaker supplies and begging while imitating a mute. François could not give authorities the name of one person who could testify on his behalf. His lack of social connections undermined his potential to earn a living or to defend himself.[105]

In his excellent study of the confinement of the poor in eighteenth-century France, Robert Schwartz clarifies the connection between the increase of imprisonment and a hardening of attitudes toward the mobile poor, who were increasingly treated with suspicion. After 1750, he writes, "mendacity became virtually a *cause célèbre*."[106] In this atmosphere, underwritten by the material conditions of the period, western European authorities associated migration with deviant behavior. Consequently, men such as Joseph Le Sage and his son were caught between the necessity to engage in seasonal migration, popular suspicion of migrants, and France's tough new legislation of 1767. Each was arrested and detained in a *dépôt de mendicité* in the late summer of 1768 for being some 26 miles from home without a job. They were out on their annual circuit of harvesting work; separated, they were caught begging on the road during a bad harvest when work was hard to find.[107]

After the creation of France's royal workhouses, the greatest rates of arrest occurred in the corridors of circular migration systems. Repression "seems to have been more intense where the problems and tensions associated with the comings and goings of seasonal migrants were more acute: in areas situated along the main arteries of migration and in the areas where migrants converged."[108] It is by arrests, then, that the police of France and elsewhere controlled the disruptive effects of immiseration in the late eighteenth century. When the shocks to rural industry added unemployment to the list of rural woes, followed by the poor harvests of 1787 and 1788, then the political and social upheaval of 1789 in France, police could no longer contain the fears of rural people. Fears of adult male strangers found their apotheosis in the Great Fear, the panic that swept rural France during the first summer of the Revolution. On August 12 of that summer, a shocking incident occurred in lower Normandy that shed light on the hatred that vagrants inspired when the inmates of the Beaulieu workhouse surged to escape. The fear of local people in the face of escaped vagabonds was fierce; the inmates were stopped in their tracks by a hostile crowd that fired on and wounded the would-be escapees.[109] Hard times had increased beggary to a point the public could not tolerate, even though the nascent Revolution had released the prisoners of the Bastille not a month before.

Few workhouse inmates were women. Indeed, women were less likely than men to be incarcerated in workhouses because the begging old woman, or mother with young children, was one of the "deserving poor," and also because women posed less of a threat to peace and property than did men. It is not women's physical threat of force but rather their sexuality that brought them to the fore of marginal migrants in the eighteenth century. To maintain the precarious health of the armed forces, French women infected with venereal diseases were confined to workhouses.[110] And to save the coffers of municipalities, single mothers were urged to reveal the identity of the "author" of their pregnancy.[111] In the underemployed generations that came of age after 1750, there were increasing proportions of single pregnant women. Local studies show a rise in illegitimate births in such diverse and widespread areas as Normandy, Paris, Lorraine, Leipzig, Frankfurt, Bavaria, and Hamburg.[112]

Vulnerability to pregnancy is women's Achilles' heel. And for migrant women, the pregnancy of the single female is a manifestation of social and economic difficulty. In every town, most urban single mothers were migrant women. There was a two-way relation between migration and illegitimacy for the eighteenth-century woman. A small proportion of single women who bore children in town was propelled to the city by a rural pregnancy; they arrived in the city with the intention of bearing their child anonymously and perhaps returning home. This was the case for about 7 percent of single mothers in eighteenth-century Bordeaux, such as Catherine Delrun, who came from a nearby town in 1773 to bear the child of a hometown carpenter. To a certain degree, then, urban illegitimacy reflects regional illegitimacy and rural illegitimacy rates appear lower than they really were. In such cases, the failure of pregnancy to produce a marriage stemmed from the difficulties of setting up a household in the face of rural immiseration.[113]

Far more common was the migrant woman who became pregnant in the city where she worked as a servant or a seamstress. Studies from the old regime confirm the argument of Louise Tilly, Joan Scott, and Miriam Cohen that associate the illegitimacy boom with the increase of young women in an urban setting without the social support that could enforce a marriage promise in case of pregnancy. Women from the port city of Nantes reported that the servant and sailor "authors" of their pregnancies had promised marriage—increasingly so across the century.[114] Cissie Fairchilds explains the importance of the marriage promise:

> . . . it was a promise of marriage that enticed a maid to sleep with a footman, a laundress with an apprentice hatmaker, a shepherdess with an agricultural laborer. Marriage was of overwhelming importance to lower-class women. Not only did it legitimize their sexual relationships in the eyes of society, and save them from the scorn accorded to spinsters, but it also provided them with their only hope of economic security. It was only within the context of a family economy, with husband,

wife, and children all working to contribute to the family income, that a lower-class woman could hope to survive.[115]

The country woman alone in the city could not enforce such a promise. Those who were poor lacked the social and economic power to do so and often had not even a parent at any distance. Over half the single mothers in Lille to the north had no father living who could bring their suitor to the altar; 70 percent had lost one parent or the other.[116] Olwen Hufton's long-standing portrait of the single mother stands confirmed: "She was emphatically a woman on her own, in so far as she lived away from her family and several miles from her native village. She had been born in the country, but her misfortune was likely to have occurred in town. In short, she belonged to that large contingent of country girls who sought employment in town."[117] Such a woman was Marie Barbe, from a small town about forty miles upriver from Bordeaux. After two years working as a servant in the city, she became pregnant but remained single after her infant was born in 1776.[118]

If the eighteenth-century migrant was an object of suspicion, a vagrant, or likely to be single mother, does this mean that people who took to the road differed from stay-at-homes? Were they more criminal, less moral, or inherently marginal types? Did leaving home engender antisocial behavior? Certainly, many migrants were distinct in that they were the poor, those who had the fewest resources with which to fight hunger and underemployment. Single migrant women did not seem to have different sexual attitudes or behavior than those who stayed at home, as the considerable rates of bridal pregnancy indicate; what distinguished them was their lack of clout to realize a marriage.[119] Finally, although many thieves and criminals were migrants, the vast majority of migrants were neither thieves nor criminals. Theft was not the sole response to hunger.

What seems to have distinguished the migrant thief from the man simply down on his luck and the single mother from the one who married before giving birth was the social support of a network of companions or relatives. It is no accident that vagrants and single pregnant women were so often orphans, or that migrants avoided traveling alone. The cohesive teams of harvest workers and labor migrants were highly moral groups because they could offer protection and aid where the lone drifter, orphaned at an early age, could have none.[120] Drifters like the orphan René Françoise were in a quite different situtation than men in an organized, collective system of circular migration.

The migrants who appeared most marginal in the late eighteenth century teach us several fundamental lessons. Those without social support suffered the most vulnerability to misfortune, robbery, or seduction. Perceptions about migrants visited immeasurable suffering upon them—in the form of exclusion, suspicion, and refusals of aid. These reactions demonstrate with force that when men and women left home, they left behind solidarities and even the limited support of a recognized identity. To be a lone foreigner—from the next valley or farther away—in and of itself bred suspicion and hostility. Hard times exacerbated this painful truth, exposing men and women to increasing harassment. The history of the migrant is the history of people often unjustly maligned and mistreated. As a consequence, one goal of this study is to bring them out of the margins of history.

MIGRATION TO EIGHTEENTH-CENTURY TOWNS AND CITIES

This was less the era of the great city than of the smaller provincial center. After a period in which the greatest urban growth was confined to the large capital and port cities, the pattern of European urban expansion changed in the eighteenth century. The impulse of large-city growth that had dominated the seventeenth century faded. On the other hand, mid-size cities prospered and capitals of rural industry grew; towns of 5,000 to 9,900 people were the urban areas most likely to grow after 1700. In this age, urbanization concentrated in 3,000 to 4,000 centers of marketing, administration, and production.[121]

Among the towns that typified urban growth in this age, industrial towns were crucial, because early industry "flourished best not as town *or* country, but as a complementary system involving both rural and urban places and the various elements of a regional urban hierarchy."[122] Textiles and other goods produced in the countryside underwent their most rudimentary transformations in the countryside, where nails were hammered, thread spun, and rough cloth woven. Often rural people marketed these goods in the small market towns of industrial regions. In towns and cities, the more delicate tasks that required great finesse were carried out: fabric was processed in fulling mills, dyed, and finished. Just as crucial, the "structural framework for these export-oriented activities—embodied in markets, merchants, and sources of credit—remained urban."[123] The city was the site of commercial information, decision making, and exchange; it was the locus of the massive capital required for large-scale trade as well as of the petty amounts doled out, bit by bit, to rural workers.[124] Although rural workers received pitiful pay, the spread of merchant capital is a fundamental mark of this era. Without merchant resources and decisions to produce in particular areas, to put out raw materials and to purchase the finished goods, rural production would have remained small-scale and local.

Although there are not enough studies to draw a general portrait of the early industrial town, one town, Verviers, has been investigated with great care and sophistication. Its growth and size are typical of the expanding urban area of the time; Verviers grew from 7,400 in 1650 to about

13,000 in 1750—after being almost unchanged for centuries.[125] Located about 15 miles east of the Belgian city of Liège, Verviers expanded as a center of the woolens industry that exported cloth primarily to German territories east of the Rhine. Until the eighteenth century, it also had substantial trade with Holland in locally produced nails for Dutch ships; this trade fell off when Dutch shipping was outflanked by the British.[126] Although Verviers was tightly linked with its surrounding villages, where it would employ 30,000 workers by 1800, it was urban in character. No peasants or farmers lived in Verviers. The households of the town included an elite of administrators and professionals (3%) and a healthy proportion of craftsmen (11%) and tradesmen (10%) in commerce, food, and lodging. Near half the town's household heads worked in the textile industry (48%), most as skilled teaselers and shearmen (19%); teaselers raised the nap of finished cloth; shearmen snipped smooth the napped product. Woolen weavers were also an important component of the Verviers populace (15%).[127]

What role did migration play in the growth of this early industrial town? According to the backward projection of its population, *net* migration played virtually no role at all until the 1770s. From the 1650s until the 1770s, town growth was fueled by high fertility (which in turn increased during boom periods when women married at younger ages). Only late in the eighteenth century did Verviers's population begin to follow an "urban" pattern: mortality increased, and deaths outnumbered births. In the 1770s and 1780s net immigration caused city growth, but not before. This finding is intriguing precisely because it distinguishes Verviers from its industrial villages, which did grow through immigration in the early stages of industrial growth. This suggests that the migration most important to early industry took place within the countryside, because village economies expanded proportionally more than those of industrial towns like Verviers.[128]

If migration did not cause small industrial centers like Verviers to grow, what role did mobility play in this system that intimately linked town and country? A regional perspective revealed that "the populations of heavily industrialized rural areas were far more mobile, both geographically and socially, than peasant populations still tied to the land."[129] Although there are no figures for gross migration in the Verviers region, certain patterns are clear. In this thriving economy where agriculture and industry coexisted, it was relatively easy for proletarian youth to shift from agriculture to industrial work. Thus young men like Henri-Joseph Delilez, son of an agricultural laborer, could apprentice themselves in cloth manufacturing after spending their youth as rural farm servants. In this case, Delilez was apprenticed to a master fuller in 1769 at age 24. Skilled workers like Delilez were among the most mobile in Europe. In this case, shearmen moved among industrial towns in the region; Verviers shearmen worked in nearby Sedan and Monshau, prizing their independence. When Delilez was tramping as a journeyman, he encountered natives of Verviers everywhere he went (even in Moravia in present-day Czechoslovakia, where he met his Belgian wife). "Foreign" workers also found work in Verviers—enough so that shearmen and weavers complained about them in the mid-eighteenth century.[130] If work in Verviers attracted skilled labor, it doubtless also attracted young women and proletarian men like the young Delilez who came from the communities strung along the region's dense network of roads. Although there are no measures of migration flows to and from Verviers, we can be sure that they were more important than net migration and that they included both skilled laborers from other towns and "betterment" migrants from the area.

Large industrial and shipping cities were also important to early industry, and, because some have been studied in depth, something is known of their migration dynamics. For example, Rouen, in northern France near the mouth of the Seine River, served as both a center for early industrial production and a node in international trade. The number of citizens housed within the walls of Rouen had been reduced from 80,000 to about 60,000 in the seventeenth century by the departure of its Protestants and the 13,000 deaths in the wake of subsistence crises and epidemics of 1693–1694. It required most of the eighteenth century to regain the population lost. On the eve of the 1789 Revolution, greater Rouen came to about 100,000 people.[131]

This gain of 20,000 in the eighteenth century masked a great turnover of population as men and women moved to and from the city. Marriage records reveal that newcomers entered the city in significant numbers; indeed, half the grooms in eighteenth-century Rouen were born elsewhere. Marriage records from other eighteenth-century cities show that migrants were a sizable proportion of city dwellers: 33 percent in Bordeaux, 46 percent in Geneva, 47 percent in Marseille. Yet these records do not include young, single folk, those most likely to move around; even citizenship records may be more inclusive, for those from Berlin show that 72 percent of *burghers* were from outside the city.[132]

Men and women also departed from cities, although traces of this movement are difficult to find. Rouen's parish records show that even families with children—the most sedentary of people—moved out of the city; of every 100 couples married in Rouen who had children, over one-fifth left, even in the prosperous years between 1750 and 1789. One of three elite families, 15 percent of artisan families, and 19 percent of worker families departed. In all, 21 percent of the couples of which the man was a native-born Rouennais and 37 percent of couples of which the man was born elsewhere would depart.[133] Likewise, for every 100 marriages in the southern port city of Marseille in 1750, 40 couples departed after the wedding, and another 10 departed after the birth of their first child.[134] The individual city, then, gained and lost people continually. An appreciation of urban population turnover is central to understanding that newcomers were a continual part of the life of cities—even cities that did not expand by net immigration.

This turnover is captured by Jean-Claude Perrot's research on Caen, a city in lower Normandy some 65 miles west and south of Rouen. Caen grew to 35,000 people in the second half of the eighteenth century—but this was a gain of only 3,000 over 1753, and in light of the 47,000 baptisms (and fewer deaths) in that period, migration appears to be of little import to this city because there was little net in-migration. Yet Perrot has uncovered a more interesting and complex story: Caen grew to 41,000 by 1775, then diminished with the outbreak of the Revolution and further diminished by 1795. Three unusual censuses allowed him to estimate emigration and immigration and changes in the flow of people to and from the city. The net growth of 3,000 people covers the entry of 20,842 people and the exit of 20,153 others. Between 1753 and 1795, from 422 to 630 people entered the city annually while 74 to 1,500 departed. Thus, although it is impossible to know the gross migration figures to and from the eighteenth-century city, Perrot's estimation suggests an impressive volume of movement.[135]

In order to understand the kinds of migration engendered by early industry and the role of large cities in this movement, we must discard the notion that the city walls of the old regime separated two distinct ways of life. The early industrial system rested on the complementarity of rural and urban. Rather than a dichotomy, rural and urban represent two ends of a continuum. The areas adjacent to city walls (the *faubourgs* in France) and villages in the immediate vicinity (the *banlieue*) must be brought into the purview of urban populations in order to comprehend mobility in early industrial areas. Without considering outlying areas, we view urban populations in a vacuum.[136] In the case of Rouen, the surrounding settlements grew much more than the population within its walls. For every 100 households added to greater Rouen between 1713 and 1772, 50 were added to the 28 villages in the immediate vicinity (*banlieue*) where an estimated 2,000 new households appeared. Settlements adjacent to the city walls (*faubourgs*) grew at a similar rate, increasing their share of the urban population by 50 percent between 1700 and 1790. To look for net immigration and population growth, then, one must look past the walls of the city to outlying areas.

The vibrant villages outside the city walls were very attractive to industrial workers because they offered significant advantages over both the city and village to spinners and weavers. Like urban workers, those in outlying villages were exempt from the notorious and onerous tax of the *taille*; they also had easy access to the markets for their goods and could bargain and sell on their own without a middleman. Like village folk, they could enrich their diet with the vegetables from their own gardens and take time for lucrative harvest work. Like the inhabitants of *faubourgs*, they could sell their garden vegetables at market as well.[137]

Unfortunately, the lives of people on the outskirts of cities like Rouen, who were so important to its vigorous industry, trade, and urban life, remain mysterious. Ignorance about these people reflects a void in the history of migration and more generally of the European population and labor force. Who were these workers settling on the outskirts of Rouen and similar cities? Were most of them industrial workers? Did they marry young and have large families like some manufacturing proletarians? Where did they come from? Were they the sons and daughters of villagers in the Pays de Caux setting out on their own? Might they also include people from the distant Jura, Alps, or central highlands in search of a better life? How did they manage in the unemployment crises set off by the 1786 treaty that opened France to the competition of English products? None of these questions yet has an answer. Until research on the early industrial center focuses on this vital area between city and countryside, these and other important questions will remain unanswered.

The most complete and even exemplary picture of urban-bound migration systems has been constructed by Jean-Pierre Poussou for eighteenth-century Bordeaux. His complex and fascinating portrait of this port city in its regional context shows how a confluence of various regional, national, seasonal, and long- and short-distance migrations streams joined to supply a growing urban area. Bordeaux was not a manufacturing city but a growing Atlantic port that became an international entrepôt of great importance in the eighteenth century. It was enriched by export markets for the grain of southwestern France and for the region's wine. Trade flourished in sugar and tobacco, goods imported from France's Caribbean colonies. Commercial expansion fed a building boom and increased population, for the city grew from 45,000 in 1700 to 60,000 in mid-century, then to 111,000 in 1790. By the outbreak of the Revolution, Bordeaux was the third largest city in France, after Lyon and Paris.[138]

This expansion took place in an era when "the major problem of so many individuals was partial or permanent underemployment."[139] By contrast with the city, southwestern France was subject to the same kind of squeeze that impoverished people in many regions. The agricultural economy was increasingly market-oriented, even for sharecroppers and the notoriously poor people of the sandy Landes region. As the population increased after 1750, landholdings became smaller, pushing peasant families below the minimum holding for independence. In an age of rising prices and rising rents, rural salaries remained rigidly low, but salaries rose by a third in the city.[140] This contrast in wages and (even more important) in the possibilities for employment generated and expanded migration into Bordeaux.

A variety of migration systems focused on the city, most of which brought newcomers from the towns and villages of southwestern France. Like other major cities, Bordeaux dominated its region and drew most of its people from there. Within the southwest, there were two privileged areas, the first a veritable "demographic basin" of a dozen cantons within about 35 miles of the city. These cantons alone produced a quarter of the city's migrant brides. The existence of such a demographic basin is crucial; it indicates that the borders of a city were like a permeable membrane through which people easily entered and exited. Moreover, the number of newcomers from nearby towns corroborates the importance of short-distance moves and step migration from smaller towns for urban populations. The second privileged source of new Bordelais was a more extended "mobile" zone along transport routes, the villages and towns along the rivers that supplied Bordeaux and its region, particularly the Garonne and Dordogne. People traveled from these locations to the city with alacrity, while those from farther inland did not.

In addition to these regional newcomers were the thousands of seasonal migrants from the upland regions of Limousin and the Auvergne, including sawyers who provided lumber to build Bordeaux, laborers who laid its streets, and masons who constructed its buildings. Urban migrants moving among the cities of France—from Paris, Lyon, and the cities that dotted the Atlantic and English channel coast—comprised a significant minority. In fact, while the people who came to Bordeaux from nearby were primarily rural people, those from farther away were more likely to come from urban areas. Many worked in Bordeaux's commerce.[141]

An elite group of migrants played an especially significant role in Bordeaux; these were the merchants and traders who ran the city's commerce. They tended to come from cities; some were foreigners like the English and German wine-traders. In this Catholic nation, a high proportion of French merchants were Protestants. Likewise, the powerful families of the region sent some of their sons into the sovereign courts, the *parlement*, of Bordeaux.[142]

Women dominated the migration systems originating near the city, making up the vast majority of migrants from the demographic basin adjacent to Bordeaux. Young women on the wine-producing plain lived in families on smallholdings who had greater need for their sons' labor in the vineyards than their daughters' work. Such families found it very difficult to amass a dowry for their daughters, who, unlike upper-class women, generally did not have the option of entering a convent if they did not marry. It was acceptable to send a daughter to the nearby city. Consequently, families put their daughters out to work as servants or in the other jobs the city offered women: lingerie worker, dressmaker, and seller of petty merchandise. It is for these reasons that women dominated the migration stream from nearby Bordeaux and why they traveled from less far than male migrants. Women were two-thirds of the migrants from Bordeaux's *département* of the Gironde; two-thirds of those who married in

Bordeaux were from the three nearest *départements*. The farther the origins of the migration stream, the more masculine its character.

The systems of circular, temporary migration to Bordeaux from the uplands were entirely masculine. Not until the nineteenth century would these migration streams include women, and women would signal the shift from circular to chain migration and increase permanent settlement in Bordeaux. In the eighteenth century, however, the men of the uplands left women behind and the women of the winegrowing plain left behind them vineyards dominated by men.[143]

An intense rhythmic interdependence between rural and urban areas linked Bordeaux with its hinterland. The demands for labor were extremely seasonal in this port city, where construction took place in the summer, trade on the high seas commenced in September, and the wine trade began a six-month season in October; thus port workers, masons, and sawyers carefully timed their travel between town and country. Coopers keyed their peak work season to the vine harvest. When grapes were ripe in the early fall, urban people would join men and women from the vineyards and farther afield in a massive, collective effort to achieve a timely *vendage*. Commercial employees and domestic servants, on the other hand, were more likely to work year-round.

Each group of migrants—from foreign merchants to construction workers and domestic servants—traveled by a distinct rhythm. Each circuit was unique: some traveled only a few miles, coming from a village in which working in the city was a normal part of the life course; workers like the masons were called "swallows" because their movement was a seasonal one; merchants' attraction to Bordeaux was an impulse guided by commercial expansion. Although Bordeaux's wine harvests and port seasons enforced seasonal itineraries, the multiplicity of itineraries applies to all cities to some degree—where bureaucrats, professionals, servants, and day-laborers each added their labor to that of the urban natives. They remind us that migration behavior, particularly in an urban case, is a complex of activities of people who are urban and rural, elite and proletarian. This observation complements the evidence of high turnover among eighteenth-century urban populations, for each kind of group had reasons to move on.

CONCLUSION

Over the course of the eighteenth century, two distinct patterns of human mobility overlay the long-standing practices of local and circular migration outlined in chapter 2. The first was a regime engendered by increased rural manufacturing and fed by capital that came into the countryside. In industrial regions, villages attracted workers who were quite sedentary because a great proportion of men and women were able to subsist at home with earnings from manufacturing. For some regions, the era of rural industry was a more settled one than earlier periods. Especially those towns linked with early industry were likely to grow in this era and the great age of urbanization still lay ahead.

By contrast, Europeans who resided in regions without early industry to bring in additional income increasingly sought work outside their home village in seasonal agricultural or urban employment. Circular migration systems expanded and in some cases spawned chain migration patterns. Articulate systems of temporary male migration for harvest work and urban labor expanded; simultaneously, dense networks attracted people on the outskirts of urban areas into the cities, the majority of whom were women. Rural laboring men came from farther afield and skilled artisans circulated among production centers. Elite merchants and officials moved among cities in a national or even international circuit. After 1750, subsistence migration increased with impoverishment, and with it vagrancy proliferated.

There are many lacunae in this sketch that can only be filled by further research. Movements to and from the early industrial center remain murky; although the industrial expansion of the eighteenth century dissolved many distinctions between urban and rural production, it is not yet known what the conflation of urban and rural meant for the movements of people around industrial cities. Little is known about the newcomers to manufacturing towns, who may have been an important component of the future factory proletariat.

More generally, it is important to discover the connections between the poor uplands that exported people and the fertile plains of crowded villages. Shreds of evidence such as travelers' reports from the 1780s suggest that some people deserted their poor villages. Theoretically, close ties existed between manufacturing and other districts because people could move between agriculture and industrial production without leaving the countryside. Nonetheless, the tendency of migration streams to follow established practices suggests that systems of temporary migration would persist to long-standing destinations, slowly adapting to new ones. Practically, there are virtually no data that link the two migration scenarios, even though they shared the same time and in some regions were in close geographic proximity.

In addition, movements of women in regions without manufacturing, such as alpine areas, will remain mysterious until the populations of small mountain towns and silk mills are better known. Their migration patterns, however limited, will teach us more about upland family and society and about the ways in which female migration is embedded in such systems, while also following the logic of women's employment.

It is certain that with the expansion of rural industry, the village laborer was more vulnerable than any landowning peasant to international markets. Throughout western Europe, men and women in villages that were in many cases quite remote depended on the international markets for the goods they produced, markets over which they had absolutely no control. This scenario, so consequential for the men and women of the eighteenth century, is also rich in implications for the subsequent era. After this period during which unprecedented numbers of Europeans made their livelihoods in a rural setting, village economies would shift drastically during the nineteenth century. Eventually, rural people would be forced from countrysides that could no longer support them.

CHAPTER

4

Migration in an Age of
Urbanization and Industrialization

The nineteenth century produced an urban society. Urbanization, the growth in the proportion of people living in cities, was a central fact of European life as urban growth outstripped rural growth. By 1900, over half the citizens of once-bucolic Britain lived in towns of over 20,000; likewise one-quarter of the population of Belgium and the Netherlands and one-fifth of Germans and French resided in cities of this size.[1] Moreover, the urban population gathered in cities that were larger than any in European history; by 1900, greater London reached 6.5 million, and Paris grew to 2.5 million. The suburbs of large cities had grown at a greater pace than the center cities, and new factory cities rose on the horizon.[2] Village society had lost its preeminence forever. Because urbanization and the growth of factory towns were exceptionally dramatic, our attention focuses on migrants like Jeanne Bouvier, who moved from village to town.

In 1865, Jeanne Bouvier was born to a peasant family in eastern France, in the region of the great city of Lyon. She passed her early childhood in the village where her father alternatively worked in the fields and in his trade as a barrel maker, a skill crucial to the local wine industry. As a young woman Bouvier worked in the silk mills south of Lyon. Like many other country girls, she spent part of her youth as a domestic servant on the periphery of urban society; this was the avenue for her entry into the capital city of Paris. By the age of 21, Jeanne Bouvier was a Parisian, a skilled and valued dressmaker in a large workshop; between her birth and her acquisition of a private couturiere's clientele in her early thirties, this peasant's daughter had become an urban woman. A visit home to her mother and family in the 1890s revealed the gulf that had opened between her and her village relatives. She could no longer understand their *patois*, and time and distance had taken a toll on their feelings for one another. Jeanne Bouvier reflects the general image of migration in the nineteenth century because she began her life in a village but became a worker in one of the vast cities of Europe.[3]

If Bouvier fits our stereotype of a nineteenth-century migrant, a close investigation of her life reveals a more complex reality. In 1876, when Bouvier was 11 years of age, an epidemic destroyed the vineyards of the Rhone valley, forcing her family to sell its land and possessions and set off on the road. They moved often, pushed by landlords, unemployment, and poverty. Jeanne first worked in the silk mills to support her family, earning a pittance for a 13-hour day at the factory. From age 11 to 14, she worked at five jobs in different towns and villages of her region—as a servant, mill girl, and harvest worker. Then her mother took Jeanne to Paris where her first job lasted one week. Too poor to return home, Jeanne suffered through four exploitative servant jobs in and around Paris during her first year, which tired her of domestic work but introduced her to city life. A cousin in Paris showed her hat-trimming work; then as wages in that trade collapsed she subsequently made her way as a dress-maker. It was insecurity that motivated Bouvier's family to move and that kept them on the road during Jeanne's early years. The shift to city life was not a single relocation, but a series of moves in her youth that were guided by her mother and aided by her extended family.

This more complex reality of rural insecurity and multiple moves may not fit the stereotype of the nineteenth-century migration, but it does resonate with the understanding of migrations that is now emerging. Recent studies observe that we must look to the countryside to understand the plethora of movement that came with the nineteenth century. Although the great urban growth of the period has led scholars to focus on the dazzling lights of the city and smokestacks of factory towns, the countryside is the key to understanding departures from home. This is partly because rural areas supported the vast majority of Europeans at the close of the Napoleonic wars in 1815, and rural population reached its peak in many places on the Continent by 1850. Because it supported so many people, the countryside was vulnerable to crises, and crises came in series during the nineteenth century—visiting region after region with the collapse of long-standing practices of agricultural employment and rural industries, the failure of particular crops, and the restructuring of local markets for goods and labor that came with the railroad.

It follows that migration to the growing cities of Europe at the expense of the countryside—urbanization—needs to be rethought. Recent studies also show that Europeans were not irrevocably attracted to the city. Rather, people moved to and from the city as their life cycle and economic circumstances dictated, and they moved with greater frequency than we have previously imagined. Indeed, migration to the city is better understood as a pulsing two-way current between town and country rather than as attraction to a magnet.[4] This more nuanced understanding of migration confirms historians' rethinking of industrialization. Western European industrialization is coming to be understood more as a long and diffuse process involving capital and labor and less as a technology-driven development of mechanized factory production. Technology, then, has come to share center stage in the drama of industrialization with movements of labor and capital.[5] This chapter interprets the role of migration in this reconceived process of industrialization.

Finally, this chapter highlights the development of farther-reaching migration systems. New itineraries developed. Even local movements within marriage markets expanded, thanks to the bicycle. With the crisis years of the 1840s the men and women of Flanders came to work in French fields and industries; the Irish flooded English cities. The new cities of the Ruhr basin were the destination of people from near and far who had previously stayed in eastern Germany, on nearby farms, or whose ancestors had migrated to Holland every summer.[6] The end of serfdom in Prussia (1807), Austria (1848), and Russia (1861) mobilized the central European labor force and eventually brought central Europeans, particularly Poles, into Germany and France. Consequently, an international labor force harvested Europe's crops, built its transport infrastructure, and worked its mines and factories.

Other migration systems reached beyond the Continent. Europeans had explored, settled, and colonized for 300 years, but these activities reached a peak in the nineteenth century as colonization expanded. The advent of the steamship, which provided cheap transoceanic fares, in combination with European population pressure, facilitated developing migration systems that reached to the western hemisphere and to Australia and New Zealand. Moreover, these migration systems carried people in both directions; many left Europe to work for only a short period in the new world. In the 1815–1914 period particularly, European migration must be seen as one part of a worldwide movement of men and women in a global labor force.[7]

These three issues—rural decline, urbanization/industrialization, and transoceanic migration—forewarn us that the nineteenth century tells a particularly complex tale, one that has at its heart the reversal of fortunes in the countryside that left many people with few alternatives to departure from home. The shifts in rural life were fundamental demographic, labor force, capital, and landholding changes that proceeded very unevenly across Britain and the Continent. The expansion of population and troubles of rural manufacture began in eighteenth-century Britain. Conditions on the Continent, by contrast, preserved rural industry longer and, indeed, rural manufacturing continued to expand in parts of Germany in the later nineteenth century. As a consequence, this chapter will refer to trends that occurred in the eighteenth and early nineteenth century in some locations and as late as the early twentieth century in others.

Nineteenth-century migrations unfolded against the backdrop of existing mobility patterns, interweaving change with continuity. Local migration systems retained a certain importance to rural markets as other kinds of mobility expanded. Between 1850 and 1914, circular migration systems came to a peak as teams of agricultural and construction workers did the crucial work of harvesting and city building. Simultaneously, chain migration from villages and small towns to cities became more important as thousands of young people sought urban livelihoods where their kin and compatriots had gone. Finally, career migration became more important than ever before for lay people as the nation state became a major employer. The bureaucratization of government functions, the growth of state postal and education systems, to say nothing of the formation of the nation states of Germany and Italy after 1850, meant that unparalleled numbers of clerks, officials, and schoolteachers were assigned to posts by their employer.

An increased visibility of women's mobility is fundamental to these shifts in migration patterns. Although women had always been important among local migrants, they came to constitute important groups in every kind of migration system. For example, many Polish sugar beet workers were women who traveled in circular migrations, wives and daughters of upland masons joined chain migration systems to major cities, and French women elementary schoolteachers assigned to remote village schools came to be a very large group of career migrants. Women were particularly attracted to the growing cities of the age, where they found work as mill operatives in textile towns and as domestic servants or needle workers in commercial centers. It is fitting that the story of a young woman opens this chapter.

This chapter first surveys the fundamental changes that altered the nineteenth-century countryside, giving a brief sketch of the eastern provinces of Germany as an example. The focus then shifts to urban growth and attendant migration, including a discussion of the social issues of nineteenth-century migration. Migration to the Americas concludes the chapter. To provide the context for these topics, I initially sketch the links between migrations and the politics of the nineteenth century.

THE CHARACTER OF THE AGE:
WAR, PEACE, AND MIGRATION

International conflicts, state restrictions, and laissez-faire policies all influenced migration in the 1815–1914 period. It was preceded by a decade of revolution in France that stretched into 25 years of conflict and political change. Revolutionary France founded a Republic whose civil wars, external wars, and political divisions sent émigrés from France and raised armies of young men throughout Europe. War and political reorganization culminated during the Napoleonic Empire when territories from the Netherlands to Rome were incorporated into the French Empire and states of western Germany were consolidated into the Confederation of the Rhine.

The revolutionary era brought on a mass movement of émigrés from France. Some 200,000 of the 26 million French people from all levels of society departed from France between 1789 and 1799, the majority of whom departed in 1793–1794 as the politics of the Republic became more divisive and deadly. About 28,000 of the émigrés were women. The royalty and wealthy nobles among them were a particularly influential minority (an estimated 18% of émigrés) in England, German territories, and friendly courts on the Continent.[8]

Within France, the Revolutionary decade began with intense population turbulence that ultimately took a heavy toll on its cities. Social and political change inspired the retreat of elites from urban areas. As a consequence, sellers of luxury goods and wigmakers, for example, fell on hard times, and the quintessential urban newcomer, the domestic servant, was no longer in demand. In fact, when the number of clerics, nobles, and rentiers fell by one-third in the eastern French city of Nancy between 1789 and 1796, the population of domestics fell by half.[9] Building projects declined after 1792, reducing the flow of seasonal laborers. Thus, the Revolutionary era was one of deurbanization in France that was especially costly to large cities; the number of people in Paris decreased by 12 percent, 1790–1806, and the nation's urban population dropped from 20.5 to 19 percent.[10]

The prolonged wars of this era affected international movements in two interrelated ways: by putting young men under arms, on one hand, and creating hostile borders, on the other. The French general call-up of August 1793 (levée en masse) assigned to combat duty single men aged 18 to 25; then, as of 1798, all men aged 20 to 25 were eligible for conscription. Under Napoleon, as many as 200,000 men left France to fight. This call-up echoed across Europe as British, Austrian, Dutch, Prussian, and Russian forces were mustered against Napoleonic forces. Young conscripts were precisely those who were most likely to be labor migrants in peacetime. All combatants had been removed from the potential pool of migrant laboring men. Not only was the pool of potential migrants reduced by wartime, but economic warfare and upheaval also reduced the demand for international migrants. The Napoleonic era was fatal, for example, to the migrations of French into Spain, who were replaced by Galicians and Asturians from northwest Iberia; even the once-successful Société Chinchon described in chapter 3 was definitively liquidated in 1823.[11]

The continental blockade boycotting British goods after 1806 stilled the merchant marine of the Atlantic coast. The port of Amsterdam was virtually closed as the number of ships entering the port dropped from 1,350 to 310 in the short period between 1806 and 1809. This collapse eliminated the need for Norwegian and German foreign sailors and reverberated throughout the Dutch economy, effecting a decline in the export market for cheese and for immigrant hay cutters. The precipitous decline of Amsterdam shipping shows how the blockade, wars, and politics of the French imperium played havoc with the labor force. The largely rural Rhineland textile industry that thrived on exports, for example, suffered because the Continental System treated all non-French areas as foreign territories; while the left bank of the Rhine, annexed into France, thrived with all the French Empire as a market, industries on the right bank, including those around the booming towns of Elberfeld and Barmen, were devastated.[12] Fortunately, it would be 100 years before the people of Europe again would see such widespread disruption and hostilities.

The nineteenth century—here defined as the period between the end of the Napoleonic wars in 1815 and the outbreak of World War I in 1914—was kinder in many ways than either the seventeenth or eighteenth centuries; in demographic and military terms it was relatively free of disaster. After the widespread wars of the French Revolution and of the Napoleonic era, the military interventions of the 1820s in Spain and Italy were mild. The revolutions and subsequent repressions of 1848, as important as they were politically, killed and exiled many fewer people than the eighteenth-century revolution in France. The next wars on the Continent, under Bismarck's leadership, each lasted only a matter of weeks. Colonial takeovers and armed conflict in the Crimea and South Africa were remote to European populations. No conflict bore the destruction of the Thirty Years' War, the mobilizations of the Napoleonic Wars, or the impact of the French Revolution.

In the century of peace that followed, only minimal state intervention touched migration practices. Working people wanted to cross borders, and they were usually free to do so. Moreover, the unification of the Italian state in 1870 and the forging of the German Empire in 1871 facilitated the movement of people within these national states. In fact, intervention in migration usually took the form of encouragement. Caribbean and South American governments looked far and wide for laborers when it was no longer legal to use slave labor.[13] Some states, like Brazil, offered subsidized travel to incoming workers. In Europe, some countries, such as England and Denmark, occasionally subsidized departures of their poor. One exception to this encouragement of migration was Britain's refusal to allow artisans or skilled mechanics to emigrate during the early industrial revolution. More important, Prussia (and, after 1871, the German Empire) regulated the movements of Polish migrants within its borders and from abroad. This intervention is discussed below.

Although state intervention in migration was relatively rare, governmental policies were fundamental to shaping mobility in this age. State building included the construction of railroads, canals, roads, and public monuments that employed seasonal migrant laborers by the thousands. Laissez-faire policies effectively encouraged movement in the global labor force and reflected the symbiosis of labor-abundant homelands and labor-hungry developing economies. Moveover, the states of western Europe colonized much of Asia and Africa in this period. Between 1876 and 1915, a quarter of the globe was distributed among a handful of nations—primarily Britain, France, Germany, Belgium, and Italy.[14] Imperial ventures moved few Europeans relative to the millions of men and women who settled in European cities and in the Americas.[15] However, the colonies of the nineteenth century would come home to roost in the form of migrations from Asia and Africa after World War II. Although less visible in one century, colonial migrations would have serious repercussions in the next.

RURAL EUROPE

Population and Landholding in the Nineteenth Century

The population increased as never before between 1815 and 1914. Not even the growth of the 1750–1800 period (when the European population expanded by 34%), as unprecedented as it was, could match that of the nineteenth century. A population that was 187 million in 1800 grew to 266 million in 1850, then to 468 million by 1913, an increase of 42 percent in the first half of the century and another 76 percent by World War I. During the nineteenth century, the number of people more than tripled in Denmark, Finland, and Great Britain; it more than doubled in Belgium, Holland, Germany, and Austria-Hungary, and doubled in Italy. Growth rates varied: France grew by a mere 55 percent over the century, and as the population of Great Britain doubled for a second time between 1850 and 1910, that of France increased by only 14 percent.[16] (See Table 4:1.)

Improvements in the production and distribution of food in the nineteenth century underwrote this population growth. Widespread improvement in the feeding of Europeans began with a first agricultural revolution in the eighteenth century (and the nineteenth century, in some regions), which brought fallow land under cultivation and introduced new fodder crops such as clover and root crops such as turnips. The gradual introduction of the potato in the late eighteenth and nineteenth centuries allowed rural people to produce adequate food on very small plots of land. Such new crops as the potato, in combination with other horticultural and technological innovations, enhanced Europe's food supply. In the case of England, for example, food production tripled between 1700 and 1870. With the grim exception of the poor harvests, high grain prices, and potato famine of the "hungry forties," food production increased.

A fall in death rates also underlay this expansion.[17] The demographic crises that had wiped out old regime populations were defeated definitively in the nineteenth century; few wars were waged on European soil, and few famines suffered, apart from the crises of the 1840s. More important, ordinary mortality gradually declined—albeit in a localized and gradual fashion. Mortality declined for adults, for children, and, finally, for infants in northern and western Europe—most slowly in unsanitary industrial cities and rural areas where infants were exposed as their mothers worked in the fields. André Armengaud rightly indicates that "this decline

TABLE 4.1
Estimated Population Growth in Western
Europe, 1800–1910
(in millions)

	c. 1800	c. 1850	c. 1900	c. 1910
Norway	0.9	1.5	2.2	2.4
Sweden	2.3	3.5	5.1	5.5
Finland	1.0	1.6	2.7	3.1
Denmark	0.9	1.6	2.6	2.9
Germany	24.5	31.7	50.6	58.5
Netherlands	2.2	3.1	5.1	5.9
Belgium	3.0	4.3	6.7	7.4
Switzerland	1.8	2.4	3.3	3.8
France	26.9	36.5	40.7	41.5
Great Britain	10.9	20.9	36.9	40.8
Ireland	5.0	6.6	4.5	4.4
Spain	11.5	15.5	18.6	19.9
Portugal	3.1	4.2	5.4	6.0
Italy	18.1	23.9	33.9	36.2

SOURCE: André Armengaud, "Population in Europe, 1700–1914," in *The Fontana Economic History of Europe*, vol. 3, *The Industrial Revolution, 1700–1914*, edited by C. Cipolla (New York: Barnes and Noble, 1976), 29.

marked a turning point in European demography" because the decline in ordinary mortality meant a sizable increase in survivors—of men and women who would reach reproductive age to bear their own children. For example, where in France only 62 percent of women survived to age 20 between 1805 and 1807, 76 percent survived into their peak childbearing years in the 1900–1902 period.[18]

These increased survivors shared finite land resources and, as a consequence, the proportion of landless laborers in rural populations increased.[19] The shift from serf to laborer was particularly swift and dramatic in Germany's eastern provinces, where in many instances serfs were freed only to become farm servants or cottagers (*Knechte* or *Instleute*) and then landless laborers who only had a small potato patch to work (*Deputant*) and were paid in kind. The social ties and shared interests binding landlord to worker were severed.[20] To return to the Saxon example cited for the eighteenth century: between 1550 and 1750, the proletariat had leapt from 26 to 61 percent of the rural population; by 1843 this proportion expanded to 79 percent of the rural population. The peasant population of the sixteenth century had been replaced by one that was only one-fifth

Map 4:1 Western Europe, 1871–1914

peasant and in which the vast majority of people owned at most their dwelling and a garden, if they owned anything at all.[21] This trend had transpired over a longer period in Britain and was less important in France, where peasant land ownership remained relatively strong outside the great farms of the north.

Population growth and proletarianization in the European countryside had clear, long-term implications for migration. Even without crises, rural areas could not support the tripled population of Denmark, Britain, or Finland; the doubled population of Belgium, Italy, the Netherlands, Austria-Hungary, or Germany; or even the 50 percent increase in France. The landless among rural-dwellers were most willing to move. In the long term, population growth and industrial development would result in a much larger, and urbanized, labor force. But before this urbanization would be effected, a series of uneven changes would rock the countryside that eventually drastically reduced sources of income. Consequently, in the short run, particularly in the period between 1850 and World War I, crises in rural economies promoted mobility.

The Disintegration of Rural Livelihoods

Western Europe saw drastic changes in rural economies in the nineteenth century, as chances to earn a living year-round by rural manufacture, agricultural work, or a combination of the two were endangered. Although the means and the timing by which rural economies were undercut varied, regional histories have in common one result: the reduction of rural people's ability to make their living at home. At the heart of rural crises two kinds of changes are discernible: the demise of old agricultural systems and the demise of rural industries—with their concomitant social systems and migration routines. In addition, crop failures played a catastrophic role in certain times and places. Of course, out-migration was only one response to rural crises; people also persisted at home, staying on in the countryside and changing the means by which they earned their bread, and living on less. Perhaps it is most useful to survey the forces that reduced the chances of rural people to earn a living at home. Why, in a general way, did each phenomenon occur? How did each change encourage migration by chipping away at people's ability to work at home?

Capitalist Agriculture and Changes in Rural Employment
In 1800, the vast majority of Europeans lived in the countryside and worked in agriculture at least part time; during the next century, changes in agricultural production and the social system it supported transformed rural routines and undermined the social structure in ways that created new migration patterns. On the Continent, large landholdings continued to increase at the expense of small ones, to the detriment of the peasant economy. Cash crops produced on a large scale made food production a more widespread capitalist venture than ever before. Continental government policies encouraged land consolidation, enclosure, and the absorption of commons. Large farms increased the food supply and employed many people, but they simultaneously undermined the social and agricultural practices that supported the peasantry and year-round farm servants and agricultural laborers.

The important institution of farm service was ill-suited to large enclosed farms. Rather than hire agricultural servants by the year, large farms tended to hire labor for shorter periods, because labor demand became focused in short seasons as farm production narrowed to one or two labor-intensive crops. The rural domestic on an annual contract became less commonplace. A great many people worked in agriculture, but a larger proportion were employed in short-term work gangs, such as teams of vine trimmers, hoers, flower cutters, hay mowers, and potato diggers. This is especially crucial because while farm owners housed and fed domestics year round, they only housed laborers during the short periods they worked the land.[22] With the collapse of farm service, then, young people lost housing and sustenance.

The decrease in farm servants began in England, when the peace of 1815 flooded the country with labor—including Joseph Mayett (whose story opened chapter 2), who never again worked as a domestic after his discharge. "Individuals decay and die; species become extinct. Servants in husbandry were creatures of the early modern economy; the institution of service was imbedded in a matrix of agricultural practices and social organization," writes Ann Kussmaul.[23] By the mid-nineteenth century, servants in husbandry had virtually disappeared from southeastern England, where large farms and enclosures were most common.[24] The decrease in farm servants was no less important to areas such as eastern Germany, where it was an end-of-century phenomenon. Between the agricultural censuses of 1895 and 1907, servants in agriculture in all of Germany fell by 29 percent, as teams of seasonal workers replaced the freed peasants of the northeast and laborers that worked on a one-year contract.[25]

Changes in agriculture produced intense, short-lived periods of rural work that made seasonal movement proliferate. The three-field system that had supported agriculture since the Middle Ages was first altered when new crops such as clover, legumes, and (in some areas) potatoes were added to the traditional crop rotation. Then in a second agricultural revolution, systems developed that included root crops and demanded more intense and shorter-term labor. Later in the century, sugar beets were added to the rotation in some regions of France, Germany, Sweden, Russia, and the Netherlands. The land became more productive and more profitable, but did so in a way that further destabilized agricultural employment. "Each step up the ladder of intensification increased the total labor input per acre but also further imbalanced the seasons, since virtually all of the new work had to be done in the warm months," observes Steve Hochstadt. "While the relationship of summer to winter work in the three-field system was 1.4:1, it changed to 1.9:1 when potatoes were introduced, and reached 2.6:1" with the introduction of the sugar beet.[26] As a result, agriculture demanded massive teams of summer workers. The records of one enterprise in West Prussia show the hiring of three different groups: general summer workers employed from April to October, who hoed, spread fertilizer, then thinned and harvested sugar beets; hay harvesters for July and August; and potato diggers for October.[27]

Across Europe, while the need for summer workers increased, the need for winter workers diminished with the introduction of the thresher. This machine performed the work that occupied 80 percent of a farmworker's time in the winter and moved that task to the end of the summer. Moreover, the thresher was used by nearly all farms over five hectares, while other farm machines for planting and harvesting were not widely used.[28] The episodic nature of farm work severely reduced the annual labor contract before World War I.

Changing rural economies forced people to find new itineraries for cash earning. In hard times and crowded places, agricultural workers could not rely on long-standing migration systems; rather, they desperately searched for work and moved when they heard it was available, keeping their ear to the ground. As long-standing, more protective social systems gave way to capitalist employers who left care in off-season, illness, and old age to the individual worker, the neat categories of seasonal and temporary labor migration overflowed as rural laborers sought work wherever and whenever they could find it.

The story of Franz Rehbein, an agricultural laborer just north of the Elbe River estuary in the 1890s, offers vivid testimony of rural migration in an age of insecurity. This mobility was not part of a system of seasonal labor but a repeated search for work. His is a rare tale; Rehbein's is the only extant account of German farm labor by a member of the rural proletariat (aside from memoirs of childhood).[29] Three times in a single year—the year of his marriage—Rehbein left home to find employment to supplement intermittent farm work. He was married one summer in his late twenties to his sweetheart, who was in service on a dairy farm. After a day and a half off work for the wedding, the couple continued to live and work separately until the fall, while Rehbein joined a work crew on a dike to protect reclaimed coastal land from the North Sea. Harvest work followed, but the wages, ordinarily adequate to support laborers for much of the year, were paid at half the usual rate because the grain was poor and labor plentiful. Then came winter unemployment. Rehbein wrote that "for the first time I learned what it meant to have to struggle along as a 'free' and married day laborer. . . . There was nothing happening on the farms. The final threshing of the grain was done by machine, and there was no chaff to separate either."[30] Desperate to make up for his poor harvest earnings and to support his wife and newborn son, Rehbein left home. Along with a few compatriots, he made a day's trip to the construction site for the Kiel Canal that would join the Baltic and North seas; there they worked as excavators until spring. Then, Rehbein was able to live with his family again while he worked on a local farm. Another stretch of unemployment came early in the summer, so he once again departed, this time for brickyards where he worked until harvest time, employed as a brick finisher and returning home on Sundays. Tense and exhausting harvest work followed. "My wife worked faithfully alongside me [binding sheaves of grain]. Up to then I'd never wanted her to work with me because it hurt me to yoke her up too. . . . But my wife said there was no way of knowing what it was going to be like next winter, and she insisted on working with me at harvesting."[31] After the harvest, Rehbein worked with a threshing machine crew for a period of weeks, laboring from 3:00 or 4:00 A.M. until as late as midnight, then sleeping on the ground. This exhausting last task of the harvest cycle would be his demise; Franz Rehbein lost a hand to the threshing machine and became unfit for farm labor. His story shows that even when he was an able-bodied farm laborer, Rehbein was unable to support himself year-round without leaving home for *ad hoc* seasonal jobs. It is important that he was engaged in the great tasks of his age as a seasonal laborer. As a laborer on the Kiel canal, Rehbein helped on the public works that altered the transport infrastructure, and, as a brickworker, he was part of the building materials industry that supplied the cities of the German Empire.

Crop Failures
Crop failures had long struck at rural people, and although starvation ceased to be a threat to the English by the seventeenth century, other areas remained mortally subject to weather conditions well into the eighteenth century. By 1815, improvements in agricultural productivity and the transport of foodstuffs considerably reduced the chances that any one area would be reduced to starvation. Nonetheless, the cold spring and summer of 1816 resulted in widespread famine after the failure of grain crops; beggars, vagrants, and emigrants all fled home areas that offered little to eat.[32] Crop failures continued to hold a powerful sway over country people, partly because rural Europe supported a much greater population in 1850 than in 1750. Fed by crops like the potato, and supported in densely populated countrysides by rural industry, rural life depended on good harvests and manufacturing prosperity.[33]

As a consequence, when crops failed, as the potato did so disastrously in the mid- to late 1840s, even more people lurched into a state of hunger and indigence. During the worst years of the potato famine (1846–1851), a million Irish perished, and another million set out for England and the United States. Germans and Dutch, also hard-hit, began a large-scale exodus to North America. The potato famine is but one part of the suffering brought on by widespread crop failure throughout western Europe during the bleak years of the "hungry forties."

With this tragic exception, crop failure in the nineteenth century struck more often at rural wages than at foodstuffs, because it affected industries with an agricultural base, such as the manufacture of silk and wine.[34] Although silk weaving was an urban art, the silk industry rested on the cultivation of mulberry trees whose leaves fed silk worms until they spun the cocoons from which raw silk was wound. In the 1850s, both silkworms and the mulberry tree were struck by disease. In the short term, people left silk-working towns and villages; more important, these crises began the long process of undermining the rural fortunes of the hill people of Lombardy and southern France.[35] The wine industry was also subject to vine-mildew, and the plague phylloxera, a vine-killer spread by aphids, proved deadly to French vines. After almost a decade in eastern Languedoc in the south, it then spread to the southwest as the 1880s approached, then to the north, and finally to the Champagne and Moselle regions in the northeast. As the disease ascended the Rhone valley, it reached the area south of Lyon where the family of Jeanne Bouvier (whose story opened this chapter) lived—until the 1876 crop losses forced them to sell their land and possessions. Because the vine was the mainstay of thousands of families, the phylloxera epidemic struck at the core of small-holders, many of whom, like the Bouviers, lost everything.[36]

The Demise of Rural Industry
The collapse of rural industries and deindustrialization of the European countryside, which withdrew capital from the hands of rural people, is as much a key to the nineteenth century as the growth of factory industry. Handicraft production had supported hundreds of thousands of villagers who worked seasonally, part time, or full time in manufacturing. During the nineteenth century—on a vast array of timetables that differ by region and industry—the markets for rural manufactured goods dried up; the capital invested in manufacturing moved to larger-scale urban sites in some regions and fled other regions altogether. "The larger dynamic at work," points out Christopher Johnson in his study of deindustrialization, "is the unevenness of capitalist development and the ability of capital to play regional and sectoral hopscotch"; capital moved faster and with greater alacrity than labor.[37] Ironically, the withdrawal of manufacturing ultimately made villages more agricultural than they had ever been. Indeed, Philippe Pinchemel concludes his study of the evolution of rural Picardy with the observation that

> If one of the weavers of 1836 returned to the canton of Rosières, if a spinner of Hornay returned to her village, they would not recognize the rural countryside and the social, human landscape. . . . Villages have become exclusively agricultural communities with a shopkeeper and some other professionals from the non-agricultural sector scattered here and there. This impoverishment of the socio-professional structure, this "ruralization" of the countryside . . . dates from the second half of the nineteenth century.[38]

Chances for village work withered, and pay rates for rural goods declined, reducing the ability of country workers to get by in their local "cottage economy."[39] Whole villages and regions scrambled for alternative ways to make a living or to reduce their consumption.[40] Women, whose "finger work" was spinning or lacemaking, often changed their tasks and remained in the village. The litany of alternatives tried by the women of Auffay (the Norman spinning village featured in the last chapter) is typical of rural possibilities. When the rates for hand-spun thread dropped, they first continued spinning, working for longer hours at reduced rates. Then, when water-powered mill spinning was established nearby, some worked in these small mills that dotted the European countryside in this period. But these mills met their demise with the centralization of steam-powered factory spinning. When factory production of thread expanded matériel, a boom in handloom weaving followed, and the women of Auffay took on the traditional male task of weaving. Two additional village alternatives grew as well: Women's agricultural work expanded with new fodder crops that required more weeding and hoeing than did traditional grain. Seamstress work also expanded in village settings with increased cloth production. Despite measures of relief from each of these alternatives—self-exploitation, rural spinning mills, weaving, agricultural labor, and sewing— women became less able to work for pay in Auffay, as in other villages.

In many textile areas, female spinners were undercut by mechanized spinning in the late eighteenth century, but rural weavers' demise came nearly a half-century later.[41] The most visible and acute hardships caused by the demise of rural industry are those that struck at men who were completely dependent upon their earnings from manufacturing, such as the handloom weavers. The little towns of eastern Languedoc that had supported wool weavers collapsed in the 1850–1870 period. Typically, the city council of Lodève reported in 1868 that over 2,000 workers had left their *pays natal* in search of work.[42] In mid-century England, weavers constituted the largest group of industrial workers; they were the third largest occupational group after agricultural laborers and domestic servants, numbering 800,000 to 840,000 along with their dependents.[43] These weavers were the first whose earnings were undercut by declining piece rates in the wake of mechanized weaving—rates that literally pushed their families to starvation.[44] As many as 70,000 Scottish weavers were forced to abandon their trade between 1840 and 1860.[45] The drop in demand for linen devastated Irish and Flemish workers and pushed thousands of Silesian families into starvation and revolt by 1844. Although English parliamentary committees and other inquiring bodies recorded the degradation and starvation rates paid to weavers who remained at the loom, the weavers who left home in hard times are less well documented.

Nonetheless, it is clear that, for many weavers, "fleeing the trade" meant also leaving their home village. Some appear, with their families, in industrial towns like Preston, where their children found work in the Lancashire textile mills. Others went to North America. Those of eastern Languedoc tended to seek work in the cities of southern France.[46] Even when the adult worker or the adult working couple continued to struggle by on lower rates and remained in the village, many children would take other work out of town. A Lancashire song at mid-century observed that

> If you go into a loom-shop, where there's three or four
>   pairs of looms,
> They all are standing empty, encumbrances of the rooms;
> And if you ask the reason why, the old mother will tell
>   you plain,
> My daughters have forsaken them, and gone to weave by
>   steam.[47]

Stagnating population figures and the loss of young adults from industrial villages and small towns reflect the departures of village workers. Births and marriages decreased as young people left. For example, the population of Auffay remained virtually the same at about 1,140 in the crisis-ridden 1796–1841 period, despite the fact that it should have grown by natural increase alone. Its population stagnation is eloquent testimony to departures—doubtless departures of some women to some of the big spinning mills on the river Seine, the Rouen mills, and domestic jobs in the city and departures of young men for the textile mills of Rouen.[48] Nineteenth-century censuses for cantons just to the south, in Picardy, recorded that villages simultaneously became smaller and more agricultural as artisans and industrial workers gave up their manufacturing and left or turned to the fields full time.[49] Dying textile towns in eastern Languedoc lost population in absolute terms; Lodève, for example, lost over a quarter of its population between 1848 and 1906.

Rural deindustrialization affected men and women differently because almost all manufacturing and agricultural tasks were sex-specific. In other words, the dissolution of rural livelihoods worked on a gendered timetable. In the little wool-producing towns of Languedoc, for example, when the women's work process of wool preparation was dropped, 1,500 female jobs were affected before men's work declined. Family units doubtless struggled and single women may have left their hometown.[50] Gullickson's exemplary research analyzes the differential effect on men and women of the disintegration of the rural textile industry in the village of Auffay and how it influenced gender relations—courtship, marriage, and childbearing. When rural economies changed, they affected both women's productive and reproductive roles.

During the "golden age of spinning," the majority of women were employed in textiles, while men worked in agriculture, crafts, and some weaving (1750–1786). In this spinning era, the vast majority of women married in the village of Auffay (only 2.2 to 7% were single, compared with 12% for the entire kingdom of France and greater proportions in other nations). And, although premarital sexual relations were common, they nearly always resulted in marriage: about one bride in five was pregnant, but fewer than one child in 30 was born out of wedlock.[51]

Employment patterns subsequently changed in such a way that dislocated men and women, producing increased proportions of single women, pregnant brides, and illegitimate children. Between 1787 and 1817, as factory spinning chipped away at women's employment, it became increasingly difficult for a pregnant woman to bring her lover to marriage. The interval between conception and marriage lengthened, so that pregnant brides were closer to term when they married, and there were more of them (one-fourth of all brides). The proportion of children born out of wedlock tripled. Political and military upheaval exacerbated the effects of declining employment for women. The French Revolution undermined Auffay's church, then ousted its priest. Moreover, the ability of women to realize a marriage, once pregnant, was weakened by conscription of village men into the army—and by the fleeting presence of national troops in the area.[52]

Nonetheless, when social and economic stability returned after the Napoleonic wars, local employment continued to disintegrate and to disrupt courtships. Most telling was the decrease in married women during this period; by 1850, fewer women were married in Auffay than in a century, as the proportion of single women climbed to 16 percent. With the complete demise of local spinning, women worked as seamstresses or as calico weavers, but fewer women could find work, and the light calicos were soon undermined by machine production.

Men, the majority of weavers whose work was undermined more slowly, were more likely than women to depart from the village, "leaving broken engagements and pregnant women."[53] Male and female migration patterns diverged with the collapse of local industry; men went to urban workshops and factories to work as spinners, weavers, and warp winders, while women were relatively less mobile.[54] In this region, which had long depended on village employment for its women, families tried to keep their daughters at home. Villagers were aware of the dangers of the notorious provincial capital of Rouen; they were wary of the factory workshop in this city where illegitimacy was high.[55] We will see in the section on urban illegitimacy that they had good reason to be cautious.

The story of Auffay alerts us to the gendered economic dynamics behind changes in rural social relations and differential migration patterns.[56] In this case, deindustrialization tore at the fabric of rural society, delaying marriage, rendering courtships unstable, and producing children out of wedlock.

Deindustrialization also promoted temporary migration. In scrambling to make a living, some manufacturing villages developed seasonal migration itineraries for farm work. Collective migration strategies are nearly invisible to the historical record, so it is impossible to know how many agricultural workers were spinners, weavers, or nailmakers in other seasons. Nonetheless, the itinerary of one village is revealed by the biography of Mémé Gardez Santerre. Early in the century the people of her village, Avesnes-les-Aubert in the north of France, had been able to live by weaving alone, but by the 1880s they were also engaged in the cultivation of Europe's fastest-growing and most labor-intensive crop, the sugar beet. When Mémé was born in the 1880s, the family could not earn enough from weaving linen to support themselves, so low were the piece-rates for handloomed linen by that time. Mémé Gardez Santerre wove linen handkerchiefs in the cellar of her village home in Avesnes with her sister and father from the age of 10; then her husband joined the family when she married. (Her brothers had left home to become agricultural laborers.) They purchased bread all winter on credit, which they paid for by lucrative summer work. They left their village in May for a large farm in the Norman Vexin owned by a Parisian company and devoted exclusively to the production of wheat and sugar beets. By becoming seasonal migrant agricultural laborers, the weavers of Avesnes were able to underwrite their weaving until the opening salvos of World War I literally destroyed their village. So, although they lived in a backwater, members of the Gardez family were at the center of the changes that altered the lives of rural people in the years before World War I.

The family carried out a routine series of agricultural tasks during their six months of agricultural labor. That they were paid differently for each task and that each was separately defined reflects the segmented nature of agricultural work and routines on capitalist farms. In May, the Gardez family hoed thistles from the wheat fields, paid by the plot. In June, they removed rocks from these same fields by hand and carried them to nearby roadways; the next task was to spread fertilizer by pitchfork in a family team. After this, they thinned sugar beets, straddling the row of beets and swinging a hoe. With the ripening of the wheat, "strapping" Flemish harvesters arrived with their scythes; Mémé and members of her family each followed a reaper, gathering the wheat into sheaves, then tying sheaves into a bale. The September task of the sugar beet harvest followed; here Mémé and her family were the harvesters, bending to pull out each beet, then stretching to throw it into the oxcart that followed them. The children of the family then worked in the barnyard, farmhouse, and vegetable garden while their parents carried out the heavy post-harvest tasks of preparing the sugar beets for pulping and finally working in the nearby processing plant used by the farm. At the end of November, the Gardez family lined up to settle accounts with the farm agent; his account would generally accord with that which Mémé kept on behalf of her illiterate parents. On this day, they would "hear an unfamiliar sound. It was gold or silver pieces clinking from hand to hand," which signaled the annual payday for the Gardez family. After one day spent on travel home by rail with their fellow villagers, they paid their debt for the previous winter's bread and began another six-month stint of weaving.[57] This migration system devised by the people of one village in northern France resonates with routines of seasonal work elsewhere.

Changing Patterns of Circular Migration

In the long run, shifts in landownership that would produce a proletarian countryside, the movement of capital to urban areas, and the concomitant shifts in the labor force would all serve to produce a metropolitan world. But in the short run, the changes described above inflated seasonal work, economic insecurity, and temporary movement. The nineteenth century saw the development of seasonal and temporary migration systems that may be unprecedented. As we have seen, at the beginning of the century roughly 300,000 men and women moved annually in seven major systems of seasonal migration (that each included over 20,000 people annually).[58] Similar migration systems, much smaller, joined city to hinterland and rural areas to regional harvests throughout western Europe. For example, southwestern France provided vine harvest workers and construction workers to the Bordeaux region; towns of the Rhineland and southern Germany each had their own hinterland. However, no system of migrant labor seems to have been required in 1800 to produce the massive grain harvests of central Europe. Rather, Baltic territories, German territories east of the Elbe, and western Russia all harvested rich grainlands with the labor of the serf-farmers who could neither move freely nor deny their labor to the lord in whose jurisdiction they dwelt. The vast estates of East Elbia drew on the local farmer-serfs and their livestock for labor and draught animals.[59]

The pattern of seasonal and temporary migration changed considerably in the years before World War I as some important seasonal migration systems atrophied and new ones developed. The North Sea system declined as the Dutch demand for labor declined; Germans moved to the United States or eventually found employment in the new industrial cities of the Rhine-Ruhr zone. Reversing a centuries-old pattern, workers from the Netherlands trekked to Germany as industry prospered there after 1875.[60] Most spectacularly, massive migration systems developed east of the Elbe River as labor force changes reverberated throughout the provinces of eastern Germany, Austria-Hungary, and western Russia. Germans from poor and upland areas harvested and performed urban work from the Tyrol north to the Baltic Sea and from Holland east to Russia.[61]

In western Europe, the numbers of agricultural laborers who migrated for short-term farm tasks recovered from the low point of the Napoleonic war period and rose to new heights. Irish and Scots came in greater numbers to harvest in England. By 1841, the number of Irish who worked in England between planting their potatoes in February and digging them up in November numbered at least 50,000 per year.[62] At mid-century over 264,000 male and 98,200 female agricultural workers in France moved in seasonal migration circuits—not including foreign harvesters like the Belgians, who cut grain in northern France. The number of people in the vine harvest—intense, short-term work—reached nearly 526,500 men and 352,100 women.[63]

The construction of the transportation infrastructure vastly expanded temporary seasonal work in the nineteenth century. New and improved roads, canals, and railroad lines provided temporary mobile employment. Because of the ubiquitous, continual, and intense nature of railroad construction, it in particular mobilized thousands of men—to excavate roadbeds in countryside and city, pierce tunnels, construct bridges, surface roadbeds, and lay rails. Railroad construction covered Britain in the 1830s and 1840s, then the low countries, France, and Germany. For example, the 2,000 kilometers of completed rail lines expanded to 17,000 between 1852 and 1869 in France, then to 33,000 by 1914. Rail work was seasonal. In relatively level lowland areas, the preparation of roadbeds could be done by local workers when there was not more pressing harvest work; but generally it was teams of migrant workers who built the railroads; only they were willing to live in makeshift barracks, located in rural areas that could be hostile and remote. Navvies were often foreigners: Irish in England, Belgians in northern France, Poles in Germany, and Italians in Germany, Switzerland, and France.[64]

On the Continent, railways went into mountainous areas that required more men, time, and labor to lay rails. The construction of tunnels and viaducts made the work more arduous and dangerous. To put the railroad through the steep 51-kilometer stretch north of the coal mines of Alès in the south of France, workers built 47 tunnels, excavating through 16 kilometers of mountain. This feat was performed by teams of men from the central highlands and from Piedmont in northwestern Italy. The Alpine tunnels were extraordinarily long and difficult to construct. For example, the Fréjus tunnel at the French-Italian border, 13 kilometers long, was built between 1857 and 1871; it was hand-mined until 1861. In the beginning, 500 men at once worked on the tunnel, but in the 1860s, up to 2,000 laborers were at work. Teams worked for nine years on the tunnel at the Gothard pass.[65] Credit for the heavy, dangerous work of constructing roads and railroads in alpine Europe goes to thousands of Italian workers. In 1900, 44,000 of them were at work in railroad construction in Switzerland alone, but they also worked in southern Germany and France. "The Chinese of Europe," Italian men were the mainstay of seasonal construction crews on the Continent.[66]

The installation of rail networks itself produced more circular migration routines, because fast delivery encouraged the production of seasonal goods for urban markets, where people would pay high prices for fresh

meat and diary products, flowers, fruits, and vegetables. The Mediterranean littoral, for example, continued to draw harvest workers into the
twentieth century, but less for grain harvests than for short, intense harvests of grapes, fruits, and flowers. By the turn of the century, wheat
harvest workers no longer came from the Cévennes mountains just west
of the Rhone River; rather, young women worked in the Rhone valley
picking strawberries in May and June, and men came to harvest tomatoes
later in the summer; then masses of montagnards appeared for the grape
harvest on the Mediterranean plain, where replanting vines after the phylloxera epidemic had transformed the littoral into a wine factory. East of
the Rhone, 15,000 Italian men and women came to Provence every year;
women grew and picked flowers, vegetables, and olives; teams of men
tilled and harvested grapes and gardened. Likewise, Bretons picked
strawberries and green beans for the Parisian market and new potatoes for
London.[67]

None of these specialized harvest teams, however, was as important as
those who took to the road for sugar beet work. No industrial crop needed
more concentrated labor power over such extensive regions or grew so
quickly, feeding a demand for animal fodder and alcohol as well as sugar
itself. By 1900, Germany produced half the world's sugar; central and eastern Germany and northern France were the two giants of sugar beet production.[68] The great demand for sugar beet workers, like the demand for
railroad workers, internationalized migrant labor within Europe in the
1850–1914 period. In Germany, sugar beet migrations began with
Sachsengängerei—"going to Saxony"—as early as the 1840s, and such migrants were still called Sachsengängerei as beet fields proliferated east of the
Elbe, attracting 119,000 international workers in 1900 and an estimated
433,000 by 1914, including Russian and Austrian Poles, Italians, Scandinavians, White Russians, and Ruthenians. The 50,000 Belgian agricultural
workers in France specialized in sugar beets.[69]

In the 1850–1914 period, rural women increasingly formed groups of
farm laborers that worked on the vast farms of eastern England and the
Continent. In southern France, groups of women came to the Rhone valley to pick flowers and strawberries. Thomas Hardy vividly portrayed the
work of Tess of the d'Ubervilles digging the large yellow turnips called
swedes; her job was to dig up the lower half of turnips whose upper half
already had been eaten off by the livestock, "to grub up the lower or
earthy half of the root with a hooked fork called a hacker."[70] In central
Europe, women began to take advantage of the chances to earn cash by
the season during the last quarter of the century. They traveled and
worked in separate groups composed primarily of single women aged 16
to 20. A Polish peasant remembers that "the women and girls . . . would
cross the Vistula River into the Russian territory to work on the fields.
. . . They would go on foot, in groups of two or three score, carrying in

big kerchiefs their clothes and food with them. They would leave home in the spring and return after the potatoes had been dug in the autumn."[71] Other Polish women trekked to the sugar beet fields of Germany and Denmark, where they outnumbered male workers.[72]

The Example of East Elbia

The German provinces east of the Elbe river provide a dramatic example of the changes in the nineteenth-century European countryside that produced responsive migration systems, which themselves altered considerably between 1815 and 1914. These provinces were East Prussia, West Prussia, Pomerania, Posen, Brandenburg, and Mecklenburg. I summarize the evolution of rural conditions and consequent migration patterns here because the links between them are dramatic and instructive. Rural East Elbian society was relatively sedentary before the nineteenth century because its people were bound to the soil by the feudal relations with landlords, but then the region quickly experienced changes that had been more gradual in the west. As serf-farmers were freed from feudal obligations in the early nineteenth century, Prussian landowners were compensated for their loss of labor from the land and incomes of their people. The situation was exacerbated by the division and enclosure of common lands that, in parts of East Prussia, made up 50 percent of agricultural land. The loss of commons meant that many peasants could not keep animals or fertilize their fields and did not have access to forests that provided firewood and building materials. The poorest could not support themselves or pay their debts from reduced plots; one scholar estimates that in eastern Prussia over 100,000 peasants lost their property. Thus, although Prussian land reforms of the nineteenth century were designed to create an independent peasantry, they created many proletarians as well.[73]

Many villagers in the eastern German provinces came to depend upon rural industry for at least part of their livelihood. They grew flax, produced wool, spun, and wove textiles; they made charcoal, forged nails, and produced tools and shoes for local use. In Brandenberg, around Berlin, textile production was particularly intense. In the agricultural provinces farther to the east, the working of flax and production of linen were a most important part of agricultural workers' livelihood. The number of looms used by part-time linen weavers in Prussia doubled in the 40 years after 1816.[74] The people of northeastern Germany, then, became more dependent on rural industry by the middle of the nineteenth century, later than in most parts of England, the low countries, France, western Germany, or Saxony.

In the 1870s and 1880s, both rural industry and rural agricultural employment collapsed. The crises that had stricken the rural linen and iron industries in western Germany earlier in the century invaded the northeastern provinces after the creation of the German Empire in 1871. Local markets that had kept industries alive collapsed—like the cottage weaving supporting Rixdorf outside Berlin and the metalworking in the ore fields near that city. The acreage of flax in Germany dropped from over 530,000 acres in 1872 to 42,000 on the eve of World War I.[75] The collapse of rural industrial employment came simultaneously with the expansion of short-term agricultural employment.

Undermined in every quarter, the people of the eastern German provinces expanded existing small-scale migration streams and created new ones to North America and to the burgeoning cities of central and western Germany (which will be discussed below). Poles from Austrian and Russian territories, attracted by the very conditions that repelled those in northeastern Germany, came to take their places in the fields because they faced greater poverty at home. Poland had been obliterated as a political entity in the late eighteenth century when it was divided into Russian, Austrian, and Prussian territory. Until Poland was returned to the political map of Europe in 1918, its people were ruled as minorities in Russia, Prussia (the German Empire, 1871–1918), and Austria (Austro-Hungary, 1867–1918). Among the most important migration systems brought Poles (particularly from Austrian Galicia) into Germany, where they replaced eastern Germans (many of whom were themselves ethnic Poles) who had been unseated by changes in the rural economy. By 1910, well over 200,000 men, women, and children from Austrian and Russian Polish provinces came annually to northeastern Germany to work in agriculture and industry.[76]

Three interdependent systems of migration developed in the northeast German provinces: one with North America, another with the provinces of industrializing western Germany, and a third with Poles from Austrian and Russian territories.[77] Emigration to North America increased dramatically for the period from the 1880s until the mid-1890s. Further, a stream of eastern Germans went to the Ruhr-Rhine zone, where mining and modern iron foundries were beginning a long expansion. Among the most distinctive groups to take this east-west trek were the ethnic Poles from German provinces who left farm labor for work in the Ruhr valley as coalminers beginning in the 1870s. One contemporary describes how miners were sought out by company "recruiting sergeants" who would come to their home village at the beginning of the year, sign on workers, pay one mark as earnest money, then organize a general dance—bringing hundreds of miners to the Ruhr valley in this way.[78]

In the west, ethnic Poles took the jobs eschewed by people from western Germany and consequently remained proletarian miners and factory workers. Poles were part of the movement of many ethnic groups from the northeastern provinces to the western provinces of Germany, a movement that outstripped German emigration to North America.[79] Indeed, migration to the west in some ways substituted for emigration; it increased in the 1880s and 1890s, while migration to North America dropped quite suddenly to a trickle in the mid-1890s with the Panic of 1893 in the United States and the simultaneous industrial boom in western Germany.[80] East Prussia, West Prussia, and Posen, each of which contributed under 20,000 citizens to Rhineland-Westphalia in 1880, had a total of 460,000 living in these western provinces by 1910.[81]

In response to the labor vacuum created by the departures of natives of the eastern German provinces and the rise of labor-intensive sugar beet culture, these provinces came to depend on migratory labor to a much greater extent than south or southwest Germany. By 1900, over 119,000 workers came from Russian Poland alone; a total of 433,000 seasonal agricultural workers legally entered Germany by 1914. They included Italians, Scandinavians, and White Russians, but the vast majority were Poles from Austrian Galicia and Russia. Over half the Poles were women, favored by employers because they were skilled at working on root crops, accepted low wages, and were perceived as docile workers.[82] The *"willig und billig"* (eager and cheap) Poles from Austrian Galicia had been undermined by the same processes as those in Prussia after the Austrian liberation from serfdom in 1848, having moved from serfdom to smallholder or cottager status on land that could ill-support their increasing numbers.[83]

The German government regulated the Poles who entered the German Reich from Austrian and Russian Poland. Because dreams of a resurrected Polish state (uniting the Poles of eastern Germany, Austria, and Russia) threatened Germany's eastern border, repressing Polish nationalism guided policy.[84] Foreign Poles could only work as temporary labor in the German Reich, and they were only allowed in eastern provinces. They were not allowed to bring dependent family members along, nor were they allowed to settle; rather, foreign Poles were required to depart from German territory before December 20 of each year and were forbidden to return before February 1. Even Poles from the eastern provinces of Germany who worked in the western industrial zone were regulated; their press and societies were controlled, their flags and emblems banned.[85]

The situation of Polish workers in prewar Germany forecast that of twentieth-century migrant workers in three ways. Regulation by the German government foreshadowed the state regulation of foreign labor that increased in the twentieth century. As a reserve army of agricultural and industrial labor, the Polish workers experienced the finale of the precipitous and complete disintegration of the social system of eastern Prussia that transformed serfs into wage earners; workers themselves were forced to absorb the perils of economic slumps, unemployment, illness, and old age. Finally, the Polish workers recruited to the German beet fields signaled the transformation of eastern Germany from a labor-exporting to a labor-importing region. Each of these trends—state regulation, worker self-support, and widespread labor importation—would become more important on the Continent in the twentieth century.

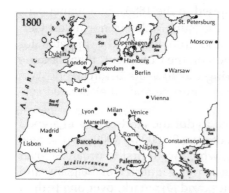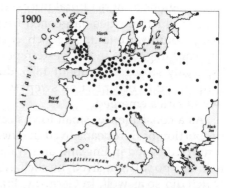

Map 4:2 European Cities of 100,000 or More in 1800 and 1900

Source: McKay, John P., Hill, Bennett D., and John Buckler, *History of Western Society*, Fourth Edition. Copyright 1991 by Houghton Mifflin Company. Used with permission.

We now turn to the cities that attracted Polish workers such as the Poles from East Prussia who became miners in the booming Ruhr valley at the close of the nineteenth century.

MIGRATION AND URBANIZATION

American observer Adna Weber voiced the sentiments of his age when he wrote in 1899 that "the most remarkable social phenomenon of the present century is the concentration of population in cities."[86] This urban population gathered in cities that were of unprecedented size in European history. Capital cities became spectacular metropolises and cities of over 100,000 proliferated; where there were only 23 European towns of over 100,000 in 1800, there were 135 a century later.[87] The great factory cities, billowing smoke from red-brick mills and foundries, provided the most striking new feature of the urban landscape. During the nineteenth century, these cities sprawled where there had once been a market town or small manufacturing center. Industry spawned new cities on such a vast scale that cities multiplied for the first time since the Middle Ages.[88] (See Map 4:2.)

Like many changes in the nineteenth century, urbanization continued on an eighteenth-century trajectory and followed an uneven history. The growth of cities accelerated first in Britain, where the first factory towns like Manchester mushroomed at the end of the eighteenth century. After the Napoleonic wars, continental capitals began to expand and new factory towns appeared, concentrating at first around the low countries. The extreme crises of the late 1840s broke the back of many rural industries while the boom years of the 1850s through 1870s expanded urban markets for labor. Subsistence agriculture subsequently faced severe depression in many regions as agricultural prices dropped in the 1880s. Simultaneously, heavy industrial cities burgeoned from the Ruhr Valley in northwest Germany southward to the French coal and iron basin. The impetus for cityward migration in the western portion on the Continent, then, became especially strong after about 1875; during the 40 years before World War I, the trend to urbanization swept western Europe and an elaborated system of cities emerged.

As a consequence, small towns came to dot the landscape and a good proportion of Europeans lived in cities of over 20,000 by 1900. As the new century dawned in England and Wales, which were first to urbanize, over half the population lived in such cities; over a quarter of Belgians and Dutch did so as well. In Germany, France, and Denmark, over one-fifth of the population lived in cities of over 20,000. A slightly smaller proportion of Spanish did so, and about one in seven Italians, Norwegians, Swiss, and Austro-Hungarians lived in such cities.[89] The proportion of rural people declined in each national population.[90]

What were the general patterns of migration that fed these growing cities? Clearly, the majority of migrants to towns and cities moved within their home region. Over half of the migrations within France, Switzerland, the Netherlands, and Norway were estimated to be within the home *département*, province, or canton.[91] The importance of these mundane movements is surprising, because the presence of long-distance migrants and foreign laborers (like the Irish in Manchester or Poles in Ruhr mining towns) was most memorable to contemporaries.[92] Nonetheless, the most reliable migration data indicate that the largest groups of migrants came from a city's immediate hinterland; from studies of the Ruhr to those of England and southern France, most urban migrants came from the next town, the next village, or a neighboring county. For example, in 1851, when "many people were not daunted by the prospect of a walk of 20 or more miles in a day to see kin or friends," 70 percent of the migrants in the textile town of Preston, Lancashire, had come from within a 30-miles radius of the city.[93] Likewise, people who resided in villages and small towns near urban areas had an overwhelming tendency to move to the city nearby. For example, half the people who left Casalecchio, in the vicinity of Bologna, in the 1865–1921 period went to that city.[94]

These short-distance movements included some sizable international migrations, such as those of the numerous Flemish, who crossed the border from Belgium into French Flanders, and the Italians, whose move to France was a short journey along the Mediterranean littoral. In addition, much regional migration went unmeasured because movements within provinces, counties, or *départements* were not recorded. Yet intraregional movements outnumbered both the vast international proletarian flows of Irish to English cities and of Poles to the cities of the Ruhr and the long-distance national flows of nationals to capital cities like Paris, London, Berlin, or Madrid.

Also, temporary movements played a crucial role in cityward migration. Moreover, these are particularly important because they reflect circular migration itineraries, the nature of nineteenth-century employment, and the insecurities of the age. Although very few historical data sources measure temporary migration, Prussian migration statistics give a sense of the volume of arrivals and departures from many cities. These data reveal that the people who arrived in and departed from Rhine-Ruhr cities in a given year varied from under 20 percent of a given city's total urban population up to 54 percent, depending on the local economy and the year.[95] Migration rates became very high after 1850 and, although it is impossible to compare them with preindustrial rates, those of the late nineteenth century may have been the highest. The proportion of migrants that stayed in the city only a short time can also be measured for some towns. In 1885 half of the newcomers in the industrial city of Duisburg, for example, left within the year.[96] The population registers of other areas also reveal high rates of population turnover.[97] Interestingly, population registers for the nineteenth century confirm both the importance of migration from the immediate hinterland, or "demographic basin," and high rates of population turnover that have been inferred from preindustrial records.

Particularly before 1850, a primary reason that men and women came to the city for only a short period of time was that much urban work (like rural work) was seasonal. Especially in the beginning stages of shaft mining, coalmining could only attract peasants and agricultural workers in the winter when they were free from field work. Early water-powered slitting mills that served metallurgy closed with summer droughts and winter freezes. Likewise, early textile mills closed in a dead season that coincided with harvests. Another employer of women, dressmaking, rose and fell with the fashion season, pulling workers between 20-hour days in high season and unemployment in others.[98]

More important, the cities of Europe were constructed by seasonal labor. The great booms in city-building that provided housing, commercial spaces, public facilities and urban infrastructures such as sewer systems were based on the summer work of men in the construction trades. Teams of excavators were followed by masons, whose articulate migration systems rendered them most visible. Like the "swallows" from Spanish Galicia and northern Portugal who built Madrid, and construction workers from Poland and Italy who labored in the Rhine-Ruhr zone, masons from the Limousin built Paris and Lyon. The *département* of the Creuse in the central highlands of France alone exported over 10,000 masons annually in 1810—whose numbers had increased to 30,000 in 1848. By 1907, over 30,000 Italians were at work in excavation and masonry in Germany, over 57,000 in construction. The brickmaking that supplied the cities of the German Reich was a specialty of Lippe in western Germany, whose region sent out 14,000 brickmakers annually by the end of the nineteenth century; brickmaking shadowed the construction season, lasting from April to October.[99]

For many workers, especially before 1850 in areas where families had viable landholdings, part-time urban work complemented, and even aided, their agricultural lives because it provided cash that enabled them to purchase and maintain land. For example, before the 1840s, temporary urban work in the industrial Stéphanois valley southwest of Lyon enabled men to participate in harvests at home and even to engage in ribbon weaving.[100] Like the masons of the central highlands, the miners and metalworkers of the Stéphanois balanced between peasant and proletarian lives, underwritten by urban capital. These sorts of urban employment for peasant workers in the early nineteenth century resonate with long-standing patterns of seasonal work for landholders.

Sheer insecurity, however, moved many laborers to and from cities. Skilled workers left cities in slumps to pursue their craft elsewhere, moving from town to town. For example, the metalworkers of the Stéphanois increasingly came from other metalworking towns as the century passed. For the unskilled worker, particularly the single man, urban employment was even less stable; it is these who were most likely to flood into—and out of—cities in hard times. The migration rates for single men outstripped those for any other social group. For example, the annual rate of immigration to the administrative and heavy industrial city of Düsseldorf was .61 for single men between 1904 and 1907, .35 for single women, and .08 and .09 for marrieds. This means that the number of single men arriving in the city was equal to 61 percent of the number already present.[101]

Although some rural-born Europeans could go back to villages in periods of unemployment, balancing between agricultural and urban work, between proletariat and peasantry, others had no such refuge. This was the case for young, unskilled Carl Dingler, a second-generation factory worker who had lived with his family in Bavaria, France, Hesse, and the Palatinate in western Germany before he arrived in the town of Esslingen in Württemberg at the age of 16. After a time there, Dingler traveled for 18 months in a vain search for steady employment from the southwest corner of Germany to Berlin. In 1863 and 1864, he worked at five jobs in Berlin, Dresden, and smaller towns, each of which lasted from six weeks to six months.[102]

Many newcomers settled in towns and cities as systems of circular migration became systems of chain migration that drew people out of their home area. Montagnards who had long worked in lowland areas for periods of months eventually took permanent work in those areas; town dwellers who did business in provincial capitals did the same.[103] Although these systems involved a great deal of movement back and forth, they left a healthy residue in the city. The classic example of seasonal migrants who become a permanent part of the urban labor force is that of rural people who worked in urban construction. For example, the masons of the Limousin who since the eighteenth century had spent summers in Paris had expanded their numbers to 30,000 by 1848. With the Parisian building boom of the 1850s and 1860s, the city became a giant construction site that had potential employment for those who lived in Paris year-round. Simultaneously, agricultural work became less attractive, women desired to leave the Creuse as well, and the railroad facilitated family moves. By 1880, there were 2,000 wives in Paris and 3,000 single Creusoises who worked as servants; children were raised at home by grandparents. Eventually, many upland families decided to raise their children in Paris and even to remain there themselves. A degree of material success, along with familial and village ties, allowed them to retire back home. By the turn of the century, over 24,000 men and women born in the Creuse resided in Paris.[104]

How do the movements of men and women compare? Women were the majority of residents in most cities since preindustrial times and women's employment expanded with textile mills, service work, and the garment trade in the nineteenth century. Does this mean that more women than men moved to cities in this period? National information comparing male and female migration patterns for the nineteenth century can be inferred from census data. These data only address movement from county to county, in the case of England, and from *département* to *département* in the case of France. Thus we can compare men and women, not as they enter the town or move from village to village, but only when they cross regional administrative borders.[105] Censuses from the 1880s are the base for Ernest Ravenstein's famous "law" that woman is the greater migrant than man.[106] An analysis of the English censuses by county for the 1861–1900 period bears this out; save in a few counties, women were more likely than men to move, especially women in the counties surrounding the city of London.[107]

In the case of France, members of each generation since 1816 were more likely to leave their *département* of birth over the course of the century (increasing from about one-fifth for the 1816 generation to over one-third for those born in the early 1890s). The curve for women, however, is steeper than that for men: women born in the 1816–1820 period were less likely to migrate than men, but since the generation of the 1886–1890 period, women have been more likely than men to leave their home *département*.[108]

In the Düsseldorf region of Germany (*Regierungsbezirk Düsseldorf*), early migration registers show movement to and from each area within the region. They measure not the number of people who moved but rather the number of moves made, supplying information on the *flow* of migrants rather than the *stock* of migrants. In the Düsseldorf registers, women comprised 37 percent of the migrants throughout the 1824–1854 period; in the last half of the nineteenth century, 44 percent of the moves were made by women. This set of comparisons, in which women move less than men, is particularly significant because it measures migration directly rather than inferring migration behavior from census data. Likewise, migration registers from outside Bologna, Italy, show that the majority of migrants were men, although women were more likely than men to leave home. Both migration registers suggest that although women were likely to relocate, they each made fewer moves in their lifetime than their male compatriots. In other words, women were very likely to move, but to move fewer times than men.[109] Unlike Carl Dingler, young women rarely searched from city to city for work.

What role did these migrant men and women play in the urbanization of Europe? On the face of it, they were responsible for city growth and rural stagnation, particularly in the light of the visible ethnic communities such as the Ruhr Poles and Lancashire Irish. Yet as spectacular as urban growth was to nineteenth-century Europe, in some regions migration played a relatively modest role because cities had become less deadly and more capable of producing (and raising to adulthood) their own young people. In other words, because urban mortality decreased, more city growth was due to natural increase rather than migration. This was particularly noticeable in England, where nineteenth-century urban death rates were exceptionally low despite the horrific conditions in some cities such as the Manchester described by Friedrich Engels. London had a self-maintaining population as of 1800, and only 16 percent of its growth between 1852 and 1891, net, was owed to immigrants. A changing balance of births and deaths gave Stockholm and the smaller cities of Sweden natural increase between the 1850s and 1860s.

Where mortality remained very high, as in Italy, migration was more crucial to city growth. It accounted for 80 to 89 percent of the growth of Rome, Turin, and Milan. Meanwhile, French cities continued to rely on immigration for urban growth because their birthrates were low: 64 percent of the net increase in the Paris population was due to immigration; the great cities of Lyon, Marseille, and Paris, like early modern cities, could not have sustained their populations without the intrepid migrant.[110]

Migrants and the Urban Economy

These observations about migration to the growing cities of the nineteenth century can be further refined, because the kinds of people who moved into any given city and the ways in which they earned a living depended a great deal on the specific urban economy. This section investigates migration to three kinds of cities—those engaged in the textile industry, heavy industry, and administration/commerce. Each urban type grew by a specific rhythm and attracted somewhat demographically distinct groups. Men and women, workers with special skills, singles and family groups were more attracted to some towns than to others. Of course, all the growing cities of western Europe attracted both men and women, families and singles; each city included various occupational groups from skilled craftsmen and bureaucrats to domestic servants. Each city had some manufacturing, some commercial functions, and some administrative offices. Nonetheless, this section will investigate cities by their general economic profile to sort out the role of labor demand in the complex patterns of urban migration in the nineteenth century.

The Textile City

Since spinning was the first manufacturing function to mechanize and gather workers in large mills, textile cities heralded urban industry. Beginning in Lancashire, mill towns proliferated as weaving mechanized and machine production spread to the Continent. Migration was important to their initial stages of growth because mill towns grew from obscure provincial centers to become major cities. For example, Barmen on the Wupper River was among the most successful: an old textile center of less than 3,800 in 1750 and a rapid innovator of about 16,500 in 1809, by 1910 the city was a major textile producer with a population of over 169,200. In peak periods, migration fueled the lion's share of this growth, despite a high birthrate that held through the 1870s. The first factory workers on a large scale were those who labored in the mills, many of whom were women and children. Consequently, the majority of migrants in Barmen, and probably in other textile cities as well, were women for whom there were mill jobs. The majority of residents in many textile towns were women; the sex ratio of Barmen, like the nearby textile cities of Krefeld and Elberfeld, was less than 100; it dropped as the industry expanded, from 98.9 in 1871 to 92.8 in 1895.[111] The textile town, then, was a very particular kind of city.

The history of one textile city, Roubaix, demonstrates the forces at work in urbanizing textile regions. Roubaix, located just south of the French-Belgian border near the ancient city of Lille, was in an area where the Flemish had spun and woven wool since Roman times. With the manufacturing expansion of the eighteenth century, Roubaix grew to 8,000 people and became one of the region's centers for finishing and marketing wool. It became a factory town as local entrepreneurs adopted English technology, including the flying shuttle and steam engine in 1820 and the machine loom in 1842. With the rural crises of the 1840s that eliminated many small producers and pushed workers from the countryside, then the economic boom of the 1850s and 1860s, Roubaix's expansion continued.[112] By the end of the century, the sleepy manufacturing center was known for its industrial vigor—and housed over 124,000 people.[113]

Roubaix's woolens industry remained linked to rural production long into the nineteenth century because rural weaving was long-lived. Rural weavers like the Santerre family (described earlier in this chapter) combined their earnings from winter weaving with their summer harvest work. Village weaving remained strong into the 1850s, when Roubaix employed at least 80,000 rural workers. Weavers were most dense around the city: 10,000 worked in greater Roubaix, and 8,000 in Wattreloos across the Belgian border. It was only in the 1860s that rural weaving was "seriously encroached upon" by the expansion of mechanical looms in Roubaix.[114]

Who peopled the industrial boomtown of Roubaix, expanding it to 30,000 people in 1851, then increasing its population fourfold by the turn of the century? How did migration help to create the industrial city? What role did the natural increase that resulted from urban births play in city growth? How can the migrants to Roubaix help us to understand the movement that peopled the textile cities of Europe?

Most migration was from nearby, from the French department of the Nord and from Flemish Belgium across the border. Like other textile cities in Britain and the Rhineland, Roubaix's labor force was overwhelmingly regional.[115] The crises of the 1840s had a particularly devastating effect on this densely populated plain supported by rural industry, and as a consequence Belgians flooded the city. Handloom weavers stayed in the countryside, but Belgians were willing to work power-driven looms and came to dominate that occupation in the 1870s and 1880s.[116]

By 1886, the majority of people in Roubaix were Belgians. Nearly all its migrant foreigners (59% of migrants) were Belgians, and of the people who had been born in Roubaix (54% of the total population) about 45 percent were Belgians. Thus, in this city of 99,779 people resided at least 25,000 migrants from Belgium and 24,000 Roubaix-born Belgians. French migrants from the *département* of the Nord in which Roubaix was located— a third of the city's migrants—comprised the largest group of non-Belgian migrants.[117]

At the beginning of the twentieth century, both French and Belgian residents of Roubaix still came from nearby. Of the migrants in the city, over a third had been born within 20 kilometers of the city, whether in France or in Belgium. One in six (15%) came from northern France, and many more—a full 40 percent—were born in Belgium, beyond a 20-kilometer radius.[118]

The Belgians who peopled Roubaix do not make this city the odd case. Irish were of similar importance to Manchester in England. Along with the Poles, the Dutch, the eastern Germans in the Ruhr valley, and the Italians in southern France, Switzerland, and Germany, the Belgians in Roubaix were an integral part of the *international labor force* to whom the economic expansion on the Continent provided employment.[119] Like the other groups of workers who crossed borders to find work, they were not homogeneous. Separate streams of Flemish men worked the power-driven looms in the weaving mills, while Walloons worked on construction sites. Young Belgian women from beyond the immediate hinterland of Roubaix were its domestic servants, and those from closer by were more likely to work in the mills. Some of the city's Belgians settled in particular neighborhoods and retained their native Flemish tongue and their unique identity in the community. Others became naturalized French citizens.[120]

As the city spread toward the border, an estimated 40,000 Belgians chose to commute to Roubaix rather than make their homes in France. They demonstrate how European workers maximized their flexibility and minimized their vulnerability at a time when there was little security for ordinary men and women. Belgian commuters were able to take advantage of France's high wages—wages were as much as 65 percent higher in France than Belgium in the mid-1880s—and of Belgium's lower prices for housing and foodstuffs. Law protected them from conscription into the armies of France, and because there was no compulsory military service in Belgium before World War I, commuters could avoid military service altogether.[121] The most visible commuters were the *frontalières*, or border-dwellers. Each morning at about six, the streets of border villages filled with workers whose sabots clattered on the streets as they walked into France. Other commuters lived farther away so that they could stay on the land, residing in villages where life was cheaper and a field could be maintained. A third group lived too far away for a daily commute; these would arrive Monday morning, rent a bed for the week, and return to their village on Saturday evening; such long-distance commuters numbered 950 at one border station alone.[122]

The extraordinary growth of Roubaix masked a greater volume of turnover and temporary movement. Machine textiles had a dead season in July, August, and September during which workers went home or to the fields to work.[123] Construction work in Roubaix was summer work. In addition, textile work was insecure in any season; the history of Roubaix is one of production crises, prolonged strikes, and layoffs that forced workers to take to the road.[124] There were doubtless many migrants who stayed in the city only a short while. Unfortunately, they cannot be counted directly from French sources. Perhaps insecurity is the reason that total migration rates (which are available for some German cities) increased over the century as textile cities grew. The Rhineland textile cities of Barmen, Elberfeld, and Krefeld, for example, had relatively low migration rates that rose to .25 around the turn of the century.[125] Yet the migration rate for any city glosses over different migration streams, disguising differences among migrant groups and between men and women.

The migration streams of women workers to the nearby textile town of Verviers in Belgium have been analyzed from population registers; they offer a clue to the ways in which population turnover worked. Like Roubaix, Verviers expanded rapidly after the early adoption of English textile technology in an area dependant upon cottage industry. There, too, urban industry remained linked with rural weaving in the hinterland of the city well after 1850. The population registers show that nearly all women born in Verviers stayed in their hometown, which had relatively good jobs for women. George Alter discerned two patterns for women migrants. Many of those who came to the city in family groups found work in the mills; they were less likely to stay on than natives, but nonetheless they were more likely to remain in Verviers than a second, more mobile migrant group. The most mobile women were the single females in their twenties and early thirties who sought employment in the city: 40 percent left in less than one year and 79 percent had departed within three years. Two-thirds of the women reported that they were returning to their last residence or to their birthplace, which suggests that they were part of a circulating pool of insecurely employed young, single women. Many of them had been orphaned before they moved and could not return to their family. Young women who left Verviers did not gain entry into the factory jobs that were relatively well paying; rather, they were the domestic servants of Verviers; they worked in an occupation that attracted migrant women because it came with room, board, and a familial setting.[126] The mobile servants of Verviers resemble the Belgian women in their twenties who came to Roubaix from beyond the city's immediate hinterland at the turn of the century, of whom over one in four was a domestic servant.[127]

Many migrants to Roubaix came as a family—and family migrants were doubtless more likely to remain in the city longer on average than young, single women or men.[128] The children of Roubaix could be employed from an early age in the mills, and by the end of the century married women worked in textiles as well. In contrast to administrative or commercial centers, cities with a mechanized textile industry readily offered family employment. It is partly for this reason that an estimated 40 percent of the migrants living in Roubaix in 1906 arrived in family groups.[129]

Despite the visibility of Roubaix's Belgians and other migrant groups, migration was far from the sole factor accounting for city growth. Natural increase played an important role in the expansion of Roubaix, because its birth rates were extremely high, like those in most textile towns, including the Rhineland cities of Krefeld, Elberfeld, and Barmen, where fertility rates were high before 1870. When Roubaix fertility began to decline after 1872, it pitched downward from the impressive level of 45.8. (A crude birth rate indicates the number of births per thousand; a rate of 45.8 means that for every 1,000 people in the total population of Roubaix, there were 45.8 births in a one-year period.) Even after this date (when fertility declined to 35.8 in 1886) the children who survived in Roubaix were more important to its growth than migration. Georges Franchomme calculated that natural increase accounted for 85 percent of city growth in the 1876–1881 period, then 77 percent of city growth in the 1881–1886 period. Roubaix had extraordinarily unsanitary housing and high infant mortality, yet even after its fertility had begun to decline in the 1870s and early 1880s, natural increase accounted for the lion's share of the city's 24,000 new citizens.[130]

In sum, an investigation of Roubaix clarifies connections between migration and industrial urbanization in several ways. We see that mobility, a constant movement of people to and from the city, was a central fact of life in Roubaix. And although this city drew on a regional labor force, it was an international labor force composed of several distinct streams. The Roubaix data also testify to the flexibility of migration as a strategy for Roubasien workers that protected them from seasonal and cyclical layoffs, one that both forced and encouraged them to keep ties with home. This flexibility eventually encouraged Belgian workers to commute across the international border. Those who came to Roubaix were in many cases family groups rather than single people. Finally, the fact that net migration did not account for all city growth but rather natural increase also helped to expand Roubaix suggests that the net effect of migration was less important to the industrial city than it had been 200 years before, when cities had been even more deadly. The role played by migrants in the textile cities of the industrial age was no chimera, yet it was more complex, and perhaps more interesting, than we have imagined.

The City of Heavy Industry
Heavy industrial cities—metallurgical centers of foundries, rolling mills, and machine construction—expanded in the wake of industrial development in order to provide the matériel for the factories, railroads, and infrastructure construction of the modern age. Like textile centers, the cities of heavy industry grew from villages and small production centers to become smoke-spitting, polluted cities, but they tended to mushroom even more quickly than textile towns. For example, by 1900, a string of boomtowns in the Ruhr area contained nearly 2 million inhabitants who produced about half the coal and one-third of the pig iron and steel of the German Empire. This population had increased sevenfold since 1850. Cities of heavy industry, like the coalmining towns that were in many cases nearby, relied on a labor force of young men; this was reflected in the high sex ratios of the Ruhr industrial cities, whose sex ratios peaked at 139 (Bochum, 1871), 120 (Dortmund, 1870), and 127 (Essen, 1871).[131] Like textile towns, then, metallurgical cities were a particular kind of place.

Duisburg, located at the confluence of the Ruhr and Rhine rivers about 250 kilometers northeast of Roubaix, was one of the region's industrial cities. Like Roubaix, it grew from a small eighteenth-century town, but Duisburg had a very different labor force because it was a city of foundry, rolling mill, and tool factory—a heavy industry town that developed an important commercial component. It is exemplary of the second kind of new factory city on the horizon in the nineteenth century, growing from a population of 8,900 in 1848 to over 106,700 in 1904.[132]

This growth is the residual of substantial migration into and out of the city and of sustained, high birthrates. Like Roubaix, the birthrate was a relatively very high 45.0 just before the 1870s, but in this case the birthrate subsequently rose to peak at 57.0 in 1875 before it dropped to 45.3 in 1900 and to 38.0 in 1910. These births partly explain population expansion, but they did so in a context of massive migration to and from Duisburg. In the

1848–1904 period, when the city gained 97,836 citizens, this gain was made at the time when city officials registered 719,903 arrivals and departures; the residue of these migrants is partly responsible for city growth. Similarly, in the metalworking city of Bochum nearby, natural increase accounted for 66 percent of city growth between 1880 and 1900, and 34 percent of growth came from 10,807 migrants. Prussian migration statistics reveal that during this period a staggering 232,098 people entered Bochum, so at least 194,800 had departed. Population turnover was extraordinary in these cities. When Duisburg began to industrialize in the 1850s, total migration rates rose from 23 percent per year to over 45 percent, meaning that the number of people entering or leaving the city every year equaled one-fifth to nearly one-half of the total population. Except during years of industrial crisis, more people arrived than departed, and it is the accumulation of the small proportion of migrants who stayed on that helped to produce city growth.[133]

Because Duisburg was a growing metallurgical center with many more jobs for men than for women, those who sought work there were more likely to be single men than women or family groups. Men were 63 percent of migrants before 1854 and three-quarters of the migrants later in the century; only about 17 percent of migrants were married in 1890. Men were more heavily represented in the migration streams to Duisburg than in the city's population, which had a sex ratio between 117 and 105 in the 1850–1914 period. This disparity stems from the fact that more men came to Duisburg to search for a job and returned to the road in hard times, when the construction season was over, or when it was time to return to the fields at home. Women were 48 percent of the city population in this period, but only 25 to 29 percent of its migrants.[134]

The highly male labor force of such cities, the importance of temporary work, and the insecurity of industrial jobs meant that migration rates were probably highest in this sort of urban economy, particularly because employers purposefully saw that single men were the last hired and first fired. Indeed, the total migration rate for the Ruhr industrial cities was higher than for either its textile centers or administrative towns; while their total migration rates peaked at 25 to 30 percent, Duisburg's and Dortmund's reached over 45 percent; that of Bochum and Essen reached nearly 60 percent.[135]

Prussian population registers permit James Jackson, Jr., not only to discern the age, gender, and marital status of "Duisburg's mobile masses" but also to estimate the number of moves an individual might make in a lifetime, and when. Jackson estimates that the migrant to nineteenth-century Duisburg, most likely a single man aged 15 to 25, might change his residence 15 to 16 times in his lifetime, and make 10 of those moves between ages 15 and 30. These frequent moves for young men help account for the fact that although women were nearly half Duisburg's residents, they did not move nearly so frequently as its men. He reminds us that for young people, moving was tied with a series of transitions that come with this stage in the life cycle: leaving family, entering the job market, finding a spouse, and establishing a separate household.[136]

Many migrants apparently returned home. Jackson's analysis of Duisburg's migration patterns suggests that migrants from Duisburg's immediate hinterland were those most likely to return home—and that they moved to the rhythms of agricultural fortunes at home.[137] Later in the century (1867–1868 and 1890), two-thirds of the single migrants from rural areas returned directly to rural areas. Single men and women were twice as likely as families to have only a short stint in the city.[138] In his study of this metallurgical center, Jackson correctly emphasizes the "magnitude and persistence of this circular migration between urban and rural areas. . . . " He indicates that "the decision to move to nineteenth-century Duisburg was not irrevocable. Migrants were not blindly being pushed out of rural areas never to return. Geographical mobility was more cautious, discerning, and reversible than that."[139] Like the villagers on the periphery of France's metalworking towns in the Stéphanois valley who went to the city for short work periods before they took proletarian status and factory work on a permanent basis, the rurals of *Düsseldorf Kreis* purposefully moved between town and country.[140]

The migration streams that fed Duisburg changed as the city changed. Migrants in Duisburg initially dominated artisanal and skilled occupations in the expanding industrial labor force. But by the 1890s, migrants were more likely to find work at unskilled occupations—perhaps as former migrants and their native-born children had a monopoly on skilled positions.[141] Among these, both in the 1860s and 1890s, came a clear stream of domestic servants who were young single women. By the 1890s, when the Duisburg economy had a stronger commercial component and the German Reich a growing bureaucracy, migrants were also important among the professional and white-collar workers of the city. Thus, even in the heavy industrial town, there were several distinct streams of migrants that included both career migrant bureaucrats and circular migrant servants.[142]

These migration streams were geographically distinct. As in Roubaix, an enormous proportion of migrants came from within a demographic basin of the immediate area. Over one in five migrants of 1890 was born within 10 kilometers of Duisburg and, in all, over one-third were born within 24 kilometers of the city. After the coming of heavy industry in the 1850s, many more people came from beyond the Düsseldorf region. Foreigners increased. By the 1890s, a large contingent of Dutch workers labored in Duisburg, and by 1910, one out of six migrants was a foreigner. Italian workers came in the greatest numbers, followed by the Dutch, both of whom worked in construction. One in five foreigners was from Austria-Hungary; this group may have been primarily Duisburg's share of the eastern Poles who were so important to the mining towns of the region such as Gelsenkirken.[143] Like the textile towns of Roubaix and Manchester, and the mining towns of northern France and the Ruhr valley, Duisburg had an international labor force.

The migration registers of Duisburg allow a direct measure of migration in the 1850–1914 period that confirms, first, the intimate links between cities and the surrounding countryside, as people moved freely between the two. Second, they demonstrate that the movement of specific groups, such as the migrant bureaucrats and their families or the Polish workers from the east, occurred in the context of massive temporary movements on the part of young, single people. We now turn to cities that had slower rates of growth and less turbulent populations.

The Commercial and Service City
Commercial and service functions were essential to the urbanizing economies of the nineteenth century—and cities primarily devoted to commerce, administration, and services expanded in the century before World War I. However, unlike many industrial cities, these were not new on the horizon; rather, commercial and administrative cities were often centuries old and of substantial size long before the nineteenth century. As a consequence, they did not experience the same kind of exponential growth as did the industrial cities that sprouted from small towns. Cologne, for example, served as a center for banking, insurance, and trade in cloth and metal in the Rhine-Ruhr zone. In 1800, it was the largest city in the area, with a population of 50,000. That population doubled by mid-century and by 1900 there were 373,000 residents, but by then the city was part of an intensely urbanized zone and was no longer outstanding in size. Capital cities like London and Paris grew as much as they did in the nineteenth century because their administrative, commercial, and service functions multiplied. Paris, for example, grew fivefold, from 547,000 to over 2.5 million, in the course of the century, attracting people from throughout France and abroad. Among commercial and administrative centers, however, provincial capitals of about 80,000 that had a regional draw were more typical than spectacular capitals such as London or Paris. Unlike mining and metallurgical centers, these cities housed a majority of women. The sex ratio of Cologne, for example, fell below 100 after 1867 and remained between 99.8 and 96.1 for the rest of the century; the sex ratio of Paris was 89 by 1901. Perhaps because there were many women in these cities and because employment may have been slightly less insecure, the extant measures of population mobility indicate that administrative cities may have had less in- and out-migration than heavy industrial centers. Cologne's total migration rate remained under 32 while that of the Ruhr metallurgy centers went up to 50 or 60 in the 1880–1910 period. Nonetheless, migrants were essential to the administrative/service center because these cities had uniquely low birthrates; they were peopled by white-collar workers, the pioneers of family limitation, and by domestic servants, who

were nearly all single and who therefore depressed the crude birth rate. For example, the birthrate in Cologne was only 42.9 in 1875 while that of the metallurgical center of Duisburg was 57.0.[144] Commercial/administrative cities, then, may be as distinct as industrial towns in terms of their growth rates and demographic composition.

The French cities of Amiens and Nîmes are typical of commercial/administrative/service cities.[145] Each was an ancient settlement that had predated Roman times, and each had become a regional center for rural industry with an important artisanal component by the eighteenth century. With the Revolution of 1789, each became the prefecture of a newly formed *département*. The administrative functions of Amiens and Nîmes grew with state bureaucracies and services in the nineteenth century, and their importance in commerce increased as each town became a railroad entrepôt. At the end of the nineteenth century, these were large cities that gained their living from institutions that included the departmental prefecture, courthouses, secondary schools, normal schools, army garrisons, convents, and orphanages. Each served as a rail crossroads, rail repair depot, and commercial center. Much of the commerce in Amiens served the remnants of its textile industry, and that of Nîmes, the wine trade. Amiens, more than Nîmes, was able to retain its textile industry, especially for male workers; by the turn of the century, both towns began to build shoe and garment manufactures. Amiens and Nîmes grew substantially after mid-century, from 50,000 to 90,000 and 80,000 respectively, but they were never rivaled boomtowns like Duisburg or Roubaix. In the case of Nîmes especially, this growth was dependant on migrants because its birth rate was a low 28.0 in the 1870s and only 16.0 in 1901.[146]

Over 40 percent of city residents in Amiens and Nîmes were migrants. The men among them were situated, first, in commerce (29% and 28% respectively in Amiens and Nîmes), then in manufacturing (26% and 18%), administration or bourgeoisie (11% and 15%), and, finally, in transport (10% and 13%). In these relatively bourgeois cities, migrant women were very likely to work as domestics; over a third in each city did so (34% and 35%). Migrant wives and daughters were most likely to sew or to keep shops for a living.

Domestic service played a crucial role in women's migration in this period. For centuries, service had been a routine part of premarital life, as young women had worked as domestics on farms and in urban families to help their families and to accrue a dowry. In the nineteenth century, the growing city expanded the demand for domestics throughout Europe, among whom migrant women were the vast majority. At the turn of the century, typically, over 90 percent of the servants in Berlin, St. Petersburg, and Paris—and the clear majority in London—were migrants. Of the 166,600 servants in Paris in 1901, 131,100 were French women born outside the city.[147] Domestic service even played an important role for the women who moved into textile towns like Roubaix and heavy industrial towns such as Duisburg. In Duisburg, fully 75 percent of the single female migrants aged 15 to 30 who were employed in unskilled positions—most of the young women who did not live with their families—worked as domestic servants in 1867.[148] Service offered the newcomer housing, a domestic atmosphere, and protection from the life of the streets. Consequently, parents were willing to allow their daughters to enter this relatively private and protected situation that addressed (at least theoretically) their daughter's need for housing and social protection.[149] Jeanne Bouvier (whose story opens this chapter) signals a trend in domestic service. Although it had traditionally served in conjunction with temporary migration, in the nineteenth century, many women did not return to rural and small-town homes, but rather they used domestic service as an entrée into the city, then moved from service into the needle trades. Domestic service, an occupation associated with temporary migration, became a means to begin urban life.[150]

Most migrants in provincial administrative cities came from areas with long-standing historical connections. Men and women came to Nîmes from the area immediately surrounding the city on the Mediterranean plain, and from the uplands of eastern Languedoc to the north. Many were from the villages and small towns that had suffered from the collapse of silk and agricultural prices in the second half of the late nineteenth century. Likewise, the men and women in Amiens came from its hinterland of Picardy, where villages and small towns had been decimated by the collapse of rural industry. The city census figures suggest that about one-third of migrants to each city came in family groups.

Particular streams of migrants were embedded in the regional supply of people to Amiens and Nîmes. Railroad workers came to Nîmes from villages along the railroad line that had been constructed through the arduous terrain to the north. Administrators, teachers, lawyers, and doctors were either the children of the educated parents in the region's small towns or bright scholarship students whose families had encouraged them to become a schoolmaster or administrator. In Nîmes, the migrant elite was disproportionately from Protestant villages and towns. Over a quarter of the domestic servants in Amiens came from very nearby, within 20 kilometers of the city; the most significant group of domestics in Nîmes was from the uplands.[151]

Although French sources reveal nothing about the process of urbanward migration, the economy and migrant labor force in Amiens and Nîmes leave important clues about population turnover. Workers in railroad depots, schools, administration, and domestic service were not subject to the same kinds of slumps and layoffs as industrial workers; rather, they had relatively steady jobs. On the other hand, young women could come and go from town because the demand for servants was great and it usually was easy to find another servant position. Like other growing cities, Amiens and Nîmes provided employment for seasonal construction workers. Also, Amiens's and Nîmes's manufacturing waned and their commercial fortunes suffered setbacks, so that migrant workers in these endeavors may have departed in times of unemployment. It is possible to speculate that commercial/administrative cities like Amiens and Nîmes—and Cologne, for whom the total migration rate stayed below 32—had a smaller proportion of temporary migrants than heavy industrial cities.

Finally, proportionally more migration in administrative centers than elsewhere moved by the logic of, and at the behest of, the employer. Career migration—movement in a pattern set by a bureaucracy—was increasingly important with the Europe-wide growth of state administrations, public education, and postal services in the nineteenth century. It was particularly crucial to cities like Nîmes and Amiens, whose prefectural administrators came from provincial centers and in some cases rose in national administration. Likewise, their teachers, judges, and church personnel moved within regional and national administrative networks.[152]

Several kinds of migration streams, then, fed the growing commercial and industrial centers. An enormous proportion of city dwellers came from village and small towns nearby, where people of every social strata had friends and contacts in town. Many of these would return home. The educated and ambitious provincial elite managed to find places in town for their children. Migrant women worked as servants, while their brothers were railroad workers, chimney sweeps, or miners, for example. Civil servants moved by a separate logic, that of their employer. None of these kinds of movements is unique to the nineteenth century, but each became more visible and more voluminous in this age of railroad commerce and bureaucratized states.

This survey of three city types permits some generalizations about migrants in urbanizing Europe. Textile cities attracted a high proportion of women migrants and had low sex ratios (i.e. relatively few men per 100 women). Most had very fertile populations whose birthrates dropped after about 1870. Despite the fact that they were among the great factory cities that mushroomed in Europe, the draw of textile cities was largely regional. Heavy industry and coalmining cities, on the other hand, attracted male laborers and had high sex ratios. They generally had a high birthrate through the 1870s. Heavy industrial towns may have had the greatest population turnover of any kind of city. Finally, commercial and administrative cities offered many jobs to women; their populations were especially female because the domestic servant, the quintessential woman migrant, was in great demand. These cities' draw depended on their size, but migrants were of particular demographic importance to administrative cities because they had the lowest crude birth rates.

The most striking feature of migration to cities is this: high rates of mobility provided the context for urbanization, and most of this mobility was accounted for by the intimate and enduring contacts between urban areas and their immediate hinterlands. This has been confirmed and measured by recent studies that employ population registers and German migration statistics. We may infer that in the 60 years before World War I especially, Europeans "were not simply urbanites or rural bumpkins, not divided neatly into agriculturalists and industrial workers. Rather, they were part of a regional network of economic opportunities and constraints, a system of shared knowledge and ramifying kinship networks."[153]

These generalizations about urban areas have their limits, of course. There is much we do not know. Only further case studies and comparative research can elucidate whether or not the relatively high turnover in various kinds of cities extends beyond the Rhine-Ruhr examples here. Our understanding of urbanizing society will be enhanced by the disaggregation of migration streams feeding into cities, which will in turn shed light on the connections among social structure and migration. Finally, although there have been some studies of urban domestic servants, we are far from understanding the part played in urbanizing Europe by women's productive and reproductive capacities.

When nineteenth-century contemporaries thought about migrants in urban areas, they focused on the degrading conditions of human life in the fast-growing cities, which shocked people of all political persuasions.[154] Beginning in Britain with Friedrich Engels's controversial, but accurate, portrait of life in Manchester, subsequent observers and reformers furnished equally indelible images of community and individual in the factory age.[155] Not only did they portray a physically unhealthy environment, but one in which theft, assault, drunkenness, prostitution, and illegitimacy were common as well.

Crime and Illegitimacy: The Marginal Migrant

The role of the migrant among urban thieves, thugs, drunks, prostitutes, and single mothers is a matter of debate. Many contemporary observers and twentieth-century sociologists see the newcomer to the city as a person who was disoriented, dislocated, and vulnerable to marginal behavior; it was the migrant who quickly would turn to theft or prostitution, "hypnotized by the city lights like the sea birds who, after sunset, fly bewildered under the beam of the lighthouse."[156] Recent research has debated this view, emphasizing the systems of chain migration that protected migrants from anomic behavior and that operated to protect even the poor from dislocation.[157] Both perceptions are found in the work of Louis Chevalier on nineteenth-century Paris. His *Laboring Classes and Dangerous Classes*, first published in 1958, portrayed an urban society torn asunder by drink, crime, and sexual misery; it contradicted his earlier study *La formation de la population parisienne*, which catalogued the systems of migration from throughout France that had built and peopled the capital.[158]

By their very nature, studies of criminality and studies of migration streams both offer misleading approaches to the question of migrants and urban marginal behavior. Urban crime studies, for example, focus only on an unsavory underside to the migrants' world that is far from the whole picture. On the other hand, studies of coherent migration streams have been accused of a rosy functionalism that glosses over the exploitation and vulnerability of migrants. Recent research that carefully compares newcomers with city natives shows that the issue of migrants and marginal behavior is more complex than either extreme perspective allows. It reveals that there is a pernicious grain of truth to the persistent notion that migrants are likely to be criminals and single mothers. This grain of truth, however, is one part of a complex picture in which other traits besides migrant status alone are related to marginal behavior. Much marginal behavior, to say nothing of dislocation or anomie, is completely beyond the grasp of the historical researcher. Finally, even if the majority of thieves in a given city were migrants, for example, the vast majority of migrants certainly were not thieves. It is necessary, then, to ask a more refined set of questions than whether or not migrants were disoriented by urban life.

The most systematic study of migrants and urban marginal behavior is William Sewell, Jr.'s, investigation of crime in Marseille.[159] Mid-century court records reveal that most cases involved theft, petty theft, assault, vagrancy, and begging. Clearly, migrants had higher rates of arrest than natives, but particular migrants and particular crimes were at issue. Very few women appeared in court; theft was their only crime, and even that applied only to a small group. Most criminals were young men, with an average age of about 25; beggars were older, with a mean age of 41. Although we do not know the length of time that the accused had been in Marseille, their origins were clear: those from a greater cultural and geographic distance from Marseille had the highest rates of crime. Italians, the poorest of migrants in Marseille, were subject to prejudicial treatment and had far and away the worst jobs in town, but they also had a coherent community and could return home easily in hard times. Consequently, they were rarely arrested for either vagrancy or assault but rather for petty theft, the crime of the poor. Corsicans in particular, who were notoriously homicidal at home, took to a narrower path and to legal behavior in a city that provided promising jobs and a supportive community.[160]

Neither all crime nor all migrants, then, were alike. Moreover, crime was most closely associated with a particular migrant neighborhood, an old port slum area where men lived in rooming houses. These were the migrants who were most likely to be temporary residents in Marseille and who were at the age associated with frequent moves. They were not a permanent "dangerous class," bred by the misery and dislocation of urban life, but rather a temporary one—temporary because they resided in the city for only a short time and also because they were in the most crime-prone stage of their lives. The vast majority of arrested migrants were not repeat offenders, but people for whom a theft, an assault, or a vagrancy conviction was a one-time occurrence. These young single men show a "somber underside of migration"; they were different individuals than those who appear in the marriage records of Marseille, steady and upwardly mobile sorts who supply most of the data about migrants in French cities.[161] Those tried for crimes constituted a small segment of the migrants who animated Europe, a minority among those with more fortunate and more orderly lives. Young men from old port rooming houses may have added more than their share to the city's crime, but they were a minor part of the vast migrations to France's third largest city, which tripled in size between 1820 and 1870.

For women, the most palpable manifestation of marginal behavior in urban areas was not criminal behavior but sexual activity and pregnancy out of wedlock. The degradation of women most prominently associated with urban growth was prostitution, but studies of migration link prostitution with migrant women only insofar as they discuss the importance of former domestic servants among the ranks of prostitutes (service being the chief occupation for newly arrived migrant women).[162] Yet prostitutes were few in comparison with the hundreds of thousands of young women who made their way into the city. These young women, vulnerable to pregnancy, partly accounted for the "illegitimacy boom" that expanded the proportion of children born out of wedlock between 1750 and 1875.[163]

The relationship between migration and illegitimate births in the city was complex. Illegitimacy rates were very high in many cities, ranging from 30 to 50 percent in the 1880s for Vienna, Prague, Rome, Paris, Stockholm, Moscow, and Budapest, but this was partly because many women who were already pregnant came to the city to deliver their child in an anonymous setting, then oftentimes to abandon it.[164] Furthermore, illegitimacy was by no means solely an urban phenomenon in western Europe; indeed, a German expression ran *Ländlich, Schändlich* (rural and shameful) because in some rural areas, premarital pregnancy and illegitimacy were particularly common.[165] Nonetheless, migrant women disproportionately bore illegitimate children in the city, and single mothers disproportionately identified themselves as domestic servants.[166]

The most finely textured analysis of urban illegitimacy distinguishes among women who married before pregnancy, those who married while they were pregnant, and those who bore children out of wedlock in the textile city of Verviers, Belgium, during the nineteenth century.[167] The women of Verviers operated in an urban society where sexual intercourse was clearly part of courtship, as it was in much of the European countryside. Understanding the ability to marry as the result of personal and social bargaining, George Alter compared women who were able to bring their partners to marry and those who lacked the clout to do so. Migrant women were most likely to bear children out of wedlock, particularly those who had not come to Verviers with their family, early in life, but rather as adults. Migration alone was not associated with bearing an illegitimate child, however; women whose fathers had died and older women were also likely to be deserted when they became pregnant. In Verviers, bearing an illegitimate child was less a matter of isolation than of low standing in the marriage market. Neither migrant status, nor the loss of a father, nor age "made illegitimacy inevitable," concludes Alter, "but they all made it more difficult to find a partner, more difficult to refuse his sexual advances without jeopardizing the relationship, and more difficult to apply social pressure to bring him to marriage."[168]

Rachel Fuchs has analyzed the records of the maternity hospital for the indigent in Paris, La Maternité, which allow an analysis of the link between illegitimacy and migration to that city at the turn of the century.[169] Nearly all the hospital patients were single mothers, and over four-fifths of these patients were migrant women. More important, some regions of the country were underrepresented in the hospital, others were overrepresented. Regions least likely to send women to La Maternité were those with long-standing migration systems and those with highly male migration streams; women from these areas had well-established contacts in the city and were likely to be married. By contrast, regions that sent more women to La Maternité had traditions of high illegitimacy. Most significantly, the sole province that sent a great many women to the hospital, considering its representation in Paris, was a province with a tradition of low illegitimacy rates. This was Brittany, whose migrants were the most recently arrived, the most female, and the least skilled of any migrant group in Paris. Its women were most likely to be domestic servants and least likely to have male kin in town. Like the single mothers of Verviers, the Breton women who bore children in La Maternité had little social or personal power in the marriage market.[170]

Information about the migrants among the population that concerned nineteenth-century reformers—the marginal and criminal—shows that the key factor in crime or single motherhood was the migrant's social and economic support. Migrant men with the least steady jobs and migrant women with the least social clout—those without a father, kin, or powerful friends—paid for their vulnerability in ways that landed them in jail and saddled them with infants to raise without a husband. More generally, the investigation into migrants and marginality reveals another way in which human contacts are at the core of the migration experience. Social contacts not only shaped migration streams and fed information back home but also played the crucial role at destination of protecting their members against homelessness, unemployment, criminal behavior, sexual exploitation, and arrest.

Although city-bound migrants were a concern to Europeans and visible to historians, so were the over 50 million who departed the Continent for new worlds. It is to them that I now turn, focusing on three questions: What was the pattern of migration to the western hemisphere? By what processes did migrants depart the Continent? And finally, what is the relationship between the movement of Europeans on the Continent and the migrations that took them across the Atlantic?

MIGRATION TO THE AMERICAS

Between the fall of Napoleon and World War I, transoceanic emigration streams grew and diffused as millions of Europeans left the Continent in what has been assessed as "the greatest transfer of populations in the history of mankind."[171] Migration from Europe was a hallmark of the nineteenth century. It was not new, but rather it greatly expanded on previous trends. For example, an estimated 1.5 million people had emigrated from Britain in the eighteenth century; a minimum of 125,000 German settlers in North America had been increased by about 17,000 mercenaries who stayed on after the American Revolution. This migration would increase with the harvest failures and economic dislocations that followed the Napoleonic wars, when 30,000 to 40,000 European migrants came to the western hemisphere annually. Eighty years of mass migrations began with the 1840s, when two important trends emerged. On one hand, the demand for labor increased in the farmlands and cities in North America and the sugar and coffee plantations of Latin America, partly because the slave trade had been abolished.[172] On the other hand, Europe's "hungry forties," the potato famine, and political struggles exacerbated suffering and unemployment. Emigration pushed into high gear as 200,000 to 300,000 Europeans departed per year in the crisis-ridden late 1840s. The number continued to be high after mid-century; an estimated 13 million embarked between 1840 and 1880, and another 13 million departed in the last 20 years of the century. In all, about 52 million migrants left Europe between 1860 and 1914, of whom roughly 37 million (72%) traveled to North America and 11 million to South America (21%). Three and a half million Europeans, primarily British, moved to Australia and New Zealand.[173] The first groups of migrants knew relatively little about their destination and could not easily return home. Later, however, the vast numbers of men and women who crossed the oceans had greater information about the work and communities that awaited them; they also were more able, and more likely, to return home.[174]

Patterns of Transatlantic Migration

The story of the mass migrations to the United States after 1840 is a familiar one. Mass migrations began with the Irish, for whom the United States was by far the most important destination.[175] Driven by the potato famine, they outnumbered any immigrant group in the 1840s, when over 780,000 arrived. In the 1850s, 914,000 Irish came to the United States. Thereafter, Irish immigration was reduced to about 435,000 per decade until the 1880s, when it rose again to over 655,000. Fewer English than Irish came to the U.S. in the 1840s through the 1870s (over 200,000 per decade); then English emigration rose in the 1870s and 1880s to nearly match the Irish at over 640,000 per decade. English immigration to the U.S. remained at this high level until World War I.[176] Like the Irish, Germans emigrated to the U.S. *en masse* in the 1840s and 1850s, when about 434,600, then 951,000 arrived. After a falling off of emigration in the 1860s and 1870s, nearly a million and a half Germans arrived in the U.S. in the 1880s. This emigration fell sharply in the 1890s, partly because German industrial development created a vast demand for labor at home.[177]

Other major immigrant groups joined the Irish, Germans, and English beginning in the 1880s and hailing from eastern and southern Europe. Emigrants from Russia increased from 39,300 in the 1870s to over 213,000 in the 1880s. Some of these were Jews escaping tzarist pogroms that increased in intensity in the early twentieth century. Others were part of the mass emigration of Poles from the regions of Russia, Austria-Hungary, and the German Empire that had divided the kingdom of Poland in the 1772–1795 period. An estimated 100,000 Poles arrived in the U.S. in the 1880s; this number would grow from 30,000 to 50,000 *per year* in the 1890s and to 130,000 to 175,000 per year before World War I.[178] Italians were also highly visible among late-century migrants to the U.S. Where nearly 56,000 immigrated in the 1870s, over 655,000 arrived in the 1880s—a number equal to the English or Irish. This migration stream remained strong until World War I. This sketch of the largest European migration groups does not include the important array of smaller groups who were so significant among their home populations (such as Norwegians, Finns, Danes, or Swedes) or the sizable numbers of Asian migrants to the United States.[179]

Although the Italians were so visible among migrants to the United States, even more Italians went to Brazil and Argentina, where they were the vast majority of immigrants until the turn of the century, when the growing migration of Spanish to Latin America superseded Italians. Although Italians, Spanish, and Portuguese all emigrated to North America, Latin America was their most important destination. Between 1854 and 1924, over three-quarters of the 11 million immigrants to Latin America were from Italy and the Iberian peninsula; 38 percent were Italians, 28 percent were Spanish, and 11 percent were Portuguese.[180]

Migration patterns look very different from the perspective of Europe. Transoceanic migrations diffused over the Continent from the northwest to the southeast during the nineteenth century. The intensity of migrations varied from nation to nation. Norwegians were the most likely transoceanic migrants; an annual average of 6.6 persons per thousand moved abroad over the entire 1861–1910 period. At the other end of the spectrum was France, from which emigrated only 0.2 persons per thousand.[181] The intensity of migration varied more within each country than from nation to nation; in some parts of Norway, one adult male in four had spent some time in the U.S. by the time of the 1920 census. Just as the tendency to migrate diffused within the Continent, it diffused from one region to another within national states, from northern to southern Italy, for example. There remained differences within regions. For example, in northern Italy, virtually no emigrants came from the province of Bologna (.05 per thousand population), while 46 people per thousand crossed the Atlantic from the Venetian province of Bulluno in the 1881–1882 period.[182]

The provinces of western Europe that sent the greatest proportion of their people abroad were mountainous regions and small islands. In Italy, they were the provinces around the Alps to the north and east of Milan and around the southern Appenines. The people most likely to leave Spain and Portugal were from their Atlantic islands (Canaries and Azores) and from the mountainous northwest corner of the Iberian peninsula— the poor regions of northern Portugal and Spanish Galicia. Scandinavian emigrants most likely came from the mountains of south-central Norway and south-central Sweden, Oland Island, and the Danish Islands of Bornholm and Lolland-Falster. The Scottish highlands sent disproportionate numbers abroad early in the century. These geographical locations enjoyed few resources and little employment because they were relatively isolated from the urban and industrial jobs that would increase over the century; their people, then, were less likely than others to join the currents of migration to the nation's cities and towns.[183]

A Global Labor Force

The vast majority of European transoceanic migrants moved to improve their economic situation. It is important to note, however, that an enormous spectrum of aspirations are encompassed under the rubric of economic motives. "There are substantial differences," observes J. D. Gould, between "Norwegian emigrants to the U.S.A. in the mid-nineteenth century, leaving a homeland of poor soil to create new farms for themselves from the wilderness; English and Scots mechanics and skilled artisans moving at about the same time to American industry in the hope . . . of encountering a better opportunity for promotion and perhaps for setting up as an independent entrepreneur; and the Italian or Balkan peasant crossing the Atlantic around the turn of the century in search of temporary work at high wages. . . . "[184] Some religious dissenters did leave Europe in the nineteenth century, including groups of Norwegians, Swedes, Germans, Danes, and Dutch. Political considerations motivated some smaller, albeit consequential, migration streams, such as those of the German liberals and Polish nationalists after their respective defeats in 1848 and 1863. Germanization policies were part of the reason that Danes emigrated from Schleswig in 1864 and Poles departed the eastern German provinces of the German Empire after 1871. However, relative to the seventeenth century, few migrants from nineteenth-century Europe were driven by political, religious, or ethnic persecution. The clearest exception to this observation is the Jews, who were persecuted in Russia and eastern Europe after 1890, deprived of political and legal rights, oppressed economically, and harassed in their social and spiritual life.[185] Although economic motives cover a range of impetuses for moving, and even they do not explain emigration in a complete way, it is true that most Europeans crossed the ocean to improve their, and their children's, level of living.

The same demographic and economic pressures underlay emigration from Europe and proletarian mass migration on the Continent. The record increase in European population made vast numbers of Europeans available to the western hemisphere—a population increase abetted by the trend to a proletarian population and the release of eastern Europeans from the constraints imposed by feudal social relations. Emigration from Europe drained off an estimated one-quarter of the Continent's population increase. Most emigrants were rural people, although the English were very likely to be from towns and cities. Both in the east and in the west, the landless population increased more than the landowning peasantry, and it was proletarians, in the vast majority of cases, who emigrated to the new world.[186] In disproportionate numbers, they left regions in which rural industry had worked to create a dense, impoverished population, susceptible to slumps in prices for handicraft and rural-produced goods. Emigration increased with harvest failures like those in Germany and the Netherlands in 1846 and 1854, in Sweden in 1867 and 1868, and most notably the potato famine in Ireland.[187]

Refined studies show that the region, rather than the nation, played the key role in transoceanic migration. Walter Kamphoefner found that areas stressed by the collapse of rural industries were very likely to send people to the new world in the 1840s and 1850s. For example, the people of Westphalia in northwestern Germany were among the first Europeans on the Continent to develop a significant migration system with the new world. Westphalia had been connected with the traditions of seasonal migration to Holland since at least the seventeenth century. In the eighteenth century, the production of linen had thrived in this area as men, women, and children set themselves to the growth and preparation of flax, to spinning, and to weaving. The seasonal patterns and gender responsibility for this work varied from place to place, but in many areas of Westphalia the practice of seasonal migration to Holland remained strong through the period of the Napoleonic wars at the turn of the century.[188] Like many areas with a strong rural industry, Westphalia had a high rate of growth in combination with small farm holdings and a dense rural population.

Regions like Minden, a crescent-shaped district located 75 kilometers east of the Dutch border, had a higher birthrate and denser population than surrounding agricultural and industrial areas.[189] Its people were the notoriously poor *Heuerlinge*, who rented small plots of land, owed service to the landlord, grew and worked flax, and in many cases emigrated seasonally to Holland to earn cash.

The *Heuerlinge* of Westphalia, especially those at work in the rural linen industry, were among the first emigrants to join the massive movement of Germans to North America in the 1840s and 1850s.[190] Their departure came in the wake of depredations to the rural linen industry that reduced it from a major export to an insignificant product: the Napoleonic wars (1803–1815), coupled with the continental blockade (1804–1815), cut off the Westphalian linen manufactures from sizable markets in the western hemisphere, particularly in South America. Although linen manufacturing benefited from the lack of British competition on the Continent during wartime, it was devastated by the fact that the British seized the South American markets and the Irish entered the handloom trade with great success while it was cut off from international trade. The industry faced decline after the wars on two additional counts: linen spinning, then weaving, machines began replacing rural production, and cotton was replacing linen throughout Europe. With less work and lower piece rates, the rural weavers and spinners of Westphalia suffered, particularly during the agricultural crises of the 1840s. The 22,594 spinner families supported by the region in 1838 were forced to thin their numbers.[191] Seasonal migration in Holland could not offer adequate compensation for the lack of resources at home; German industry in the Rhine Valley and mining in the Ruhr were not yet adequately developed to offer work. Westphalians' solution was to go to the United States, where a node of kin and friends founded farms in the state of Missouri.

Where poverty and population growth combined with traditions of emigration, the likelihood of migration abroad became very strong; personal relations produced what Sune Åkerman terms a "multiplier effect," reinforcing the structural changes that encouraged emigration.[192] J. D. Gould puts it another way, observing that the metaphor of migration fever is an apt one, first because it communicates a certain psychological excitement, and second, and more important, because it is spread "by personal transmission."[193] In some regions a veritable "emigrant culture" made migration a particularly important strategy for money-earning. This had always been true for pockets of the European population; nonetheless, the population growth and economic changes of the nineteenth century meant that more regions—from Sweden to Iberia and from Ireland to Greece—developed important migration streams abroad. For example, the men of northern Portugal, who had long emigrated to Brazil, also worked in Argentina and Spain. The Irish from western counties who had harvested grain in England moved to English cities and virtually emptied some regions as they emigrated to North America. Among emigrant cultures, the Italians are probably the best known for the workers they sent throughout France, Switzerland, and Germany, as well as for the large contingents of men and women from Italy who went to the United States, Argentina, and Brazil. In addition, Italians from the villages and small towns of their native land populated the growing cities of Turin, Milan, Rome, and Palermo.

Migrants to the western hemisphere were responding to a more distant but enormous demand for labor in North and South America between 1860 and 1914. Millions of Europeans traveled to the United States alone, where the 1862 Homestead Act beckoned land-hungry Europeans to the prairies. In addition, heavy industry, construction, mining, commerce, food production, urban manufacturing, and services all demanded expanded numbers of workers. Argentina's grain region and Brazil's coffee plantations required a vast labor force. By 1910, immigrants accounted for one-fifth of the workers in the United States and one-third of its industrial operatives. Until 1885, when contract labor was outlawed in the U.S., labor recruiting agents came to Europe from the United States; subsequently, emigration agents and steamship companies took up migrant recruitment. Mass recruitment to Argentina and Brazil began in the 1880s.[194] Pulses in labor demand recruited or discouraged potential immigrant workers; particularly after the 1860s, immigration responded to the North and South American business cycles.[195]

This is partly because transport technology sped communications and eased the costs of travel as the steamship gradually replaced the sailing vessel. In 1867, the average sailing time from Europe to the U.S. was 44 days, but in that same year, steamers made the trip in 14 days; the trip from northern Europe to New York was reduced to 10 days by the 1880s and to a week after 1900. This speed allowed the development of seasonal migration across the ocean, such as that of Italian and Spanish *golondrinas* (swallows); these were men who would travel to the Argentine pampas for fall harvests of wheat and fruit. Before returning home in May, some would work in Brazil's southern coffee districts.[196] The cost of the trip was also reduced with the steamship and competition among shipping companies and booking agents. In addition, travel subsidies for laborers sometimes reduced the cost of a voyage to Brazil to virtually nothing.[197]

The development of transport technology, in conjunction with the openness of the new world to immigrants and the overflow of people from the Continent, provided three essential elements for the mass transoceanic migrations of the nineteenth century. Indeed, these great migrations are in a sense the result of a race between the pressure of numbers in Europe, on one hand, and the development of employment opportunities for the increased population, on the other.[198] The world labor force was integrated by the mutually reinforcing, unprecedented supply of proletarians in peripheral areas of Europe and demand for labor in the core regions of Europe and the new world.[199] In terms of core and periphery areas, the industrial and commercial core regions of Britain and western Europe exerted the same demand for labor as did the Americas; the densely populated peripheral areas—particularly Ireland, Italy, and Polish provinces—provided labor to prosperous regions in both the Americas and western Europe.[200] The transoceanic mass migrations of the nineteenth century redistributed the world labor force.

The Process of Transatlantic Migration

The vast majority of emigrants from Europe moved in systems of chain migration that diffused information about their journey and destination; these systems maintained themselves by letters and prepaid tickets sent by relatives and compatriots across the ocean. Case studies of migrant groups, such as those from Sicily who lived on Manhattan, Italian harvesters in Argentina, or German farmers in Missouri, reveal rich, lively contacts among compatriots. A study of Sweden's Langosjö parish and its emigrants specifies family relations and transatlantic moves, mapping how kin and home contacts acted as the life blood of systems that moved people across the ocean.[201] Likewise, more general statistical analyses like that of British emigration to the United States uncover countywide migration traditions that held throughout the nineteenth century.[202] The "consolidating effects of feedback" among migrants focused overseas migration streams at particular destinations; among Italians alone, Venetians went to South Brazil, those from the small town of Caserta north of Milan went to Providence, Rhode Island, and the natives of Sambuca in Sicily settled on Elizabeth Street in New York's Little Italy. Migrants often specialized in particular occupations; miners, for example, came to North America and sought work through specific webs of contact. Many groups originated with young men and came to include women in their numbers as they became permanently settled and formed families.[203] Migrants traveling such great distances were part of a work crew that arrived together, or they had compatriots or relatives to greet them. (The relatives, of course, were usually husbands, parents, or siblings who had made their way and now sent for loved ones. Alternatively, they were men who had found work for a cousin or compatriot.) On the eve of World War I, nearly 80 percent of immigrants to the U.S. had a relative waiting for them; 15 percent were joining friends.[204]

Women formed a substantial minority among migrants from western Europe to North America. In the 1820–1928 period, they were 40 percent or more of the English, Scottish, Swedish, and German migrants to the United States—and nearly half of the Jewish migrants from eastern Europe and the Irish. Women figured less large in the late-century migration groups from Italy and southeastern Europe because a large proportion of those groups were men who came to work in North America for only a short time; in these cases, women's labor was crucial to keeping the family enterprise going at home while men were absent. Thus, a complex of factors at home and in the Americas shaped women's transatlantic migrations. As men settled in the new world, the demand for domestic labor called for wives, sweethearts, and arranged marriages with women from home. The vast majority of single women came to work. For example, although about 40 percent of German adult women declared an occupation when they entered the United States in 1910, nearly 80 percent of single German women did so.[205] Irish women comprised the majority of Irish who came to the United States in some of the post-famine years. They came to work in North America because the possibilities for work or marriage at home had disintegrated precipitously with the crises of the 1840s.[206]

Migration streams began with a successful pioneer who maintained contacts with home, with a labor recruiter, or with a shipper's agent. The individual pioneer was in many cases a hardy soul who acted from desperation like the first Norwegians who, because they wanted to farm and lacked money, headed for the free land of the American frontier—or like the Norwegian family that stopped in Chicago where there was good work to be had instead of pushing on to farmland. Little is known about pioneers who reconnoitered, serving as "antennae, the nerve ends of the body of workers in their home towns," like the Italian street musicians who perused the Continent, then New York and Toronto for employment opportunities. The pioneer who inspired migration from a village was often not a local but rather an emigrant from a nearby village who returned to tell about the new world or who wrote letters that were passed from hand to hand and even copied and circulated.[207] Recruiters and labor agents acted widely and forcefully, seeking out industrial workers and iron miners, organizing construction crews in North American cities (until contract labor was outlawed in 1885), cane-cutting crews in Louisiana, and shiploads of agricultural laborers in Argentina and Brazil. Emigration agents in the pay of shipping companies were very influential, despite the fact that they merely recruited travelers to fill a boat and did not arrange employment; an energetic agent started migration from many a Polish, German, and Danish village.[208]

Once Europeans left home, however, their local system of movement could be expanded or cut short by personal communications. Agents could not successfully promote a system without positive feedback; they were unable, for example, to keep German workers on Brazilian coffee plantations (or Poles on Hawaiian sugar cane plantations!). Likewise, personal contacts entered and mixed with agent-sponsored systems. This was demonstrated most forcefully to Italian government investigators who interviewed laborers boarded for the trip to South America; they found that friendship, village ties, and agent relationships were mixed in the same groups. Chain migration was not mechanistic but rather the result of multiple decisions and contacts.[209]

Although the history of transoceanic migration may be coherent in terms of world-scale labor, it is also elucidated by—and indeed, inspired by—local contacts and considerations. It is for this reason that the local and regional focus is particularly informative about the evolution of migration. The history of migration from the one Polish village illustrates how migration to the new world was added to the local migration repertoire. When Polish ethnographer Franciszek Bujak visited the western Galician village of Maszkienice (in Austrian Poland) in 1899, he found a community where half the landowning peasants could not support themselves but rather needed to earn cash elsewhere. An additional quarter of the population was proletarian. The men of the village had worked constructing the rail lines from Vienna and from Crakow to Lvov and the cement factory in a nearby town. In 1899, 40 percent of its young adults left, most for seasonal work in Austrian coal mines in Ostrava (80), in Danish sugar beet fields (17), or in the region's cities. People from neighboring villages had been traveling to the United Stated for some time, and their earnings were well known, but until the previous year Maszkienicans had stayed in Austria and Denmark. Migration to America had begun when a miner was persuaded by a neighboring villager to join him digging coal in Pennsylvania rather than in Ostrava. Agents from Austrian mining companies, transatlantic steamship companies, and German agricultural estates all had come to Maszkienice on the railroad train to offer their enticements abroad—from low ship fares to cigars and schnapps.

In 1911, the ethnographer returned to see the changes wrought by a decade of letters, verbal exchange, and kin contacts about emigration. He found that seasonal emigration had increased by 50 percent and emigration to the U.S. had multiplied fourteenfold. Twenty percent of emigrants were in the U.S., and an equal portion in Germany (including many young women); only 28 percent worked in the coal mines of Ostrava in Austria, and the rest (nearly a third) worked in the cities of Austrian Poland.[210]

The emigrants from Europe are significant to this study, most obviously because the departure of such vast numbers of men and women relieved a pressure on resources (land, jobs, and food) that would otherwise have been immeasurably greater. The political, social, and economic consequences of a Germany supporting 6 million more people, a Britain with 10 million more citizens, and an Italy with a population greater by 8 million doubtless would have been considerable. It is for this reason that Britain supported emigration programs (as well as the transport of convicts). Even some German states and Denmark for a time promoted emigration of their poorest and least desirable citizens.[211]

Many migrants returned home. After about 1860, transatlantic migration was increasingly a temporary move and was conceived of as such by many. Of the migrants to the U.S. in the 1870s, an estimated 25 percent returned; of 1890s migrants, an estimated 45 percent returned home.[212] Thousands of Italian and Spanish workers harvested grain and fruit in Argentina beginning in October; some then worked in Brazilian coffee plantations, then returned home in May. They may have numbered from 25,000 to nearly 100,000 annually in the 1880–1914 period.[213] Portuguese worked in Brazil with every intention of returning home, and as many as 66 percent of all migrants to Brazil returned to Europe.[214] An obscure but illuminating example is that of the English interior decorators who spent a season in London, another in the English countryside, and a third in New York; more common were the "some hundreds" of English masons and stonecutters who worked in the United States from spring until fall.[215] Returns are notoriously difficult to trace, but it is possible to estimate the proportion of returns to Europe from the United States between 1907 and World War I, by which time return migrations were common. At this time, nearly 48 percent of English and north Italians, about 42 percent of south Italians, 33 percent of Portuguese and Poles, and 20 percent of Germans returned. Some groups were unlikely to seek out their homeland: only 16 percent of Irish, whose homeland was bereft of opportunity, and 7 percent of Jews, most of whose homeland was a very unsafe Russia, returned. Europeans were more likely to return home from Latin America than from the U.S.; nearly half came home again (50 percent of Italians, 43 percent of Spanish).[216]

Those who returned home were primarily men who had worked in construction gangs or factories for a few years. Return migration was primarily the movement of working-aged people (15–45), who could use their income at home; although women's patterns echoed men's in any one migrant group, men were more likely to return to Europe. For example, in the 1909–1928 period, when Italian male immigrants outnumbered women by over two to one, male returnees outnumbered their female counterparts by over seven to one. Generally, the groups that returned most migrants to their home country were the most male groups—those who sent men to earn money abroad while their wives and daughters remained at home. Nearly half the Irish and the Jews, who usually remained in the U.S., were women.[217] Many of these temporary immigrants were single, but Lars-Göran Tedebrand's study of Swedish remigration shows that some were married men who had left their families behind, and others were women who had worked for a time as domestic servants in the United States.[218]

These returns are significant for understanding that the transatlantic migrant was consciously operating in a global labor market. Subject to however narrow a labor experience, however exploited, European proletarians who came from one hemisphere to work in another purposefully acted in a world that stretched far beyond their own village or town. That many chose to return home confirms the sophistication, intentionality, and instrumentality of their moves. For the Italian laborer who had long worked abroad within Europe for short periods, wrote Francesco Coletti in 1911, "the whole world is a homeland."[219] This observation offers an important corollary to preindustrial migration itineraries, which went well beyond the periphery of the localized world we envision for seventeenth-century people. In both cases, European migrants lived in a far larger world than the one assigned to them by history.

Transatlantic migration brought money into European towns and villages as emigrants sent remittances in the form of postal orders and cash slipped into letters home. Work in North and South America, like migrants' labor on the Continent, served to repay debts, build houses, and purchase land.[220] In some instances, migrant earnings brought a significant rise in the standard of living of the migrant's family back home.

The destinations and careers of returnees are unfortunately shrouded in mystery and have been aptly compared to the farther side of the moon. This dark lunar surface currently is being illuminated bit by bit by individual case studies. Lars-Göran Tedebrand's investigation of remigrants from Västnorrland in Sweden shows that returns were disproportionately destined for rural areas, despite the fact that Sweden was becoming urbanized. Tedebrand's fine data allow him to see that when emigrants returned, the vast majority (78% to 90%) returned to their home area. More importantly, remigration was strongest to peasant areas; people were less likely to return home to industrial parishes or parishes of landless rural workers. Time in America allowed farmers' children to earn money in order to continue on the land, which was more attractive than the Swedish alternative of following an urban and proletarian itinerary. Swedish returnees, like temporary migrants over the centuries, used income from migration to stay on the land.[221]

Fulfilling this aspiration, however, seems to have had the effect of conserving the status quo in village society. Generally speaking, rural polities and landowning systems stayed much the same; migrant income neither allowed a permanent deferral of proletarian status nor financed significant and permanent upward mobility.[222] Donna Gabaccia's very refined study of migration and the Sicilian town of Sambuca gives a more nuanced understanding of this general observation. Sambucesi's destinations were Louisiana, Chicago, and New York in the main. They were more likely than Swedes to return home (25% vs. 10%, approximately), particularly the poorest among them who had gone to cut sugar cane in Louisiana. The returnees were neither "as upwardly mobile, as socially exclusive, nor as politically conservative as might be expected."[223] They returned to the same neighborhoods where, like Swedish returnees, many of the men worked at the same occupation as their father and many of the women married men who worked at their father's occupation. But there was upward and downward mobility as well. Consequently, although money-earning in America little changed Sambuca's overall social structure, it moved people within it. As migrants' offspring intermarried, groups that had little contact in the nineteenth century became kin in the twentieth. As a result, experiences in migration and intermarriage produced a more fluid society.

What were the connections between transoceanic migration and migration within Europe? Extant studies suggest that migration to the new world was an integral part of mobility patterns in many parts of Europe, particularly in regions adjacent to international ports. Scandinavian case studies reveal that many of those who emigrated to America from cities had arrived in those cities from the countryside a few years previously. The majority of emigrants from Stockholm, for example, had not come from this city but rather from smaller towns. Emigrants from Norwegian cities also moved in stages. The fine detail of Swedish migration data indicates that many emigrants to the new world first left the village or small town for another town, and finally for Stockholm—living and working at each location for a time—before crossing the Atlantic. This is corroborated by Danish materials. Many city dwellers who emigrated, then, were part of the streams of village and small-town dwellers creating urban lives for themselves.[224] One Swedish study reports that these "stage emigrants" were more likely to be women than men because servant work was so important for female migrants in the city; it was thus a traditional itinerary that took women to the city. Among Irish men, cityward migration before emigration may have been more characteristic of skilled workers and tradesmen than of unskilled laborers.[225] Many people emigrated directly from their home village, however; village dwellers from central Europe, for example, were transferred by emigration agents by train directly to a port city like Bremen or Hamburg where they soon boarded their vessel. Nonetheless, even these emigrants—like the people of Maszkienice who went to Pennsylvania—participated in the expanding patterns of mobility that characterized all of Europe in the century before World War I; their trek abroad was one of the several paths that broadened the horizons of their village.[226]

CONCLUSION

The nineteenth century was a mobile age. The young agricultural worker, the country artisan, and the rural young woman were all likely to leave home. As migration systems expanded and proliferated, Europeans would travel farther than their ancestors and would be more likely to stay away. Their moves were inspired by the same fundamental factors that long had shaped human mobility: a changing configuration of demographics, capital, and labor needs. Generally, rapid population increase, the growth of urban capital, and ultimate loss of rural manufacturing or steady agricultural employment and proliferation of urban jobs promoted a shift away from local rural migration to circular migration systems, chain migrations to urban areas, and career migration.

Women played a greater role in more distant moves than before. As villagers, they sought work and married farther from home than before. Young women played an especially significant role among migrants into textile, commercial, and administrative cities. Their participation in agricultural team labor, and in emigration to the new world, increased.

Migrants played a complex of roles in the remarkable city growth of the century. They certainly fed the initial impulses of growth that transformed villages and small towns into industrial cities. However, the earliest historical data that directly measure migration make it very clear that the movements of men and women to and from continental towns far outstripped net urban growth. Although migrants contributed to city growth and remained important to urban populations, then, such movement was only a partial manifestation of much greater mobility. In addition, massive mobility accompanied urbanization, but was not its sole cause because declining urban death rates allowed cities themselves to contribute significantly to their own growth.

The specific histories of migration varied considerably from region to region. Large farms and capitalist agriculture expanded early on in the wheat belts, drawing in annual teams of harvest workers, while peasant production persisted elsewhere; the sugar beet production that demanded a massive seasonal labor force became important only late in the century. Rural industry thrived until the 1840s in many regions on the Continent, only damaged with the coming of the railroad later in the century. Pockets of cottage production that allowed people to remain in their villages persisted until World War I. By contrast, the early textile mill towns like Manchester, Verviers, and Elberfeld attracted workers early on; heavy industry towns, which required a distinct labor force, expanded later in the century.

It is probable that the rate of mobility increased in most regions over the course of the 1815–1914 period. The best evidence, for large German cities, certainly suggests that mobility increased dramatically and peaked in the late nineteenth century. Yet these data are not conclusive because we have no comparable records for earlier times and because these only apply to a subset of German regions.[227] It is indisputable, however, that major shifts in migration systems created movement that covered greater distances. At the extreme, new migration systems evolved that took German cottage industry workers not to Holland or the next village, but to the United States. The liberated population of Russian and Austrian Poland traveled not only to the Rhine-Ruhr zone, but also to North America. In a more mundane fashion, marriage contacts were made not in the next village but progressively farther afield.[228] The average trek was a longer one. This trend is manifested in an increasing proportion of people who crossed various administrative boundaries and thus added themselves to the bureaucratic count of people away from home, be they in another commune, county, *département* or *Kreise*.

In the end, the men, women, and children who took to the road produced a very different population in 1914 than a century earlier. This was a free, urbanized, and proletarian population. Legally free to move, a decreasing proportion of people were kept in place, or even in the countryside, by landownership. By the end of the century, the boom in city-building had slacked and work in metallurgy and mining became more steady.[229] The combined result of these two trends was to give more people permanent work at the expense of seasonal employment, and a greater proportion of workers were constrained neither by possessions nor by the law to stay in place. The labor force in western Europe was an international one, in which Belgians, Italians, Irish, and Poles in particular worked across an international boundary—if not across the Atlantic—from home.

Free movements of these working people would stop suddenly with World War I, which froze international borders and trapped nearly 200,000 Poles in a foreign land. Armies quickly absorbed the young men who would otherwise be out searching for work. This military and political interregnum would announce a new era in the history of migration.

CHAPTER

5

Migration in the Twentieth Century

Young parents Mémé and Auguste Santerre were stacking hay bundles "in the overpowering heat, surrounded by the strong odor of freshly cut hay and the sweat of the workers" when the outbreak of World War I was announced with the traditional alarm of church bells. The Santerres and their fellow workers were alerted when, "suddenly, at the neighborhood church, a furious, irregular, extraordinary bell-ringing broke out."[1] The war that followed decimated the Santerre's home village and killed up to 13 million people, including civilians.

World War I proved to be a death-knell, not only for millions of Europeans, but for free migration as well. The 1815–1914 era of relatively free mobility gave way to a time in which states directly sponsored, regulated, and forced migration. The status of foreigners became more salient in questions of citizenship, juridical rights, suffrage, and political discussion.[2] In wartime, neither armies nor civilians moved by choice but rather were displaced by battle and state policy, for reasons of their nationality or ethnicity. In the European wars of the twentieth century, borders were crossed by millions "whose passports were guns and whose visas were bullets. They set in motion millions of others who marched unarmed between streams of blood and tears."[3]

State control of foreign workers between the wars, and after World War II, had a different rationale than wartime displacements. Workers were allowed across borders in great numbers in response to a labor shortage, and often in response to recruiting efforts or bilateral government agreements. For example, the West German and Turkish governments cooperatively initiated migration to West Germany after the construction of the Berlin Wall in 1961 cut off its supply of eastern European workers.[4] Germany in the 1960s, like the German Empire of the prewar period that hired so many Poles, sought a labor force that would enter the country in a reversible flow, so its foreign workers were called guest workers, or *gastarbeiter*. However, in the 1960s, it was not only Germany that imported labor but France, Britain, Belgium, the Netherlands, Luxembourg, and Sweden as well. State intervention and control of international migration is central to the history of migration in this century; the movements of wartime and of imported postwar labor have this in common. For this reason, the Naumoff family and Kemal Altun, whose movements were controlled by governments and international agencies, represent two of the twentieth century's most significant migrant groups.

Peter and Anna Naumoff left home precipitously in 1944. German occupation forces rounded them up with other Ukrainian farmers. Their trip west was a brutal three-week journey in a cattle car. They were shipped, ahead of the Soviet army, into Austria, where they were installed in a factory camp to work for the Third Reich. At the war's end, they had nobody to go home to, so the couple, now with an infant son, were placed in a refugee camp to the west. By 1950 they were in a fourth camp with a fourth child. Because Peter Naumoff had contracted tuberculosis at the wartime factory, it would be 1960 before a country could be persuaded to accept them and they would begin civilian life again.[5] The Naumoffs were among the 30 million Europeans displaced by the World War II.

The departure of Kemal Altun from home was considerably slower. Only after four trips across his country to Istanbul, applications, bribes, then tests for literacy and job skills, and finally an examination for tuberculosis, diabetes, and syphilis, was he allowed to board a train for western Europe in 1974. The process took seven years.[6] Altun was among the 893,000 Turks—and over 8 million foreign nationals—who lived in western Europe in the early 1970s. Economic crises soon struck their host nations, and European governments encouraged Kemal Altun and his compatriots to return home.

The regulation of immigration and foreign labor intensified during World War I with the institution of offices, mechanics, and ideologies of labor recruitment and control that would be used long into the century. State regulation of international labor did not mean that workers no longer drew on kin and compatriot contacts in systems of chain and circular migration; rather, those contacts and migration systems operated in the context of (and often purposefully evaded) state interest and control. Generally speaking, foreign labor would continue—albeit under more formal auspices—to play the same role as in earlier centuries, that of an exportable secondary labor force that would perform the most arduous and unpleasant tasks in mining, construction, and agriculture.[7]

The history of worker migration between nations in this century is sharply divided into two periods. Initially a "second thirty years' war" decimated the population and halted the movement of free labor from 1914 to 1945. International labor migration was controlled by hostilities until 1919; subsequent postwar rebuilding took the energies of the members of the native labor forces that survived the war; transatlantic migration was squelched when the United States dramatically narrowed its acceptance of immigrants in 1921 and 1924; the international depression of the 1930s reduced the demand for labor so drastically that some nations closed their borders to foreign workers; finally, the hostilities of World

War II kept free labor behind the lines and put men into battle. Generally, during this period, repatriates, refugees, and some contract "coolie" labor replaced the free movement of men and women across international borders.[8] Although there were massive displacements at the end of both wars, the impetus for those migrations was fundamentally different than in the eighteenth and nineteenth centuries.

A decade after the end of World War II, a familiar migration scenario appeared. Men and women came to European cities to work temporarily, performing menial and difficult tasks—often in order to earn money that would enable them to retain or upgrade their family landholdings. In some cases, the new migrants sent for their wives or married a compatriot. They visited home and talked to others about making the trip. In this way, systems of circular migration became the systems of chain migration that are so important to history. In this case, however, two important distinctions separated postwar migrations from those of previous centuries: the newcomers were from the countries of southern Europe, the wider Mediterranean basin (North Africa, Yugoslavia, Greece, and Turkey), sub-Sahara Africa, and far-flung former colonies of Europe. Many migrants differed from northern Europeans in their ethnicity, race, or religious tradition. Also, the states of western Europe took an active part in this movement, if not as recruiters, then at least as agencies that attempted to control the volume and direction of migration. By 1981, over 11 million foreign nationals from southern Europe, North Africa, and the British New Commonwealth lived in the United Kingdom and northwestern Europe.[9]

The international migrations of the twentieth century—both the forced migrations of the 1914–1945 period and postwar streams of foreign workers—occurred against a backdrop of internal migrations that depleted the countrysides and inflated the sprawling cities. As localized peasant societies collapsed even in France, rural marriage markets became regional. Young men and women increasingly could imagine their futures only in an urban area, so the shift from circular to chain migration to the city was completed because fewer people returned home before retirement. The rural exodus or *"landflucht"* was a great concern in the interwar period as well as after World War II. The native-born young people became more highly educated and more likely to take white-collar work than before, and as a consequence it was they who inflated the ranks of career migrants, moving by the direction of the bank, the post office, or the educational system.

Demographics, labor force demands, and movements of capital all played a role in this phase of urbanization and industrial development. As European fertility dropped precipitously to all-time low levels, the Continent sent few migrants to the Americas and needed to import labor.[10] Although less prolific, rural populations still produced all the farmers Europe needed without keeping everyone at home, because jobs were in the cities, where non-farm capital gathered. It was no longer landownership but wages that provided a living for the lion's share of Europeans.

This chapter tells three distinct yet interconnected stories—of wartime Europe, of the urbanward shift in internal migration, and of international labor in the postwar period. They are interlocking pieces of the same demographic, economic, and political units that formulated the Common Market in 1957 and prepared the European Economic Community for 1992. Migration patterns for this population resulted from European economic conditions, the political economy of migrants' home nations, and European political and ethnic relations. The chapter first relates the tale of human movements across national borders during the 1914–1945 period, then it turns to the ways in which internal migration shifted in the twentieth century. Finally, it analyzes the waves of international migration into the northwestern portion of the Continent since 1960. I close with a historian's perspective on the European future.

MIGRATION AMONG EUROPEAN NATIONS, 1914–1945

When war began in the late summer of 1914, migrations overseas nearly ceased. The voluminous movement between Britain and the new worlds changed drastically: England had lost 200,000 to 240,000 people per year from emigration in the 1911–1913 period; in 1914, only 91,000 British emigrated overseas, and this figure was reversed in the next year, when 20,000 people immigrated to Britain from across the Atlantic, "expatriates, who rushed back to the motherland to join in the fight." Emigration from Germany and France were minimal; nonetheless, even these movements were reduced. On the Continent, the majority of Germans and Austrians in France quickly departed for home. Some, like the people of northern France (including Auguste and Mémé Santerre) were not so lucky; as Germany invaded France over a million and a half refugees fled for *départements* to the west and south.[11]

Some foreign workers could not return home. In the interests of the German state, over 300,000 Russian-Polish seasonal industrial and agricultural workers were kept on; where they had been forced to return home annually before the war, they were now forbidden to return. Russian Poles, particularly those of military age, were retained so that they could not join enemy armies, while most Austrians were released to the German Empire's ally. Germany also augmented its wartime labor force with Belgian workers, recruited by force in the winter of 1916–1917, when over 100,000 Dutch and Belgians worked behind the German lines. In all, over 2 million volunteers, civilian prisoners, and prisoners of war were at the disposal of the German war economy.[12]

France augmented its labor force with prisoners of war and contract labor from two hastily created services. An Arms Ministry service brought in over 82,000 workers from Greece, Portugal, Spain, and Italy; the Ministry of Agriculture service imported over 113,000 agricultural workers from Spain and Portugal, accompanied by over 35,000 additional women and children. These arrangements began continuing streams of Spanish and Italian workers, who were joined by smaller groups of Algerians and other North African colonials, Indochinese, and Chinese.[13]

When hostilities ceased with the Armistice of November, 1919, a vast movement of people began. In fact, although surviving soldiers and wartime workers could go home, a return was impossible for most exiles, repatriates, and refugees. The war, then revolution and civil war in Russia from 1914 to 1923, yielded a stream of refugees and exiles into Germany (500,000), France (400,000), Poland (70,000), and other new central European nations that would only stop when the border of the U.S.S.R. closed in 1923. Five years of war had decimated Polish territories and evacuated its people so that an estimated 700,000 were repatriated by 1923. An estimated 200,000 Germans were repatriated, many from the eastern provinces of the Reich that were returned to reconstructed Poland after the Versailles settlement. In the west, about 120,000 Germans from Alsace-Lorraine fled into the Rhineland, and 50,000 French moved into Alsace-Lorraine as it once again became part of France. The Great War, then, not only leveled the population of Europe at its 1914 numbers, but it also was the impetus for the movement of Russians, Poles, and Germans to the west and the resettling of people around Alsace and the Rhineland. It set off the first refugee crisis of the twentieth century.[14]

In the years that followed the war, "beyond the push and pull of the labor market and population, the individual immigrant was manipulated by the agencies of the . . . state, corporate business, and his or her home government."[15] Legislation passed in the United States in 1921 and 1924 instituted restrictive quotas on the numbers of southern and eastern Europeans who could enter the U.S., cutting off the emigration of Poles and Italians that had been so significant before the war. Immigration to Germany was reduced as well; the 2 million foreigners in the country in 1918 were reduced to 174,000 foreign workers by 1924, when the country was plagued by inflation and unemployment. Despite these decreased numbers, Germany continued to regulate and control foreign labor, particularly in agriculture, where some 50,000 Polish workers came in for the beet and potato harvests in 1920.[16]

By contrast, the French state was liberal in its policies toward refugees and in need of foreign labor. Not only did Russian and Polish émigrés settle in Paris, but also the state signed bilateral treaties for labor to rebuild towns, restore factories, and fill in trenches in northern France soon after the war's end. The government facilitated the entry of over a million foreigners between 1919 and 1924, of whom many worked in reconstruction teams. In addition, commercial recruiters operating in the interests of mines and large farms recruited Polish contract labor in the 1920s. By 1923, over 33,000 Poles harvested sugar beets in northern France and cut wheat in the Ile-de-France. The iron and coal mines of France recruited over 139,000 Polish miners between 1919 and 1929. Some of these were young, single workers who came directly from Poland, but a core of the miners were *Ruhrpoles* from the mines of Westphalia who had come from Germany's eastern provinces to its western mines before World War I began. Recruited into France along with their wives and children, these miners became a cohesive and important minority in the French Polish community.[17]

In addition, the number of Spanish workers in France, already increased in wartime, expanded for the annual vineyard harvests in the southwest. The number of Italians working in France increased until the late 1920s, when Italian fascist policy began to vigorously discourage emigration. Belgian workers in France decreased at the same time, partly because Poles competed with and replaced Belgian labor in the northern provinces. Nonetheless, France employed foreign labor as did no other country in the 1920s. On the eve of the Depression, France's nearly 1.6 million foreign workers included over 475,000 Italians, 287,000 Poles, 194,000 Spaniards, 156,000 Belgians, and 386,000 others, such as Germans, Swiss, Algerians, Russians, Yugoslavs, Czechs, and Rumanians. Growing streams of government-approved workers increasingly came from eastern Europe and Algeria.[18]

This flow of workers into France—and throughout Europe—altered dramatically with the international economic depression of the 1930s. All national groups in France reduced their numbers as the French encouraged repatriation, restricted entries, and placed quotas on the hiring of foreigners in certain industries. As a consequence, although 360,000 foreigners arrived in the 1931–1936 period, there were 541,000 departures. Among Poles and Italians (and probably Portuguese, Greeks, Czechs, and Algerians), departures far outnumbered arrivals. However, France maintained a significant bedrock of 2.2 million foreign residents because its labor force had been so depleted by the war and by its long-standing low birth rate.

Germany, by contrast, closed its doors during the Depression. By 1932, a total of only 108,000 foreign workers remained, most of whom were longtime residents with permanent visas; these included only 5,000 agricultural laborers—only a handful by German standards. By 1933, 30 percent of the German labor force, which included the numerous children born between 1890 and 1914, was registered as unemployed. As a consequence, even the limited market for central Europeans' migrant labor virtually disappeared.[19]

Refugees again increased in the 1930s as fascist victories ousted political enemies and specific ethnic groups, particularly Jews. For the victims of fascism in Italy, Germany, and Spain, France was the most important asylum on the Continent. Most of the estimated 10,000 who left Italy with Mussolini's victory joined the sizable Italian community in France. An estimated 65,000 Germans left the Reich in 1933, about 80 percent of whom were Jews; 150,000, about a quarter of its "non-Ayran" population, departed before 1939. These refugees of the 1930s faced walls of restrictions, bureaucratic sluggishness, and anti-Semitism. Those who left the Continent went primarily to the U.S., where the immigration quotas of the 1920s stayed in force. Nonetheless, 80 to 85 percent of the Germans who went to the United States were Jews, and 17,200 Germans found asylum between 1935 and 1937. About one-fifth of German prewar refugees found refuge in Palestine. The Jews of Poland, Rumania, and Hungary, who far outnumbered German Jews, were also in flight. Their home states explicitly envisioned the emigration of Jews and increasingly persecuted Jews in the 1930s. As central European conditions deteriorated, Polish Jews predominated among the nearly 62,000 who found refuge in Palestine in 1935. On the eve of World War II, 110,000 Jewish refugees were spread throughout Europe, many of whom were actively attempting to leave the Continent altogether. There were probably 40,000 in France, about 8,000 in Switzerland, and many among the 50,000 people who found asylum in England in the 1933–1939 period. France was literally awash with refugees in 1939, as some 450,000 Spanish republicans who came in the wake of Franco's fascist victory joined refugee Italians and Jews.[20]

The worst was yet to come. A few months after the hostilities of World War II began in Poland, Germany invaded the low countries in the spring of 1940; masses of Dutch, Luxemburgers, and Belgians fled into northern France with German armies at their heels. At the end of May, the Red Cross reported that 2 million French, 2 million Belgians, 70,000 Luxemburgers, and 50,000 Dutch in northern France were seriously destitute. With the invasion of France, an estimated one-fifth of the French population fled as all roads to the south filled. Although many refugees would return home, 1 million remained uprooted in southern France a year later. In the summer of 1940, 100,000 French were cast out from Alsace-Lorraine when Germany repossessed its former territory.

Displacements in France, incalculably dislocating as they were, were less severe than on Germany's eastern front. This war was marked by the "deliberate uprooting of great masses of people," particularly in the east, where both the Nazi policy of *Lebensraum* and brutal displacements by Soviets were in force.[21] When the war began, Germany divided Poland into a western zone that was incorporated into the Reich and a "General Government" to the east that was designated as a home for unskilled slave labor. In a racial purge, 1.5 million Poles (including 300,000 Jews) were quickly deported to the General Government to make room for the favored German ethnics who would now be welcomed into the Reich, the *Auslandsdeutsche*. The Russian armies who also invaded Poland in September of 1939 drove Poles and Jews behind the lines and far to the east. All of these dislocations (and those to come), even the "voluntary" relocations of favored Baltic Germans into the new provinces of the Reich, were brutal transports by freight train, taken with minimal care to the health or feeding of the uprooted.[22]

In the first two years of the war, European Jews were caught between two forces: avenues of escape disappeared, while Nazis adopted a policy of rounding up Jews. The British negotiated with Palestine an agreement that severely limited immigration of Jews the very year war began, so that in the 1939–1942 period, only 40,000 Jews reached Palestine, half of whom were illegal entrants. In all, only 58,000 were able to immigrate in the 1940–1945 period. For the first time, the United States allowed the full quota of Germans and Austrians to enter in 1939; over 23,000 entered that year and 26,000 the next (the majority of whom were Jews); in June of 1941, however, Jewish immigration to the U.S. was curtailed by new restrictive legislation. Although Spain and Portugal provided passage to perhaps 40,000 Jews in 1940 and 1941, by the end of 1941, virtually all prospects of escape were blocked.

Simultaneously, the German Reich ceased to encourage Jews to leave and began instead to round them up into ghettos and camps. At this time, the Nazi policy of concentration was the preliminary stage of a plan to expel all Jews from the Reich, and all of Europe, after the war. Massive deportations from the Reich into the General Government began in 1941. This policy was fatal to the Jews of Europe. For example, by the spring of 1941, 130,000 people were forced into the ghetto of Warsaw, where hunger and disease took a heavy toll. An estimated one-fifth of the Jews of Poland died before October of 1941, when the final solution became defined as the murder of all Europe's Jews. Emigration was blocked and the construction of death camps began when Jews were already gathered, concentrated together, and trapped.[23]

Other European men and women were pulled into the German Reich as the Nazi regime used labor as a spoil of conquest. In an extension of World War I and prewar labor practices, the war government used foreign labor on an astonishing scale. Two million men and women in the defeated western nations and 2 million prisoners of war were coerced (or persuaded by propaganda) to work in German fields and factories early on in the war. But as the Blitzkrieg turned to a protracted and bloody war in the east, "like a giant pump, the German Reich sucked in Europe's resources and working population."[24] By 1944, one worker in five was a foreign civilian or prisoner of war; at that time, Germany's forced laborers numbered over 7 million, including 2.7 million Soviet citizens, 1.7 million Poles, and 1.25 million French, over 585,000 Italians, and over 250,000 each of Belgians and Dutch.[25]

This did not last. As the tide of war began to turn in 1943, and the Nazi regime collapsed in 1945, forced laborers and prisoners of war swiftly returned home. Despite destroyed communications and transport, the roads of Germany were like "swollen mountain torrents in the spring, a Babel of people and languages, all former slaves of the Third Reich."[26] Those heading west had the aid of British and American forces and were repatriated most rapidly. Before the winter of 1945–1946 closed in, the majority of the 11 million requiring repatriation had returned to their home nation. Displaced persons like Peter and Anna Naumoff, whose story was told near the beginning of this chapter, required more time.

The German retreat from the east between 1943 and 1945 produced two major, permanent shifts of European peoples and the second great refugee crisis of the century. The first is a move from east to west that included forced laborers like Peter and Anna Naumoff. The advance of the Russian army sent Germans fleeing into the Reich—even old, established German minorities that had been in the east since the Middle Ages, or at least since the days of Peter the Great. "Nearly one and one-half centuries before," wrote one ethnic German who fled Russia, "our fathers had moved from Prussia. . . . We were repeating the trek, only somewhat poorer, less certain about the future, and in the opposite direction."[27] *Volksdeutsch* refugees, as Germans who had been so favored under the Third Reich, had earned the hatred of the non-Germans around them. They continued to be expelled long after their removal was formalized by the Potsdam Agreement of August 1945; 12 million would reach the zones of occupied Germany by 1950. The German retreat marked a reversal in the historic eastward settlement of Germans and the evisceration of an ethnic group that was important to central Europe.[28]

Jews in western and central Europe were destroyed. This is chilling testimony to the effectiveness of Nazi genocidal policy in a brief three-year period. Of Poland's Jewish community of greater than 3 million people before the war, only some 31,000—a meager 2.4 percent—remained. The anticipated million Jewish refugees were not to be found at the time of the German surrender. In their stead remained, for example, 40,000 skeletal and traumatized inmates (and 10,000 corpses) in the German camp of Bergen-Belsen, of whom 13,000 perished soon after liberation. Most surviving Jews wanted neither to return home nor to remain in Europe. Pressure on Palestine mounted and 48,000 made their way there between January of 1946 and May of 1948 (of whom 30,000 were illegal immigrants). When Palestine became independent of the British in May of 1948 and the Jewish state was formed, the new nation opened its doors. In the first 18 months after independence, 340,000 Jews arrived from Europe.[29]

All told, the number of people displaced by the 1939–1945 war in Europe amount to 30 million—a number that is unfathomable in terms of human lives. These men and women of eastern, central, and western Europe were displaced, deported, or transplanted in wartime. Their story continues to resonate in the European experience.

The dramatic movements of Europeans across the borders of the Con-

tinent, forced in wartime and for voluntary labor in times of peace, occurred against a backdrop of the more quotidian and less visible moves
that have been the subject of most of this study. As mundane as these
other migrations were, they shaped the peacetime lives of western Europeans and transformed the labor force of the Continent. The following
section returns to the story of internal migration and urbanization.

POPULATION, MIGRATION, AND
URBANIZATION AFTER 1914

On the same day that agricultural laborers Auguste and Mémé Santerre
heard bells announcing the outbreak of war in 1914, church bells rang out
in Brittany where they were heard by peasants and farm servants. In the
summer of 1914, not everyone in the fields was a harvest worker like
Mémé Santerre or the Poles massed into the German and Danish fields,
but peasants and farm servants also continued to work European soil as
well. There were regions, like Brittany, where young men and women still
made their reputations as farm servants while they saved for marriage to
a compatriot from a nearby village, then settled on their own land.[30] A
wide range of rural economies and regional migration patterns, then, persisted into this century. All eventually were affected by the shortage of
rural resources and the upgrading of urban possibilities in the twentieth
century, the century that saw a final push of European urbanization.

The fundamental shape of the rural population would change after
1914, as the rapid population growth of the nineteenth century gave way
to much slower growth. As had happened earlier in France, birth rates
began an inexorable decline in the majority of provinces of Europe between 1890 and 1920, and plummeted particularly steeply between 1900
and 1930.[31] Because infant and child mortality declined as well, the population continued to grow, but it grew quite slowly. As a consequence,
although an expanding rural population and proletarianization were twin
causes of emigration from rural areas in the past, they were not key issues
in the twentieth century because the countryside was no longer crowded.
Low agricultural prices, mechanization, and a lack of jobs decimated rural
jobs. Employment and capital—in short, a future—lay in towns and cities
for most of the children of Europe.

Italian studies demonstrate the connections between migration and aspirations to permanent urban work. Constant movement around and into
cities included a sizable proportion of people who would stay on; for example, as the population of the industrial city of Turin doubled from
300,000 in 1881 to 630,000 in 1939, 50 migrants departed for every 100
arrivals. A sizable majority of 60 percent from the Piedmont village of
Valdoria remained, however. They moved into Turin's working class and

increasingly traversed blue-collar positions for white-collar work, as the generation of the 1870s gave way to the generations of the 1920s and 1930s. Men born in Valdoria during the 1873–1891 period who worked in Turin were in most cases (62%) more or less skilled workers at the end of their working lives, while only 7 percent were in white-collar jobs. By contrast, those in the 1926–1937 cohort were less likely to be workers (38%) and more likely to be white-collar employees, bureaucrats, or managers (36%) when they retired. Turin-born workers, over the same generations, were somewhat less likely to be workers (75%, then 52%), but many fewer became white-collar employees (3%, then 25%). The migrants in Turin suggest that workers who entered the industrial city after World War I experienced increasing social mobility and rarely followed in their father's footsteps.[32]

Between the wars, concern with the "rural exodus" again reached a peak as scholars and journalists expressed their keen worry that the rural life was in decline. These fears, compounded by the shock of World War I, gave many people the sense that the modern age was essentially a destructive one.[33] This concern seized upon a grain of truth—that rural life was perceived as untenable by many young men and women who saw no future in the countryside. In many places, this was particularly true of young women, who had no landownership or viable rural livelihood to which to aspire.[34] They avoided marriage with a man who worked the land; this is evidenced by the high proportions of single men among European agriculturalists in the twentieth century. Women became more likely than men to depart many rural areas and to leave at a younger age. The 1931 French census revealed what many village people already knew: that women born at around the turn of the century were more likely than men to leave their home area.[35]

The story of one young woman's decision to depart from her village shows the occupational, social, and personal components at work in the rural exodus. Marie Daudet was age 20 when she decided to leave her small village in the 1930s. The incident that set off her departure was related to rural work. Part of her job in the local bakery was the delivery of bread to the farms around her village; one late afternoon, when it was nearly dark as she drove the horse van, the horse spooked and bolted at a sharp corner of the road. The isolation in which this dangerous incident occurred so frightened Marie Daudet that she left the job the next day and came to Paris to find a childhood friend whose parents had a hotel in the city. There was already a chain of friendship that could give her an entrée into urban life. Marie Daudet had been engaged to a man in her village, but the engagement had been broken; as she later confided, "I had to go, I had known a young man."[36] The end of this relationship signaled the end of any hope for a social life or marriage in her village. Marie Daudet continued bakery work but spent the rest of her days in Paris because of dim marital prospects and unattractive work at home, combined with a contact in the city.[37] Similar prospects and contacts moved a large proportion of young, single rural people.

Village marriage records reflect the opening of rural societies. Endogamous marriages decreased as young people formed associations at greater distances from home and married partners who lived in a variety of locations. For example, in the villages of the mountainous Ardèche in southern France—many of which had long-lived contacts with silk-making upland towns and sites of seasonal migration on the Mediterranean littoral—nearly 52 percent of marriages had joined people from the same village in the 1860s. By the turn of the century, 39 percent of marriages were endogamous. In the 1930s, just over a third of marriages were endogamous, and one marriage in five included a partner from over 50 kilometers' distance. By the 1960s, men and women from all over France married in Ardechois villages, and only one wedding in eight joined two residents of the same village. Those who married locally were most likely to be farmers.[38] The intense migrations of the 1960s and early 1970s left village populations that were less demographically vital and less economically varied than ever before. Rural areas became even more agriculturalized in the twentieth century than they had been in the nineteenth century.[39] Manufacturing, commercial, bureaucratic, and professional work was primarily urban.

Restructuring of the labor market gave preeminence to permanent urban jobs and resulted in less movement between town and country. Rates of migration to and from German cities dropped from about 15 percent per year in the 1870–1914 period to less than 10 percent in the 1920s and afterward. Zurich followed the same pattern. This trend had come earlier to the more urbanized English economy, where migration between counties had declined for some time. Elsewhere, in Holland and Sweden, migration decreased in the 1930s. Likewise, the French were less likely to live outside their *département* of birth between the wars. The great economic depression partly accounts for the low migration rates of the 1930s; without opportunities, more people stayed home. When they left home, however, they moved fewer times than in the past and departures were for the long term. On the Continent, then, a less voluminous mobility surrounded urbanization after 1914 than in the past.[40]

Urbanization and emigration from farms occurred after World War II, as rural and agricultural work declined precipitously. Sweden is perhaps typical: its agricultural labor force numbered 725,000 in 1920, then 578,000 in 1950, and finally 315,000 in 1970.[41] Although the Swedish population increased, albeit slowly, those who tilled the land decreased, and in areas with low birth rates, the rural population declined absolutely. These trends were encouraged by the fall of customs barriers among Common Market countries, initially West Germany, Belgium, the Netherlands, Luxembourg, Italy, and France.[42] Farmers faced competition from a wide market and adopted such efficiency measures as cooperatives and mechanization. Between 1950 and 1972, the agricultural labor force in Italy and France decreased by more than half, and that of West Germany and Belgium by two-thirds. Simultaneously, urban areas continued to grow at the expense of rural populations throughout western Europe. Between 1950 and 1970 urbanization was particularly marked in France, West Germany, Sweden, Denmark, Finland, Norway, Ireland, Spain, and Italy; it was less important in the United Kingdom and the Netherlands, because they were already thoroughly urban. By 1970, the vast majority of Europeans lived in urban areas: 91 percent of the British, 78 percent of the French, 85 percent of the West Germans, 69 percent of the Italians, and 87 percent of the Swedes resided in urban areas.[43]

Interregional migrations in the 1960s were marked by particularly intense exchanges among prosperous urban regions, overlaid by net flows of migrants from declining rural and old mining or industrial regions to economically vital areas where industries and commerce thrived. In Italy, net movements went from southern to northern industrial regions; in Spain, to Madrid and the Mediterranean coast; in Britain, from Scotland, northern England, and Wales to the south; in France, from the central highlands and northeast to the Paris basin and the Midi.[44] Cities sprawled, and the term "megalopolis" was coined in 1961, when it applied equally well to the Washington, D.C.-to-Boston corridor in the United States as to several areas in western Europe, including southeast England, Randstand Holland, and the Rhine-Ruhr zone. A densely populated urban core wound from southern England through Randstand Holland and Belgium east to the Rhine-Ruhr zone, then turned south through Bavaria. Along with Naples, Rome, Madrid, Turin, Paris, and Berlin, the urban core shines so brightly that it was strikingly captured by nocturnal satellite photographs in the 1970s.[45]

A reverse of the trend to urbanization followed in the 1970s with migration to the countryside and broader areas around large cities. Migration into the metropolitan areas of Italy, France, West Germany, Sweden, and the Netherlands all fell—and even London lost population.[46] This trend of "counterurbanization" was due to city sprawl and the enhanced standard of living that enabled urban people to purchase more living space and second homes so that they could live outside center cities, either permanently or during holidays. It serves as a reminder that, by the 1960s, the migrants within European countries were a relatively well-educated and highly paid group. For example, French migrants in the 1980s were no longer poor montagnards who could not support themselves at home. In fact, managers and members of the liberal professions were most likely to move; mobility declined with social class to manual laborers. The least likely to move were families with property ties—farmers and shopkeepers. "Internal migration," observed geographer Paul White in the 1980s, "was an activity of the poor; today it is becoming more and more an activity of the rich."[47] Indeed, the indigenous labor forces of Europe were in 1960 much better educated and culturally homogeneous than fifty years previously, having been forged by compulsory education, language training, and the politics of two world wars.[48]

The indigenous labor force, however, was not adequate to the needs of the booming northwestern European economies of the postwar age. The nations of northwestern Europe all needed workers to replace soldiers and civilians killed in war, and the older labor force was reduced by wartime casualties, shorter work hours, and retirements. The falling birthrates of the interwar years reduced the cohort of men and women going to work in the 1950s. Moreover, educational and labor patterns exacerbated the labor shortage, because young men and women stayed in school longer and then were trained for new white-collar and skilled positions. A small labor force was particularly problematic in the boom years of the 1950s and 1960s. Gaps were partially filled by migrants from rural areas and by the women who entered the labor force in greater numbers after the war, but more workers were needed.[49] And so it was that an old trend vigorously was renewed; in response to the sizable demographic and economic demand for labor, foreigners were recruited to work in northwestern Europe.

FOREIGN LABOR IN POSTWAR EUROPE

Foreign laborers and their families arrived in unprecedented numbers in the 1960s. By the mid-1970s, over 8 million foreign men, women, and children resided in northwestern Europe. One in seven manual laborers in Germany and Britain was an immigrant; one in four industrial workers in France, Switzerland, and Belgium was a foreigner. They came primarily from nine countries in southern Europe and North Africa: Portugal, Spain, Italy, Yugoslavia, Greece, Turkey, Tunisia, Morocco, and Algeria. Their destinations were France, Germany, Switzerland, the Netherlands, Belgium, Luxembourg, and Sweden. Over a million more people from the worldwide British Commonwealth resided in Britain.[50] By and large, the countries of northwest Europe initially received workers from the nations of southern Europe or former colonies. After the Common Market was formed, workers from member nations gradually were allowed free movement within countries of the European Economic Community (EEC) beginning in 1961; workers from southern European countries (and from the Mediterranean basin) initially entered by agreements between home and host nation. Italians traveled under EEC auspices as of 1968, Greeks as of 1981, Portuguese and Spanish workers as of 1990.[51]

This highly diverse foreign labor force echoed historical patterns and processes. These men and women entered the labor market at times when deaths and low birth rates required new workers to substitute for a demographic lacuna; the twentieth-century migrants filled places left by the World War II dead and by the low birthrates of the depression just as previous migrants filled places left by the Hundred Years' War, Spanish *reconquista*, and demographic crises of the seventeenth century. The newcomers complemented the place of the native-born in the labor force by taking the difficult, low-status jobs that Europeans avoided.[52] Like the migrants in eighteenth- and nineteenth-century Europe, most postwar immigrants came from regions short on capital and long on population, regions much poorer than northwestern Europe. Moreover, the migration processes were similar to those of the past: Most postwar migration streams were pioneered by men but came to include a significant proportion of women. Like earlier migrants, the men who founded these migration streams to northwestern Europe intended to maintain or enhance their lives at home with money earned abroad; they came for months or years, but they did not intend to remain in Europe. As they had in the past, however, many stayed, sent for their families, and became a permanent part of European society.

On the other hand, these migration streams break with historical patterns on two significant dimensions. First, as labor migrants, postwar immigrants operated in a state-regulated context that was relatively unusual before 1914. Postwar governments self-consciously recruited laborers, then supervised migration, albeit not always effectively or with the desired outcome. The protracted and often violent process of decolonization brought an important minority of newcomers to postwar Europe. These included Europeans and non-Europeans from French Algeria, the Dutch East Indies, and Britain's New Commonwealth (India, Pakistan, Bangladesh, and the West Indies). Some citizens of the New Commonwealth, for example, came for economic reasons because they were allowed entry and citizenship. Others, however, came essentially as refugees, as losers in violent political struggles for liberation. Among these were the some 80,000 Algerian Harkis loyal to the French colonial administration, who arrived in France in 1961 and 1962 after the Algerian struggle for independence.[53]

Further, ethnic minorities were important among these migrants, particularly in cases where migration streams originated in Muslim or Arab countries, like Pakistan, Algeria, and Turkey. In most cases, ethnic minorities were former subject people of the colonies, as were the Surinamese in the Netherlands. Such groups were especially large in France and Britain. The 55,000 black Africans in France in the 1960s from former sub-Saharan colonies more than doubled in the 1970s. Northern Africans, particularly Algerians, numbered over 810,000 by 1981. In Britain, Indians, Pakistanis, and West Indians easily outnumbered other migrant groups.[54] Because newcomers originated in the Mediterranean basin and beyond, they made Europe more ethnically heterogeneous. Migrants' languages, gender relations, cultural habits, religion, reproductive patterns, education, and race all set them farther apart from mainstream western European culture than were the village migrants of the eighteenth and nineteenth centuries. They were more different than the Irish from the English, or the Poles from Rhineland Germans. Some immigrants, then, faced levels of hostility and racism that few nineteenth-century migrants had to endure.

This section sketches the history of migration streams to northwestern Europe in the thirty years after 1960 as they developed from teams of recruited workers to settled families. It gives special attention to the groups forming ethnic minorities, examining Turks as an exemplary group of this kind. I address three questions: What does a historical perspective reveal about postwar migrants in Europe? Why did members of migrant groups remain in Europe in the 1970s and 1980s, despite considerable efforts to remove them? Finally, what are the prospects for these postwar migrants?

Foreign laborers worked at jobs the native-born avoided, many of which had earlier been specialties of native-born rural migrants: agricultural labor, construction, and mining. This was already visible in France's interwar foreign labor force: 67 percent of foreign workers (in contrast to 40% of native-born workers) performed blue-collar tasks. Between 1906 and 1931, when French nationals abandoned mining, construction, metallurgy, and stonework to foreigners, the proportion of self-employed and white-collar foreign workers decreased, but the proportion of white-collar and commercial workers among the native-born was on the rise.[55] In the highly segmented postwar labor force, employers hired migrants for positions that the native population found most disagreeable and disruptive, like those that required work on night shifts, exposed workers to the most danger, and were the dirtiest. Hence, in the 1970s, when the city of Geneva tunneled a comprehensive drainage system underneath the city, it hired men from Italy, Spain, and Yugoslavia to do the job. When the textile manufacturers of Roubaix required work on three shifts, they hired Algerian men for work Belgians would no longer take and French women could not legally accept under protective legislation.[56] Foreign women became domestic servants, because this occupation had become intolerable to most native-born women.[57] Just as a seventeenth-century observer asked who would do the work in Spain if not the French migrant, John Berger posed this question in the 1970s: "Who was to build the new buildings and motorways, make the castings, clean the cities, man the assembly lines, quarry the minerals, bury the pipe lines?" The migrant worker. And Berger acutely observed, "He has been there from the beginning."[58] Migrants' place in the labor force arguably has enabled indigenous Europeans to acquire and monopolize highly skilled, white-collar, and professional work.[59]

Like past migrants, these workers come from regions with too little capital for their growing populations. In the Mediterranean basin and

New Commonwealth, high rates of natural increase, low incomes, and underemployment were common. In the mid-sixties, the populations of Greece, Spain, and Portugal increased at 1 to 1.2 percent per year; Turkey at 2.7 percent, and the British Commonwealth countries of Jamaica and Pakistan at 3.1 percent. The population of Algeria increased by 3.4 percent annually. These growing populations fed their children on some of the lowest incomes in the world; the annual per capita gross national product in the mid-1960s was simultaneously $125 for Pakistan, $520 for Jamaica, $353 for Turkey, $822 for Spain, and $1,272 for Italy—this compared with $1,977 for Britain and $2,324 for France.[60] Changes in rural landholding and agriculture discouraged these increasing populations from staying on the land; they flooded long-standing migration streams. Thus, Turks, for example, inundated shantytowns on the outskirts of Ankara and Istanbul. By the 1960s, additional destinations were required.

The balance between an enormous supply of foreign labor and European demand initially was negotiated via bilateral government agreements. Because migration streams each had unique histories related to both the sending and receiving nation, I briefly survey their origin and initial development.[61] (See Table 5:1.[62])

France, with its history of immigration, initially had the greatest foreign population. The Office National d'Immigration was established in 1945 to recruit workers and, in many cases, their families as well in order to bolster the low birthrate. Most migrants came from Italy and Spain, then from the colony of Algeria. This was not tightly regulated immigration; by the late 1960s, over four migrants in five were arriving clandestinely—that is, traveling on tourist visas and arriving without work permits. At that time, over 2.75 million foreigners lived in France, largely from Spain, Italy, and Algeria.[63]

Germans expelled from central and eastern Europe at the end of World War II added 8 million to the population of the Federal Republic of Germany; they substituted for foreign labor in the years of rebuilding immediately following the war. In the interests of stability, the postwar governments quickly integrated these ethnic Germans into the population by distributing them throughout the allied sectors. This was successful because the newcomers were by law citizens and voting members of the polity. They blended into this society that itself was "in the throes of demographic relocation and change."[64] West Germany was the last nation to recruit foreign workers, but when it did so, recruitment was carefully organized by the Federal Labor Office (*Bundesanstalt für Arbeit*) and more foreigners moved to West Germany than to any other nation. A bilateral recruiting agreement was made with Italy in 1955 and with Greece in 1960, but when construction of the Berlin Wall stopped the flow of East Germans into the West in the summer of 1961, the government quickly made recruiting agreements with Turkey, Morocco, Portugal, Tunisia, and Yugoslavia. By the end of the sixties, nearly 3 million foreigners lived in

TABLE 5.1
**Foreigners Residing in Selected European Countries by Country
of Citizenship and Labor Force Participation, Early 1960s, Early
1970s, and 1981 (in thousands)**

Host Country

Country of Citizenship	Belgium	France	Germany	Netherlands	Switzerland
Italy					
All Migrants					
Early 1960s	200.1	629.0	196.7	. . . .	346.2
Early 1970s	249.5	572.8	629.6	19.4	587.3
1981	. . . .	452.0	624.5	21.1	417.3
Economically Active					
Early 1960s	69.1	305.0	177.6	5.6	303.1
Early 1970s	90.3	220.0	370.0	9.6	338.0
1981	90.5	157.6	316.1	10.5	234.9
Spain					
All Migrants					
Early 1960s	15.8	441.7	44.2	. . . .	13.5
Early 1970s	67.5	570.6	272.7	30.7	125.3
1981	. . . .	412.5	177.0	22.8	99.7
Economically Active					
Early 1960s	7.2	213.0	38.9	1.3	. . . .
Early 1970s	27.9	260.0	165.0	20.2	83.2
1981	32.0	128.9	85.9	12.7	63.4
Portugal					
All Migrants					
Early 1960s	0.9	50.0	0.8	. . . .	0.4
Early 1970s	7.2	812.0	121.5	7.6	. . . .
1981	. . . .	859.4	109.4	9.3	13.1
Economically Active					
Early 1960s	. . . .	30.1	0.3	0.1	. . . .
Early 1970s	3.1	385.0	85.0	4.4	4.1
1981	6.2	434.6	57.1	5.6	9.3
Turkey					
All Migrants					
Early 1960s	10.8	. . . .	6.7	. . . .	0.6
Early 1970s	20.3	45.4	1,027.8	53.7	26.6
1981	. . . .	118.1	1,546.3	148.2	42.9

TABLE 5.1 (continued)

Host Country

Country of Citizenship	Belgium	France	Germany	Netherlands	Switzerland
Economically Active					
Early 1960s	0.1	. . . .	4.4	0.1	. . . .
Early 1970s	7.1	33.0	590.0	32.5	16.5
1981	23.0	. . . .	637.1	59.5	22.7
Yugoslavia					
All Migrants					
Early 1960s	4.8	. . . .	16.4	. . . .	1.2
Early 1970s	5.2	79.3	707.8	11.9	37.9
1981	. . . .	67.8	637.3	14.2	49.1
Economically Active					
Early 1960s	. . . .	. . . .	12.1	0.2	. . . .
Early 1970s	. . . .	58.0	470.0	9.4	28.4
1981	3.1	. . . .	357.7	8.4	34.3
Greece					
All Migrants					
Early 1960s	9.8	. . . .	42.1	. . . .	2.4
Early 1970s	22.4	10.1	406.4	3.9	10.8
1981	. . . .	. . . .	299.3	4.2	9.1
Economically Active					
Early 1960s	3.6	. . . .	35.1	0.2	. . . .
Early 1970s	8.5	5.0	225.0	2.2	6.2
1981	10.7	. . . .	132.2	2.3	4.9
Algeria					
All Migrants					
Early 1960s	0.2	350.5	. . . .	. . . .	0.2
Early 1970s	6.6	845.7	4.3	. . . .	. . . .
1981	. . . .	816.9	5.0	0.5	. . . .
Economically Active					
Early 1960s	0.1	208.6	. . . .	. . . .	. . . .
Early 1970s	2.0	450.0	2.0	. . . .	. . . .
1981	3.2	382.1	. . . .	0.2	. . . .

TABLE 5.1 (continued)

Host Country

Country of Citizenship	Belgium	France	Germany	Netherlands	Switzerland
Morocco					
All Migrants					
Early 1960s	0.5	33.0	1.0	. . . .	0.2
Early 1970s	39.3	269.7	24.0	30.1	. . . .
1981	. . . .	444.5	39.4	93.2	. . . .
Economically Active					
Early 1960s	0.1	19.7	. . . .	. . . .	. . . .
Early 1970s	15.7	145.0	15.0	24.1	. . . .
1981	37.3	171.9	. . . .	40.2	. . . .
Tunisia					
All Migrants					
Early 1960s	0.2	26.6	0.4	. . . .	0.2
Early 1970s	2.2	148.8	17.5	1.1	. . . .
1981	. . . .	193.2	24.1	2.5	. . . .
Economically Active					
Early 1960s	. . . .	12.4	. . . .	. . . .	. . . .
Early 1970s	0.9	85.0	11.0	0.9	. . . .
1981	4.7	73.2	. . . .	1.5	. . . .
Total					
All Migrants					
Early 1960s	243.1	1,531.1	308.3	. . . .	364.9
Early 1970s	420.2	3,354.4	3,211.6	158.4	787.9
1981	. . . .	3,364.4	3,462.3	316.0	631.2
Economically Active					
Early 1960s	80.2	788.8	268.4	7.5	303.1
Early 1970s	155.5	1,641.0	1,933.0	103.3	476.4
1981	210.7	1,348.3	1,586.1	140.9	369.5

Note: Total is for migrants from countries listed in this table only. Germany is the Federal Republic of Germany.
SOURCE: Excerpted from Rosemarie Rogers, "Post-World War II European Labor Migration: An Introduction to the Issues," in *Guests Come to Stay* (Boulder, Colo.: Westview Press, 1985), 5–9.

West Germany, primarily from Italy, Yugoslavia, EEC nations, and Turkey.[65]

The largest groups of migrants to Britain came from former colonies as England granted independence and thereby created the New Commonwealth of nations in the Indian subcontinent and West Indies. After World War II, Indians, Pakistanis, and West Indians soon joined long-standing streams of Irish immigrants to England. By 1966, over 2.5 million people from the Commonwealth, Ireland, EEC countries, and southern Europe lived in Britain.[66]

The smaller nations of northwest Europe were just as likely to recruit foreign labor. Switzerland recruited fewer immigrants in absolute numbers than these larger nations, yet its historic dependence on foreign labor increased in the 1950s and 1960s.[67] Switzerland's postwar labor recruitment was the most thoroughly controlled of any nation; it encouraged temporary guestworkers by tight surveillance of entries and by hiring seasonal labor and borderland commuters. Employers recruited labor, but admissions and residence were state-controlled. Nonetheless, by the end of the 1960s, nearly a million foreigners lived in Switzerland, over half of whom were Italian.[68]

The Netherlands drew people from their East Indian colonies and did not recruit from southern Europe until the 1960s, when bilateral agreements were reached with Italy, Spain, Portugal, Turkey, Greece, Morocco, Yugoslavia, and Tunisia. By 1970, a quarter of a million foreigners lived in the Netherlands, primarily from West Germany, Turkey, Spain, Belgium, and Morocco. Belgium organized recruitment immediately after the war through bilateral labor agreements, the *contingentensysteem*, to bring Italian workers, especially, to its mines and mills. After 1963, when the *contingentensysteem* ceased, workers continued to come on their own. By 1970, over 700,000 foreigners lived in Belgium, over a third of whom were Italians. Just as northwestern Europe allowed workers to move within EEC countries, Scandinavian nations of Denmark, Norway, Iceland, Sweden, and Finland formed the Nordic Labor Market in 1954. This allowed Finns to enter Sweden in great numbers. In the sixties, Swedish firms privately recruited workers farther afield, in Yugoslavia, Greece, and Turkey. By 1970, 191,000 foreigners resided in Sweden, half of whom were Finns.[69]

The history of migration of these diverse groups generally followed three stages: non-colonial groups (and many colonials as well) began as labor migrants recruited to work in systems of circular migration. Family reunification combined with diminished recruitment produced growing systems of chain migration. Finally, migrants became permanent residents, national and ethnic minorities whose children (and grandchildren) were in many cases born and raised in northwestern Europe.

In the first phase of postwar migration, when Italians, Spaniards, and Turks were recruited in large numbers for specific public works or factory jobs, the overwhelming majority of migrants were young men who lived in employer dormitories or *Heime*. These migrants' experiences and working lives were recorded in prose, photographs, and poetry by John Berger and Jean Mohr in their invaluable document, *A Seventh Man*. Of the foreign migrant's essential isolation, Berger wrote that "His solitude is like iron in the rain/his palms are red with rust/on the foreign side of the river. . . ."[70] Like the *Hollandsgänger* of the seventeenth century and the temporary migrants in the United States observed by Michael Piore, these workers lived without family and spent as little as possible on themselves in order to save for a return home.[71]

In the 1960s and 1970s, new migration streams entered the countries of northwestern Europe, and others faded. Italians began to travel to West Germany more than to France, where demand for workers was on the rise and pay was better. Also, France was flooded with competitors in the persons of *Pieds Noirs*, ethnic French from Algeria, and with ethnic Algerians after Algeria became independent in 1962. A massive Portuguese migration to France began that would come to rival Algerian immigration and that would outnumber Spanish and even Italian immigration. In Britain in the 1970s, Indians, Pakistanis, and Bangladeshis replaced West Indians.[72]

In the years between 1967 and 1973, the number of foreigners in northwestern Europe skyrocketed to an all-time high and migration streams began to change dramatically as family reunification became more important. By the early seventies, over 8 million people from Italy, Spain, Portugal, Greece, Turkey, Yugoslavia, Morocco, Algeria, and Tunisia lived in northwestern Europe. Over half of these foreigners were wives, children, and other relatives who were not working (or did not report employment).[73] Workers' wives had been recruited as laborers in their own right or had come as dependents; many children were brought along or born in the host country. The migrant community was changing composition, and its new structure was more one of a long-term immigrant community than of a migrant labor community.

Historical experience explains why postwar migrants became permanent residents. The long-standing phenomenon of chain migration reminds us that migration systems grew from the "migration fever" transmitted by letters and by word of mouth. Given the numbers of migrants and the dramatic differences in standard of living between home and destination, it was predictable that postwar migration streams would maintain themselves. How, for example, could a 1973 migration system involving 605,000 Turkish workers in Germany have disappeared without a very considerable trace, particularly considering the relatively humble conditions in most Turkish towns and villages at that time?[74]

Historical experience also confirms the importance of family integrity to the migration process. Married migrant laborers have been willing to live without their families only for short periods or under the direst of circumstances. For example, poverty impelled Galician Poles to work in

German agriculture, returning home for only a few weeks per year; difficulty of travel forced men to work in seventeenth-century Spain for years before returning to their families. Workers in systems of circular migration historically have been willing to distort their lives considerably—to work at difficult, demeaning, and dangerous jobs; to tolerate very bad housing—as long as those conditions were temporary. However, migrant workers were not willing to forego all hope of a family life permanently. They arranged periodic returns home, married at destination, or sent for wives.

The international oil crisis, inflation, and recession that began in 1973 sharpened hostility to foreign workers. European prejudices—irritated by the phenotypical distinctiveness of many foreigners, their visibility in local labor markets, and their numbers in many cities—fed off social stress and fueled antiforeign incidents. Algerians were murdered in southern France and their wives were denied residence permits in the north. Similar actions against Pakistanis in Britain and against Turks in Germany reflected growing hostility to the increased numbers of immigrants, particularly to those who were distinct in race or ethnicity.[75] Resentment was fueled as Europeans realized that with dependents, foreigners were more visible and expensive than laboring groups of single men, who were housed by their employers and kept apart from society. Migrants' children entered school systems and child welfare programs; social welfare programs attended to their families and housing programs attempted to eradicate the shantytowns that had spread on the edge of many a metropolis.

The economic crisis of the early 1970s brought on efforts to stop immigration altogether. In November of 1973, West Germany banned entries of workers from non-EEC countries and within a year several other governments did the same. France banned the entry of dependents as well as of workers, albeit ineffectively. It then offered a repatriation allowance to workers who would give up residence and work permits and take their family home. Germany instituted vocational training programs for some returnees; both the Netherlands and Germany began assistance plans for Yugoslavia and Turkey. No country except Switzerland, however, instituted the stringent measures necessary to keep foreigners out—efficaciously barring the entry of dependents.[76] Northwest European countries did not take such measures for humanitarian reasons; they believed that migrants had certain social rights, including the right to family life. They also realized that the jobs performed by migrant workers (as undesirable as they were) were an important structural part of their labor forces and that migrants, although they did not live well, did provide a market that was important to European economies, especially in the troubled times of the early 1970s.[77]

The attempt to shut off migration, as one shuts off a faucet, was unsuccessful. In fact, attempts to cut off immigration inadvertently encouraged family reunifications because workers, no longer able to risk a visit home, remained in Europe and urged their families to join them. Relatives who intended to settle in Europe arrived on tourist visas and stayed on illegally.[78] The absolute number of foreign residents increased by 13 percent in West Germany between 1974 and 1982, by 33 percent in France (1969–1981), and by 13 percent in Britain (1971–1981). Thus, although migrants did not continue to arrive in net flows that matched those of the 1966–1973 period, their numbers did not diminish.[79]

In addition, deeper demographic, economic, and social forces encouraged migrants to stay on in northwestern Europe. The balance between scarce resources and persistent population expansion in home countries continued to encourage men and women willing to leave for northwestern Europe. Both internalized and social norms in home societies encouraged continued migration.[80]

During the 1980s, it became clear in Europe that foreign nationals were becoming resident minorities rather than migrant laborers who would return home—despite political hostility, racial and ethnic prejudice, poor housing, social problems, and high personal costs to the migrants themselves. Migration streams had been transformed by family reunifications to permanent ethnic minorities. The institutions of immigrant subcultures, from ethnic grocery stores to mosques, studded the cities of western Europe. It is no accident that two of the most comprehensive English-language books on immigrants in Europe published in the 1980s were titled *Guests Come to Stay* and *Here for Good*.[81]

The fall in the northern European birth rate in the 1970s forecasts an ongoing need for foreign workers in the 1990s and beyond.[82] Yet the prospects for the social and economic position of migrant minorities varied considerably from group to group. To illustrate the range of immigrant experiences, I briefly contrast two of the largest migrant groups, Portuguese in France (who numbered 859,400 in 1981) and Turks in the Federal Republic of Germany (who numbered 1,546,300 in 1981).

FROM MIGRANT LABOR TO EEC
PARTNERS: THE PORTUGUESE
IN FRANCE

The continued presence of foreign labor was not problematic in the case of the Portuguese in France, the second largest foreign group in all of northwestern Europe in the early 1980s. Like Spain and Italy, Portugal had a considerable history of emigration, but until the late 1950s, most migration was to Brazil and to Spain—and involved only men.[83] Once Portuguese began to enter France, however, they came in droves. Their numbers were difficult to ascertain because a very large proportion arrived illegally, because the authoritarian Sulazarist regime discouraged male migration, drafted young men into the army, and forbade the emigration of women. In the early 1960s, only 50,000 Portuguese resided in France; this group blossomed to 812,000 by the early 1970s.[84]

Although the Portuguese language is distinct from French and Portuguese migration to France relatively new, this migrant culture was relatively congruent with that of the French. Portuguese shared peasant backgrounds and the tradition of the Catholic faith with many French. Moreover, Portuguese women came to France with the tradition of work and childbearing in the absence of men, who had long been migrant workers on their own. By the mid-1970s, women were as prominent among Portuguese migrants as among the long-standing Spanish and Italian groups; over one in five was a woman, compared with one in 12 Algerians, one in 20 Poles, one in 30 Tunisians or Moroccans, and one in 40 Yugoslavs. Portuguese women were distinctive among migrants in France by their high rates of labor force participation (over 50% were employed in 1974).

These trends carried special importance in the French context, because the sizable numbers of Algerians in France integrated less easily into French culture. The Muslim women from Algeria labored under the tradition of *purdah* and other social and personal restrictions. Only 18 percent of Algerian women worked for pay. And Portuguese women worked at jobs that caused them and their families to interact with the French. Single women worked as domestic servants, married women as cleaning ladies (*femmes de ménage*), and mothers as *concièrges* (porters) in order to take care of their children while they worked. Portuguese women's work resembled that of migrant women in earlier centuries and of Spanish migrant women, but differed from that of Algerian women, who took semiskilled and unskilled industrial jobs.[85]

Their occupational patterns gave Portuguese a relatively integrated position in the French labor force. Similarly, their housing was integrated with French housing.[86] Finally, unlike some Muslim and African immigrants, Portuguese were not singled out for racial and cultural attack. Portugal's entry into the EEC in 1990 assured Portuguese continued residence in France and assimilation into the labor force.

FROM MIGRANT LABOR TO ETHNIC MINORITY: THE TURKS IN GERMANY

Among the immigrant groups from cultures whose religious practices and appearance were distinct from those of northwestern Europeans, the Turks are most important. The story of their migration and residence in Europe is particularly crucial because the largest migration stream in postwar Europe was that from Turkey to Germany.

Conditions in Turkey illustrate the dramatic differences between host and home society that characterized the southeast Mediterranean: unprecedented increase in population, the unseating of rural people, and unemployment. Reduced mortality and high birth rates created intense demographic pressure, tripling the population of Turkey in the 50 years following the founding of the Republic of Turkey in 1923. Simultaneously, changes in agricultural production, transport, and marketing (like earlier changes in Europe) forced sharecroppers and peasant smallholders off the land; these changes caused both shifts in landownership and massive migrations from eastern and central Turkey to the urban centers in the west and south, particularly Istanbul, Ankara, and Izmir. In cities as well as in the countryside, there was considerable unemployment and underemployment, estimated to include a total of 3 million people in the early 1970s. Overpopulation and underemployment created a sharp contrast between Turkish and western European standards of living; in 1973, the per capita income of Turks was $563, while that of West Germans was $3,739 and of French, $3,403.[87]

Likewise, the migration of Kemal Altun, related near the beginning of this chapter, is one of extreme contrasts between his home village and destination—all the more extreme because his home village of Yesilyazi was in the mountains of Kurdistan, which were primitive in comparison with the cities and towns of western and central Turkey. There men and women eked out a living on land that was not their own by caring for sheep and goats and by harvesting wheat and beans. Summers were green; winters were long and idle periods when, aside from rug-weaving, there was no work besides clearing the snow from the earthen roofs threatened with collapse. Without roads, running water, plumbing, or electricity, Yesilyazi was 30 years behind the villages of central Anatolia.[88]

Turkish migration to Europe was first and foremost migration to West Germany. Germany looked to Turkey for workers because the two nations had a history of relatively cordial relations, Turkey was a strategically located ally, and the labor force of Turkey was underemployed. Over 8,700 Turks had entered the country by the end of 1961, when government agreements instituted this migration system—a number that grew to 72,476 in 1965. By 1974, when Kemal Altun arrived in Europe, 1,027,800 Turks resided in West Germany; they were a quarter of the foreign population.[89]

In the late 1960s, German employers began to seek out Turkish women workers. They recruited low-paid female workers for electronics, textile, and garment work; thus Turkish women entered the German labor force, manufacturing car parts, folding factory-made stockings, assembling blue jeans, canning food, and packing candies.[90] Their fathers and husbands in Turkey encouraged them, urging women to take up industrial work abroad so that they could secure positions for their male relatives at a time when jobs for men were in decline. Many single women and married women were able to obtain jobs or dependent visas for their father, husband, or brother. Simultaneously, married men began to bring their wives to Germany. After 1967, about a third of Turkish entrants were women.[91]

When Germany attempted to quell this growing migration in November of 1973 by banning worker immigration from non-EEC countries, nearly a million Turks resided in Germany. Many of these migrants dared not leave the country out of fear they would not be allowed to return, so they sent for their wives and children rather than visit home. So in 1973, the proportion of Turks who entered Germany as workers (rather than as dependents) fell below 50 percent; it never again rose above that figure. Some workers went home, but more stayed and brought in relatives. Since 1975, Turkish families have become part of urban Germany. By 1981, 30 percent of Turks had already been in West Germany for 10 years or more, and an equally large group had been in the country for six to nine years.[92]

The presence of family was made all the more beneficial by the humane German social system. While foreign workers were in demand, Turkey negotiated with West Germany for agreements based on the principle of equal treatment in matters of sickness, accident, unemployment, old-age insurance, and children's allowances.[93] Children's allowances (*Kindergeld*) played a primary role in family reunifications. In 1975, differential rates of children's allowances went into effect for children living outside of West Germany; as a consequence, parents of four children gained 205 DM per month if their children lived in Germany. The response to this measure was completely unforeseen: the immigrant community began a massive importation of family members, so that over 31 percent of the newcomers to Germany in 1975 through 1977 were dependents.[94]

The systems of migration that have joined Turkey to Europe for over 30 years have had vast and varied repercussions on Turkish life, which only can be touched on here. The prolonged absence of adult males has affected family and village life. Just as in seventeenth-century French villages from which men absented themselves for years at a stretch in Spain, the women in Turkish villages have taken greater financial and administrative responsibilities than was previously the norm. In this Muslim country where women did not engage in market activities, many have taken responsibility for remittances sent from their husbands. Although case studies suggest that patterns of authority between husbands and wives have changed little in small villages, apparently the authority of in-laws over married women whose husbands have departed has been diluted.[95]

Questions of gender, sex roles, and social lives are especially painful for Muslim immigrants such as Turkish men and women. In Turkey, unmarried women did not work outside the home, and women wore a scarf (although not a veil) and were covered from head to foot. Hence, women recruited to Germany as workers had not previously worked before outside their home or village; and none of those who lived in employer dormitories (*Heime*) previously had lived apart from their families. In

European cities, married women were separated from their husband's parents, whom they had been raised to rely upon, and instead had to rely on other Turks.[96] Opportunities to work changed (and continue to change) migrants' social norms. Women who were sent into the labor force in advance of their husband or father acted as guides for males who followed. Finally, many women who remained in the European workplace have a more egalitarian and companionate marriage than they would in a Turkish village.[97]

The most intractable difficulty for both Turkish families and German society is the second generation—immigrant's children. In 1980, nearly half the immigrant children aged 16 to 20 in Germany were neither in school, nor in an apprenticeship, nor working at a regular job; two-thirds aged 15 to 19 had no vocational training. Incomplete schooling and training exacerbated the social and linguistic isolation suffered by these children, producing what one scholar dubbed "a generation of bilingual illiterates."[98] Without roots in their parents' home country, the social or linguistic skills of native-born Germans, or training, they became a growing group of unemployed young people with little hope for a place in the labor force. Even those born in Germany remained legal foreigners, excluded from citizenship and suffrage. Turkish children were less integrated into German society than those of Italian, Greek, Spanish, or Yugoslav parentage. Torn between the social customs and authority structures of their family and of the society around them, they experienced the great distance between home and European culture and occupied a particularly vast no-man's land.[99]

In many senses, it is the children who took the brunt of social, political, and economic disaffection. Although their fathers or mothers were recruited as workers, they were untrained and regarded as unemployable, objects of the considerable hostility palpable in the antiforeign politics and neo-fascist political movements that have become more acceptable not only in Germany but in England and France as well.[100] Heinrich Böll's Letta, the heroine of *Group Portrait with Lady* who had a penchant for relationships with the outcasts of postwar society, took up with a Turkish worker at the end of the novel, first published in 1971.[101] As labor migrants, the lone men who could not speak German and were isolated from German neighborhoods and folkways were pariahs in Germany. Yet Turkish families and long-term residents were perhaps as marginalized as male labor migrants. They continue to hold unskilled and semiskilled positions and to earn wages far below average; their rates of unemployment are considerably higher than those of German nationals; and their housing is segregated.[102] Many Turks have neither good prospects in Germany nor plans to return to their homeland. The fact that Turkey has not been allowed to join the EEC at this writing, despite protracted and earnest negotiations, reflects in part a broad unwillingness to freely allow Turks into Europe.

Difficulties for groups like Turks in Germany operate on all levels—from national politics to the most intimate relationships. Rightist political parties like France's National Front in Belgium, Germany, Denmark, Norway, Sweden, and Switzerland espoused the expulsion of foreigners in the 1980s and feed off hostility to foreign migrants—particularly Turks.[103] Muslims' condemnation of *Satanic Verses* by Indian immigrant Salman Rushdie in 1989, a book they consider blasphemous, reflects the profound moral problems faced by those who cross cultural borders as well as the enduring power of religious doctrine to enflame hatred.[104] Within families, the struggles between spouses and between generations over how to live among Europeans and authority within the family destroy harmony and dissolve some families.[105] Finally, the identity of the "guests come to stay" is itself divided; as one child of immigrants put it, "On my birth certificate it is written that I am a 'Turk.' But in the full sense, more correctly, with my thinking, I am not completely a Turk. I do not want to be a German either."[106]

CONCLUSION

The state-sponsored and controlled migrations that have characterized the twentieth century were an outgrowth of the strong national states of the late nineteenth century. Recruitment of foreign workers and the use of prisoner-of-war labor in World War I was followed by both recruitment and exclusion of foreign labor during the interwar years. State policies grew out of labor needs created by capital placement and indigenous demography. Thus, for example, the French recruited Spanish fieldworkers to bolster the labor force during the crucial wine harvests of its southwest in the 1920s. From 1933 to 1945, ethnic and racial hatred dominated the population policies of the Third Reich, which brutally uprooted and murdered millions of Europeans. Since that war, economic self-interest again has guided national migration policies, muted by political necessity in the era of decolonization, when Britain, France, and the Netherlands opened their borders to their former colonials.

As newcomers from East Germany and the Soviet bloc flooded into West Germany in the fall of 1989, it became clear that the long-standing, large-scale migration to the west from central and eastern Europe had been staunched only temporarily by Soviet and cold war policies, and then only for a short period of some 28 years between the building of the Berlin Wall in 1961 and its demise in 1989. In 1990, an estimated 1.3 million people left the dissolving Soviet bloc. Central and eastern Europeans, with proof of German ancestry from early modern colonists, took advantage of German citizenship legislation allowing them to come home to their prosperous, albeit distant, relations in reunited Germany. Others prevailed upon Germany's relatively liberal laws of policial asylum. As in the nineteenth century, Germany once again became a bridge from east to west, and as in the years following World War II, it was swollen with new residents and their dependents—many of whom were ethnic Germans (*Aussiedler*) although their language and culture was not necessarily German. To the south, people from Albania and Yugoslavia pushed into Italy.[107]

As western Europe unites under the EEC rubric, then, it faces the challenge of an enlarged and redefined Europe as the tidy divisions of east and west are called into question. Newcomers from poorer European countries to the east will continue to arrive; history suggests that, barring new political restrictions, they will continue to do so until their homelands can offer employment and material well-being.

Central and eastern Europeans settling in the west may face both hostility and hardship, but less so than the more culturally and ethnically diverse migrants from former colonies and the southern Mediterranean basin. These "guests come to stay" and their children—from former British, Dutch, and French colonies in Asia and Africa and from Turkey—are the unanticipated legacy of postwar policies that exploited the enormous gap in income between Europe and sending nations, while ignoring the historical lesson that circular migration systems evolve into expanding systems of chain migration. With the exception of the Turks, they are also an unanticipated legacy of European imperial politics of past centuries. Some of these migrant groups are at risk of enduring a long period as an underclass marked by underemployment. Those from poor Muslim countries with expanding populations will continue to seek entry into Europe where their presence challenges the hegemony of white Christian culture. Only intense, extensive, and expensive programs of schooling, housing, and training can avoid protracted, explosive social and economic problems.[108] Unfortunately, it is perhaps unlikely that such programs will be initiated in the political and social atmosphere of the 1990s. From this perspective, it is perhaps fortunate that western Europe is no longer a key draw for the global labor force; for Asians, East Africans, and many eastern Mediterranean migrants, "the European honeypot has given way to that of the Middle East."[109]

Within the common market, capital may move with more ease than labor in the coming decades, so that, as industries relocate, migration among the national states of the EEC may become less significant than in the 1970s and 1980s. In any case, citizens of EEC countries migrate freely among nations. Italian, Spanish, Portuguese, and Greek workers move as easily as Dutch or German technicians.

Geographically and historically, the European Economic Community is of long standing, and the movements of workers among nations are reminiscent of old patterns. Where the French once worked in Spain, the Germans in the Netherlands, and the Irish in England, those flows of migrants continue and in some cases reverse. Indeed, this book is a study of the European Economic Community that has existed in reality for over three centuries. In historical perspective, it has suffered an interregnum most recently and most seriously in the wars and hostilities of the 1914–1945 period. From the ashes of those hostilities, however, emerged an impulse for peace and unity that hopefully will outlast the destructive forces of nationalism and ethnic arrogance. The hope for lasting unity in the EEC and peace within the wider Continent lies in Europe's ability to develop and affirm pluralistic societies within its own borders.

Notes

1. PUTTING MIGRATION INTO HISTORY

1. The village of Pradelles and its migrants are compiled from portraits in Abel Poitrineau, *Remues d'hommes: Essai sur les migrations montagnardes en France, 17e–18e siècles* (Paris: Aubier Montaigne, 1983).

2. Poitrineau, *Remues d'hommes*; Robert Schwartz, *Policing the Poor in Eighteenth-Century France* (Chapel Hill: University of North Carolina Press, 1988).

3. For an excellent discussion of this process, see Steve Hochstadt, "Socioeconomic Determinants of Mobility in Nineteenth-Century Germany," forthcoming in *Global Moves, Local Contexts: European Migrants in International Perspective*, ed. D. Hoerder and L. P. Moch.

4. Dirk Hoerder, "An Introduction to Labor Migration in the Atlantic Economies, 1815–1914," in *Labor Migration in the Atlantic Economies: The European and North American Working Classes During the Period of Industrialization*, ed. D. Hoerder (Westport, Conn.: Greenwood Press, 1985); Eva Morawska, "Labor Migrations of Poles in the Atlantic World Economy," *Comparative Studies in Society and History* 31 (1989), 237–72.

5. Paul White and Robert Woods, "The Geographical Impact of Migration," in *The Geographical Impact of Migration*, ed. P. White and R. Woods (London: Longman, 1980), 42.

6. Charles Tilly, "Demographic Origins of the European Proletariat," in *Proletarianization and Family History*, ed. D. Levine (Orlando, Fla.: Academic Press, 1984), 1–85.

7. Charles Tilly, *As Sociology Meets History* (New York: Academic Press, 1981), 164.

8. John Hajnal, "European Marriage Patterns in Perspective," in *Population in History: Essays in Historical Demography*, ed. D. V. Glass and D. E. Eversley (London: Edward Arnold, 1965), 101–43.

9. For expansion and debate on this point, see chapter 2. Alan Sharlin, "Natural Decrease in Early Modern Cities: A Reconsideration," *Past and Present* 79 (1978), 126–38.

10. East of the Elbe River, serfdom was eliminated in 1807 in Prussia, 1848 in Austria, and 1861 in Russia. Serfdom in the west limited the movement of rural people, although it did not stop it altogether; see Zvi Razi, "The Erosion of the Family-Land Bond in the Late Fourteenth and Fifteenth Centuries: A Methodological Note," in *Land, Kinship and Life-Cycle*, ed. R. M. Smith (Cambridge: Cambridge University Press, 1984), 295–304. For mobility in Baltic Europe, see Andrejs Plakans, "Peasant Farmsteads and Households in the Baltic Littoral, 1797," *Comparative Studies in Society and History* 17 (1975), 2–35. For the large-scale state-sponsored moves in eastern Europe before the nineteenth century, see Hans Fenske, "International Migration: Germany in the Eighteenth Century," *Central European History* 13 (1980), 332–47; Dirk Hoerder, "Migration in the Atlantic Economies: Regional European Origins and Worldwide Expansion," forthcoming in *Global Moves, Local Contexts*.

11. Susan Cotts Watkins, *From Provinces into Nations: Demographic Integration in Western Europe, 1870–1960* (Princeton: Princeton University Press, 1991).

12. I use a functional definition of the state, to include states from the principalities and free cities of the Holy Roman Empire in the seventeenth century to the bureaucratic national states of the mid-twentieth century: "Let us define states

as coercion-wielding organizations that are distinct from households and kinship groups and exercise clear priority in some respects over all other organizations within substantial territories. The term therefore includes city-states, empires, theocracies, and many other forms of government, but excludes tribes, lineages, firms, and churches as such." Charles Tilly, *Coercion, Capital, and European States, AD 990–1990* (Cambridge, Mass.: Basil Blackwell, 1990), 1–2.

13. Aristide Zolberg, "International Migration Policies in a Changing World System," in *Human Migration: Patterns and Policies*, ed. W. McNeill and R. Adams (Bloomington: Indiana University Press, 1978), 241–86.

14. For a review of the arguments regarding British enclosure, see Michael Turner, *Enclosures in Britain, 1750–1830* (London: Macmillan, 1984).

15. For a discussion of connections between the state and agrarian regimes, see Catharina Lis and Hugo Soly, *Poverty and Capitalism in Pre-Industrial Europe* (Atlantic Highlands, N.J.: Humanities Press, 1979), 97–104.

16. Tilly, *Coercion, Capital, and European States*, 123.

17. Indeed, in frustration over the loss of montagnard conscripts, the French state timed the conscription lotteries in villages like Pradelles to occur when migrants were at home; Abel Poitrineau, "Aspects de l'émigration temporaire et saisonnière en Auvergne à la fin du XVIIIe siècle et au début du XIXe siècle," *Revue d'histoire moderne et contemporaine* 9 (1962), 41. The unique and massive inquiry into temporary migration in the Napoleonic era is a result of the concern with draft dodging on the part of the French Imperium; the inquiry is discussed below in this chapter and in Jan Lucassen, *Migrant Labour in Europe, 1600–1900* (London: Croom Helm, 1987), 7–17. See also chapter 3.

18. James Scott, *Weapons of the Weak: Everyday Forms of Peasant Resistance* (New Haven, Conn.: Yale University Press, 1985).

19. Kingsley Davis, "The Migrations of Human Populations," *Scientific American* 231, no. 3 (1974), 96.

20. Philip Curtin, "Migration in the Tropical World," in *Immigration Reconsidered*, ed. V. Yans-McLaughlin (New York: Oxford University Press, 1990), 21–36; Dirk Hoerder, "Migration in the Atlantic Economies"; Eric Wolf, *Europe and the People without History* (Berkeley, Calif.: University of California Press, 1982).

21. Eric Hobsbawm, *The Age of Empire, 1875–1914* (New York: Pantheon, 1987), 59.

22. See, for example, Eugene Kulischer, *Europe on the Move: War and Population Changes, 1917–1947* (New York: Columbia University Press, 1948); Michael Marrus, *The Unwanted: European Refugees in the Twentieth Century* (New York: Oxford University Press, 1985); Aristide Zolberg, Astri Suhrke, Sugio Aguayo, *Escape from Violence: Conflict and the Refugee Crisis in the Developing World* (New York: Oxford University Press, 1989).

23. Tilly, *Coercion, Capital, and European States*, 98–99.

24. See, for example, Kertzer and Hogan, "On the Move: Migration in an Italian Community, 1865–1921," *Social Science History* 9 (1985), 1–23.

25. Maurice Garden, "Le bilan démographique des villes: Un système complexe," *Annales de démographie historique* (1982), 267–75.

26. Roger Schofield, "Age-Specific Mobility in an Eighteenth-Century Rural English Parish," *Annales de démographie historique* (1970), 261–74; Emmanuel Todd, "Mobilité géographique et cycle de vie en Artois et en Toscane au XVIIIe siècle," *Annales: Economies, sociétés, civilisations* 30 (1975), 726–44.

27. For a debate concerning the concept of family strategies, see Leslie Page Moch, Nancy Folbre, Daniel Scott Smith, Laurel Cornell, and Louise Tilly, "Family Strategies: A Dialogue," *Historical Methods* 20 (1987), 113–25.

28. For the link between poverty and family disintegration, see Cissie Fair-

childs, *Poverty and Charity in Aix-en-Provence, 1549–1789* (Baltimore: Johns Hopkins University Press, 1976); Olwen Hufton, *The Poor of Eighteenth-Century France, 1750–1789* (Oxford: Clarendon Press, 1974), esp. chap. 12.

29. Although most discussions of migration were gender-blind until the 1980s, specific discussions of migrants themselves were usually limited to men, partly because data on women's work are relatively poor and partly because women were less likely than men to be labor migrants. See, for example, Klaus Bade, ed., *Population, Labour, and Migration in 19th and 20th Century Germany* (Leamington Spa: Berg, 1987); Abel Chatelain, *Les migrants temporaires en France de 1800 à 1914*, 2 vols. (Lille: Université de Lille III, 1977); Dirk Hoerder, "An Introduction to Labor Migration," 3–31; Michael Piore, *Birds of Passage: Migrant Labor and Industrial Societies* (Cambridge: Cambridge University Press, 1979).

30. Caroline Brettell, "Hope and Nostalgia: The Migration of Portuguese Women to Paris" (Ph.D. diss. Brown University, 1978); *idem.*, *We Have Already Cried Many Tears: The Stories of Three Portuguese Migrant Women* (Cambridge, Mass.: Schenkman, 1982); Nancy Foner, "Women, Work, and Migration: Jamaicans in London," *Urban Anthropology* 4 (1975), 229–49; Annie Phizacklea, ed. *One Way Ticket: Migration and Female Labour* (London: Routledge & Kegan Paul, 1983); Rita Simon and Caroline Brettell, eds., *International Migration: The Female Experience* (Totowa, N.J.: Rowman and Allanheld, 1986); special issue of the *International Migration Review* 18, no. 4 (1984).

31. Notable exceptions include Peter Clark, "Migration in England during the Late Seventeenth and Early Eighteenth Centuries," *Past and Present* 83 (1979), 57–90; William Sewell, Jr., *Structure and Mobility: The Men and Women of Marseille* (Cambridge: Cambridge University Press, 1985); Emmanuel Todd, "Mobilité géographique."

32. For a discussion of this paradox, see Donna Gabaccia, "Women of the Mass Migrations: From Minority to Majority, 1820–1930," forthcoming in *Global Moves, Local Contexts*.

33. See for example Poitrineau, *Remues d'hommes*.

34. See, for example, Gay Gullickson, *Spinners and Weavers of Auffay: Rural Industry and the Sexual Division of Labor in a French Village, 1750–1850* (Cambridge: Cambridge University Press, 1986).

35. Abel Chatelain, "Migrations et domesticité féminine urbaine en France, XVIIIe siècle—XXe siècle," *Revue d'histoire économique et sociale* 47 (1969), 506–28; Rachel Fuchs and Leslie Page Moch, "Pregnant, Single, and Far from Home: Migrant Women in Nineteenth-Century Paris," *American Historical Review* 95 (1990), 1007–31.

36. Donna Gabaccia, "Women of the Mass Migrations"; Dirk Hoerder, "From Migrants to Immigrants: Acculturation in a Societal Framework," forthcoming in *Global Moves, Local Contexts*. Marie Hall Ets, *Rosa* (Minneapolis, Minn.: University of Minnesota Press, 1970) is the moving biography of an Italian immigrant woman who came to the United States specifically to provide domestic labor for her husband and his coworkers in a Missouri mining town.

37. A study of this issue is found in Fuchs and Moch, "Pregnant, Single, and Far from Home"; for a more general review, see Mirjana Morokvasic, "Birds of Passage Are also Women . . . ," *International Migration Review* 18 (1984), 896–99.

38. There is a large body of information on such concepts, among which the most useful may be Thorsten Hägerstrand, "Migration and Area," *Lund Studies in Geography*, ser. B, 13 (1957), 27–158.

39. Sune Åkerman, "Towards an Understanding of Emigrational Processes," in *Human Migration: Patterns and Policies*, ed. W. H. McNeill and R. Adams (Bloomington, Ind.: Indiana University Press, 1978), 287–306; for a theoretical perspec-

tive, see Charles Tilly, "Migration in Modern European History," in *Human Migration*, 50–55.

40. David Kertzer and Dennis Hogan, "On the Move," 19–20.

41. James Jackson, Jr., and Leslie Page Moch, "Migration and the Social History of Modern Europe," *Historical Methods* 22 (1989), 27–36.

42. Charles Tilly, "Migration in Modern European History," 50–55.

43. Philip Curtin, "Migration in the Tropical World," 27; David Eltis estimates that about 8 million Africans arrived in the Americas before 1820, compared with some 2.3 million Europeans, in "Free and Coerced Transatlantic Migrations: Some Comparisons," *American Historical Review* 88 (1983), 252–55. For coerced and colonizing migrations, see William Peterson, *Population*, 3rd. ed. (New York: Macmillan, 1975), 317–26; Walter Nugent, "Frontiers and Empires in the Late Nineteenth Century," *The Western Historical Quarterly* 20 (1989), 395–406; Charles Tilly, "Transplanted Networks," in *Immigration Reconsidered*, 88–90.

44. Jan de Vries, *European Urbanization, 1500–1800* (Cambridge, Mass.: Harvard University Press, 1984), 200.

45. Arthur Ravenstein, "The Laws of Migration," *Journal of the Royal Statistical Society* 48 (1885), 167–235, and 52 (1889), 241–305. ([Reprint edition] New York: Arno Press, 1976).

46. This inquiry is in the French National Archives, series F.20, 434–35, Renseignements fournis par les préfets relative à l'émigration et à l'immigration d'ouvriers, 1807–1812.

47. Arthur Ravenstein, "The Laws of Migration"; for a survey of subsequent work, see James Jackson, Jr., and Leslie Page Moch, "Migration and the Social History of Modern Europe," 27–36; Everett Lee, "A Theory of Migration," *Demography* 31 (1966), 47–57; R. Paul Shaw, *Migration: Theory and Fact* (Philadelphia: Regional Science Research Institute, 1975); White and Woods, "The Geographical Impact of Migration."

48. Steve Hochstadt, "Migration and Industrialization in Germany," *Social Science History* 5 (1981), 445–46; *idem.*, "Migration in Germany: An Historical Study" (Ph.D. diss., Department of History, Brown University, 1983); Steve Hochstadt and James Jackson, Jr., " 'New' Sources for the Study of Migration in Early Nineteenth-Century Germany," *Historical Social Research/Historische Sozialforschung* 31 (1984), 85–92; James Jackson, Jr., "*Alltagsgeschichte*, Social Science History and the Study of Migration in Nineteenth-Century Germany," *Central European History* 23 (1990), 242–63; *idem.*, "Migration and Urbanization in the Ruhr Valley, 1850–1900" (Ph.D. diss., Department of History, University of Minnesota); *idem.*, "Migration in Duisburg, 1867–1890: Occupational and Familial Contexts," *Journal of Urban History* 8 (1982), 235–70.

49. Sydney Goldstein, "The Extent of Repeated Migration: An Analysis Based on the Danish Population Register," *Journal of the American Statistical Association* 59 (1964), 1121–32; Myron Gutmann and Etienne van de Walle, "New Sources for Social and Demographic History: The Belgian Population Registers," *Social Science History* 2 (1978), 121–43; Ann-Sofie Kälvemark, "The Country That Kept Track of Its Population: Methodological Aspects of Swedish Population Records," in *Time, Space and Man: Essays on Microdemography*, edited by J. Sundin and E. Soderlund (Atlantic Highlands, N.J.: Humanities Press, 1979), 221–43.

50. George Alter, *Family and the Female Life Course: The Women of Verviers, Belgium, 1849–1880* (Madison: University of Wisconsin Press, 1988); Dennis Hogan and David Kertzer, "Longitudinal Methods for Historical Migration Research," *Historical Methods* 18 (1985), 20–30; David Kertzer and Dennis Hogan, "On the Move," 1–23.

51. Alter, *Family and the Female Life Course*; Hochstadt and Jackson, " 'New' Sources"; Hogan and Kertzer, "Longitudinal Methods."

52. Hogan and Kertzer's study covers through 1921; interestingly, it reveals no significant break in local migration patterns with World War I; see Kertzer and Hogan, "On the Move." Judging from Maurizio Gribaudi's study of Turin, work from registers of the twentieth century promises to be controversial and path-breaking; see Maurizio Gribaudi, *Itinéraires ouvriers: Espaces et groupes sociaux à Turin au début du XXe siècle* (Paris: Editions de l'Ecole des Hautes Etudes en Sciences Sociales, 1987).

53. Myron Gutmann, *Toward the Modern Economy: Early Industry in Europe, 1500–1800* (New York: Knopf, 1988); Steve Hochstadt, "Migration in Preindustrial Germany," *Central European History* 16 (1983), 195–224; Lucassen, *Migrant Labour in Europe*; David Souden, "Movers and Stayers in Family Reconstitution Populations, 1660–1780," *Local Population Studies* 33 (1984), 11–28.

54. De Vries, *European Urbanization*, 200; Tilly, "Demographic Origins of the European Proletariat," 1–85.

55. De Vries, *European Urbanization*; Gutmann, *Toward the Modern Economy*. The magisterial reconstruction by E. Anthony Wrigley and Roger Schofield, *The Population History of England, 1541–1871: A Reconstruction* (Cambridge, Mass.: Harvard University Press, 1981), is least useful for this study because it seeks to reconstruct national population change and is thus unconcerned with internal migrations; the authors consider London and market towns that attract migrants a distraction because they are "very unlike the country at large" (48). Net emigration, inferred from estimates of missing deaths, is estimated in the study only out of concern for calculating rates of fertility, nuptiality, and mortality (219–28).

56. Christopher Johnson, *The Life and Death of Industrial Languedoc* (Oxford: Oxford University Press, forthcoming); Michael Hanagan, *Nascent Proletarians: Class Formation in Post-Revolutionary France* (Oxford: Basil Blackwell, 1989); Donald Reid, *The Miners of Decazeville: A Genealogy of Deindustrialization* (Cambridge, Mass.: Harvard University Press, 1985); Charles Tilly, "Flows of Capital and Forms of Industry in Europe, 1500–1900," *Theory and Society* 12 (1983), 123–42.

2. MIGRATION IN PREINDUSTRIAL EUROPE

1. Ann Kussmaul, *Servants in Husbandry in Early Modern England* (Cambridge: Cambridge University Press, 1981), 85–93; see also Joseph Mayett, *The Autobiography of Joseph Mayett of Quainton, 1783–1839* (Aylesbury: Buckinghamshire Record Society, 1986).

2. Jan de Vries, *European Urbanization, 1500–1800* (Cambridge, Mass.: Harvard University Press, 1984), 234.

3. Peter Clark, "Migration in England during the Late Seventeenth and Early Eighteenth Centuries," *Past and Present* 83 (1979), 64–67, 72; this information is from witness biographies in English ecclesiastical courts; unfortunately, there is no comparable information from other western European countries.

4. Jean-Pierre Poussou, "Mobilité et migrations," in *Histoire de la population française*, ed. J. Dupaquier, vol. 2, *De la renaissance à 1789* (Paris: Presses Universitaires de France, 1988), 98–137.

5. In the past, the term "preindustrial" usually referred to the period before the development of mechanized industry; this designation is no longer so appropriate, since the significance of large-scale rural industry before mechanization, often called "protoindustry," became apparent to scholars in the 1970s and 1980s.

198 / Notes to pages 24–27

However, it is difficult to focus on preindustrial areas, because the artisanal production of goods for local consumption on a small scale was ubiquitous in rural areas; moreover, larger-scale export production dates far back in some regions and grew unevenly, so rural industry is difficult to trace.

6. For comments regarding terminology and periodization, see Myron Gutmann, *Toward the Modern Economy: Early Industry in Europe, 1500–1800* (New York: Knopf, 1988), 6–7.

7. De Vries, *European Urbanization*, 69–77, Appendix 1; de Vries refers to cities of under 40,000, 257–58. Eric Hobsbawm, "The Overall Crisis of the European Economy in the Seventeenth Century," *Past and Present* 5 (1954), 33–53; Gutmann, *Toward the Modern Economy*, 90–111; Emmanuel Le Roi Ladurie, *Peasants of Languedoc* (Urbana: University of Illinois Press, 1974), 290–93; Roger Mols, "Population in Europe, 1500–1700," in *The Fontana Economic History of Europe*, vol. 2, *The Sixteenth and Seventeenth Centuries* (London: Fontana, 1974), 7–82.

8. Paul Hohenberg and Lynn Lees, *The Making of Urban Europe, 1000–1950* (Cambridge, Mass.: Harvard University Press, 1985), 113–20.

9. Pierre Goubert, *Louis XIV and Twenty Million Frenchmen* (New York: Random House, 1966), 179–83, 211–17.

10. Pierre Goubert, *Beauvais et le Beauvaisis de 1600 à 1730* (Paris: SEVPEN, 1960), 592–93.

11. For an evocative reminder of the small scale of life in preindustrial Europe, see Peter Laslett, *The World We Have Lost: England before the Industrial Age*, 3d ed. (New York: Scribner's, 1983), chap. 3.

12. De Vries, *European Urbanization*, 74, Appendix 1; Mols, "Population in Europe," 39–40.

13. Olwen Hufton, *The Poor of Eighteenth-Century France, 1750–1789* (Oxford: Clarendon Press, 1974), 72.

14. For a discussion of the constraints of serfdom, see Jerome Blum, *The End of the Old Order in Europe* (Princeton: Princeton University Press, 1978); Andrejs Plakans, "Seigneurial Authority and Peasant Family Life," *Journal of Interdisciplinary History* 6 (1975), 638–40; *idem.*, "Peasant Farmsteads and Households in the Baltic Littoral, 1797," *Comparative Studies in Society and History* 17 (1975), 9.

15. Jean-Pierre Kintz, "La Mobilité humaine en Alsace. Essai de présentation statistique, XIVe-XVIIIe siècles," *Annales de démographie historique* (1970), 168–69; Olivier Zeller, *Les Recensements lyonnais de 1597 et 1636: Démographie historique et géographie sociale* (Lyon: Presses Universitaires de Lyon, 1983), 235–36.

16. Edward I expelled Jews from England in 1290; subsequent persecutions of Jews were particularly virulent following outbreaks of the bubonic plague, but all fundamentally sought justification in Christians' labeling Jews as the killers of Christ. John Edwards, *The Jews in Christian Europe, 1400–1700* (London: Routledge, 1988), 11, 27–29. Sources for the history of European Jews include Salo Wittmayer Baron, *A Social and Religious History of the Jews*, 18 vols., 2nd, revised ed. (New York: Columbia University Press and Jewish Publication Society of America, 1952–); Jonathan Israel, *European Jewry in the Age of Mercantilism, 1550–1750* (Oxford: Clarendon Press, 1985); Yves Lequin, *La mosaïque France: Histoire des étrangers et de l'immigration* (Paris: Larousse, 1988).

17. Edwards, *The Jews in Christian Europe*, 11–12, 26. Many Spanish Jews also went to North Africa and to the eastern Mediterranean; generally, Italian Jews went to Balkan territories and German Jews to Poland. See also Israel, *European Jewry*, 23–28.

18. Edwards, *The Jews in Christian Europe*, 12, 104–13.

19. Edwards, *The Jews in Christian Europe*, 114–19.

20. Edwards, *The Jews in Christian Europe*, 93–103, 110.

21. E. Anthony Wrigley and Roger Schofield, *The Population History of England, 1541–1871: A Reconstruction* (Cambridge, Mass.: Harvard University Press, 1981), 219–28.

22. English Protestants also took refuge in the Netherlands and some Huguenots went to North America. Jon Butler, *The Huguenots in America: A Refugee People in New World Society* (Cambridge, Mass.: Harvard University Press, 1983); Carlo Cipolla, *Before the Industrial Revolution: European Society and Economy* (New York: Norton, 1980), 191–92; Cees Cruson, "French Huguenot Refugees in Seventeenth-Century Amsterdam" (Erasmus Universiteit Rotterdam, 1984); Kintz, "La mobilité humaine en Alsace"; Gerald Soliday, *A Community in Conflict: Frankfurt Society in the Seventeenth and Early Eighteenth Centuries* (Hanover, N.H.: University Press of New England, 1974), 35; Zeller, *Les Recensements lyonnais de 1597 et 1636*, 231–35.

23. Christopher Friedrichs, *Urban Society in an Age of War: Nördlingen, 1580–1720* (Princeton: Princeton University Press, 1979), chap. 1; Sigfrid Steinberg, *The Thirty Years' War and the Conflict for European Hegemony, 1600–1660* (London: E. Arnold, 1966); Günther Franz provides the best analyses of the effect of the Thirty Years' War on the population, *Der 30jK und das deutsche volk* (Jena, 1940); he is cited in Theodore Rabb, "The Effects of the Thirty Years' War on the German Economy," *The Journal of Modern History* 34 (1962), 47–49. Great power battle deaths alone are estimated at 2,071,000 for the Thirty Years' War and at 1,251,000 for the War of the Spanish Succession; Charles Tilly, *Coercion, Capital, and European States, AD 990–1990* (Cambridge, Mass.: Basil Blackwell, 1990), 165–66.

24. The port of Seville, for example, saw the arrival of 16 million kilograms of silver and 185,000 kilograms of gold between 1503 and 1650. Poitrineau, *Les Espagnols de l'Auvergne et du Limousin du XVIIIe au XIXe siècle* (Aurillac: Malroux-Mazel, 1985), 19.

25. Poitrineau, *Les Espagnols de l'Auvergne et du Limousin*, 72, 198.

26. Cruson, "French Huguenot Refugees."

27. Simon Hart, "Gens de mer à Amsterdam au XVIIe siècle," *Annales de démographie historique* (1974), 145–63; *idem.*, "Geschrift en getal. Onderzoek naar samenstelling van de bevolking van Amsterdam in de 17e en 18e eeuw op grond van gegevens over migratie, huwelijk beroep en alfabetisme," in *Geschrift en getal* (Dordrecht, 1976), 115–81, cited in de Vries, *European Urbanization*, 185.

28. Jan Lucassen, *Migrant Labour in Europe, 1600–1900* (London: Croom Helm, 1987), 148–53.

29. Poitrineau, *Les Espagnols de l'Auvergne et du Limousin*, 15.

30. Clark, "Migration in England."

31. Asian women married before age 21 and in some regions at a considerably earlier age. For an introduction to the vast literature on European family, see Richard Evans and W. R. Lee, eds., *The German Family: Essays on the Social History of the Family in Nineteenth- and Twentieth-Century Germany* (London: Croom Helm, 1981); John Hajnal, "Age at Marriage and Proportions Marrying," *Population Studies* 7 (1953), 111–36; *idem.* "Two Kinds of Preindustrial Household Formation Systems," in *Family Forms in Historic Europe*, ed. R. Wall and P. Laslett (Cambridge: Cambridge University Press, 1983), 65–104; Tamara Hareven, "The History of the Family and the Complexity of Social Change," *American Historical Review* 96 (1991), 95–124; Peter Laslett and Richard Wall, eds., *Household and Family in Past Time* (Cambridge: Cambridge University Press, 1972); Michael Mitterauer and Reinhard Sieder, *The European Family: Patriarchy to Partnership from the Middle Ages to the Present* (Chicago: University of Chicago Press, 1977); Lawrence Stone, *The Family, Sex and Marriage in England: 1500–1800* (London: Weidenfeld and Nicolson, 1977); Louise Tilly and Miriam Cohen, "Does the Family Have a History? A Review of Theory and Practice in Family History," *Social Science History* 6 (1982), 131–79;

Susan Watkins, ed., *Journal of Family History* 9, no. 4 (1984), special issue on spinsterhood.

32. Pierre Goubert, "Family and Province: A Contribution to the Knowledge of Family Structures in Early Modern France," *Journal of Family History* 2 (1977), 179–95; Hans Medick, "The Proto-industrial Family Economy: The Structural Function of Household and Family during the Transition from Peasant Society to Industrial Capitalism," *Social History* 3 (1976), 291–315; Mitterauer and Sieder, *The European Family*; Laslett and Wall, *Household and Family in Past Time*; Lutz Berkner, "The Stem Family and the Developmental Cycle of the Peasant Household: An Eighteenth-Century Austrian Example," *American Historical Review* 77 (1972), 398–418.

33. David Herlihy, "Family," *American Historical Review* 96 (1991), 1–16; Mitterauer and Sieder, *The European Family*, 5–10; Laslett, *The World We Have Lost*, 2; Emmanuel Le Roy Ladurie, *Montaillou: The Promised Land of Error* (New York: Braziller, 1978).

34. Leslie Page Moch, "The Family and Migration: News from the French," *Journal of Family History* 11 (1986), 193–203.

35. John Hajnal, "Two Kinds of Pre-industrial Household Formation Systems," 65–104.

36. Alan Macfarlane, "The Myth of the Peasantry: Family and Economy in a Northern Parish," in *Land, Kinship and Life-Cycle* (Cambridge: Cambridge University Press, 1984), 343; Roger Schofield, "Age-Specific Mobility in an Eighteenth-Century Rural English Parish," *Annales de démographie historique* (1970), 261–74.

37. Kussmaul, *Servants in Husbandry*, 5.

38. Goubert, "Family and Province," 180, 185, 187.

39. Kussmaul, *Servants in Husbandry*, 49–59; Emmanuel Todd, "Mobilité géographique et cycle de vie en Artois et en Toscane au XVIIIe siècle," *Annales: E.S.C.* 30 (1975), 729–30.

40. Hajnal, "Two Kinds of Pre-Industrial Household Formation Systems," 95–97; Alan Macfarlane, *The Family Life of Ralph Josselin. A Seventeenth-Century Clergyman: An Essay in Historical Anthropology* (Cambridge: Cambridge University Press, 1970), 343; Macfarlane, "The Myth of the Peasantry," 343; Richard Wall, "The Age of Leaving Home," *Journal of Family History* 3 (1978), 181–202.

41. Hajnal, "Two Kinds of Pre-Industrial Household Formation Systems," 94; Kussmaul, *Servants in Husbandry*, 4, 19, 34; Schofield, "Age-Specific Mobility," 261–74; Keith D. M. Snell, *Annals of the Labouring Poor: Social Change and Agrarian England, 1660–1900* (Cambridge: Cambridge University Press, 1985), chap. 2.

42. Kussmaul, *Servants in Husbandry*, 54.

43. Ann Kussmaul, "The Ambiguous Mobility of Farm Servants," *Economic History Review* 34 (1981), 225; this precious data is from a Lancashire farm record. There is very little comparable information for farm servants in early modern France aside from Todd, "Mobilité géographique." A more sedentary variation on service work prevailed in central Europe, where the young were often relatives who spent years in the house of an uncle, for example, before taking on more mobile service work in late adolescence. Mitterauer and Sieder, *The European Family*, xi, chap. 5, esp. 98–99; Richard Wall suggests that kin arrangements may have also been made in England in "The Age of Leaving Home."

44. Lawrence Stone, "Family History in the 1980s," *Journal of Interdisciplinary History* 12 (1981), 62–63; Poussou, "Mobilité et migrations," 105; Poussou notes, however, that there has been no study of farm servants in France, 124.

45. Kussmaul, *Servants in Husbandry*, 85–92.

46. Macfarlane, "The Myth of the Peasantry," 209; Kussmaul, *Servants in Husbandry*, 77; Wall, "The Age of Leaving Home."

47. Kussmaul, *Servants in Husbandry*, 77; emphasis in the original.

48. Emmanuel Todd, *The Explanation of Ideology: Family Structures and Social Systems* (London: Basil Blackwell, 1985), 19–20.

49. Goubert, *Beauvais et le Beauvaisis de 1600 à 1730*, 65–67.

50. See, for example, Poussou, "Mobilité et migrations," 102. Also, David Sabean, "Household Formation and Geographical Mobility: A Family Register Study for a Württemberg Village, 1760–1900," *Annales de démographie historique* (1970), 275–94.

51. The parish, Banize, was analyzed by Marie-Annie Moulin in *Les maçons de la Haute-Marche au XVIIIe siècle* (Clermont-Ferrand: Institut d'Etudes du Massif Central, 1986), 273–74, and presented in Poussou, "Mobilité et migrations," 101–102, 106–107.

52. For a study of the effects of legal and economic change on family inheritance behavior, see Margaret Darrow, *Revolution in the House: Family, Class and Inheritance in Southern France, 1775–1825* (Princeton: Princeton University Press, 1989); for one analysis of household and inheritance systems, see Emmanuel Le Roi Ladurie, "Système de la coutume. Structures familiales et coutume d'héritage en France au XVIe siècle." *Annales: E.S.C.* 27 (1972), 825–46.

53. Pierre Goubert, "Family and Province," 179–95; Lutz Berkner and Franklin Mendels, "Inheritance Systems, Family Structure, and Demographic Patterns in Western Europe, 1700–1900," in *Historical Studies of Changing Fertility* (Princeton: Princeton University Press, 1978), 209–223.

54. Laurence Fontaine, "Solidarités familiales et logiques migratoires en pays de montagne à l'époque moderne," *Annales: E.S.C.* 45 (1990), 1433–50; Macfarlane, "The Myth of the Peasantry," 346–47.

55. Extended household did not include married daughters, who usually lived with their spouse's family; in the case of Italian sharecroppers, young women also left before marriage to work as servants. Todd, "Mobilité géographique."

56. Goubert, "Family and Province," 190.

57. Goubert, "Family and Province," 179–95, esp. 190; Louise Tilly and Joan Scott, *Women, Work, and Family* (New York: Holt, Rinehart and Winston, 1978), chaps. 1 and 2.

58. Poussou, "Mobilité et migrations," 103.

59. Poussou, "Mobilité et migrations."

60. Natalie Davis, *The Return of Martin Guerre* (Cambridge, Mass.: Harvard University Press, 1983), 6–7.

61. Macfarlane, "The Myth of the Peasantry," 343.

62. For these contrasting models, see Clark, "Migration in England"; Macfarlane, "The Myth of the Peasantry"; Poussou, "Migrations et mobilité."

63. David Gaunt, "Pre-industrial Economy and Population Structure: Elements of Variance in Early Modern Sweden," *Scandinavian Journal of History* 2 (1977), 194–98.

64. Gaunt, "Pre-industrial Economy and Population Structure," 196.

65. Todd, "Mobilité géographique," 733.

66. Clark, "Migration in England," 64–67.

67. Macfarlane, "The Myth of the Peasantry," 209–10.

68. Davis, *The Return of Martin Guerre*; the film *Le retour de Martin Guerre*, directed by Daniel Vigne, was released in 1984.

69. Davis, *The Return of Martin Guerre*, 7–26.

70. Hart, "Les Gens de mer à Amsterdam," 145–63; Steve Hochstadt, "Migration in Preindustrial Germany," *Central European History* 16 (1983), 195–224; Jean Jacquart, *La crise rurale en Ile-de-France, 1550–1670* (Paris: Colin, 1974), 262–63, 486, 493, 741–43; Lucassen, *Migrant Labour in Europe*, chap. 6, 166.

71. Peat was cut or scooped out of the ground (depending on its relation to the

water table) and used for fuel in households and industry; for example, it fueled the brick ovens that created the building materials for Dutch cities. Madder is a plant whose root was a source of red dye until the creation of chemical dyes. See Lucassen, *Migrant Labour in Europe*, chap. 4.

72. In 1650, however, the Dutch economy was no longer in a state of expansion; Jan de Vries, *The Economy of Europe in an Age of Crisis, 1600–1750* (Cambridge: Cambridge University Press, 1976).

73. Lucassen, *Migrant Labour in Europe*, 53.

74. An acre is 2.47 hectares.

75. Lucassen, *Migrant Labour in Europe*, 97–99, 144.

76. Lucassen, *Migrant Labour in Europe*, 149–53.

77. Walter Kamphoefner, *The Westfalians: From Germany to Missouri* (Princeton: Princeton University Press, 1987); Lucassen, *Migrant Labour in Europe*, chap. 9.

78. Hans's words are from *Romanzieke Juffer* by Pieter Bernagie, cited by Lucassen, *Migrant Labour in Europe*, 44–45.

79. Slenderhinke's words are from Pieter Langendijk's *De zwester*, cited by Lucassen, *Migrant Labour in Europe*, 47.

80. Lucassen, *Migrant Labour in Europe*, 47–49.

81. This line is from the poetry of Lucas Rotgans published in 1715, cited in Lucassen, *Migrant Labour in Europe*, 54.

82. Lucassen, *Migrant Labour in Europe*, 54–55.

83. This characteristic of migrants to the present day was particularly noted by Michael Piore, *Birds of Passage: Migrant Labor and Industrial Societies* (Cambridge: Cambridge University Press, 1979).

84. Lucassen, *Migrant Labour in Europe*, 45, 48, 97.

85. Peter Clark and Paul Slack, *English Towns in Transition, 1500–1700* (London: Oxford University Press, 1974), 119; Maurice Garden, "Le Bilan démographique des villes: Un système complexe," *Annales de démographie historique* (1982), 267–75; Hochstadt, "Migration in Preindustrial Germany"; Michel Terrisse, "Méthode de recherches démographiques en milieu urbain ancien (XVIIe–XVIIIe)," *Annales de démographie historique* (1974), 249–62.

86. Jean-Pierre Bardet, *Rouen aux XVIIe et XVIIIe siècles: Les mutations d'un espace social*, 2 vols. (Paris: Société d'Edition d'Enseignement Supérieur, 1983), 108; Clark and Slack, *English Towns in Transition*, 65; Viven Brodsky Elliot, "Single Women in the London Marriage Market: Age, Status and Mobility," in *Marriage and Society*, ed. R. Outhwaite (London: Europa Publications, 1981), 84; Hochstadt, "Migration in Preindustrial Germany," 202–203, 208–209; Emmanuel Le Roi Ladurie, *Histoire de la France urbaine*, vol. 3, *La ville classique* (Paris: Seuil, 1981), 53, 56, 303; Steve Rappaport, *Worlds within Worlds: Structures of Life in Sixteenth-Century London* (Cambridge: Cambridge University Press, 1989), 76, 79.

87. This is partly because painstaking family reconstitutions are hardly feasible for large populations, and they yield uncertain information about migration. There have been partial family reconstitutions for some urban groups and some parishes. The most useful for the study of migration is Bardet, *Rouen aux XVIIe et XVIIIe siècles*. The backward projection techniques developed for measuring fertility and nuptiality have been used in only one study to assess net migration. This study of Verviers region of Belgium will be discussed in chapter 3; Myron Gutmann, *Toward the Modern Economy*.

88. For a survey of English towns on this question, see Clark and Slack, *English Towns in Transition*, 85–91.

89. Clark and Slack, *English Towns in Transition*, 85–91; de Vries, *European Urbanization*, 195; E. Anthony Wrigley and Roger Schofield, *The Population History of*

England, 1541–1871: A Reconstruction (Cambridge, Mass.: Harvard University Press, 1981), Tables 6.4 and A3.1.

90. Christopher Friedrichs, *Urban Society in an Age of War*, 35–52.

91. De Vries, *European Urbanization*, 199–231.

92. Goubert, *Beauvais et les Beauvaisis*, 66.

93. De Vries, *European Urbanization*, 206, 213; Emmanuel Le Roy Ladurie estimates the proportion of departures from rural areas at 10 to 15 percent, *Histoire de la France rurale*. Vol. 2, *L'âge classique des paysans, 1340–1789* (Paris: Seuil, 1975), 282–83.

94. Allan Sharlin, "Natural Decrease in Early Modern Cities: A Reconsideration," *Past and Present* 79 (1978), 126–38.

95. Elliot, "Single Women in the London Marriage Market," 84–90; de Vries, *European Urbanization*, 190–95.

96. See, for example, Pierre Deyon, *Amiens, capitals provinciale. Etude sur la société urbaine au 17e siècle* (Paris: Mouton, 1967), 39–41; de Vries, *European Urbanization*, 193, 197–98.

97. A. M. van der Woude, "Population Developments in the Northern Netherlands (1500–1800) and the Validity of the 'Urban Graveyard' Effect," *Annales de démographie historique* (1982), 55–75. See also David Eversley, "Population, Economy and Society," in *Population in History: Essays in Historical Demography*, ed. D. V. Glass and D. E. C. Eversley (London: Edward Arnold, 1965), 53.

98. De Vries, *European Urbanization*, chap. 10.

99. Robert Darnton, "Workers Revolt: The Great Cat Massacre of the Rue Saint-Séverin," in *The Great Cat Massacre and Other Episodes in French Cultural History* (New York: Basic Books, 1984), 74–104; Peter Laslett, *The World We Have Lost*, 1–4.

100. De Vries, *European Urbanization*, 178; Roger Mols, *Introduction à la démographie historique des villes d'Europe du XIVe au XVIIIe siècle*, vol. 2 (Louvain: Publications Universitaires, 1955), 183–91, 195–99, 218–22.

101. Jean Pierre Poussou, *Bordeaux et le sud-ouest au XVIIIe siècle* (Paris: Editions de l'Ecole des Hautes Etudes en Sciences Sociales, 1983), chap. 3, 63–101; Poussou, "Mobilité et migrations," 116–18; Leslie Page Moch, "The Importance of Mundane Movements: Small Towns, Nearby Places and Individual Itineraries in the History of Migration," in *Migrants in Modern France: Population Mobility in the Later 19th and 20th Centuries*, ed. P. E. Ogden and P. E. White (London: Unwin Hyman, 1989), 97–117.

102. For Norwich apprentices, see Penelope Corfield, "A Provincial Capital in the Late Seventeenth Century: The Case of Norwich," in *The Early Modern Town*, ed. P. Clark (London: Longman, 1976), 240. Apprenticeships records are widely used in studies of the early modern city. See, for example, Maurice Garden, *Lyon et les Lyonnais au XVIIIe siècle* (Paris: Belles Lettres, 1970).

103. Clark, "Migration in England," 64–67.

104. Corfield, "A Provincial Capital," 240; Deyon, *Amiens, capitale provinciale*, 350–52.

105. For Britain, see Clark and Slack, *English Towns in Transition*, 21, 57, 64.

106. Catharina Lis and Hugo Soly, *Poverty and Capitalism in Pre-Industrial Europe* (Atlantic Highlands, N.J.: Humanities Press, 1979), chap. 4.

107. Corfield, "A Provincial Capital," 238.

108. Clark, "Migration in England," 68; because Clark's study is based on court witness biographies, it does not include beggars and vagrants, who were England's long-distance "subsistence migrants." Josef Konvitz, "Does the Century 1650–1750 Constitute a Period in Urban History? The French Evidence Reviewed,"

Journal of Urban History 14 (1988), 430–42; *idem., The Urban Millennium* (Carbondale, Ill.: Southern Illinois University Press, 1985), chap. 3.

109. Martin Lister, *A Journey to Paris in the Year 1698*, ed. Raymond Stearns (London: Johnson, 1699; Urbana, Ill.: University of Illinois Press, 1967), 19–20.

110. Poussou, "Mobilité et migrations," 107; see Moulin, *Les maçons de la Haute-Marche au XVIIIe siècle*, 15–17.

111. Clark, "Migration in England"; Clark and Slack, *English Towns in Transition*, 33, 42–43; Hochstadt, "Migration in Preindustrial Germany," 199–201; Bernard Petit, "Démographie d'une ville en gestion: Versailles sous Louis XIV," *Annales de démographie historique* (1977), 49–84; Poussou "Mobilité et migrations," 116–22.

112. For example, a backward projection technique is able to measure the role of net migration in changes in city size, but is unable to estimate gross migration flows; Gutmann, *Toward the Modern Economy*, chap. 5.

113. Clark, "Migration in England," 64–68; Allan Sharlin and John Sammis "Migration and Urban Population in Pre-Industrial Europe: Würzburg in the Late Seventeenth and Early Eighteenth Centuries" (University of California, Berkeley, 1982), cited by Hochstadt, "Migration in Preindustrial Germany," 204. I would like to thank Steve Hochstadt for sending me Sharlin and Sammis's paper.

114. Exact figures for out-migration of families are only given for after 1750; these will be reported in chapter 3; Bardet, *Rouen aux XVIIe et XVIIIe siècles*, vol. 1, 377; Hochstadt, "Migration in Preindustrial Germany," 203–205; Poussou, "Mobilité et migrations," 120.

115. For the role that being orphaned may have played in the decision to remain in the city, see Elliot, "Single Women in the London Marriage Market," 90–91.

116. For insight into subsistence migration, see Margaret Spufford, *Contrasting Communities: English Villagers in the Sixteenth and Seventeenth Centuries* (London: Cambridge University Press, 1974); Hufton, *The Poor of Eighteenth-Century France*, chaps. 3, 8; Lis and Soly, *Poverty and Capitalism in Pre-Industrial Europe*, chap. 4.

117. Corfield, "A Provincial Capital," 239, 240, 245, 252–54, 257.

118. More important cities were Lyon with 97,000, Marseille with 75,000, Rouen with 64,000, Bordeaux with 50,000, and Nantes with 42,000; Amiens, Rennes, Strasbourg, and Tours all numbered at about 30,000 in 1700; population figures are from de Vries, *European Urbanization*, Appendix I.

119. Pierre Deyon, *Amiens, capital provinciale*, 7–9.

120. Deyon, *Amiens, capitale provinciale*, 13.

121. Goubert, *Beauvais et les Beauvaisis*, 85–89.

122. Goubert, *Beauvais et le Beauvaisis*, 256–59.

123. Goubert, *Beauvais et le Beauvaisis*, 293.

124. Goubert, *Beauvais et le Beauvaisis*, 66.

125. Goubert, *Beauvais et le Beauvaisis*, 593.

126. Goubert, *Beauvais et le Beauvaisis*, 130, 594–95.

127. De Vries, *European Urbanization*, 141.

128. Hohenberg and Lees, *The Making of Urban Europe*, 4–5.

129. Geoffrey Cotterell, *Amsterdam: Life of a City* (Boston: Little, Brown and Co., 1971), 72, 79–80, 83, 86.

130. Cotterell, *Amsterdam*.

131. The latter figure is from Robert Mols, "Population in Europe," 61.

132. Jan de Vries, "The Population and Economy of the Preindustrial Netherlands," *Journal of Interdisciplinary History* 15 (1985): 661–82. Because trade in the Baltic Sea was a crucial part of Dutch shipping, many Norwegians, Swedes, and Danes also married in Amsterdam. Of the seamen grooms in this period, 21 percent were from Amsterdam, 22 percent from elsewhere in the United Provinces, 19 percent were Germans, 16 percent were Norwegians, 7 percent were Swedes,

and 6 percent were Danes; in all, 42.5 percent were Dutch and 57.5 percent were foreigners. Simon Hart, "Gens de mer à Amsterdam au XVIIe siècle," 157.

133. De Vries, *European Urbanization*, 210–12.

134. De Vries, *European Urbanization*, 212; John Wareing, "Migration to London and Transatlantic Emigration of Indentured Servants, 1683–1775," *Journal of Historical Geography* 7 (1981), 363; Wrigley and Schofield, *The Population History of England*, 219.

135. Rappaport, *Worlds within Worlds*, 76, 79; E. Anthony Wrigley, "A Simple Model of London's Importance in Changing English Society and Economy, 1650–1750," in *Towns in Societies: Essays in Economic History and Historical Sociology*, ed. P. Abrams and E. A. Wrigley (Cambridge: Cambridge University Press, 1978), 215–43; Clark and Slack, *English Towns in Transition*, 64, 65, 86, 87.

136. Macfarlane, "The Myth of the Peasantry," 343. For a cautionary note, see Wall, "The Age of Leaving Home."

137. David Souden, " 'East, West—Home's Best'? Regional Patterns in Migration in Early Modern England," in *Migration and Society in Early Modern England*, ed. P. Clark and D. Souden (Totowa, N.J.: Barnes and Noble, 1988), 292–332, esp. 305–307.

138. The sex ratio statistic is for 40 London parishes; Clark and Slack, *English Towns in Transition*, 88; see also Abel Chatelain, "Migrations et domesticité féminine urbaine en France, XVIIIe siècle-XXe siècle," *Revue d'histoire économique et sociale* 47 (1969); de Vries, *European Urbanization*, 178; Roger Mols, *Introduction à la démographie historique des villes d'Europe du XIVe au XVIIIe siècle*, 3 vols. (Louvain: Publications Universitaires, 1954–56), vol. 2, 179–89. Steve Rappaport reports an earlier sex ratio of 116 (52% male) for London in 1552; this calculation is based on the sex ratio of burial records, *Worlds within Worlds*, 51.

139. Elliot, "Single Women in the London Marriage Market," 91–93.

140. Clark and Slack, *English Towns in Transition*, 64.

141. Elliot, "Single Women in the London Marriage Market," 90–95.

142. Elliot, "Single Women in the London Marriage Market," 86–87, 94–95, 99. For a report of the age of marriage of migrant German women in Amsterdam and migrant women in Geneva, see de Vries, *European Urbanization*, 190–92.

143. Elliot, "Single Women in the London Marriage Market," 99–100.

144. Clark and Slack, *English Towns in Transition*, 65.

145. Clark and Slack, *English Towns in Transition*, 120.

146. Caroline Barron, "Richard Whittington: The Man Behind the Myth," in *Studies in London History Presented to Philip Edmund Jones*, ed. A. E. J. Hollaender and W. Kellaway (London, 1969), 197–248; L. Stephen and S. Lee, eds., *The Dictionary of National Biography*, 21 vols. (London, 1901), vol. 21, 153–57; these works are cited by Rappaport, *Worlds within Worlds*, 367–69.

147. Cited in Wareing, "Migration to London," 358.

148. Clark and Slack, *English Towns in Transition*, 65.

149. Peter Laslett, *The World We Have Lost*, 5, 21.

3. MIGRATION IN THE AGE OF EARLY INDUSTRY

1. This portrait is drawn from Abel Poitrineau, *Remues d'hommes: Essai sur les migrations montagnardes en France, aux 17e–18e siècles* (Paris: Aubier Montaigne, 1983), 5, 8–19, 49–59; idem. "Aspects de l'émigration temporaire et saisonnière en Auvergne à la fin du XVIIIe siècle et au début du XIXe siècle," *Revue d'histoire moderne et contemporaine* 9 (1962), 5–50.

2. Gay Gullickson, *Spinners and Weavers of Auffay: Rural Industry and the Sex-*

ual Division of Labor in a French Village, 1750–1850 (Cambridge: Cambridge University Press, 1986), chap. 4.

3. Gullickson, *Spinners and Weavers of Auffay*, chap. 3.

4. For a study of human mobility, the term early industry is far more appropriate than protoindustry because the latter term implies continued industrial development, particular agricultural configurations, and rural processes. All of these are especially problematic when the role of mobility is considered. First, protoindustry was originally conceived as marking the first stage of the industrialization process that leads to mechanized production. This focus is particularly inappropriate for a study of migration, because "protoindustry" was not always a precursor to factory production; in many areas, rural deindustrialization, rather than mechanized production, came on the heels of rural industry. See chapter 4 below. Second, the literature on protoindustry originally emphasized particular configurations of agriculture and commerce, yet seasonal underemployment and the impulse of merchant capital appear to be more fundamental; a focus on these two elements is more helpful in translating the dialectic between circular migration and rural industry. Finally, the term early industry clearly refers to urban processes as well as to rural work. Because non-mechanized production always had important urban components, and because migration to the city in this age is a key to understanding human mobility, the urban component is vital. See Leslie Clarkson, *Proto-Industrialization: The First Phase of Industrialization?* (London: Macmillan, 1985); Gullickson, *Spinners and Weavers of Auffay*, chap. 3; Myron Gutmann, *Toward the Modern Economy: Early Industry in Europe, 1500–1800* (New York: Knopf, 1988), 5–6; Myron Gutmann and René Laboutte, "Rethinking Protoindustrialization and the Family," *Journal of Interdisciplinary History* 14 (1984), 587–607; Paul Hohenberg and Lynn Lees, *The Making of Urban Europe, 1000–1950* (Cambridge, Mass.: Harvard University Press, 1985), 125–29; Rabb Houston and Keith D. M. Snell, "Protoindustrialization? Cottage Industry, Social Change, and Industrial Revolution," *The Historical Journal* 27 (1984), 473–92; Franklin Mendels, "Proto-industrialization: The First Phase of the Industrialization Process," *Journal of Economic History* 32 (1972), 241–61.

5. Hohenberg and Lees, *The Making of Urban Europe*, 130–31, 179–86.

6. Michael Anderson, *Population Change in North-Western Europe, 1750–1850* (London: Macmillan, 1988), 23, 26; Jan de Vries, *European Urbanization, 1500–1800* (Cambridge, Mass.: Harvard University Press, 1984); see also the section on cities in this chapter.

7. Hans Fenske, "International Migration: Germany in the Eighteenth Century," *Central European History* 13 (1980), 342–46.

8. Bernard Bailyn, *Voyagers to the West: A Passage in the Peopling of America on the Eve of the Revolution* (New York: Knopf, 1986), 24–26; Fenske, "International Migration," 343–44.

9. Gutmann, *Toward the Modern Economy*, 51; E. Anthony Wrigley, "The Growth of Population in Eighteenth-Century England: A Conundrum Resolved," *Past and Present* 98 (1983), 122.

10. Anderson, *Population Change in North-Western Europe*, 21–24.

11. For an assessment of the causes of mortality decline, see Anderson, *Population Change in North-Western Europe*, 53–64.

12. Wrigley, "The Growth of Population," 126–33.

13. Rudolf Braun, "Early Industrialization and Demographic Change in the Canton of Zurich," in *Historical Studies of Changing Fertility*, ed. Charles Tilly (Princeton: Princeton University Press, 1978), 289–334; de Vries, *European Urbanization*, 238; David Levine, *Family Formation in an Age of Nascent Capitalism* (New

York: Academic Press, 1977), chap. 5; Hans Medick, "The Proto-industrial Family Economy: The Structural Functioning of Household and Family during the Transition from Peasant Society to Industrial Capitalism," *Social History* 3 (1976), 291–315.

14. Gullickson, *Spinners and Weavers of Auffay*, chap. 7; Gutmann, *Toward the Modern Economy*, 169–72; Gutmann and Laboutte, "Rethinking Protoindustrialization and the Family"; Houston and Snell, "Protoindustrialization?"

15. See, for example, Herbert Kisch, *From Domestic Manufacture to Industrial Revolution: The Case of the Rhineland Textile Districts* (Oxford: Oxford University Press, 1989), 95–153, 221; Catharina Lis and Hugo Soly, *Poverty and Capitalism in Pre-Industrial Europe* (Atlantic Highlands, N.J.: Humanities Press, 1979); Charles Tilly, "The Demographic Origins of the European Proletariat," in *Proletarianization and Family History*, ed. David Levine (Orlando, Fla.: Academic Press, 1984), 26–52; Jean-Pierre Poussou, *Bordeaux et le sud-ouest au XVIIIe siècle* (Paris: Editions de l'Ecole des Hautes Etudes en Sciences Sociales, 1983), 292–301.

16. Karlheinz Blaschke, *Bevölkerungsgeschichte von Sachen bis zur industriellen Revolution* (Weimar: Böhlhaus, 1967), 190–91, as reported in Tilly "The Demographic Origins of the European Proletariat," 30–32.

17. Lis and Soly, *Poverty and Capitalism in Pre-Industrial Europe*, 133, 171; Albert Soboul, *La Civilisation et la Révolution française*, 3 vols. (Paris: Arthaud, 1970), vol. 1, 125–26.

18. Tilly, "The Demographic Origins of the European Proletariat," 26–52.

19. David Levine, "Production, Reproduction, and the Proletarian Family in England, 1500–1851," in *Proletarianization and Family History*, 104–15; Tilly, "Demographic Origins of the European Proletariat," 38–44.

20. Gutmann, *Toward a Modern Economy*, 174.

21. For case studies and general discussion, see Gutmann, *Toward the Modern Economy*, chap. 5; Levine, "Production, Reproduction, and the Proletarian Family"; *idem.*, *Family Formation in an Age of Nascent Capitalism*; Tilly, "Demographic Origins of the European Proletariat."

22. Lis and Soly, *Poverty and Capitalism in Pre-Industrial Europe*, 97–104.

23. For estimates of the poor in eighteenth-century Europe, see Lis and Soly, *Poverty and Capitalism in Pre-Industrial Europe*, 171–73.

24. For the description of this migration system, see chapter 2 and Jan Lucassen, *Migrant Labour in Europe, 1600–1900* (London: Croom Helm, 1987), Part I; Poitrineau, "Aspects de l'émigration temporaire et saisonnière en Auvergne à la fin du XVIIIe siècle et au début du XIXe siècle," 5–50.

25. Lutz Berkner and Franklin Mendels, "Inheritance Systems, Family Structure, and Demographic Patterns in Western Europe, 1700–1900," in *Historical Studies of Changing Fertility*, 209–23; Laurence Fontaine, "Family Cycles, Peddling and Society in Upper Alpine Valleys in the Eighteenth Century," in *Domestic Strategies: Work and Family in France and Italy, 1600–1800*, ed. S. Woolf (Cambridge: Cambridge University Press, 1991), 43–68; Louise Tilly and Miriam Cohen, "Does the Family Have a History? A Review of Theory and Practice in Family History," *Social Science History* 6 (1982), 131–79; Louise Tilly and Joan Scott, *Women, Work and Family* (New York: Holt, Rinehart and Winston, 1978).

26. Leslie Page Moch, Nancy Folbre, Daniel Scott Smith, Laurel Cornell, and Louise Tilly, "Family Strategies: A Dialogue," *Historical Methods* 20 (1987), 113–25.

27. Olwen Hufton, *The Poor of Eighteenth-Century France, 1750–1789* (Oxford: Oxford University Press, 1974), 69–127.

28. De Vries, *European Urbanization*, 222; Ann Kussmaul, *Servants in Husbandry in Early Modern England* (Cambridge: Cambridge University Press, 1981), 86; Jan

Lucassen, *Migrant Labour in Europe*, 95–99; Roger Schofield, "Age-Specific Mobility in an Eighteenth-Century Rural English Parish," *Annales de démographie historique* (1970), 265–66.

29. For a survey of rural industry, see Lis and Soly, *Poverty and Capitalism in Pre-industrial Europe*; Gullickson, *Spinners and Weavers of Auffay*, 69; Gutmann, *Toward the Modern Economy*, chaps. 5, 6, and 7.

30. Lutz Berkner, "Family, Social Structure, and Rural Industry: A Comparative Study of the Waldviertel and the Pays de Caux in the Eighteenth Century" (Ph.D. diss., Harvard University, 1973), 139–40.

31. Berkner, "Family, Social Structure, and Rural Industry," 154–60.

32. Paul Bairoch, "International Industrialization Levels from 1750 to 1980," *Journal of European Economic History* 11 (1982), 281.

33. Lucassen, *Migrant Labour in Europe*, chap. 5.

34. Clarkson, *Proto-Industrialization: The First Phase of Industrialization?*, 20; Levine, in *Family Formation in an Age of Nascent Capitalism*, compares the freeholding villages of Shepshed with the manor-dominating village of Bottsford; Joan Thirsk, "Industries in the Countryside," in *The Rural Economy of England: Collected Essays* (London: Hambledon Press, 1984), 217–33.

35. After the Thirty Years' War, the Silesian nobility welcomed Czech and Moravian Protestant refugees, whom they settled on their estates as spinners and weavers of linen; in the next century, after Silesia became part of Prussia, several hundred new colonies of foreign spinners and weavers were established in mountain and forest areas. By the time of the first census, in 1748, over 19,800 looms were at work in Silesia; by 1790, there were some 28,700 looms employing over 50,000 weavers. Herbert Kisch, "The Textile Industries in Silesia and the Rhineland: A Comparative Study in Industrialization," in *Industrialization before Industrialization: Rural Industry in the Genesis of Capitalism*, ed. P. Kriedte, H. Medick, and J. Schlumbohm (Cambridge: Cambridge University Press, 1981), 179–82.

36. Berkner, "Family, Social Structure, and Rural Industry," 164–203.

37. Berkner, "Family, Social Structure, and Rural Industry," 369–70, 283–91.

38. Peter Clark, "Migration in England during the Late Seventeenth and Early Eighteenth Centuries," *Past and Present* 83 (1979), 81–83; Anne-Lise Head, "Quelques remarques sur l'émigration des régions préalpines," *Revue suisse d'histoire* 29 (1979), 181–93.

39. Steve Hochstadt, "Migration and Industrialization in Germany, 1815–1977," *Social Science History* 5 (1981), 448–49; David Souden, "Movers and Stayers in Family Reconstitution Populations, 1660–1780," *Local Population Studies* 33 (1984), 20–21, 24.

40. While there were only 583 weddings in the 69 years before 1749, 1,249 nuptials took place in the subsequent 39 years. Levine, *Family Formation in an Age of Nascent Capitalism*, 4–6, 36–41.

41. Levine, *Family Formation in an Age of Nascent Capitalism*, 43.

42. This section is based on Gullickson, *Spinners and Weavers of Auffay*, 16, 134, 136, 953–54.

43. Gutmann, *Toward the Modern Economy*, chaps. 5–6, 71–72, 136–47, 159.

44. Annual net migration rates are the proportion of the population that moves, net, in any given year, and these are net in-migration rates; they signify that the balance of moves to and from the villages increased the village populations by 6.6 to 6.8 percent annually. The net migration rates fell to .059 in 1700 and .048 in 1705. *Net* annual migration rates are not the same as *gross* migration rates. A net annual migration rate of .000 does not indicate a sedentary population; it means that whatever the volume of arrivals, they are offset by the number of departures from a given place. A net annual migration rate of .068 indicates that *in addition to*

arrivals and departures that offset each other, there are arrivals that equal 6.8 percent of the original population figure. Therefore, when net migration rates to the villages around Verviers fell below .048, this does not indicate that the population ceased to move; rather, it indicates that arrivals to and departures from any given village more nearly balanced each other out. Gross migration rates—the total movement of people from commune to commune—are not available for any rural industrial population. They simply cannot be calculated from the sources for eighteenth-century population studies: parish registers, *Bürgerbucher*, parish lists, or the occasional census.

45. Robert Schwartz, *Policing the Poor in Eighteenth-Century France* (Chapel Hill, N.C.: University of North Carolina Press, 1988), 139–40. See also Gullickson, *Spinners and Weavers of Auffay*, 96–107.

46. Lis and Soly, *Poverty and Capitalism in Pre-Industrial Europe*, 189–90; Schwartz, *Policing the Poor*, 149–50.

47. Lucassen, *Migrant Labour in Europe*, 233–34, 263–64.

48. I am indebted to Jan Lucassen for his survey of migration systems taken from the French Imperial survey of 1811. See Lucassen, *Migrant Labour in Europe*, chap. 6.

49. For assessments of the Napoleonic survey, see, for example, Roger Beteille, "Les migrations saisonnières en France sous le Premier Empire: Essai de synthèse," *Revue d'histoire moderne et contemporaine* 17 (1970), 424–41; Abel Chatelain, *Les migrants temporaires en France de 1800 à 1914*, 2 vols. (Lille: Publications de l'Université de Lille III, 1977), vol. I, 24–25; Lucassen, *Migrant Labour in Europe*, chaps. 1–2; Georges Mauco, "Les migrations ouvrières en France au début du XIXe siècle d'après les rapports des préfets de l'Empire, de 1808 à 1813" (Doctoral diss., University of Paris, 1932).

50. Chatelain, *Les migrants temporaires en France*, vol. 1, 48, 111–12, 162–69, vol. 2, 615; Lucassen, *Migrant Labour in Europe*, 232–33.

51. Lucassen, *Migrant Labour in Europe*, chaps. 2, 4.

52. Ruth-Ann Harris, "Seasonal Migration between Ireland and England Prior to the Famine," in *Canadian Papers in Rural History*, vol. 7 (Gananoque: Langdale Press, 1989), 363–86; Joel Mokyr and Cormac Ó Gráda, "Emigration and Poverty in Prefamine Ireland," *Explorations in Economic History*, ser. 2, 19 (1982), 361; David Morgan, *Harvesters and Harvesting, 1840–1900* (London: Croom Helm, 1982), 84; Cormac Ó Gráda, "Seasonal Migration and Post-Famine Adjustment in the West of Ireland," *Studia Hibernica* 13 (1973), 49–50; Edward P. Thompson, *The Making of the English Working Class* (London: Harmondsworth, 1981), 471; Arthur Redford, *Labour Migration in England* (Manchester: Manchester University Press, 1976), 133.

53. Lucasssen, *Migrant Labour in Europe*, 235–60.

54. Lucassen, *Migrant Labour in Europe*, 235–59.

55. Antonio Meijide Pardo, *La emigración Gallega intrapeninsular en el siglo XVIII* (Madrid: Instituto Balmes de Sociologia, 1960), chap. 4.

56. Chatelain, *Les migrants temporaires en France*, 49, 110, 169–78.

57. Abel Poitrineau, *La vie rurale en Basse Auvergne au XVIIIe siècle* (Paris: Presses Universitaires Françaises, 1966), 120.

58. Poussou, *Bordeaux et le sud-ouest au XVIIIe siècle*, 298.

59. Poitrineau, *La vie rurale en Basse Auvergne*, 120. It was not until the nineteenth century that potatoes (which could increase the food supply) came to this region.

60. Poitrineau, "Aspects de l'émigration saisonnière et temporaire de l'Auvergne," 6–7.

61. For a catalogue of upland specialties, see Poitrineau, *Remues d'hommes*, 96–143; Hufton, *The Poor of Eighteenth-Century France*, 68–106.

62. Chatelain, *Les migrants temporaires en France*, vol. 1, 561–62; Alain Corbin, *Archaïsme et modernité en Limousin au XIXe siècle (1845–1880)*, 2 vols. (Paris: Marcel Rivière, 1975), vol. 1, 177–225; Marie-Annie Moulin, *Les maçons de la Haute-Marche au XVIIIe siècle* (Clermont-Ferrand: Publications de l'Institut d'Etudes du Massif Central, 1986), 47.

63. Hufton, *The Poor of Eighteenth-Century France*, 76–77.

64. There were 87 boys and 103 girls in residence under the age of 14, but only 43 boys and 44 girls over that age. Messance, *Recerces sur la population des généralités d'Auvergne, de Lyon, de Rouen* (Paris: Durand, 1766), 13.

65. Maurice Garden, *Lyon et les Lyonnais au XVIIIe siècle* (Paris: Belles Lettres, 1970), 49–50.

66. Poitrineau, "Aspects de l'émigration saisonnière et temporaire en Auvergne," 41–42.

67. Chatelain, *Les Migrants temporaires en France, passim.*; Lucassen, *Migrant Labour in Europe*, chap. 4; Poitrineau, *Remues d'hommes*, 69–85.

68. Poitrineau, "Aspects de l'émigration saisonnière et temporaires de l'Auvergne," 17.

69. Lucassen, *Migrant Labour in Europe*, 50–51; Poitrineau, *Remues d'hommes*, 149–81, 306–308; Alain Lottin, "Naissance illegitimes et filles-mères à Lille au XVIIIe siècle," *Revue d'histoire moderne et contemporaine* 17 (1970), 315.

70. Poitrineau, *Remues d'hommes*, 195–204.

71. Poitrineau, "Aspects de l'émigration saisonnière et temporaire de l'Auvergne," 41–46.

72. Laurence Fontaine, "Les migrations marchandes des hautes vallées alpines à l'époque moderne; phénomène de rupture ou signe d'une organisation de la migration villageoise?", paper presented at Colloquium "L'Emigration: Une Réponse Universelle à une Situation de Crise?" July 1991, Le Châble, Switzerland; *idem.*, "Family Cycles, Peddling, and Society in Upper Alpine Valleys in the Eighteenth Century."

73. Poitrineau, *La vie rurale en Basse Auvergne*, 570–71, draws on M. Legrand, *Voyage fait en 1787 et 1788 dans la ci-devant haute et basse-Auvergne*, 3 vols. (Paris: L'Imprimerie des Sciences et Arts, 1794–1795).

74. Poitrineau, *Remues d'hommes*, 213, 221–23; Poussou, *Bordeaux et le sud-ouest*, 131.

75. Tilly, "The Demographic Origins of the European Proletariat," 46.

76. Abel Poitrineau, *Les espagnols de l'Auvergne et du Limousin du XVIIIe au XIXe siècle* (Aurillac: Malroux-Mazel, 1985), 8.

77. Poitrineau, *Les espagnols de l'Auvergne et du Limousin*, 8.

78. Poitrineau, *Les Espagnols de l'Auvergne et du Limousin*, 19, 23.

79. Poitrineau, *Les Espagnols de l'Auvergne et du Limousin*, 23, 66.

80. Poitrineau, *Les Espagnols de l'Auvergne et du Limousin*, 139.

81. Poitrineau, *Les Espagnols de l'Auvergne et du Limousin*, 66, 247, 249, 250.

82. Poitrineau, *Les Espagnols de l'Auvergne et du Limousin*, 156–61.

83. Poitrineau, *Les Espagnols de l'Auvergne et du Limousin*, 129, 131.

84. Poitrineau, *Les Espagnols de l'Auvergne et du Limousin*, 81.

85. The minute-books of 33 notaries in the highlands record the deaths of over 200 eighteenth-century emigrants. Poitrineau, *Les Espagnols de l'Auvergne et du Limousin*, 80.

86. Geneste received 848 wills, of which 466 were women's; among these, 82 came from spinsters belonging to lay orders. Poitrineau, *Les Espagnols de l'Auvergne et du Limousin*, 207.

87. Poitrineau, *Les Espagnols de l'Auvergne et du Limousin*, 56–57.

88. Poitrineau, *Les Espagnols de l'Auvergne et du Limousin*, 62–63.

89. Poitrineau, *Les Espagnols de l'Auvergne et du Limousin*, 67; *idem.*, "Aspects de l'émigration temporaire et saisonnière en Auvergne," 31.

90. If fertility was little affected by migration, it was because the men, not the women, married late. Poitrineau, *Les Espagnols de l'Auvergne et du Limousin*, 76

91. Poitrineau, *Remues d'hommes*, 218–19; *idem.*, *Les Espagnols de l'Auvergne et du Limousin*, 70.

92. Poitrineau, *Les Espagnols de l'Auvergne et du Limousin*, 72–73.

93. Poitrineau, *Les Espagnols de l'Auvergne et du Limousin*, 9.

94. *Gavachos*, the rather insulting name for the French, was either taken from *gardevaches*, cowherd, or was derived from the name for the French highland province of Gévaudan. Poitrineau, *Les Espagnols de l'Auvergne et du Limousin*, 14, 111.

95. Poitrineau, *Les Espagnols de l'Auvergne et du Limousin*, 237.

96. Hufton, *The Poor of Eighteenth-Century France*, xx; Schwartz, *Policing the Poor*, 144–50.

97. See, for example, Hufton, *The Poor of Eighteenth-Century France*, 69–106; Lis and Soly, *Poverty and Capitalism in Pre-Industrial Europe*, 171–94.

98. Poitrineau, *Remues d'hommes*, 181.

99. Lis and Soly, *Poverty and Capitalism in Pre-Industrial Europe*, 171–94.

100. Lis and Soly, *Poverty and Capitalism in Pre-Industrial Europe*, 187–88; Schwartz, *Policing the Poor*, 137.

101. Cissie Fairchilds, *Poverty and Charity in Aix-en-Provence, 1549–1789* (Baltimore, Md.: Johns Hopkins University Press, 1976); Lis and Soly, *Poverty and Capitalism in Pre-Industrial Europe*, 187–88; Schwartz, *Policing the Poor*, 138.

102. Schwartz, *Policing the Poor*, 187–98.

103. For a nuanced portrait of the orphanage, see Fairchilds, *Poverty and Charity*.

104. Schwartz, *Policing the Poor*, 226–29; the fate of their other children is unknown.

105. Hufton, *The Poor of Eighteenth-Century France*, 117–27; Schwartz, *Policing the Poor*, 229, 232.

106. Schwartz, *Policing the Poor*, 154, 169, 241; Lis and Soly discuss the *Tuchthuizen*, *hôpitaux généraux*, workhouses, and *Zuchthäusern* that combined craft production with incarceration of paupers beginning in the seventeenth century, *Poverty and Capitalism in Pre-Industrial Europe*, 117, 128, 197, 211.

107. Schwartz, *Policing the Poor*, 153.

108. Schwartz, *Policing the Poor*, 165.

109. Schwartz, *Policing the Poor*, 242–44.

110. For a striking portrait of the fate of the *vénérienne*, see Hufton, *The Poor of Eighteenth-Century France*, 238–39, 312–13.

111. For information and debate about the single mothers of eighteenth-century France and the *déclarations de grossesse* through which they can be perceived, see Jacques Depauw, "Amour illegitime et société à Nantes au XVIIIe siècle," *Annales: E.S.C.* 27 (1972), 1155–81; Cissie Fairchilds, "Female Sexual Attitudes and the Rise of Illegitimacy: A Case Study," *Journal of Interdisciplinary History* 8 (1978), 627–67; Alain Lottin, "Naissances illegitimes et filles-mères à Lille"; Jean-Pierre Poussou, *Bordeaux et le sud-ouest au XVIIIe siècle*, 152–64; Edward Shorter, "Female Emancipation, Birth Control, and Fertility in European History," *American Historical Review* 78 (1973), 605–40; Louise Tilly, Joan Scott, and Miriam Cohen, "Women's Work and European Fertility Patterns," *Journal of Interdisciplinary History* 6 (1976), 447–76. See also Peter Laslett, Karla Oosterveen, and Richard Smith, eds., *Bastardy and Its Comparative History* (London: Edward Arnold, 1980).

112. Edward Shorter, "Illegitimacy, Sexual Revolution, and Social Change in Modern Europe," *Journal of Interdisciplinary History* 2 (1971), 262–72.

113. Lottin, "Naissances illegitimes et filles-mères à Lille," 304–305; Poussou, *Bordeaux et le sud-ouest au XVIII siècle*, 161–63. See also chapter 4 below.

114. Depauw, "Amour illegitime et société à Nantes," 1166; Fairchilds, "Female Sexual Attitudes and the Rise of Illegitimacy," 654–59; Tilly, Scott, and Cohen, "Women's Work and European Fertility Patterns," 235–48.

115. Fairchilds, "Female Sexual Attitudes and the Rise of Illegitimacy," 641.

116. Lottin, "Naissances illegitimes et filles-mères à Lille," 305.

117. Hufton, *The Poor of Eighteenth-Century France*, 324.

118. Poussou, *Bordeaux et le sud-ouest au XVIII siècle*, 155.

119. For comparisons between women who bore illegitimate children and those who were married during their pregnancy, see George Alter, *Family and the Female Life Course: The Women of Verviers, Belgium, 1849–1880* (Madison: University of Wisconsin Press, 1988), chap. 5; Ann-Sofie Kälvemark, "Illegitimacy and Marriage in Three Swedish Parishes in the Nineteenth Century," in *Bastardy and Its Comparative History*, 328.

120. Poitrineau, *Remues d'hommes*, 69–87; Poussou, *Bordeaux et le sud-ouest au XVIII siècle*, 180–81.

121. De Vries, *European Urbanization*, 68–69; see also Philip Benedict, "Was the Eighteenth Century an Era of Urbanization in France?" *Journal of Interdisciplinary History* 21 (1990), 179–215.

122. Hohenberg and Lees, *The Making of Urban Europe*, 130.

123. Hohenberg and Lees, *The Making of Urban Europe*, 130.

124. Gullickson, *Spinners and Weavers of Auffay*, 45–46, 65–67.

125. De Vries, *European Urbanization*, 101–102, 142; Gutmann, *Toward the Modern Economy*, 138.

126. Gutmann, *Toward the Modern Economy*, 195–99, 206–207.

127. George Alter, *Family and the Female Life Course*, 16; Gutmann, *Toward the Modern Economy*, 158–60.

128. Gutmann, *Toward the Modern Economy*, 137–42, 147.

129. Gutmann, *Toward the Modern Economy*, 175.

130. Gutmann, *Toward the Modern Economy*, 176–79, 183–85. Delilez's story is recounted in Gutmann (176–77) and in H. Carton de Wiart, "Le vie et les voyages d'un ouvrier foulon du pays de Verviers au XVIIIe siècle d'après un manuscrit inédit," *Academic Royale de Belgique. Classe des Lettres, Mémoires* (in-8) 2nd. ser., 13 (1921), 1–59.

131. Jean-Pierre Bardet, *Rouen aux XVIIe et XVIIIe siècles: Les mutations d'un espace sociale*, 2 vols. (Paris: Société d'Edition d'Enseignement Supérieur, 1983), vol. I, 209; Michel Mollat, *Histoire de Rouen* (Toulouse: Privat, 1979), 209, 219, 221.

132. Results reported in Bardet, *Rouen aux XVIIe et XVIIIe siècles*, vol. I, 211, 216–17; Steve Hochstadt, "Migration in Preindustrial Germany," *Central European History* 16 (1983), 201.

133. Bardet, *Rouen aux XVIIe et XVIIIe siècles*, vol. I, 209.

134. Michel Terrisse, "Méthode de recherches démographiques en milieu urbain ancien (XVIIe-XVIIIe)," *Annales de démographie historique* (1974), 249–62.

135. De Vries, *European Urbanization*, 205–206; Jean-Claude Perrot, *Genèse d'une ville moderne: Caen au XVIIIe siècle*, 2 vols. (Paris: Mouton, 1975), vol. I, 99–142, 158–66.

136. Maurice Garden, "Le bilan démographique des villes: Un système complexe," *Annales de démographie historique* (1982), 267–75.

137. Bardet, *Rouen aux XVIIe et XVIIIe siècles*, vol. I, 211; see also Philippe Guignet, *Mines, manufactures et ouvriers du Valenciennois au XVIIIe siècle* (New York: Arno Press, 1977), 214.

138. Poussou, *Bordeaux et le sud-ouest au XVIIIe siècle*, 20, 235–60.

139. Poussou, *Bordeaux et le sud-ouest au XVIIIe siècle*, 30.
140. Poussou, *Bordeaux et le sud-ouest au XVIIIe siècle*, 330.
141. Poussou, *Bordeaux et le sud-ouest au XVIIIe siècle*, 82, 139.
142. Poussou, *Bordeaux et le sud-ouest au XVIIIe siècle*, 122, 142–47.
143. Poussou, *Bordeaux et le sud-ouest au XVIIIe siècle*, 131; Poitrineau, *Remues d'hommes*, 49–66.

4. MIGRATION IN AN AGE OF URBANIZATION AND INDUSTRIALIZATION

1. Adna Weber, *The Growth of Cities in the Nineteenth Century* (1899, reprint edition Ithaca, N.Y.: Cornell University Press, 1965), frontispiece.
2. André Armengaud, "Population in Europe, 1700–1914," in *The Fontana Economic History of Europe*, vol. 3, *The Industrial Revolution, 1700–1914*, ed. C. Cipolla (New York: Barnes and Noble, 1976), 32–33; Maurice Garden, "Le bilan démographique des villes: Un système complexe," *Annales de démographie historique* (1982), 267–75.
3. Jeanne Bouvier, *Mes mémoires: Ou 59 années d'activité industrielle, sociale et intellectuelle d'une ouvrière, 1876–1935* (Paris: Maspéro, 1983), 35–96.
4. Dieter Langewiesche, "Wanderungsbewegungen in der Hochindustrialisierungs-periods. Regionale, interstädtische und innerstädtische Mobilität in Deutschland 1880–1914," *Vierteljahrschrift fur Sozial- und Wirtschaftsgeschichte*, 64. Band (1977), 19; noted in Steve Hochstadt, "Städtische Wanderungsbewegungen in Deutschland 1850–1914," in *Deutschland und Europa in der Neuzeit: Festschrift für Karl Otmar Freiherr von Aretin zum 65. Geburtstag*, ed. Ralph Melville, Claus Scharf, Martin Vogt, and Ulrich Wengenroth (Stuttgart: Franz Steiner Verlag, 1988), 594.
5. Charles Tilly, "Flows of Capital and Forms of Industry in Europe, 1500–1900," *Theory and Society* 12 (1983), 123–42; David Levine, "Production, Reproduction, and the Proletarian Family in England, 1500–1851," in *Proletarianization and Family History*, ed. D. Levine (Orlando, Fla.: Academic Press, 1984), 115; Myron Gutmann, *Toward the Modern Economy: Early Industry in Europe, 1500–1800* (New York: Knopf, 1988), chap. 8.
6. See, for example, Pierre Guillaume, *La population de Bordeaux au XIXe siècle: Essai d'histoire sociale* (Paris: Armand Colin, 1972); Jan Lucassen, *Migrant Labour in Europe, 1600–1900* (London: Croom Helm, 1987), 172–95.
7. See, for example, Dirk Hoerder, *Labor Migration in the Atlantic Economies: The European and North American Working Classes during the Period of Industrialization* (Westport, Conn.: Greenwood, 1985).
8. The revolutionary exiles are less important to the history of France or western Europe than the Protestants who had fled France in the 1680s because, unlike the earlier refugees, most émigrés returned. The social status of over 90,600 émigrés is known; 27 percent were clergy, 21 percent peasants, 19 percent bourgeoisie, 18 percent noble, and 16 percent manual laborers; Jacques Dupaquier and Joseph Goy, "Révolution et population," in Jacques Dupaquier, *Histoire de la population française*, vol. 3, *De 1789 à 1914* (Paris: Presses Universitaires Françaises, 1988), 68, 76. For debate and comment on the numbers of émigrés, also see Donald Greer, *The Incidence of the Emigration during the French Revolution* (Cambridge, Mass.: Harvard University Press, 1951); Jean Vidalenc, *Les émigrés français, 1789–1825* (Caen: Association des publications de la Faculté des Lettres et Sciences Humaines de l'Université de Caen, 1963).
9. Likewise, the number of domestics in the Norman city of Caen quickly dropped from 3,000 to 1,500 between the beginning of the Revolution and the

214 /   Notes to pages 106–112

execution of King Louis XVI in January of 1793. Dupaquier and Goy, "Révolution et population," 78.

10. Philip Benedict, "Was the Eighteenth Century an Era of Urbanization in France?", *Journal of Interdisciplinary History* 21 (1990), 210; Dupaquier and Goy use the INED measure of 2,000 to define urban areas in "Révolution et population," 80, 168.

11. Dupaquier and Goy, "Révolution et population," 76–77; Jan Lucassen, *Migrant Labour in Europe*, 7.

12. Herbert Kisch, *From Domestic Manufacture to Industrial Revolution: The Case of the Rhineland Textile Districts* (Oxford: Oxford University Press, 1989), 206–11; Lucassen, *Migrant Labour in Europe*, 17.

13. See, for example, Carl H. Senior, "German Immigrants in Jamaica, 1834–8," *Journal of Caribbean History* 10–11 (1978), 25–53; *idem.* "Irish Slaves for Jamaica," *Jamaica Journal* 42 (1978), 104–16. I would like to thank Stanley Engerman for supplying these references. See also Philip Curtin, "Migration in the Tropical World," in *Immigration Reconsidered*, ed. V. Yans-McLaughlin (New York: Oxford University Press, 1990), 21–36.

14. Eric Hobsbawm, *The Age of Empire, 1875–1914* (New York: Pantheon, 1987), 59.

15. Walter Nugent, "Frontiers and Empires in the Late Nineteenth Century," *The Western Historical Quarterly* 20 (1989), 393–406.

16. Armengaud, "Population in Europe," 28–30. Early French fertility decline is primarily responsible for relatively little population growth in that country; see E. Anthony Wrigley, "The Growth of Population in Eighteenth-Century England: A Conundrum Resolved," *Past and Present* 98 (1983), 121–50.

17. For emphasis on the role played by earlier marriages in the increase in European proletarians, see David Levine, "Production, Reproduction, and the Proletarian Family."

18. Armengaud, "Population in Europe," 39, 49. For a study of rising infant mortality in the nineteenth century, see W. Robert Lee, "The Impact of Agrarian Change on Women's Work and Child Care in Early-Nineteenth-Century Prussia," in *German Women in the Nineteenth Century: A Social History* (London: Holmes and Meier, 1984), 234–55. For a survey of cities, see Paul Hohenberg and Lynn Lees, *The Making of Urban Europe, 1000–1950* (Cambridge, Mass.: Harvard University Press, 1985), 259.

19. For a discussion of the mechanics by which the English proletariat "made itself" and increased at a much greater rate than the peasant population, see Levine, "Production, Reproduction, and the Proletarian Family in England."

20. Steve Hochstadt, "Socioeconomic Determinants of Mobility in Nineteenth-Century Germany" (Mainz: Institut für Europäische Geschichte, 1985), 9–10; J. A. Perkins, "The Agricultural Revolution in Germany, 1850–1914," *Journal of European Economic History* 10 (1981), 101–103. Serfdom was abolished in 1807 in Prussia, 1848 in Austria, and 1861 in Russia.

21. Charles Tilly, "Demographic Origins of the European Proletariat," in *Proletarianization and Family History*, 30–33. See also essays in this volume by David Levine, "Production, Reproduction, and the Proletarian Family," 87–127; and John Gillis, "Peasant, Plebian, and Proletarian Marriage in Britain, 1600–1900," 129–62.

22. Ann Kussmaul, *Servants in Husbandry in Early Modern England* (Cambridge: Cambridge University Press, 1981), chap. 7, 122–24.

23. Kussmaul, *Servants in Husbandry*, 120.

24. Kussmaul, *Servants in Husbandry*, 121, 127, 131; see also the rare first-hand account of Franz Rehbein in Alfred Kelly, ed., *The German Worker: Working-Class*

Autobiographies from the Age of Industrialization (Berkeley, Calif.: University of California Press, 1987), 188–98.

25. Steve Hochstadt, "Socioeconomic Determinants," 14.

26. Hochstadt, "Socioeconomic Determinants," 12.

27. Hochstadt, "Socioeconomic Determinants," 13.

28. Hochstadt, "Socioeconomic Determinants," 12–13.

29. Kelly, *The German Worker*, 188–203.

30. Kelly, *The German Worker*, 192–93.

31. Kelly, *The German Worker*, 194.

32. John D. Post, *The Last Great Subsistence Crisis in the Western World* (Baltimore: The Johns Hopkins University Press, 1977), 86–107.

33. Redcliffe Salaman, *The History and the Social Influence of the Potato* (Cambridge: Cambridge University Press, 1949).

34. These are not the only industrial crops whose cultivation required a migrant labor force; for crops such as madder, see Lucassen, *Migrant Labour in Europe*, chap. 4; Abel Chatelain, *Les migrants temporaires en France de 1800 à 1914*, 2 vols. (Lille: Publications de l'Université de Lille III, 1977), vol. 2, 670–731.

35. Maurice Agulhon, Gabriel Désert, and Roger Specklin, *Apogée et crise de la civilisation paysanne, 1789–1914*, vol. 3. *Histoire de la France rurale*, ed. Georges Duby and Armand Wallon (Paris: Seuil, 1976), vol. 3, 392–94; Leslie Page Moch, *Paths to the City: Regional Migration in Nineteenth-Century France* (Beverly Hills, Calif.: Sage Publications, 1983), 44–48; Louise Tilly, "Lyonnais, Lombardy, and Labor in Industrialization," in *Proletarians and Protest: The Roots of Class Formation in an Industrializing World*, ed. Michael Hanagan and Charles Stephenson (New York: Greenwood Press, 1986), pp. 134–35.

36. Agulhon, Désert, and Specklin, *Apogée et crise de la civilisation paysanne*, vol. 3, 388–91.

37. Christopher Johnson, *The Life and Death of Industrial Languedoc* (Oxford: Oxford University Press, forthcoming), chapter 12.

38. Philippe Pinchemel, *Structures sociales et dépopulation rurale dans les campagnes picardes de 1836 à 1936* (Paris: Colin, 1957), 208.

39. David Levine, *Reproducing Families: The Political Economy of English Population History* (Cambridge: Cambridge University Press, 1987), chaps. 2 and 3.

40. Johnson documents the shifts in the family economy and attempts of the wool town of Lodève and other textile towns of the eastern Languedoc region to find alternative industries in *The Life and Death of Industrial Languedoc*, chap. 10.

41. Gay Gullickson, *Spinners and Weavers of Auffay: Rural Industry and Sexual Division of Labor in a French Village, 1750–1850* (Cambridge: Cambridge University Press, 1986), chaps. 5 and 6.

42. Johnson, *The Life and Death of Industrial Languedoc*, chaps. 10 and 11.

43. English handloom weavers were outnumbered only by agricultural laborers and domestic weavers at mid-century. The estimate of their numbers originates in the parliamentary Select Committee of 1834–1835; see Edward P. Thompson, *The Making of the English Working Class* (New York: Viking, 1963), 311.

44. See Thompson, *Making of the English Working Class*, 286 and chap. 9 for an evocative summary of the conditions into which weavers declined. For an industrial study, see Julia De Lacey Mann, *The Cloth Industry in the West of England from 1640 to 1880* (Gloucester: Alan Sutton, 1987), 242–43.

45. Duncan Blythell, *The Handloom Weavers: A Study in the English Cotton Industry during the Industrial Revolution* (Cambridge: Cambridge University Press, 1969), 174, 251; Norman Murray, *The Scottish Hand Loom Weavers, 1790–1850: A Social History* (Edinburgh: John Donald Publishers, 1978), 71–75.

46. Michael Anderson, *Family Structure in Nineteenth-Century Lancashire* (Cambridge: Cambridge University Press, 1971), 40; Johnson, *The Life and Death of Industrial Languedoc*, chap. 10.

47. J. Harland, *Ballads and Songs of Lancashire* (1865), 253; cited by Thompson, *The Making of the English Working Class*, 308.

48. Gullickson, *Spinners and Weavers of Auffay*, chaps. 5 and 6.

49. Gullickson, *Spinners and Weavers of Auffay*, chaps. 5 and 6; Pinchemel, *Structures sociales et dépopulation rurale*, chap. 7.

50. Johnson, *Life and Death of Industrial Languedoc*, chap. 10.

51. Gullickson, *Spinners and Weavers of Auffay*, 133–34, 181.

52. In 1800, 74 young men who were serving as soldiers were absent from this village of about 1,150. Gullickson, *Spinners and Weavers of Auffay*, 133, 138, 179.

53. Gullickson, *Spinners and Weavers of Auffay*, 190.

54. Gullickson, *Spinners and Weavers of Auffay*, 133–38; 178–91.

55. Gullickson, *Spinners and Weavers of Auffay*, 137. One-fifth to one-fourth of the children were illegitimate in the first half of the nineteenth century and thousands of infants, the majority of whom were illegitimate, were abandoned in Rouen. See Jean-Pierre Bardet, *Rouen aux XVIIe et XVIIIe siècles: Les mutations d'un espace social*, 2 vols. (Paris: Société d'Edition d'Enseignement Supérieur, 1983), vol. 1, 320–46; Etienne van de Walle, "Illegitimacy in France during the Nineteenth Century," in *Bastardy and Its Comparative History*, ed. P. Laslett, K. Oosterveen, and R. M. Smith (Cambridge: Cambridge University Press, 1980), 264–77.

56. On the other hand, prolonged male emigration produced a society in which neither single women nor infants born out of wedlock were condemned. See Caroline Brettell, *Men Who Migrate, Women Who Wait: Population and History in a Portuguese Parish* (Princeton: Princeton University Press, 1986).

57. Chatelain, *Les migrants temporaires en France*, vol. 2, 670–72, map II-20; Serge Grafteaux, *Mémé Santerre: A French Woman of the People* (New York: Schoken Books, 1985), pp. 19–31.

58. Migration systems came to light primarily through an inquiry of the French Imperial government between 1808 and 1813. Because its primary concern was military personnel and the inquiry was carried out in a period of protracted warfare, responses are unreliable to a degree and the reported numbers of migrants were probably below the norm. Nevertheless, this inquiry, in conjunction with local studies, permitted Jan Lucassen to describe seven major systems of temporary migration. The inquiry is in the French National Archives, series F.20, 434–35, Renseignements fournis par les préfets relative à l'émigration et à l'immigration d'ouvriers, 1807–1812. For analyses and critiques of this source, see Roger Beteille, "Les migrations saisonnières en France sous le Premier Empire: Essai de synthèse," *Revue d'histoire moderne et contemporaine* (1970), 424–41; Abel Chatelain, *Les migrants temporaires en France*, vol. 1, 24–25; Lucassen, *Migrant Labour in Europe*, 7–17; Georges Mauco, "Les migrations ouvrières en France au début du XIXe siècle d'après les rapports des préfets de l'Empire, de 1808 à 1813" (Doctoral diss., University of Paris, 1932).

59. Lucassen, *Migrant Labour in Europe*, 125–26; see W. Sombart, *Die deutsche Volkswirtschaft im neunzehnten Jahrhundert und im Anfang des 20. Jahrhunderts* (Berlin, 1919), 51–52.

60. Jan Lucassen, "Dutch Migration, 1600–1900" (Amsterdam: International Institute of Social History, 1990); *idem.*, *Migrant Labour in Europe*, chap. 9.

61. See Dirk Hoerder, "An Introduction to Labor Migration in the Atlantic Economies, 1815–1914," in *Labor Migration in the Atlantic Economies*, 14.

62. Ruth-Ann Harris, "Seasonal Migration between Ireland and England Prior to the Famine," in *Canadian Papers in Rural History*, vol. 7 (Ganagoque: Langdale

Press, 1989), 370–72. See also *idem.*, *The Nearest Place that Wasn't Ireland: A Study of the Pre-famine Seasonal Migration of the Irish People to Britain* (Ames, Iowa: Iowa State University Press, forthcoming in 1992).

63. Abel Chatelain, *Les migrants temporaires en France* vol. 1, 107–47. The number of vine harvesters is very high in France because it was counted by employers and as a consequence includes both urban workers and harvesters who worked more than one vineyard. Jean-Pierre Poussou, Bernard Lepetit, Daniel Courgeau, and Jacques Dupâquier, "Migrations et peuplement," in *Histoire de la population française*, 171, 178; Arthur Redford, *Labour Migration in England, 1800–1850* (Manchester: Manchester University Press, 1976), 142.

64. See, for example, Chatelain, *Les migrants temporaires en France*, vol. 2, 813–19; Nancy Green, " 'Filling the Void': Immigration to France before World War I," in *Labor Migration in the Atlantic Economies*, 143–61; Gianfausto Rosoli, "Italian Migration to European Countries from Political Unification to World War I," in *Labor Migration in the Atlantic Economies*, 95–116.

65. Chatelain, *Les migrants temporaires en France*, vol. 2, 818, 849–71, treats life in rural rail construction sites.

66. For the employment of rail workers in France, see Yves Bravard, "Sondages à propos de l'emigration dans les Alpes du Nord," *Revue de géographie alpine* 45 (1957), 118–20; Chatelain, *Les migrants temporaires en France*, vol. 2, 813; Joseph Jacquet, *Les cheminots dans l'histoire sociale de la France* (Paris: Editions Sociales, 1967), 32–33. For the story of rail construction and out-migration of villagers to railroad centers, see Moch, *Paths to the City*, chaps. 2 and 5. Rosoli, "Italian Migration to European Countries," 100, 109, 112.

67. Armand Boyer, "Les migrations saisonnières dans la Cévenne vivaroise," *Revue de géographie alpine* 22 (1934), 571–609; Rosoli, "Italian Migration to European Countries," 106.

68. In 1889, France produced 7.140 million metric tons of sugar beets, Germany 9.2. In the early twentieth century, the major producers were:

Nation	1900 output (in metric tons)	1913 output
Germany	7,092,000	9,714,000
France	8,590,000	7,990,000
Netherlands	1,509,000	1,665,000
Italy	476,000	2,819,000
Denmark	382,000	930,000
Sweden	819,000	858,000

There are no figures of sugar beet production for the United Kingdom. Brian R. Mitchell, *European Historical Statistics, 1750–1970* (New York: Columbia University Press, 1978), Table C2, 96–125.

69. J. A. Perkins, "The Agricultural Revolution in Germany, 1850–1914," *Journal of European Economic History* 10 (1981), 106–107; Chatelain, *Les Migrants temporaires en France*, vol. 2, 704.

70. Thomas Hardy, *Tess of the d'Ubervilles* (London: Everyman, 1984), 275–76, 303–304.

71. Jan Sloma, *From Serfdom to Self-Government: Memoirs of a Polish Village Mayor, 1842–1927* (London: Minerva, 1941), 57; quoted in Morawska, *For Bread*

with Butter: The Life-Worlds of East-Central Europeans in Johnstown, Pennsylvania, 1890–1914 (Cambridge: Cambridge University Press, 1985), 53.

72. Lucassen, *Migrant Labour in Europe*, plate 20; Perkins "The Agricultural Revolution," 107–108; Poussou et al., "Migrations et peuplement," 179.

73. Steve Hochstadt, "Socioeconomic Determinants," 9–10.

74. Hochstadt, "Socioeconomic Determinants," 18; Perkins, "The Agricultural Revolution," 101–103.

75. Steve Hochstadt, "Socioeconomic Determinants," 20.

76. See Eva Morawska, "Labor Migrations of Poles in the Atlantic Economy, 1880–1914," *Comparative Studies in Society and History* 31 (1989), 237–72.

77. The following section is dependent on Klaus Bade, "German Emigration to the United States and Continental Immigration to Germany in the Late Nineteenth and Early Twentieth Centuries," *Central European History* 13, no. 4 (1980), 348–77.

78. Christopher Klessman, "Long-Distance Migration, Integration and Segregation of an Ethnic Minority in Industrial Germany: The Case of the 'Ruhr Poles,' " in *Population, Labour, and Migration in 19th- and 20th-Century Germany*, ed. Klaus Bade, 102–03 (Leamington Spa: Berg, 1987). See Wolfgang Köllmann, "The Population of Barmen before and during the Period of Industrialization," in *Population in History: Essays in Historical Demography*, ed. D. V. Glass and D. E. C. Eversley, 588–607 (London: Edward Arnold, 1965).

79. For a study of foreign laborers in a mixed economy of western Germany, see Karl Marten Barfuss, *"Gastarbeiter" in Nordwestdeutschland, 1884–1918* (Bremen: Staatsarchiv der Freien Hansestadt Bremen, 1986).

80. Bade, "German Emigration to the United States and Continental Migration to Germany," 365.

81. Bade, "German Emigration to the United States and Continental Migration to Germany," 357. These figures include ethnic Poles from the three provinces.

82. Perkins, "The Agricultural Revolution in Germany," 107–108.

83. Morawska, "Labor Migrations of Poles in the Atlantic Economy," 237–72.

84. Bade, "Labour, Migration, and the State: Germany from the Late 19th Century to the Onset of the Great Depression," in *Population, Labour, and Migration in 19th- and 20th-Century Germany*, 66–67.

85. Bade, "Labour, Migration, and the State," 107–109.

86. Weber, *The Growth of Cities*, 1.

87. Armengaud, "Population in Europe," 32–33; Maurice Garden, "Le bilan démographique des villes," 267–75.

88. Jan de Vries, *European Urbanization: 1500–1800* (Cambridge, Mass.: Harvard University Press, 1984), 77, 258–60.

89. Adna Weber, *The Growth of Cities*, frontispiece.

90. Only in the case of France (where natural increase was exceptionally low because the French birthrate was low) did the growth of cities significantly detract from rural areas in absolute numbers. Few enough French children were born in the countryside so that there was net *emigration* from many rural areas by the 1850s. Paul E. White, "Internal Migration in the Nineteenth and Twentieth Centuries," in *Migrants in Modern France: Population Mobility in the Later Nineteenth and Twentieth Centuries*, ed. P. E. White and P. E. Ogden (London: Unwin Hyman, 1989), 17–22.

91. Weber, *The Growth of Cities*, 249–55.

92. Christopher Klessman, "Long-Distance Migration, Integration and Segregation," 101–14; William J. Lowe, *The Irish in Mid-Victorian Lancashire: The Shaping of a Working-Class Community* (New York: Peter Lang, 1989).

93. Anderson, *Family Structure in Nineteenth Century Lancashire*, 37. According to William H. Sewell, Jr., *Structure and Mobility: The Men and Women of Marseille,*

1820–1870 (Cambridge: Cambridge University Press, 1985), even the great port city of Marseille drew most of its immigrants from its provençal hinterland (62% of the men and 72% of the women) and from nearby Italy in the 1820s, 162, 171; unfortunately, these figures from marriage records represent only a small fraction of all migrants. Most migrants in the southern French provincial capital of Nîmes were from eastern Languedoc in 1906; 70 percent were from its own *département* of the Gard and the contiguous *départements* of the Hérault, Lozère, and the Ardèche; see Moch, *Paths to the City*, 89.

94. David Kertzer and Dennis Hogan, "On the Move: Migration in an Italian Community, 1865–1921," *Social Science History* 9 (1985), 9–10; see also Leslie Page Moch, "The Importance of Mundane Movements: Small Towns, Nearby Places and Individual Itineraries in the History of Migration," in *Migrants in Modern France: Population Mobility in the Later Nineteenth and Twentieth Centuries*, ed. P. E. Ogden and P. E. White (London: Unwin Hyman, 1989), 97–117.

95. The cities had total migration rates from .20 to .54. James Jackson, Jr., "Migration in Duisburg, 1867–1890: Occupational and Familial Contexts," *Journal of Urban History* 8 (1982), 244–45; Steve Hochstadt, "Migration and Industrialization in Germany, 1815–1977," *Social Science History* 5 (1981), 445–68; Steve Hochstadt and James Jackson, Jr., " 'New' Sources for the Study of Migration in Early Nineteenth-Century Germany," *Historical Social Research/Historische Sozialforschung* 31 (1984), 85–92.

96. Hochstadt, "Städtische Wanderungsbewegungen in Deutschland"; *idem.*, "Urban Migration in Imperial Germany: Towards a Quantitative Model," *Historical Papers/Communications Historiques* (1986), 197–210; James Jackson, Jr., "Migration and Urbanization in the Ruhr Valley, 1850–1900" (Ph.D. diss., University of Minnesota, 1980), 64.

97. Kertzer and Hogan, "On the Move."

98. For the case of French miners, see Rolande Trempé, *Les mineurs de Carmaux: 1848–1914*, 2 vols. (Paris: Les Editions Ouvrières, 1971); Michael Hanagan, *Nascent Proletarians* (Oxford: Basil Blackwell, 1989), 31–33, chap. 3.

99. Brettell, *Men Who Migrate, Women Who Wait*, chap. 2; Chatelain, *Les migrants temporaires en France*, vol. 2, 820–21; Steve Hochstadt, "Migration in Germany: An Historical Study" (Ph.D. diss., Brown University, 1983), 320; Dirk Hoerder, "An Introduction to Labor Migration," 20; Antonio Meijide Pardo, *La emigración Gallega intrapeninsular en el sigló XVIII* (Madrid: Instituto Balmes de Sociologia, 1960), 461–606; Rosoli, "Italian Migration to European Countries from Political Unification to World War I," 109.

100. Hanagan, *Nascent Proletarians*, 31–37; see also Heilwig Schomerus, "The Family Life-Cycle: A Study of Factory Workers in Nineteenth-Century Württemberg," in *The German Family: Essays on the Social History of the Family in Nineteenth- and Twentieth-Century Germany*, ed. R. J. Evans and W. R. Lee (London: Croom Helm, 1981), 180.

101. Hochstadt, "Urban Migration in Imperial Germany," 208.

102. Schomerus, "The Family Life-Cycle," 178–79.

103. See, for example, Abel Poitrineau, *Remues d'hommes: Essai sur les migrations montagnards en France, aux 17e-18e siècles* (Paris: Aubier Montagne, 1983), chap. 9, conclusion; Chatelain, *Les migrants temporaires en France*, vol. 2, 1101–07.

104. Chatelain, *Les migrants temporaires de la France*, vol. 2, 821–25, 988–995, 1101–1107; Ministère du Commerce, de l'Industrie, des Postes et des Télégraphes, *Résultats statistiques du recensement général de la population effectué le 24 mars 1901*, 4 vols. (Paris: Imprimerie Nationale, 1906), vol. 4, 476.

105. For the problems of making inferences about migration from census data, see chapter 1. Data on rates of migration between administrative units are not

comparable between England and France, for example, because the English county is considerably smaller than the French *département*.

106. Ernest Ravenstein, *The Laws of Migration* (New York: Arno Press, 1976).

107. Dudley Baines, *Migration in a Mature Economy: Emigration and Internal Migration in England and Wales, 1861–1900* (Cambridge: Cambridge University Press, 1985), 235–37, 285–98.

108. Yves Tugault, *La mésure de la mobilité: Cing études sur les migrations internes* (Paris: INED, 1973), 36.

109. Kertzer and Hogan, "On the Move," 10–13. The Düsseldorf region included industrializing towns as well as agricultural areas, however, and the migration of women varied considerably from one area to another. Area-level data tell us little. Steve Hochstadt, "Migration in Germany," 205.

110. Weber, *The Growth of Cities*, 233–41.

111. The sex ratio in nearby textile towns of Elberfeld and Krefeld was likewise low; see Jackson, "Migration in Duisburg," 246; Köllmann, "The Population of Barmen," 589, 596–98. I have not found a measure from German migration registers that compares the migration rates of men and women into textile towns.

112. Claude Fohlen, *L'industrie textile au temps du Second Empire* (Paris: Plon, 1956), 339, 341; Raman, "Croissance d'un centre textile," 481–82.

113. Michel Raman, "Mésure de la croissance d'un centre textile: Roubaix de 1789 à 1913," *Revue d'histoire économique et sociale* 51 (1973), 473.

114. Fohlen, "Industrie textile," 234–35, 339, 343; Raman "Croissance d'un centre textile," 474.

115. Köllmann, "The Population of Barmen," 594–97; Anderson, *Family Structure in Nineteenth-Century Lancashire*, 34–37.

116. Fohlen, "Industrie textile," 341.

117. Georges Franchomme, "L'évolution démographique et économique de Roubaix dans le dernier tiers du XIXe siècle," *Revue du Nord* 51 (1969), 210. The year 1886 is the first date for which birthplace data are available.

118. These data are from a systematic sample of individuals in 10 percent of the households listed in the Roubaix census of 1906. See Leslie Page Moch and Louise A. Tilly, "Joining the Urban World: Occupation, Family, and Migration in Three French Cities," *Comparative Studies in Society and History* 27 (1985), 36, 39–47.

119. In the 1850s and 1860s, one in seven residents of Manchester, and about one in five residents of Liverpool, was born in Ireland. One-third of the entire population of Lancashire was born in Ireland throughout the 1841–1891 period. William J. Lowe, *The Irish in Mid-Victorian Lancashire*, 47; see also Lynn Lees, *Exiles of Erin: Irish Migrants in Victorian London* (Ithaca, N.Y.: Cornell University Press, 1979). For Italian migrants and others, see Nancy Green, " 'Filling the Void': Immigration to France before World War I"; Madelyn Holmes, *Forgotten Migrants: Foreign Workers in Switzerland before World War I* (Rutherford, N.J.: Farleigh Dickinson University Press, 1988); Köllmann, "The Population of Barmen," 588–607; Rosoli, "Italian Migration to European Countries."

120. Leslie Page Moch, "Infirmities of the Body and Vices of the Soul: Migrants, Family, and Urban Life in Turn-of-the-Century France," in *Essays on the Family and Historical Change* ed. L. Moch and G. Stark (College Station, Tex.: Texas A & M University Press, 1983), 55.

121. Franchomme, "Evolution démographique et économique," 211–12.

122. Raoul Blanchard, *La Flandre: Etude géographique de la plaine flamande en France, Belgique et Hollande* (Lille: Imprimerie Danel, 1906), 398–99; Blanchard's information was gleaned from the stationmaster at Herseaux; Franchomme, "Evolution démographique et économique," 212.

123. Raman, "Croissance d'un centre textile," 474.

124. Franchehomme, "L'évolution démographique et économique," 201–47; Michelle Perrot, *Les ouvriers en grève, France 1870–1890*, 2 vols. (Paris: Mouton, 1974), vol. 2, 352–56; Raman, "Croissance d'un centre textile," 470–91.

125. Jackson, "Migration in Duisburg," 244.

126. George Alter, *Family and the Female Life Course: The Women of Verviers, Belgium, 1849–1880* (Madison: University of Wisconsin Press, 1988), 67, 82.

127. Moch, "Infirmities of the Body and Vices of the Soul," 55.

128. See, for example, Jackson, "Migration in Duisburg," 248–55.

129. See Moch and Tilly, "Joining the Urban World"; Louise Tilly, "Occupational Structure, Women's Work and Demographic Change in Two French Industrial Cities, Anzin and Roubaix, 1872–1906," in *Time, Space and Man: Essays on Microdemography*, ed. J. Sundin and E. Soderlund (Atlantic Highlands., N.J.: Humanities Press, 1979), 107–32. This estimate is doubtless high because it is an inference from census data. Because migrant family groups tended to stay longer than single migrants, they are disproportionately represented in the census.

130. Franchomme, "Evolution démographique et économique," 208; this reflects a broader trend in urban demography; see de Vries, *European Urbanization*, 233–34; Jackson, "Migration in Duisburg," 247; Tilly, "Occupational Structure," 120–26.

131. Jackson, "Migration in Duisburg," 235, 246. Many metalworking towns, like those of the Stephanois valley in France, had economies and demographic characteristics that were more mixed. For sensitive studies of the labor forces in these towns, see Elinor Accampo, *Industrialization, Family Life, and Class Relations: Saint Chamond, 1815–1914* (Berkeley: University of California Press, 1989); Michael Hanagan, *Nascent Proletarians*.

132. Information on Duisburg comes from Jackson, "Migration in Duisburg," and from James Jackson, Jr., "Migration and Urbanization in the Ruhr Valley, 1850–1900," (Ph.D. diss., University of Minnesota, 1980).

133. David Crew, *Town in the Ruhr: A Social History of Bochum, 1860–1914* (New York: Columbia University Press, 1979), 60; Jackson, "Migration and Urbanization," 247–49; see also Hochstadt, "Migration in Germany," 213–22.

134. Jackson, "Migration in Duisburg," 246, 252; Hochstadt, "Migration in Germany," 202; Jackson, "Migration and Urbanization," 142.

135. Crew, *Town in the Ruhr*, 63–64; Jackson, "Migration in Duisburg," 244–45.

136. Jackson, "Migration and Urbanization," 169; see also John Modell, Frank Furstenburg, Jr., and Theodore Hershberg, "Social Change and the Transitions to Adulthood in Historical Perspective," *Journal of Family History* 1 (1976), 7–32.

137. Hochstadt, "Migration in Germany," 231.

138. Jackson, "Migration and Urbanization," 155, 157.

139. Jackson, "Migration and Urbanization," 157.

140. Hanagan, *Nascent Proletarians*, chap. 3.

141. For cities in which this pattern holds, see Sewell, *Structure and Mobility*, chap. 9; Moch, *Paths to the City*, chap. 5.

142. Jackson, "Migration and Urbanization," 143–45.

143. Hochstadt, "Migration in Germany," 319–20, 334; James Jackson, Jr., "Migration in Duisburg, 1821–1914," paper presented at the Symposium on Continental European Migration and Transcontinental Migration to North America: A Comparative Perspective, Bremerhaven, August 1991. For a breakdown of migration streams to the mining boomtown of Gelsenkirchen, see Köllmann, "The Population of Barmen."

144. Jackson, "Migration in Duisburg, 1867–1890," 247.

145. This section relies heavily on Moch and Tilly, "Joining the Urban World," 33–56.

146. Moch, *Paths to the City*, 136.

147. Gareth Stedman Jones, *Outcast London: A Study in the Relationship between Classes in Victorian Society* (Oxford: Oxford University Press, 1971); Weber, *The Growth of Cities*, 375; David Ransel, *Mothers of Misery: Child Abandonment in Russia* (Princeton: Princeton University Press, 1988), 164; Ministère du Commerce, *Résultats statistiques du recensement général de la population effectué le 24 mars 1901*, vol. 1, 329.

148. Jackson, "Migration in Duisburg, 1867–1890," 264.

149. There were shortcomings of this work and of the protection offered by live-in service; these are summarized in Rachel Fuchs and Leslie Page Moch, "Pregnant, Single, and Far from Home: Migrant Women in Nineteenth-Century Paris," *American Historical Review* 95 (1990), 1019–20.

150. See Barbara Franzoi, *At the Very Least She Pays the Rent: Women and German Industrialization, 1871–1914* (Westport, Conn.: Greenwood, 1985), 54–55, 94–95; Theresa McBride, *The Domestic Revolution: The Modernization of Household Service in England and France, 1820–1920* (New York: Holmes and Meier, 1976). For the autobiography of Doris Viersbeck, who came from a Holstein village and became a domestic in Hamburg, see Doris Viersbeck, *Erlebnisse eines Hamburger Dienstmädchens* (Munich: Ernest Reinhardt Verlag, 1910); for the autobiography of Juliette Sauget, whose career in Paris began with domestic service, see Marthe-Juliette Mouillon, "Un exemple de migration rurale: De la Somme dans la capitale. Domestique de la Belle Epoque à Paris (1902–1912)," *Etudes de la région parisienne* 44 (1970), 1–9.

151. Moch and Tilly, "Joining the Urban World," 42–48.

152. For an example of the constraints and policies surrounding career migration, see Leslie Page Moch, "Government Policy and Women's Experience: The Case of Teachers in France," *Feminist Studies* 14 (1988), 301–24.

153. Kertzer and Hogan, "On the Move," 16–17.

154. For an overview of the city in the industrial age, see Lewis Mumford, *The City in History* (Harmondsworth: Penguin Books, 1961).

155. See Armand Audiganne, *Les populations ouvrières et les industries de la France* (1860; reprint ed., New York: Burt Franklin, 1970); Friedreich Engels, *The Condition of the Working Class in England*, trans. W. O. Henderson and W. H. Chaloner (Oxford: Blackwell, 1971); Andrew Lees, "Debates about the Big City in Germany, 1890–1914," *Societas* 5 (1975), 31–47; Andrew Mearns, *The Bitter Cry of Outcast London. An Inquiry into the Condition of the Abject Poor* (Boston: Cupples, Upham, 1883); Jacob Riis, *How the Other Half Lives: Studies Among the Tenements of New York* (New York: Scribner's Sons, 1890); Georg Simmel, "Die Grossstädte und das Geistesleben," in *Die Grossstädte: Vorträge und Aufsätze zur Städteausstellung*, ed. R. Petermann et al. (Dresden: Zahn und Jaensch, 1903), 183–206; Max Weber, *The City* (New York: Basic Books, 1958).

156. Emile Vandervelde, *L'exode rural et le retour aux champs* (Paris: Alcan, 1903), 18–19. The most influential essay from American sociologists on this question is Robert Park, "Human Migration and the Marginal Man," *The American Journal of Sociology* 33 (1928), 881–93.

157. For example, see Janice Perlman, *The Myth of Marginality: Urban Poverty and Politics in Rio de Janeiro* (Berkeley, Calif.: University of California Press, 1976); Jackson, "Migration and Urbanization," chap. 6; *idem.*, "Overcrowding and Family Life: Working-Class Families and the Housing Crisis in Late Nineteenth-Century Duisburg," in *The German Family. Essays on the Social History of the Family in Nineteenth- and Twentieth-Century Germany*, ed. R. J. Evans and W. R. Lee (London: Croom Helm, 1981), 194–220; Moch, *Paths to the City*.

158. Louis Chevalier, *La formation de la population parisienne au XIXe siècle* (Paris: Presses Universitaires Françaises, 1950); *idem.*, *Laboring Classes and Dangerous*

Classes in Paris during the First Half of the Nineteenth Century (New York: Fertig, 1973).

159. Sewell, *Structure and Mobility*, chap. 8, esp. 214–26.

160. James Donovan, "The Uprooting Theory of Crime and the Corsicans of Marseille, 1825–1880," *French Historical Studies* 13 (1984), 500–28.

161. Sewell, *Structure and Mobility*, 232.

162. For studies of nineteenth-century prostitutes, see Alain Corbin, *Les filles de noce: Misère sexuelle et prostitution aux 19e et 20e siècles* (Paris: Aubier, 1978); Jill Harsin, *Policing Prostitution in Nineteenth-Century Paris* (Princeton: Princeton University Press, 1985); Richard Evans, "Prostitution, State and Society in Imperial Germany," *Past and Present* 70 (1976), 108; Alexandre Jean-Baptiste Parent-Duchâtelet, *De la prostitution dans la ville de Paris, considerée sous le rapport de l'hygiene publique, de la morale et de l'administration; ouvrage appuyé de documents statistiques puisés dans les archives de la préfecture de police* (Paris: Baillière et fils, 1936). I know of no study of migration that systematically investigates migration and prostitution.

163. Louise Tilly, Joan Scott, and Miriam Cohen, "Women's Work and European Fertility Patterns," *Journal of Interdisciplinary History* 6 (1976), 447–76.

164. See Rachel Fuchs, *Abandoned Children* (Albany, N.Y.: SUNY Press, 1984), chap. 3; Fuchs and Moch, "Pregnant, Single, and Far from Home," 1012–13; Ransel, *Mothers of Misery.*

165. John Knodel and Steve Hochstadt, "Urban and Rural Illegitimacy in Imperial Germany," in *Bastardy and Its Comparative History*, ed. P. Laslett, K. Oosterveen, and R. M. Smith (Cambridge, Mass.: Harvard University Press, 1980), 284–312; Martine Segalen, *Mari et femme dans la société paysanne* (Paris: Flammarion, 1980); Edward Shorter, John Knodel, and Etienne van de Walle, "The Decline of Non-Marital Fertility in Europe, 1880–1940," *Population Studies* 25 (1971), 375–93.

166. Anne Martin-Fugier reports that over half the single mothers delivering in Paris hospitals were domestics in 1890, "La bonne," in *Misérable et glorieuse: La femme du XIXe siècle* (Paris: Fayard, 1980), 35.

167. Alter, *Family and the Female Life Course*, chap. 5.

168. Alter, *Family and the Female Life Course*, 131.

169. Rachel Fuchs, *Poor and Pregnant in Paris* (New Brunswick, N.J.: Rutgers University Press, forthcoming in 1992).

170. Fuchs and Moch, "Pregnant, Single, and Far from Home."

171. Armengaud, "Population in Europe," 70.

172. Latin America's need for labor stemmed partly from the abolition of the slave trade in the western hemisphere; beginning in 1840, the number of Europeans crossing the Atlantic to the Americas regularly surpassed that of enslaved Africans for the first time. Before 1820, about 8 million Africans arrived in the Americas (primarily in Latin America), compared with an estimated 2.3 million Europeans. Philip Curtin, "Migration in the Tropical World," 27; David Eltis, "Free and Coerced Transatlantic Migrations: Some Comparisons," *American Historical Review* 88 (1983), 252–55.

173. Armengaud, "Population in Europe," 62, 66–67; Magnus Mörner and Herold Sims, *Adventurers and Proletarians: The Story of Migrants in Latin America* (Paris: United Nations Education, Scientific and Cultural Organization, 1985), 47.

174. J. D. Gould, "European Inter-Continental Emigration: The Role of 'Diffusion' and 'Feedback,' " *Journal of European Economic History* 9 (1980), 311.

175. For migration to the U.S. before 1840 see, for example, Bernard Bailyn, *Voyagers to the West: A Passage in the Peopling of America on the Eve of the Revolution* (New York: Knopf, 1986). On Irish migrations, see Kerby Miller, *Emigrants and*

Exiles: Ireland and the Irish Exodus to North America (New York: Oxford University Press, 1985).

176. A comprehensive study of English emigration is Baines, *Migration in a Mature Economy*.

177. For an overview of immigration to the U.S., see Leonard Dinnerstein, Roger Nichols, and David Reimers, *Natives and Strangers: Ethnic Groups and the Building of America* (New York: Oxford University Press, 1979), 87, 101. For emigration from England and Wales, see Baines, *Migration in a Mature Economy*.

178. Eva Morawska, "Labor Migrations of Poles in the Atlantic World Economy," 253; Dinnerstein, Nichols, and Reimers, *Natives and Strangers*, 101.

179. Entries into studies of Scandinavian migration are provided by, for example, Kristian Hvidt, *Flight to America: The Social Background of 300,000 Danish Emigrants* (New York: Academic Press, 1975); Harald Runblom and Hans Norman, eds., *From Sweden to America: A History of the Migration* (Minneapolis: University of Minnesota Press, 1976). Two sources that provide an introduction into studies of Asian migration to North America are: Sucheng Chan, "European and Asian Immigration into the United States in Comparative Perspective, 1820s to 1920s," in *Immigration Reconsidered*, 37–75; James T. Fawcett and Benjamin V. Carino, eds., *Pacific Bridges: The New Immigration from Asia and the Pacific Islands* (Staten Island, N.Y.: Center for Migration Studies, 1987).

180. Mörner and Sims, *Adventurers and Proletarians*, chaps. 3 and 4.

181. French participation in transatlantic migrations was minimal, partly because its exceptionally low birthrate meant that the nation could support its citizens and could spare few people. Philip Ogden, "International Migration in the Nineteenth and Twentieth Centuries," in *Migrants in Modern France*, 35–38.

182. Gould, "The Role of 'Diffusion' and 'Feedback,' " 282–89, 295.

183. Comparable data are not available for all locations; see Gould, "The Role of 'Diffusion' and 'Feedback,' " 289–91. For a detailed explanation of the migration systems developed from more and less isolated locations, see John Gjerde, "Chain Migrations from the West Coast of Norway: A Comparative Study," in Rudolph Vecoli and Suzanne Sinke, eds., *A Century of European Migrations, 1830–1930* (Champaign, Ill.: University of Illinois Press, forthcoming in 1992).

184. J. D. Gould, "The Role of 'Diffusion' and 'Feedback,' " 267.

185. J. D. Gould, "The Role of 'Diffusion' and 'Feedback,' " 268; Jonathan Sarna, "The Myth of No Return: Jewish Return Migration to Eastern Europe, 1880–1914," in *Labor Migration in the Atlantic Economies*, 423–34; M. Wischnitzer, *To Dwell in Safety: The Story of Jewish Migration Since 1800* (Philadelphia, Jewish Publication Society of America, 1948).

186. Baines, *Migration in a Mature Economy*, chaps. 3, 6, 9; Hvidt, *Flight to America*, chap. 10, 118; Walter Kamphoefner, *The Westfalians: From Germany to Missouri* (Princeton: Princeton University Press, 1987), 180–83; David Levine, "Production, Reproduction, and the Proletarian Family," 99–118; Mörner and Sims, *Adventurers and Proletarians*, 53–55; Morawska, "Labor Migrations of Poles in the Atlantic World Economy," 253; Charles Tilly, "Demographic Origins of the European Proletariat," 1–85.

187. Kamphoefner, *The Westfalians*, 178–79.

188. Lucassen, *Migrant Labour in Europe*, 29–41; Jürgen Schlumbohm, "Seasonal Fluctuations and Social Division of Labour: Rural Linen Production in the Osnabrück and Bielefeld Regions and the Urban Woolen Industry in the Niederlausitz, c. 1770–c. 1850," in *Manufacture in Town and Country before the Factory*, ed. Maxine Berg, Pat Hudson, and Michael Sonenscher (Cambridge: Cambridge University Press, 1983), 92–123.

189. Kamphoefner, *The Westfalians*, 18–25.

190. Kamphoefner, *The Westfalians*, 18–25.
191. Kamphoefner, *The Westfalians*, 19.
192. Sune Åkerman, "Towards an Understanding of Emigrational Processes," in *Human Migration: Patterns and Policies*, ed. William McNeill and Ruth Adams (Bloomington, Ind.: Indiana University Press, 1978), 303.
193. Gould, "The Role of 'Diffusion' and 'Feedback,' " 304.
194. Mörner and Sims, *Adventurers and Proletarians*, 41–42; Morawska, "Labor Migrations of Poles in the Atlantic World Economy," 252–53.
195. Walter Kamphoefner, *The Westfalians*, 178; Mörner and Sims, *Adventurers and Proletarians*, 64–65; Morawska, "Labor Migrations of Poles in the Atlantic World Economy," 250–51.
196. J. D. Gould, "European Inter-Continental Emigration 1815–1914: Patterns and Causes," *Journal of European Economic History* 8 (1979), 613; Mörner and Sims, *Adventurers and Proletarians*, 43.
197. A range of prices for passage is discussed in Philip Taylor, *The Distant Magnet* (New York: Harper and Row, 1971), chap. 5. Brazil was not the only nation to assist immigrants (Australia, New Zealand, and Argentina all offered aid at one time), but conditions on Brazil's coffee plantations and the fact that Brazil was encouraging immigrants to replace its slave labor meant that without subsidies, Brazil could not compete with Argentina, for example. Slavery was ended in Brazil in 1888. See Gould, "The Role of 'Diffusion' and 'Feedback,' " 272–82.
198. Gould, "Patterns and Causes," 667.
199. The Eurocentric focus here is appropriate for this volume, but it does not attend to the excellent work appearing on the role of the Asian, African, and indigenous American labor force in the world economy. For examples, see Lucie Cheng and Adna Bonacich, eds., *Labor Migration under Capitalism: Asian Workers in the United States before World War II* (Berkeley, Calif.: University of California Press, 1984).
200. A most articulate explanation of the fit between Europe and North America into the core-periphery model is Morawska, "Labor Migrations of Poles in the Atlantic World Economy," 237–72.
201. Among the numerous and excellent studies of the origins and workings of migrant groups are Donna Gabaccia, *From Sicily to Elizabeth Street: Housing and Social Change among Italian Immigrants, 1880–1930* (Albany, N.Y.: SUNY Press, 1984); Kamphoefner, *The Westfalians*. See Åkerman, "Towards an Understanding of Emigrational Processes," 287–306. For a survey of the volume of letters and prepaid tickets sent home, see Hvidt, *Flight to America*, chap. 15. For histories of contacts that began specific migration streams, see Vecoli and Sinke, eds., *A Century of European Migrations*.
202. Baines, *Migration in a Mature Economy*, chap. 6.
203. Donna Gabaccia, "Women of the Mass Migrations: From Minority to Majority, 1820–1930," forthcoming in Dirk Hoerder and Leslie Page Moch, eds., *Global Moves, Local Contexts*. J. D. Gould, "European Inter-Continental Emigration. The Road Home: Return Migration from the U.S.A.," *Journal of European Economic History* 9, (1980), 78; Scandinavian migration, however, tended to originate with farm families and become more of a movement of individual workers over time. See, for example, Hvidt, *Flight to America*, chap. 9.
204. U.S. Congress, Senate, *Reports of the Immigration Commission* (U.S. Printing Office, Washington, D.C., 1911), 360–65. Reported in Kamphoefner, *The Westfalians*, 188.
205. For a comprehensive study of female migrants to the United States, see Donna Gabaccia, "Women of the Mass Migrations: From Minority to Majority, 1820–1930."

206. Irish women from the provinces of Connaught and Munster were most likely to outnumber men. Miller, *Emigrants and Exiles*, 582; Janet Nolan, *Ourselves Alone: Women's Emigration from Ireland* (Lexington, Ky.: University Press of Kentucky, 1989).

207. Gould, "Patterns and Causes," 656–67; Odd S. Lovoll, "A Pioneer Chicago Colony from Voss, Norway: Its Impact on Overseas Migration, 1836–1860," in *A Century of European Migrations, 1830–1930*; John E. Zucchi, "Precursors of the 'New Immigration': Italian Street Musicians, 1815–1885" (McGill University, 1986).

208. Gould, "The Role of 'Diffusion' and 'Feedback,' " 272–82; Hvidt, *Flight to America*, chap. 1.

209. Emilio Franzina, "The Commerce of Migration. Aspects of Recruitment of Italian Workers for Argentina and Brazil in the Nineteenth Century (1867–1887)" (Universita degli studi di Verona, 1986, photocopy); Tadeusz Gasinski, "Polish Contract Labor in Hawaii, 1896–1899," *Polish American Studies* 39 (1982), 14–27; Gjerde, "The Chain Migrations from the West Coast of Norway: A Comparative Study." Some of the failed migration systems were attempts on the part of Caribbean and South Americans to replace slave labor.

210. Where in 1899 a team of 17 women had gone for farm work in Denmark, there were 50 in 1911; where 80 men had gone into the Ostrava mines, there were only 63. Franciszek Bujak, *Maszkienice, Wieś Powiatu Brzeskiego: Stosunki Gospodar-cze i Społeczne* (Krakow: G. Gebethner, 1901), and *idem.*, *Maszkienice. Wieś Powiatu Brzeskiego: Rozwój or R.1900 do R. 1911* (Lvov: B. Bebethner, 1914), cited by Morawska, "Labor Migrations of Poles in the Atlantic World Economy," 256–61 and *idem.*, *For Bread with Butter* (Cambridge: Cambridge University Press, 1985), 39.

211. Gould, "Patterns and Causes," 617; Hvidt, *Flight to America*, 20–23. In addition, the nineteenth century allowed migration as part of the liberal politics that replaced mercantilism in that age; see Hvidt, *Flight to America*, chap. 2.

212. Gould, "Patterns and Causes," 606.

213. Mörner and Sims, *Adventurers and Proletarians*, chap. 4, 43.

214. Gould, "Patterns and Causes," 607.

215. Raphael Samuel, "Comers and Goers," in *The Victorian City: Images and Realities*, 2 vols., ed. H. J. Dyos and M. Wolff (London: Routledge and Kegan Paul, 1973), vol. 1, 124.

216. Gould, "Patterns and Causes," 604–607; idem., "Return Migration from the U.S.A.," 60.

217. Donna Gabaccia, "Women of the Mass Migrations"; Gould, "Return Migration from the U.S.A.," 50–63; Mörner and Sims, *Adventurers and Proletarians*, 69–70. Gould draws on Massimo Livi-Bacci, *L'Immigrazione e l'Assimilazione degli Italiani negli Stati Uniti secondo le Statistiche Demografiche Americane* (Milano: Guiffrè, 1961). For an assessment of studies on return migration to Europe, see Dirk Hoerder, "Immigration and the Working Class: The Remigration Factor," *International Labor and Working Class History* 21 (1982), 28–41.

218. Lars-Göran Tedebrand, "Remigration from America to Sweden," in *Labor Migration in the Atlantic Economies*, 374; see also Francesco Cerase, "Expectations and Reality: A Case Study of Return Migration from the United States to Southern Italy," *International Migration Review* 8 (1974), 245–62; Gabaccia, "Women of the Mass Migrations"; Günther Moltmann, "American-German Return Migration in the Nineteenth and Early Twentieth Centuries," *Central European History* 13 (1980), 378–92; Karen Schniedewind, "The Structure and Motivation of German Return Migration to Bremen, 1850–1924" (Paper delivered at the Fifteenth Annual Meeting of the Social Science History Association, Minneapolis, Minnesota, October 20, 1990).

219. "Tutto il mondo è un paese," Francesco Coletti, *Dell'Emigrazione Italiana* (Milan: Ulrico Hoepli, 1912), 180; quoted in Gould, "Return Migration from the U.S.A.," 76.

220. For examples, see Brettell, *Men Who Migrate, Women Who Wait*; Morawska, "Labor Migrations of Poles in the Atlantic World Economy," 263–67; Tedebrand, "Remigration from America to Sweden," 369–72.

221. Tedebrand, "Remigration from America to Sweden," 372; also, see Morawska, "Labor Migrations of Poles in the Atlantic World Economy," 263–66; Tilly, "Demographic Origins of the European Proletariat," 46.

222. See, for example, Tedebrand, "Remigration from America to Sweden," 378–79; Morawska, "Labor Migrations of Poles in the Atlantic World Economy," 266.

223. Donna Gabaccia, *Militants and Migrants: Rural Sicilians Become American Workers* (New Brunswick, N.J.: Rutgers University Press, 1988), 158.

224. Baines, *Migration in a Mature Economy*, chap. 9; Sten Carlsson, "Chronology and Composition of Swedish Emigration to America," in *From Sweden to America*, 56–61.

225. Lynn Lees, "The Irish Transatlantic Migration System in the Nineteenth Century" (University of Pennsylvania, 1982, photocopy); Hans Norman and Harald Runblom, "Migration Patterns in the Nordic Countries," in *Labor Migration in the Atlantic Economies*, 50–51.

226. For a reflection on this phenomenon, see Franco Ramella, "Emigration from an Area of Intense Industrial Development: The Case of Northwestern Italy," in *A Century of European Migrations*.

227. Steve Hochstadt, "Migration and Industrialization in Germany," 445–68; idem., "Städtische Wanderungsbewegungen in Deutschland 1850–1914." Some information about mobility levels can be gained from national figures regarding proportion of population in parish or commune of birth; see Ravenstein, *The Laws of Migration*.

228. For the case that workers in rural industry were most likely to emigrate to North America, see Kamphoefner, *The Westfalians*, 178–80. For the geographical expansion of the rural marriage market, see Moch, *Paths to the City*, chap. 2; Philip Ogden, "Migration, Marriage and the Collapse of Traditional Peasant Society in France," in *The Geographical Impact of Migration*, ed. Paul E. White and Robert Woods (London: Longman, 1980), 151–79.

229. For a case study of this shift, see Hanagan, *Nascent Proletarians*.

5. MIGRATION IN THE TWENTIETH CENTURY

1. Serge Grafteaux, *Mémé Santerre: A French Woman of the People* (New York: Schocken Books, 1985), 75.

2. For a discussion of these issues, see Gérard Noiriel, *Le creuset français: Histoire de l'immigration, XIXe-XXe siècles* (Paris: Seuil, 1988), chap. 2.

3. Eugene Kulischer, *Europe on the Move: War and Population Changes, 1917–1947* (New York: Columbia University Press, 1948), 255.

4. Nermin Abadan-Unat, "Turkish Migration to Europe, 1960–1975: A Balance Sheet of Achievements and Failures," in *Turkish Workers in Europe, 1960–1975: A Socio-Economic Reappraisal* (Leiden: Brill, 1976), 6.

5. Yul Brynner, *Bring Forth the Children: A Journey to the Forgotten People of Europe and the Middle East* (New York: McGraw-Hill, 1960), 24–25.

6. Kemal Altun is a pseudonym; André Coquart, "Du village de Yesilyazi au

quartier des Chamards à Dreux (Eure et Loire)," *Hommes et migrations: Documents* 1021 (1981), 3–23.

7. For migrants in the secondary labor force, see Michael Piore, *Birds of Passage: Migrant Labor and Industrial Societies* (Cambridge: Cambridge University Press, 1979), chap. 4.

8. Kulischer, *Europe on the Move*, 250–51.

9. Rosemarie Rogers, "Post-World War II European Labor Migration: An Introduction to the Issues," in *Guests Come to Stay: The Effects of European Labor Migration on Sending and Receiving Countries* (Boulder, Colo.: Westview Press, 1985), 6–11. The receiving countries included in this calculation were Austria, Belgium, France, West Germany, the Netherlands, Sweden, and Switzerland.

10. Ansley Coale and Roy Treadway, "A Summary of the Changing Distribution of Overall Fertility, Marital Fertility, and the Proportion Married in the Provinces of Europe," in *The Decline of Fertility in Europe* (Princeton: Princeton University Press, 1986), 37–39.

11. The figures for British immigration and emigration are net figures. Jacques Dupâquier, "La population pendant la première guerre mondiale," in *Histoire de la population française*, ed. J. Dupâquier, vol. 4, *De 1914 à nos jours* (Paris: Presses Universitaires de France, 1988), 66; Colin Dyer, *Population and Society in Twentieth Century France* (New York: Holmes and Meier, 1978), 31; Grafteaux, *Mémé Santerre*, 75–77; Brian R. Mitchell, *European Historical Statistics, 1750–1970* (New York: Columbia University Press, 1978), 47; Jay Winter, *The Great War and the British People* (London: Macmillan, 1986), 266–67.

12. Ulrich Herbert, *A History of Foreign Labor in Germany, 1880–1980* (Ann Arbor: University of Michigan Press, 1990), 87–108.

13. Gary Cross, *Immigrant Workers in Industrial France: The Making of a New Laboring Class* (Philadelphia: Temple University Press, 1983), 33–42; Dupâquier, "La population pendant la première guerre mondiale," 66–67.

14. Kulischer, *Europe on the Move*, 167–68; Michael Marrus, *The Unwanted: European Refuges in the Twentieth Century* (New York: Oxford University Press, 1985), 58–60; Aristide Zolberg, Astri Suhrke, and Sergio Aguayo, *Escape from Violence: Conflict and the Refugee Crisis in the Developing World* (New York: Oxford University Press, 1989), 17–20.

15. This statement about France holds equally well for Germany and Italy; Cross, *Immigrant Workers*, 122.

16. Herbert, *A History of Foreign Labor in Germany*, 121–26.

17. Christopher Klessman, "Comparative Immigrant History: Polish Workers in the Ruhr Area and the North of France," *Journal of Social History* 20 (1986), 335–53; Noiriel, *Le creuset français*, chap. 6; Zolberg, Suhrke, and Aguayo, *Escape from Violence*, 18.

18. Cross, *Immigrant Workers*, 18–19, 53, 54, 56, 58, 83, 84, 92, 100, 112–19, 120, 128.

19. Maurice Garden and Hervé Le Bras, "La population française entre les deux guerres," in *Histoire de la population française*, ed. J. Dupâquier, vol. 4, *De 1914 à nos jours*, 107; Herbert, *A History of Foreign Labor in Germany*, 126; Kulischer, *Europe on the Move*, 186; Philip Ogden, "International Migration in the Nineteenth and Twentieth Centuries," in *Migrants in Modern France: Population Mobility in the Later Nineteenth and Twentieth Centuries*, ed. Philip E. Ogden and Paul E. White (London: Unwin Hyman, 1989), 44–47.

20. Marrus, *The Unwanted*, 126–30, 136–58.

21. Marrus, *The Unwanted*, 197.

22. Kulischer, *Europe on the Move*, 255–59; Marrus, *The Unwanted*, 196–97, 201, 220–27.

23. Marrus, *The Unwanted*, 206, 227, 275–76, 278.

24. Kulischer, *Europe on the Move*, 264.

25. Herbert, *A History of Foreign Labor in Germany*, chap. 4, 154, 156.

26. Alexander Donat (pseud.), *The Holocaust Kingdom: A Memoir* (New York, 1965), 318–19; Malcolm Proudfoot, *European Refugees: 1939–1952* (London: Faber and Faber, 1957), 158–59; quoted by Marrus, *The Unwanted*, 299–300.

27. Frank Epp, *Mennonite Exodus: The Rescue and Resettlement of the Russian Mennonites since the Communist Revolution* (Altona, Manitoba, 1962), 357; quoted by Marrus, *The Unwanted*, 239; Zolberg, Suhrke, and Aguayo, *Escape from Violence*, 20–23.

28. Kulischer, *Europe on the Move*, 264–73; Marrus, *The Unwanted*, 303, 325–30.

29. Marrus, *The Unwanted*, 307, 332–39.

30. Pierre-Jakez Hélias, *The Horse of Pride* (New Haven, Conn.: Yale University Press, 1978), chap. 1.

31. Ansley Coale and Roy Treadway, "A Summary of the Changing Distribution of Overall Fertility," 37–39.

32. Maurizio Gribaudi, *Itinéraires ouvriers: Espaces et groupes sociaux à Turin au début du XXe siècle* (Paris: Editions de l'Ecole des Hautes Etudes en Sciences Sociales, 1987), 15–16, 70–75; David Kertzer and Dennis Hogan, "On the Move: Migration in an Italian Community, 1865–1921," *Social Science History* 9 (1985), 1–23.

33. H. Boker and F. W. von Bulow, *The Rural Exodus in Germany* (Geneva: International Labour Office, 1933); R. Heberle and Fritz Meyer, *Die Grossstädte im Strome der Binnenwanderung* (Leipzig: Hirzel, 1937); Robert E. Park, "Human Migration and the Marginal Man," *The American Journal of Sociology* 33 (1928): 881–93; C. S. Schorske, "The Idea of the City in European Thought: Voltaire to Spengler," in *The Historian and the City* (Boston: MIT Press, 1963), 95–114. Interwar concerns also drew on earlier unease about rural-urban migration; see Max Weber, *The City* (New York: Basic Books, 1958).

34. The extreme case is Ireland; see Robert E. Kennedy, Jr., *The Irish: Emigration, Marriage and Fertility* (Berkeley, Calif.: University of California Press, 1973); Janet Nolan, *Ourselves Alone: Women's Emigration from Ireland* (Lexington, Ky.: University Press of Kentucky, 1989). For an instructive counterexample in a region in which women owned land, but from which emigration was blocked, see Caroline Brettell, *Men Who Migrate, Women Who Wait: Population and History in a Portuguese Parish* (Princeton: Princeton University Press, 1986).

35. Philip Ogden, "Migration, Marriage and the Collapse of Traditional Peasant Society in France," in *The Geographical Impact of Migration*, ed. P. E. White and R. Woods (London: Longman, 1980), 173–76; Yves Tugault, *La mésure de la mobilité: Cinq études sur les migrations internes* (Paris: INED, 1973), 32–38; Georges Jegouzo, "L'ampleur de célibat chez les agriculteurs," *Economie et statistique* 58 (1972), 13–22.

36. Marie Daudet is a pseudonym; Isabelle Bertaux-Wiame, "The Life History Approach to the Study of Internal Migration," *Oral History* 7 (1979), 31.

37. Bertaux-Wiame, "The Life History Approach," 31.

38. Ogden, "Migration, Marriage and the Collapse of Traditional Peasant Society in France," 164–73.

39. Paul White, "Migration Loss and the Residual Community: A Study in Rural France, 1962–1975," in *The Geographical Impact of Migration*, 198–222; *idem.*, "Internal Migration in the Nineteenth and Twentieth Centuries," in *Migrants in Modern France*, 15. For a detailed study of this phenomenon, see Philippe Pinchemel, *Structures sociales et dépopulation rurale dans les campagnes picardes de 1836 à 1936* (Paris: Colin, 1957).

40. Dov Friedlander and R. J. Roshier, "A Study of Internal Migration in En-

gland and Wales: Part I," *Population Studies* 19 (1966), 239–79; Dorothy Swaine Thomas, *Social and Economic Aspects of Swedish Population Movements, 1750–1933* (New York: Macmillan, 1941), Appendix D; United Nations Department of Economic and Social Affairs, "Methods of Measuring Internal Migrations," *Population Studies* 47 (1970), 52; cited in Steve Hochstadt, "Migration and Industrialization in Germany, 1815–1977," *Social Science History* 5 (1981), 454–55; White, "Internal Migration in the Nineteenth and Twentieth Centuries," 15.

41. Kingsley Davis, "The Effect of Outmigration on Regions of Origin," in *Internal Migration: A Comparative Perspective* (London: Academic Press, 1977), 152; cited by Philip E. Ogden, *Migration and Geographical Change* (Cambridge: Cambridge University Press, 1984), 57.

42. Subsequent members were Britain and Denmark (1973), Greece (1981), Spain and Portugal (1986).

43. Ogden, *Migration and Geographical Change*, 58–59; these figures are based on individual national definitions of urban areas.

44. Peter Wood, "Inter-Regional Migration in Western Europe: A Reappraisal," in *Migration in Post-War Europe: Geographical Essays*, ed. J. Salt and H. Clout (London: Oxford University Press, 1976), 52–60.

45. Jan de Vries, *European Urbanization, 1500–1800* (Cambridge, Mass.: Harvard University Press, 1984), 171, 265.

46. Ogden, *Migration and Geographical Change*, 59; White, "Internal Migration in the Nineteenth and Twentieth Centuries," 15–16; Hilary Winchester, "The Structure and Impact of the Postwar Rural Revival: Isère," in *Migrants in Modern France*, 142–59.

47. White, "Internal Migration in the Nineteenth and Twentieth Centuries," 25–27.

48. Susan Cotts Watkins, *From Provinces into Nations: Demographic Integration in Western Europe, 1870–1960* (Princeton: Princeton University Press, 1991).

49. Stephen Castles, Heather Booth, and Tina Wallace, *Here for Good: Western Europe's New Ethnic Minorities* (London: Pluto Press, 1984), 25; Stephen Castles and Godula Kosak, *Immigrant Workers and Class Structure in Western Europe* (London: Oxford University Press, 1973), 26–27. An explanation of the substitution function of migrant labor is found in Herman Korte, "Labor Migration and the Employment of Foreigners in the Federal Republic of Germany since 1950," in *Guests Come to Stay*, 41–43; Rogers, "Post-World War II European Labor Migration," 21.

50. John Berger and Jean Mohr, *A Seventh Man: Migrant Workers in Europe* (New York: Viking, 1979), 12; Castles, Booth, and Wallace, *Here for Good*, 43; Rogers, "Post-World War II European Labor Migration," in *Guests Come to Stay*, 4–11.

51. The Commonwealth includes Canada, Australia, and New Zealand; the New Commonwealth includes India, Pakistan, Bangladesh, and the West Indies. Rosemarie Rogers, "Western Europe in the 1980s: The End of Immigration?" in *Guests Come to Stay*, 296; Heinz Werner, "Migration and Free Movement of Workers in Western Europe," in *Les Travailleurs Etrangers en Europe Occidentale*, ed. Philippe Bernard (Paris: Mouton, 1976), 65–85.

52. Korte, "Labor Migration and the Employment of Foreigners in the Federal Republic of Germany since 1950," 41–43.

53. Zolberg, Suhrke, and Aguayo, *Escape from Violence*, 227–34.

54. Castles, Booth, and Wallace, *Here for Good*, 43, 55.

55. Cross, *Immigrant Workers in Industrial France*, 161–63.

56. Robert Berrier, "The French Textile Industry: A Segmented Labor Market," in *Guests Come to Stay*, 51–68; Berger and Mohr, *A Seventh Man*, 152–71.

57. J. S. MacDonald and L. B. MacDonald, *The Invisible Immigrants* (London: Runnymede Trust, 1972); Leslie Page Moch and Louise A. Tilly, "Immigrant

Women in the City: Comparative Perspectives," Center for Research on Social Organization, University of Michigan, 1979.

58. Berger and Mohr, *A Seventh Man*, 113, 122.

59. Herbert, *A History of Foreign Labor in Germany*, 216–18.

60. *United Nations Demographic Yearbook 1967* (New York: United Nations), 116; *United Nations Yearbook 1968*, 591 ff., cited in Castles and Kosak, *Immigrant Workers and Class Structure*, 27–28.

61. The material in this section is based on the work of Castles, Booth, and Wallace, in *Here for Good*, chap. 3.

62. Differences in numbers of total migrant residents between Table 5:1 and the text are accounted for by the fact that the table includes only migrants from the nine listed sending countries.

63. Castles, Booth, and Wallace, *Here for Good*, 50–56.

64. Herbert, *A History of Foreign Labor in Germany*, 200–201.

65. Castles, Booth, and Wallace, *Here for Good*, 71–85.

66. Castles, Booth, and Wallace, *Here for Good*, 41–47.

67. Madelyn Holmes, *Forgotten Migrants: Foreign Workers in Switzerland before World War I* (Rutherford, N.J.: Fairleigh Dickinson University Press, 1988).

68. Castles, Booth, and Wallace, *Here for Good*, 66–71.

69. Castles, Booth, and Wallace, *Here for Good*, 47–50, 57–66.

70. Berger and Mohr, *A Seventh Man*, 204.

71. Piore, *Birds of Passage*, 52–59.

72. Rogers, "Post-World War II European Labor Migration," 5–7; John Salt, "A Comparative Overview of International Trends and Types, 1950–1980," *International Migration Review* 23 (1989), 442.

73. Rogers, "Post-World War II European Labor Migration," 4–9.

74. For the "explosive" nature of chain migration, see a special issue of the *International Migration Review*, 23, no. 4 (1989).

75. Berrier, "The French Textile Industry," 64; Castles, Booth, and Wallace, *Here for Good*, 52. For a comprehensive introduction to this enormous social problem, see Castles, Booth, and Wallace, *Here for Good*, chap. 7.

76. Klaus Bade, "German Emigration to the United States and Continental Immigration to Germany in the Late Nineteenth and Early Twentieth Centuries," *Central European History* 13 (1980), 370–74; Castles, Booth, and Wallace, *Here for Good*, 70; A. Lebon and G. Falchi, "New Developments in Intra-European Migration Since 1974," *International Migration Review* 14 (1980), 549–50; Rogers, "Western Europe in the 1980s," 289.

77. Rogers, "Post-World War II European Labor Migration," 17.

78. Korte, "Labor Migration and the Employment of Foreigners," 32; Lebon and Falchi, "New Developments in Intra-European Migration Since 1974," 542.

79. Castles, Booth, and Wallace, *Here for Good*, 43, 55, 73.

80. See, for example, Nermin Abadan-Unat, "Turkish Migration to Europe," 1–49; Berger and Mohr, *A Seventh Man*, chaps. 1 and 3.

81. Castles, Booth, and Wallace, *Here for Good*; Rogers, *Guests Come to Stay*.

82. Coale and Treadway, "A Summary of the Changing Distribution," 37–39; Korte, "Labor Migration and the Employment of Foreigners."

83. For the history and impact of this important migration tradition, see Brettell, *Men Who Migrate, Women Who Wait*, chap. 2.

84. Caroline Brettell, *We Have Already Cried Many Tears* (Cambridge, Mass.: Schenkman Publishing, 1982), 16–31; Rogers, "Post-World War II European Labor Migration," 5.

85. Brettell, *We Have Already Cried Many Tears*, 26–29; Moch and Tilly, "Immigrant Women in the City."

86. Colette Callier Boisvert, "Working-Class Portuguese Families in a French Provincial Town: Adaptive Strategies," in *Migrants in Europe: The Role of Family, Labor, and Politics*, ed. H. Beuchler and J.-M. Beuchler (New York: Greenwood Press, 1987); Caroline Brettell, "Hope and Nostalgia: The Migration of Portuguese Women to Paris" (Ph.D. dissertation, Brown University, 1978); Moch and Tilly, "Immigrant Women in the City."

87. Abadan-Unat, "Turkish Migration to Europe," 6–7; Mübeccel Kiray, "The Family of the Immigrant Worker," in *Turkish Workers in Europe, 1960–1975*, 210–11; Otto Neuloh, "Structural Unemployment in Turkey: Its Relation to Migration," in *Turkish Workers in Europe, 1960–1975*, 54; Ray Rist, *Guestworkers in Germany: The Prospects for Pluralism* (New York: Praeger, 1976), 102; Yücel, "Turkish Migrant Workers in the Federal Republic of Germany," in *Migrants in Europe*, 120–21.

88. Coquart, "Du Village de Yesilyazi au quartier des Chamards à Dreux (Eure et Loire)," 3–23; Berger and Mohr, *A Seventh Man*, 47–57.

89. Abadan-Unat, "Turkish Migration to Europe," 6–7; Booth, *Guestworkers or Immigrants? A Demographic Analysis of the Status of Migrants in West Germany*, Monographs in Ethnic Relations, no. 1 (Warwick: Center for Research in Ethnic Relations, 1985), Tables 1 and 2; Castles, Booth, and Wallace, *Here for Good*, 76; Rogers, "Post-World War II European Labor Migration," 6.

90. Charity Goodman, "A Day in the Life of a Single Spanish Woman in West Germany," in *Migrants in Europe*, 210–11; Godula Kosack, "Migrant Women: The Move to Western Europe—A Step Towards Emancipation?", *Race and Class* 17 (1976), 374–77; Yücel, "Turkish Migrant Workers in the Federal Republic of Germany," 127–38.

91. Nermin Abadan-Unat, "Implications of Migration on Emancipation and Pseudo-Emancipation of Turkish Women," *International Migration Review* 11 (1977), 31; idem., "Turkish Migration to Europe," 6–7; Mirjana Morokvasic, "Birds of Passage Are Also Women. . . ," *International Migration Review* 18 (1984), 886–907.

92. Booth, *Guestworkers or Immigrants?*, Tables 7 and 80; Korte, "Labor Migration and the Employment of Foreigners," 33.

93. Abadan-Unat, "Turkish Migration to Europe," 32–34.

94. This proportion had been well under 10 percent during the 1960s and had moved from 12 to 24 percent in the early 1970s. Booth, *Guestworkers or Immigrants?*, Table 16.

95. Lenie Brouwer and Marijke Priester, "Living in Between: Turkish Women in Their Homeland and in the Netherlands," in *One Way Ticket: Migration and Female Labour*, ed. A. Phizacklea (London: Routledge and Kegan Paul, 1983), 113–29; Mübeccel Kiray, "The Family of the Immigrant Worker," 210–34.

96. Brouwer and Priester, "Living in Between."

97. Abadan-Unat, "Implications of Migration on Emancipation and Pseudo-Emancipation of Turkish Women"; Kosack, "Migrant Women: The Move to Western Europe," 374–77.

98. Herbert, *A History of Foreign Labor in Germany*, 242–43.

99. See Coquart, "Du village de Yesilyazi au quartier des Chamards à Dreux"; Castles, Wallace, and Booth, *Here for Good*, chap. 6; Korte, "Labor Migration and the Employment of Foreigners in the Federal Republic of Germany"; Herbert, *A History of Foreign Labor in Germany*, 251; Rist, *Guestworkers in Germany*; Mehmet Yaşin, "Gather up the Bales, We Are Going Back," in *Turkish Workers in Europe: An Interdisciplinary Study*, ed. İlhan Başgöz and Norman Furniss (Bloomington, Ind.: Indiana University Press, 1985), 175–91.

100. Castles, Booth, and Wallace, *Here for Good*, chap. 7.

101. Heinrich Böll, *Gruppenbild mit Dame* (Cologne: Kiepenheuer and Witsch, 1971).

102. James O. Huff and Brigitte Waldorf, "A Predictive Model of Residential Mobility and Residential Segregation," *Papers of the Regional Science Association* 65 (1988), 59–77.

103. For the reporting of this phenomenon in the U.S. press, see Richard Bernstein, "Fanning French Fears," *The New York Times Magazine*, October 4, 1987; "Rightist Parties Forming in Europe," *New York Times* November 22, 1987.

104. See, for example, the reporting in Gerald Marzorati, "Salman Rushdie: Fiction's Embattled Infidel," *The New York Times Magazine*, January 29, 1989.

105. See, for example, Nermin Abadan-Unat, "Identity Crisis of Turkish Migrants," in *Turkish Workers in Europe*, 3–22; Castles, Booth, and Wallace, *Here for Good*, chap. 6; Nancy Foner, "Sex Roles and Sensibilities: Jamaican Women in New York and London," in *International Migration*; and the essays in *Turkish Workers in Europe* and *One Way Ticket*. I would like to thank Fatma Müge Göçek for sending me Başgöz and Furniss, *Turkish Workers in Europe*.

106. Abadan-Unat, "Identity Crisis of Turkish Migrants"; Joyce Mushaben, "A Crisis of Culture: Isolation and Integration among Turkish Guestworkers in The German Federal Republic," in *Turkish Workers in Europe*, 125–50; Yaşin, "Gather up the Bales," 191.

107. Herbert, *A History of Foreign Labor in Germany*, 255–57; Judith Miller, "Strangers at the Gate," *New York Times Magazine* September 15, 1991; John Tagliabue, "European Fleeing West in Search of a Better Life," *New York Times* August 11, 1991. The figure of 1.3 million is from the United Nations High Commissioner for Refugees in Bonn.

108. See also Herbert, *A History of Foreign Labor in Germany*, 255–57.

109. Salt, "A Comparative Overview of International Trends and Types, 1950–1980," *International Migration Review* 23 (1989), 432.

Bibliography

Abadan-Unat, Nermin. "Identity Crisis of Turkish Immigrants: First and Second Generation." In *Turkish Workers in Europe: An Interdisciplinary Study*, edited by I. Başgöz and N. Furniss, 3–22.

———. "Implications of Migration on Emancipation and Pseudo-Emancipation of Turkish Women." *International Migration Review* 11 (1977): 31–57.

———. "Turkish Migration to Europe, 1960–1975: A Balance Sheet of Achievements and Failures." In *Turkish Workers in Europe, 1960–1975*, edited by N. Abadan-Unat, 1–49.

———,ed. *Turkish Workers in Europe, 1960–1975: A Socio-Economic Reappraisal.* Leiden: Brill, 1976.

Accampo, Elinor. *Industrialization, Family Life, and Class Relations: Saint Chamond, 1815–1914.* Berkeley: University of California Press, 1989.

Agulhon, Maurice, Gabriel Désert, and Roger Specklin. *Apogée et crise de la civilisation paysanne, 1789–1914.* Vol. 3 of *Histoire de la France rurale*, edited by G. Duby and A. Wallon. Paris: Seuil, 1976.

Åkerman, Sune. "Towards an Understanding of Emigrational Processes." In *Human Migration: Patterns and Policies*, edited by W. McNeill and R. Adams, 287–306.

Alter, George. *Family and the Female Life Course: The Women of Verviers, Belgium, 1849–1880.* Madison, Wisc.: University of Wisconsin Press, 1988.

Anderson, Michael. *Family Structure in Nineteenth-Century Lancashire.* Cambridge: Cambridge University Press, 1971.

———. *Population Change in North-Western Europe, 1750–1850.* London: Macmillan, 1988.

Armengaud, André. "Population in Europe, 1700–1914." In *The Fontana Economic History of Europe*, vol. 3, *The Industrial Revolution, 1700–1914*, edited by C. Cipolla, 22–76. New York: Barnes and Noble, 1976.

Audiganne, Armand. *Les populations ouvrières et les industries de la France.* 1860. Reprint. New York: Burt Franklin, 1970.

Bade, Klaus. "German Emigration to the United States and Continental Immigration to Germany in the Late Nineteenth and Early Twentieth Centuries." *Central European History* 13 (1980): 348–77.

———. "Labour, Migration, and the State: Germany from the Late 19th Century to the Onset of the Great Depression." In *Population, Labour, and Migration in 19th- and 20th-Century Germany*, edited by K. Bade, 59–85.

———, ed. *Population, Labour, and Migration in 19th- and 20th-Century Germany.* Leamington Spa: Berg, 1987.

Bailyn, Bernard. *Voyagers to the West: A Passage in the Peopling of America on the Eve of the Revolution.* New York: Knopf, 1986.

Baines, Dudley. *Migration in a Mature Economy: Emigration and Internal Migration in England and Wales, 1861–1900.* Cambridge: Cambridge University Press, 1985.

Bairoch, Paul. "International Industrialization Levels from 1750 to 1980." *Journal of European Economic History* 11 (1982): 269–333.

Bardet, Jean-Pierre. *Rouen aux XVIIe et XVIIIe siècles: Les mutations d'un espace social.* 2 vols. Paris: Société d'Edition d'Enseignement Supérieur, 1983.

Başgöz, İhan, and Norman Furniss, eds. *Turkish Workers in Europe: An Interdisciplinary Study.* Bloomington, Ind.: Indiana University Press, 1985.

Benedict, Philip. "Was the Eighteenth Century an Era of Urbanization in France?" *Journal of Interdisciplinary History* 21 (1990): 179–215.

Berg, Maxine, Pat Hudson, and Michael Sonenscher, eds. *Manufacture in Town and Country before the Factory.* Cambridge: Cambridge University Press, 1983.

Berger, John, and Jean Mohr. *A Seventh Man: Migrant Workers in Europe.* New York: Viking Press, 1975.

Berkner, Lutz. "Family, Social Structure, and Rural Industry: A Comparative Study of the Waldviertel and the Pays de Caux in the Eighteenth Century." Ph.D. diss., Harvard University, 1973.

———. "The Stem Family and the Developmental Cycle of the Peasant Household: An Eighteenth-Century Austrian Example." *American Historical Review* 77 (1972): 398–410.

———, and Franklin Mendels. "Inheritance Systems, Family Structure, and Demographic Patterns in Western Europe, 1700–1900." In *Historical Studies of Changing Fertility,* edited by C. Tilly, 209–23.

Berrier, Robert. "The French Textile Industry: A Segmented Labor Market." In *Guests Come to Stay,* edited by R. Rogers, 51–68.

Bertaux-Wiame, Isabelle. "The Life History Approach to the Study of Internal Migration." *Oral History* 7 (1979): 26–32.

Beteille, Roger. "Les migrations saisonnières en France sous le Premier Empire: Essai de synthèse." *Revue d'histoire moderne et contemporaine* 17 (1970): 424–41.

Blanchard, Raoul. *La Flandre: Etude géographique de la plaine flamande en France, Belgique et Hollande.* Lille: Imprimerie Danel, 1906.

Blythell, Duncan. *The Handloom Weavers: A Study in the English Cotton Industry during the Industrial Revolution.* Cambridge: Cambridge University Press, 1969.

Boisvert, Colette Callier. "Working-Class Portuguese Families in a French Provincial Town: Adaptive Strategies." In *Migrants in Europe: The Role of Family, Labor, and Politics,* edited by H. Beuchler and J.-M. Beuchler, 61–76. New York: Greenwood Press, 1987.

Boker, H., and F. W. von Bulow. *The Rural Exodus in Germany.* Geneva: International Labour Office, 1933.

Booth, Heather. *Guestworkers or Immigrants? A Demographic Analysis of the Status of Migrants in West Germany.* Monographs in Ethnic Relations, no. 1. Warwick: Center for Research in Ethnic Relations, 1985.

Bouvier, Jeanne. *Mes mémoires: Ou 59 années d'activité industrielle, sociale et intellectuelle d'une ouvrière, 1876–1935.* Paris: Maspéro, 1983.

Boyer, Armand. "Les migrations saisonnières dans la Cévenne vivaroise." *Revue de géographie alpine* 22 (1934): 571–609.

Braun, Rudolf. "Early Industrialization and Demographic Change in the Canton of Zurich." In *Historical Studies of Changing Fertility,* edited by C. Tilly, 289–334.

Brettell, Caroline. "Hope and Nostalgia: The Migration of Portuguese Women to Paris." Ph.D. diss., Brown University, 1978.

———. *Men Who Migrate, Women Who Wait: Population and History in a Portuguese Parish.* Princeton: Princeton University Press, 1986.

———. *We Have Already Cried Many Tears: Portuguese Women and Migration.* Cambridge: Schenkman Publishing, 1982.

Brouwer, Lenie, and Marijke Priester. "Living in Between: Turkish Women in Their Homeland and in the Netherlands." In *One Way Ticket: Migration and Female Labour,* edited by A. Phizacklea, 113–29. London: Routledge and Kegan Paul, 1983.

Carlsson, Sten. "Chronology and Composition of Swedish Emigration to America." In *From Sweden to America*, edited by H. Runblom and H. Norman, 114–48.
Castles, Stephen, Heather Booth, and Tina Wallace. *Here for Good: Western Europe's New Ethnic Minorities*. London: Pluto Press, 1984.
Castles, Stephen, and Godula Kosak. *Immigrant Workers and Class Structure in Western Europe*. London: Oxford University Press, 1973.
Cerase, Francesco. "Expectations and Reality: A Case Study of Return Migration from the United States to Southern Italy." *International Migration Review* 8 (1974): 245–62.
Chan, Sucheng. "European and Asian Immigration into the United States in Comparative Perspective, 1820s to 1920s." In *Immigration Reconsidered*, edited by V. Yans-McLaughlin, 37–75.
Chatelain, Abel. "Migrations et domesticité féminine urbaine en France, XVIIIe siècle-XXe siècle." *Revue d'histoire économique et sociale* 47 (1969): 506–28.
———. *Les migrants temporaires en France de 1800 à 1914*. 2 vols. Lille: Publications de l'Université de Lille III, 1977.
Chevalier, Louis. *La formation de la population parisienne au XIXe siècle*. Paris: Presses Universitaires Françaises, 1950.
———. *Laboring Classes and Dangerous Classes in Paris during the First Half of the Nineteenth Century*. New York: Fertig, 1973.
Clark, Peter. "Migration in England during the Late Seventeenth and Early Eighteenth Centuries." *Past and Present* 83 (1979): 57–90.
———, and Paul Slack. *English Towns in Transition, 1500–1700*. London: Oxford University Press, 1974.
Clarkson, Leslie. *Proto-Industrialization: The First Phase of Industrialization?* London: Macmillan, 1985.
Coale, Ansley, and Roy Treadway. "A Summary of the Changing Distribution of Overall Fertility, Marital Fertility, and the Proportion Married in the Provinces of Europe." In *The Decline of Fertility in Europe*, edited by A. Coale and S. C. Watkins, 1–30. Princeton: Princeton University Press, 1986.
Coquart, André. "Du village de Yesilyazi au quartier des Chamards à Dreux (Eure et Loire)." *Hommes et migrations: Documents* 1021 (1981): 1–23.
Corbin, Alain. *Archaïsme et modernité en Limousin au XIXe siècle (1845–1880)*. 2 vols. Paris: Marcel Rivière, 1975.
Corfield, Penelope. "A Provincial Capital in the Late Seventeenth Century: The Case of Norwich." In *The Early Modern Town*, edited by P. Clark, 233–72. London: Longman, 1976.
Cotterell, Geoffrey. *Amsterdam: Life of a City*. Boston: Little, Brown and Co., 1972.
Cressy, David. *Migration and Communication between England and New England in the Seventeenth Century*. Cambridge: Cambridge University Press, 1987.
Crew, David. *Town in the Ruhr: A Social History of Bochum, 1860–1914*. New York: Columbia University Press, 1979.
Cross, Gary. *Immigrant Workers in Industrial France: The Making of a New Laboring Class*. Philadelphia: Temple University Press, 1983.
Cruson, Cees. "French Huguenot Refugees in Seventeenth-Century Amsterdam." Erasmus Universiteit Rotterdam. Photocopy, 1984.
Curtin, Philip. "Migration in the Tropical World." In *Immigration Reconsidered*, edited by V. Yans-McLaughlin, 21–36.
Davis, Kingsley. "The Migrations of Human Populations." *The Scientific American* 231, no. 3 (1984): 92–105.
Davis, Natalie Z. *The Return of Martin Guerre*. Cambridge, Mass.: Harvard University Press, 1983.

Depauw, Jacques. "Amour illegitime et société à Nantes au XVIIIe siècle." *Annales: E.S.C.* 27 (1972): 1155–81.

de Vries, Jan. *European Urbanization, 1500–1800.* Cambridge, Mass.: Harvard University Press, 1984.

———. *The Economy of Europe in an Age of Crisis, 1600–1750.* Cambridge: Cambridge University Press, 1976.

———. "The Population and Economy of the Preindustrial Netherlands." *Journal of Interdisciplinary History* 15 (1985): 661–82.

Deyon, Pierre. *Amiens, capitale provinciale. Etude sur la société urbaine au 17e siècle.* Paris: Mouton, 1967.

Donovan, James. "The Uprooting Theory of Crime and the Corsicans of Marseille, 1825–1880." *French Historical Studies* 13 (1984): 500–28.

Dupâquier, Jacques. *Histoire de la population française.* 4 vols. Paris: Presses Universitaires Françaises, 1988.

Edwards, John. *The Jews in Christian Europe, 1400–1700.* London: Routledge, 1988.

Elliot, Vivien Brodsky. "Single Women in the London Marriage Market: Age, Status and Mobility." In *Marriage and Society,* edited by R. Outhwaite, 81–100. London: Europa Publications, 1981.

Eltis, David. "Free and Coerced Transatlantic Migrations: Some Comparisons." *American Historical Review* 88 (1983): 251–80.

Engels, Friedrich. *The Condition of the Working Class in England.* Trans. W. O. Henderson and W. H. Chaloner. Oxford: Blackwell, 1971.

Evans, Richard, and W. Robert Lee, eds. *The German Family: Essays on the Social History of the Family in Nineteenth- and Twentieth-Century Germany.* London: Croom Helm, 1981.

Fairchilds, Cissie. "Female Sexual Attitudes and the Rise of Illegitimacy: A Case Study." *Journal of Interdisciplinary History* 8 (1978): 627–67.

———. *Poverty and Charity in Aix-en-Provence 1549–1789.* Baltimore: Johns Hopkins University Press, 1976.

Fenske, Hans. "International Migration: Germany in the Eighteenth Century." *Central European History* 13 (1980): 332–47.

Flinn, Michael. *The European Demographic System, 1500–1820.* Baltimore: Johns Hopkins University Press, 1981.

Fohlen, Claude. *L'industrie textile au temps du Second Empire.* Paris: Plon, 1956.

Foner, Nancy. "Sex Roles and Sensibilities: Jamaican Women in New York and London." In *International Migration: The Female Experience,* edited by R. Simon and C. Brettell, 133–51.

———, "Women, Work and Migration: Jamaicans in London." *Urban Anthropology* 4 (1975): 229–49.

Fontaine, Laurence. "Family Cycles, Peddling and Society in Upper Alpine Valleys in the Eighteenth Century." In *Domestic Strategies: Work and Family in France and Italy, 1600–1800,* edited by S. Woolf, 43–68. Cambridge: Cambridge University Press, 1991.

———. *History of Peddlers in Europe.* Cambridge: Polity Press, forthcoming.

———. "Solidarités familiales et logiques migratoires en pays de montagne à l'époque moderne." *Annales: E.S.C.* 45 (1990): 1433–50.

Franchomme, Georges. "L'évolution démographique et économique de Roubaix dans le dernier tiers du XIXe siècle." *Revue du Nord* 51 (1969): 201–47.

Franzoi, Barbara. *At the Very Least She Pays the Rent: Women and German Industrialization, 1871–1914.* Westport, Conn.: Greenwood, 1985.

Friedlander, Dov, and R. J. Roshier. "A Study of Internal Migration in England and Wales: Part I." *Population Studies* 19 (1966): 239–78.

Friedrichs, Christopher. *Urban Society in an Age of War: Nördlingen, 1580–1720.* Princeton: Princeton University Press 1979.

Fuchs, Rachel G. *Poor and Pregnant in Paris.* New Brunswick, N.J.: Rutgers University Press, forthcoming in 1992.

————, and Leslie Page Moch. "Pregnant, Single, and Far from Home: Migrant Women in Nineteenth-Century Paris." *American Historical Review* 95 (1990): 1007–31.

Gabaccia, Donna. *From Sicily to Elizabeth Street: Housing and Social Change among Italian Immigrants, 1880–1930.* Albany, N.Y.: SUNY Press, 1984.

————. *From the Other Side: Women, Gender, and Immigrant Life in the United States, 1820–1980.* Bloomington, Ind.: Indiana University Press, forthcoming.

————. *Militants and Migrants: Rural Sicilians Become American Workers.* New Brunswick, N.J.: Rutgers University Press, 1988.

————. "Women of the Mass Migrations: From Minority to Majority, 1820–1930." Forthcoming in *Global Moves, Local Contexts*, edited by D. Hoerder and L. P. Moch.

Garden, Maurice. "Le bilan démographique des villes: Un système complexe." *Annales de démographie historique* (1982): 267–75.

————. *Lyon et les Lyonnais au XVIIIe siècle.* Paris: Belles Lettres, 1970.

Gaunt, David. "Pre-Industrial Economy and Population Structure: The Elements of Variance in Early Modern Sweden." *Scandinavian Journal of History* 2 (1977): 183–210.

Gillis, John. "Peasant, Plebian, and Proletarian Marriage in Britain, 1600–1900." In *Proletarianization and Family History*, edited by D. Levine, 129–62.

Glass, David V., and David E. Eversley, eds. *Population in History: Essays in Historical Demography.* London: E. Arnold, 1965.

Goldstein, Sydney. "The Extent of Repeated Migration: An Analysis Based on the Danish Population Register." *Journal of the American Statistical Association* 59 (1964): 1121–32.

Goodman, Charity. "A Day in the Life of a Single Spanish Woman in West Germany." In *Migrants in Europe: The Role of Family, Labor, and Politics*, edited by H. Buechler and J.-M. Buechler, 207–19. New York: Greenwood, 1987.

Goubert, Pierre. *Beauvais et le Beauvaisis de 1600 à 1730.* Paris: SEVPEN, 1960.

————. *Louis XIV and Twenty Million Frenchmen.* New York: Random House, 1966.

————. "Family and Province: A Contribution to the Knowledge of Family Structures in Early Modern France." *Journal of Family History* 2 (1977): 179–95.

Gould, J. D. "European Inter-Continental Emigration, 1815–1914: Patterns and Causes." *Journal of European Economic History* 8 (1979): 593–679.

————. "European Inter-Continental Emigration. The Road Home: Return Migration from the U.S.A." *Journal of European Economic History* 9 (1980): 41–112.

————. "European Inter-Continental Emigration: The Role of 'Diffusion' and 'Feedback.' " *Journal of European Economic History* 9 (1980): 267–315.

Grafteaux, Serge. *Mémé Santerre: A French Woman of the People.* New York: Schoken Books, 1985.

Green, Nancy. " 'Filling the Void': Immigration to France before World War I." In *Labor Migration in the Altantic Economies*, edited by D. Hoerder, 143–61.

————. "L'Histoire comparative et le champ des études migratoires." *Annales: E.S.C.* 45 (1990): 1335–50.

————. *The Pletzl of Paris: Jewish Immigrant Workers in the "Belle Epoque."* New York: Holmes and Meier, 1986.

Greer, Donald. *The Incidence of the Emigration during the French Revolution.* Cambridge, Mass.: Harvard University Press, 1951.

Gribaudi, Maurizio. *Itinéraires ouvriers: Espaces et groupes sociaux à Turin au début du XXe siècle.* Paris: Editions de l'Ecole des Hautes Etudes en Sciences Sociales, 1987.

Guignet, Philippe. *Mines, manufactures et ouvriers du Valenciennois au XVIIIe siècle.* New York: Arno Press, 1977.

Guillaume, Pierre. *La population de Bordeaux au XIXe siècle: Essai d'histoire sociale.* Paris: A. Colin, 1972.

Gullickson, Gay. *Spinners and Weavers of Auffay: Rural Industry and the Sexual Division of Labor in a French Village, 1750–1850.* Cambridge: Cambridge University Press, 1986.

Gutmann, Myron. *Toward the Modern Economy: Early Industry in Europe, 1500–1800.* New York: Knopf, 1988.

———, and René Laboutte. "Rethinking Protoindustrialization and the Family." *Journal of Interdisciplinary History* 14 (1984): 587–607.

———, and Etienne van de Walle. "New Sources for Social and Demographic History: The Belgian Population Registers." *Social Science History* 2 (1978): 121–43.

Hägerstrand, Thorsten. "Migration and Area." *Lund Studies in Geography,* ser. B. 13 (1957): 27–158.

Hajnal, John. "European Marriage Patterns in Perspective." In *Population in History,* edited by D. V. Glass and D. E. Eversley, 101–43.

———. "Two Kinds of Pre-industrial Household Formation Systems." In *Family Forms in Historic Europe,* edited by R. Wall and P. Laslett, 65–104. Cambridge: Cambridge University Press, 1983.

Hanagan, Michael. *Nascent Proletarians: Class Formation in Post-Revolutionary France.* Oxford: Basil Blackwell, 1989.

Hareven, Tamara. "The History of the Family and the Complexity of Social Change." *The American Historical Review* 96 (1991): 95–124.

Harris, Ruth-Ann. *The Nearest Place that Wasn't Ireland: A Study of the Pre-famine Seasonal Migration of the Irish People to Britain.* Ames, Iowa: Iowa State University Press, forthcoming in 1992.

———. "Seasonal Migration between Ireland and England Prior to the Famine." In *Canadian Papers in Rural History,* vol. 7, edited by D. H. Akenson, 363–86. Gananoque: Langdale Press, 1989.

Hart, Simon. "Gens de mer à Amsterdam au XVIIe siècle." *Annales de démographie historique* (1974): 145–63.

Head, Anne-Lise. "Quelques remarques sur l'émigration des régions préalpines." *Revue suisse d'histoire* 29 (1979): 181–93.

Herbert, Ulrich. *A History of Foreign Labor in Germany, 1880–1980.* Ann Arbor: University of Michigan Press, 1990.

Herlihy, David. "Family." *The American Historical Review* 96 (1991): 1–16.

Hobsbawm, Eric. *The Age of Empire, 1875–1914.* New York: Pantheon, 1987.

———. "The Overall Crisis of the European Economy in the Seventeenth Century." *Past and Present* 5 (1954): 33–53.

Hochstadt, Steve. "Migration and Industrialization in Germany, 1815–1977." *Social Science History* 5 (1981): 445–68.

———. "Migration in Germany: An Historical Study." Ph.D. diss., Brown University, 1983.

———. "Migration in Preindustrial Germany." *Central European History* 16 (1983): 195–224.

————. "Socioeconomic Determinants of Mobility in Nineteenth-Century Germany." Mainz: Institut für Europaïsche Geschichte, 1985, photocopy.

————. "Städtische Wanderungsbewegungen in Deutschland 1850–1914," in *Deutschland und Europa in der Neuzeit: Festschrift für Karl Otmar Freiherr von Aretin zum 65. Geburtstag,* 2 vols., edited by R. Melville, C. Scharf, M. Vogt, and U. Wengenroth, 2: 575–98. Stuttgart: Franz Steiner Verlag, 1988.

————. "Urban Migration in Imperial Germany: Towards a Quantitative Model." *Historical Papers/Communications Historiques* (1986): 197–210.

————, and James Jackson, Jr. " 'New' Sources for the Study of Migration in Early Nineteenth-Century Germany." *Historical Social Research/Historische Sozialforschung* 31 (1984): 85–92.

Hoerder, Dirk. "An Introduction to Labor Migration in the Atlantic Economies, 1815–1914." In *Labor Migration in the Atlantic Economies,* edited by D. Hoerder, 3–31.

————. "From Migrants to Immigrants: Acculturation in a Societal Framework." Forthcoming in *Global Moves, Local Contexts,* edited by D. Hoerder and L. P. Moch.

————. "Immigration and the Working Class: The Remigration Factor." *International Labor and Working Class History* 21 (1982): 28–41.

————. "Migration in the Atlantic Economies: Regional European Origins and Worldwide Expansion." Forthcoming in *Global Moves, Local Contexts,* edited by D. Hoerder and L. P. Moch.

————, ed. *Labor Migration in the Atlantic Economies: The European and North American Working Classes during the Period of Industrialization.* Westport, Conn.: Greenwood Press, 1985.

————, and Leslie Page Moch, eds. *Global Moves, Local Contexts: European Migrants in International Perspective.* Forthcoming.

Hogan, Dennis, and David Kertzer. "Longitudinal Methods for Historical Migration Research." *Historical Methods* 18 (1985): 20–30.

Hohenberg, Paul, and Lynn Lees. *The Making of Urban Europe, 1000–1950.* Cambridge, Mass.: Harvard University Press, 1985.

Holmes, Madelyn. *Forgotten Migrants: Foreign Workers in Switzerland before World War I.* Rutherford, N.J.: Farleigh Dickinson University Press, 1988.

Houston, Rabb, and Keith D. M. Snell. "Protoindustrialization? Cottage Industry, Social Change, and Industrial Revolution." *The Historical Journal* 27 (1984): 473–92.

Huff, James O., and Brigitte Waldorf. "A Predictive Model of Residential Mobility and Residential Segregation." *Papers of the Regional Science Association* 65 (1988): 59–77.

Hufton, Olwen. *The Poor of Eighteenth-Century France 1750–1789.* Oxford: Clarendon Press, 1974.

Hvidt, Kristian. *Flight to America: The Social Background of 300,000 Danish Emigrants.* New York: Academic Press, 1975.

Israel, Jonathan. *European Jewry in the Age of Mercantilism, 1550–1750.* Oxford: Clarendon Press, 1985.

Jackson, James, Jr. "*Alltagsgeschichte,* Social Science History and the Study of Migration in Nineteenth-Century Germany." *Central European History* 23 (1990): 242–63.

————. "Migration and Urbanization in the Ruhr Valley, 1850–1900." Ph.D. diss., University of Minnesota, 1980.

————. "Migration in Duisburg, 1821–1914." Paper presented at the Symposium on Continental European Migration and Transcontinental Migration to North America: A Comparative Perspective, Bremerhaven, August 1991.

———. "Migration in Duisburg, 1867–1890: Occupational and Familial Contexts." *Journal of Urban History* 8 (1982): 235–70.

———. "Overcrowding and Family Life: Working-Class Families and the Housing Crisis in Late Nineteenth-Century Duisburg." In *The German Family*, edited by R. J. Evans and W. R. Lee, 194–220.

———, and Leslie Page Moch. "Migration and the Social History of Western Europe." *Historical Methods* 22 (1989): 27–36.

Jegouzo, Georges. "L'ampleur de célibat chez les agriculteurs." *Economie et statistique* 58 (1972): 13–22.

Johnson, Christopher. *The Life and Death of Industrial Languedoc.* Oxford: Oxford University Press, forthcoming.

Jones, Gareth Stedman. *Outcast London: A Study in the Relationship between Classes in Victorian Society.* Oxford: Oxford University Press, 1971.

Kälvemark, Ann-Sofie. "Illegitimacy and Marriage in Three Swedish Parishes in the Nineteenth Century." In *Bastardy and Its Comparative History*, edited by P. Laslett, K. Oosterveen and R. M. Smith, 327–35.

———. "The Country That Kept Track of Its Population: Methodological Aspects of Swedish Population Records." In *Time, Space and Man: Essays on Microdemography*, edited by J. Sundin and E. Soderlund, 221–43. Atlantic Highlands, N.J.: Humanities Press, 1979.

Kamphoefner, Walter. *The Westfalians: From Germany to Missouri.* Princeton: Princeton University Press, 1987.

Kelly, Alfred, ed. *The German Worker: Working-Class Autobiographies from the Age of Industrialization.* Berkeley, Calif.: University of California Press, 1987.

Kennedy, Robert E., Jr. *The Irish: Emigration, Marriage and Fertility.* Berkeley, Calif.: University of California Press, 1973.

Kertzer, David, and Dennis Hogan. "On the Move: Migration in an Italian Community, 1865–1921." *Social Science History* 9 (1985): 1–23.

Kintz, Jean-Pierre. "La mobilité humaine en Alsace: Essai de présentation statistique, XIVe–XVIIIe siècles." *Annales de démographie historique* (1970), 157–83.

Kiray, Mübeccel B. "The Family of the Immigrant Worker." In *Turkish Workers in Europe, 1960–1975*, edited by N. Abadan-Unat, 210–34.

Kisch, Herbert. *From Domestic Manufacture to Industrial Revolution: The Case of the Rhineland Textile Districts.* Oxford: Oxford University Press, 1989.

———. "The Textile Industries in Silesia and the Rhineland: A Comparative Study in Industrialization." In *Industrialization before Industrialization: Rural Industry in the Genesis of Capitalism*, edited by P. Kriedte, H. Medick, and J. Schlumbohm. Cambridge: Cambridge University Press, 1981.

Klessman, Christopher. "Comparative Immigrant History: Polish Workers in the Ruhr Area and the North of France." *Journal of Social History* 20 (1986): 335–53.

———. "Long-Distance Migration, Integration and Segregation of an Ethnic Minority in Industrial Germany: The Case of the 'Ruhr Poles.' " In *Population, Labour and Migration in 19th- and 20th-Century Germany*, edited by K. Bade, 101–14.

Knodel, John and Steve Hochstadt. "Urban and Rural Illegitimacy in Imperial Germany." In *Bastardy and Its Comparative History*, edited by P. Laslett, K. Oosterveen, and R. M. Smith. Cambridge, Mass.: Harvard University Press, 1980.

Köllmann, Wolfgang. "The Population of Barmen before and during the Period of

Industrialization." In *Population in History: Essays in Historical Demography*, edited by D. V. Glass and D. E. C. Eversley, 588–607.

Konvitz, Josef. "Does the Century 1650–1750 Constitute a Period in Urban History? The French Evidence Reviewed." *Journal of Urban History* 14 (1988): 430–42.

———. *The Urban Millennium*. Carbondale, Ill.: Southern Illinois University Press, 1985.

Korte, Hermann. "Labor Migration and the Employment of Foreigners in the Federal Republic of Germany Since 1950." In *Guests Come to Stay*, edited by R. Rogers, 29–49.

Kosak, Godula. "Migrant Women: The Move to Western Europe—a Step Towards Emancipation?" *Race and Class* 17 (1976): 369–79.

Kulischer, Eugene. *Europe on the Move: War and Population Changes, 1917–1947*. New York: Columbia University Press, 1948.

Kussmaul, Ann. *Servants in Husbandry in Early Modern England*. Cambridge: Cambridge University Press, 1981.

———. "The Ambiguous Mobility of Farm Servants." *Economic History Review* 34 (1981): 222–35.

Laslett, Peter. *The World We Have Lost: England before the Industrial Age*. 3d ed. New York: Scribner's, 1983.

———, and Richard Wall, eds. *Household and Family in Past Time*. Cambridge: Cambridge University Press, 1972.

Lebon, A., and G. Falchi. "New Developments in Intra-European Migration Since 1974." *International Migration Review* 14 (1980): 539–79.

Lee, Everett. "A Theory of Migration." *Demography* 31 (1966): 47–57.

Lee, W. Robert. "The Impact of Agrarian Change on Women's Work and Child Care in Early-Nineteenth-Century Prussia." In *German Women in the Nineteenth Century: A Social History*, edited by J. C. Fout, 234–55. London: Holmes and Meier, 1984.

Lees, Lynn. *Exiles of Erin: Irish Migrants in Victorian London*. Ithaca, N.Y.: Cornell University Press, 1979.

Lequin, Yves. *La mosaïque France: Histoire des étrangers et de l'immigration*. Paris: Larousse, 1988.

———. *Les ouvriers de la région lyonnaise (1848–1914)*. Lyon: Presses Universitaires de Lyon, 1977.

Le Roy Ladurie, Emmanuel. *Montaillou: The Promised Land of Error*. New York: Braziller, 1978.

———. *Peasants of Languedoc*. Urbana: University of Illinois Press, 1974.

———. "Système de la coutume. Structures familiales et coutume d'héritage en France au XVIe siècle." *Annales: E.S.C.* 27 (1972): 825–46.

———. *Histoire de la France rurale*, vol. 2, *L'âge classique des paysans, 1340–1789*. Paris: Seuil, 1975.

———. *Histoire de la France urbaine*, vol. 3, *La ville classique*. Paris: Seuil, 1981.

Levine, David. *Family Formation in an Age of Nascent Capitalism*. New York: Academic Press, 1977.

———. "Production, Reproduction, and the Proletarian Family in England, 1500–1851." In *Proletarianization and Family History*, edited by D. Levine, 87–127.

———. *Reproducing Families: The Political Economy of English Population History*. Cambridge: Cambridge University Press, 1987.

———, ed. *Proletarianization and Family History*. Orlando, Fla.: Academic Press, 1984.

Lis, Catharina, and Hugo Soly. *Poverty and Capitalism in Pre-Industrial Europe*. Atlantic Highlands, N.J.: Humanities Press, 1979.

Lottin, Alain. "Naissance illegitimes et filles-mères à Lille au XVIIIe siècle." *Revue d'histoire moderne et contemporaine* 17 (1970): 278–322.

Lowe, William J. *The Irish in Mid-Victorian Lancashire: The Shaping of a Working-Class Community.* New York: Peter Lang, 1989.

Lucassen, Jan. "Dutch Migration, 1600–1900." Paper presented at the 17e Congrès International des Sciences Historiques, Madrid, July 1990.

———. *Migrant Labour in Europe, 1600–1900.* London: Croom Helm, 1987.

MacDonald, John, and Leatrice MacDonald. *The Invisible Immigrants.* London: Runnymede Trust, 1972.

Macfarlane, Alan. *The Family Life of Ralph Josselin, A Seventeenth Century Clergyman: An Essay in Historical Anthropology.* Cambridge: Cambridge University Press, 1970.

———. "The Myth of the Peasantry: Family and Economy in a Northern Parish." In *Land, Kinship and Life-Cycle,* edited by R. M. Smith, 333–50.

Mann, Julia De Lacey. *The Cloth Industry in the West of England from 1640 to 1880.* 1971. Reprint. Gloucester: Alan Sutton, 1987.

Marrus, Michael. *The Unwanted: European Refugees in the Twentieth Century.* New York: Oxford University Press, 1985.

Mauco, Georges. "Les migrations ouvrières en France au début du XIXe siècle d'après les rapports de préfets de l'Empire, de 1808 à 1813." Doctoral diss., University of Paris, 1932.

Mayett, Joseph. *The Autobiography of Joseph Mayett of Quainton, 1783–1839.* Aylesbury: Buckinghamshire Record Society, 1986.

McBride, Theresa. *The Domestic Revolution: The Modernization of Household Service in England and France, 1820–1920.* New York: Holmes and Meier, 1976.

McNeill, William. "Human Migration in Historical Perspective." *Population and Development Review* 10 (1984): 1–18.

———, and Ruth Adams, eds. *Human Migration: Patterns and Policies.* Bloomington, Ind.: Indiana University Press, 1978.

Medick, Hans. "The Proto-industrial Family Economy: The Structural Functioning of Household and Family during the Transition from Peasant Society to Industrial Capitalism." *Social History* 3 (1976): 291–315.

Meijide Pardo, Antonio. *La emigración Gallega intrapeninsular en el siglo XVIII.* Madrid: Institute Balmes de Sociologia, 1960.

Mendels, Franklin. "Protoindustrialization: The First Phase of the Industrialization Process." *Journal of Economic History* 32 (1972): 241–61.

Messance. *Recherches sur la population des généralités d'Auvergne, de Lyon, de Rouen.* Paris: Durand, 1766. Reprint. Paris: Editions d'Histoire Sociale, 1973.

Mik, Ger, and Mia Verkoren-Hemelaar. "Segregation in the Netherlands and Turkish Migration." In *Turkish Workers in Europe, 1960–1975,* edited by N. Abadan-Unat, 253–83.

Miller, Kerby. *Emigrants and Exiles: Ireland and the Irish Exodus to North America.* New York: Oxford University Press, 1985.

Mitchell, Brian R. *European Historical Statistics, 1750–1970.* New York: Columbia University Press, 1978.

Mitterauer, Michael, and Reinhard Sieder. *The European Family: Patriarchy to Partnership from the Middle Ages to the Present.* Chicago: University of Chicago Press, 1977.

Moch, Leslie Page. "Government Policy and Women's Experience: The Case of Teachers in France." *Feminist Studies* 14 (1988): 301–24.

———. "Infirmities of the Body and Vices of the Soul: Migrants, Family, and Urban Life in Turn-of-the-Century France." In *Essays on the Family and*

Historical Change, edited by L. P. Moch and G. Stark, 35–64. College Station, Tex.: Texas A & M University Press, 1983.

———. "The Family and Migration: News from the French." *Journal of Family History* 11 (1986): 193–203.

———. "The Importance of Mundane Movements: Small Towns, Nearby Places and Individual Itineraries in the History of Migration." In *Migrants in Modern France*, edited by P. E. Ogden and P. E. White, 97–117.

———. *Paths to the City: Regional Migration in Nineteenth-Century France*. Beverly Hills, Calif.: Sage Publications, 1983.

———, Nancy Folbre, Daniel Scott Smith, Laurel Cornell, and Louise Tilly. "Family Strategies: A Dialogue." *Historical Methods* 20 (1987): 113–25.

———, and Louise A. Tilly. "Immigrant Women in the City: Comparative Perspectives." Center for Research on Social Organization, University of Michigan. Photocopy, 1979.

———, and Louise Tilly. "Joining the Urban World: Occupation, Family, and Migration in Three French Cities." *Comparative Studies in Society and History* 27 (1985): 33–56.

Modell, John, Frank Furstenburg, Jr., and Theodore Hershberg. "Social Change and the Transitions to Adulthood in Historical Perspective." *Journal of Family History* 1 (1976): 7–32.

Mokyr, Joel, and Cormac Ó Gráda. "Emigration and Poverty in Prefamine Ireland." *Explorations in Economic History* ser. 2, 19 (1982): 360–82.

Mollat, Michel. *Histoire de Rouen*. Toulouse: Privat, 1979.

Mols, Roger. *Introduction à la démographie historique des villes d'Europe du XIVe au XVIIIe siècle*. 3 vols. Louvain: Publications universitaires, 1954–56.

———. "Population in Europe, 1500–1700." In *The Fontana Economic History of Europe*, vol. 2, *The Sixteenth and Seventeenth Centuries*, edited by C. Cipolla, 7–82. London: Fontana, 1974.

Moltmann, Günther. "American-German Return Migration in the Nineteenth and Early Twentieth Centuries." *Central European History* 13 (1980): 378–92.

Morawska, Eva. *For Bread with Butter: The Life-Worlds of East Central Europeans in Johnstown, Pennsylvania, 1890–1940*. Cambridge: Cambridge University Press, 1985.

———. "Labor Migrations of Poles in the Atlantic Economy, 1880–1914." *Comparative Studies in Society and History* 31 (1989): 237–72.

Morgan, David. *Harvesters and Harvesting, 1840–1900*. London: Croom Helm, 1982.

Mörner, Magnus, and Herold Sims. *Adventurers and Proletarians: The Story of Migrants in Latin America*. Paris: United Nations Education, Scientific and Cultural Organization, 1985.

Morokvasic, Mirjana. "Birds of Passage Are also Women. . . . " *International Migration Review* 18 (1984): 886–907.

———. "Women in Migration: Beyond the Reductionist Outlook." In *One-Way Ticket: Migration and Female Labour*, edited by A. Phizacklea, 13–31. London: Routledge and Kegan Paul, 1983.

Mouillon, Marthe-Juliette. "Un exemple de migration rurale: De la Somme dans la capitale. Domestique de la Belle Epoque à Paris." *Etudes de la région parisienne* 44 (1970): 1–9.

Moulin, Marie-Annie. *Les maçons de la Haute-Marche au XVIIIe siècle*. Clermont-Ferrand: Publications de l'Institut d'Etudes du Massif Central, 1986.

Mumford, Lewis. *The City in History*. Harmondsworth: Penguin Books, 1961.

Murray, Norman. *The Scottish Hand Loom Weavers, 1790–1850: A Social History*. Edinburgh: John Donald Publishers, 1978.

Mushaben, Joyce. "A Crisis of Culture: Isolation and Integration among Turkish Guestworkers in the German Federal Republic." In *Turkish Workers in Europe: An International Study*, edited by İ. Başgöz and N. Furniss, 125–50.

Neuloh, Otto. "Structural Unemployment in Turkey: Its Relation to Migration." In *Turkish Workers in Europe, 1960–1975*, edited by N. Abadan-Unat, 50–73.

Noiriel, Gérard. *Le creuset français: Histoire de l'immigration, XIXe-XXe siècles*. Paris: Seuil, 1988.

Nolan, Janet. *Ourselves Alone: Women's Emigration from Ireland*. Lexington, Ky.: University Press of Kentucky, 1989.

Norman, Hans, and Harald Runblom. "Migration Patterns in the Nordic Countries." In *Labor Migration in the Atlantic Economies*, edited by D. Hoerder, 35–68.

Nugent, Walter. "Frontiers and Empires in the Late Nineteenth Century." *The Western Historical Quarterly* 20 (1989): 393–406.

Ogden, Philip E. "International Migration in the Nineteenth and Twentieth Centuries." In *Migrants in Modern France*, edited by P. E. Ogden and P. E. White, 34–59.

———. *Migration and Geographical Change*. Cambridge: Cambridge University Press, 1984.

———. "Migration, Marriage and the Collapse of Traditional Peasant Society in France." In *The Geographic Impact of Migration*, edited by P. E. White and R. Woods, 151–79.

———, and Paul E. White, eds. *Migrants in Modern France: Population Mobility in the Later Nineteenth and Twentieth Centuries*. London: Unwin Hyman, 1989.

Ó Gráda, Cormac. "Seasonal Migration and Post-Famine Adjustment in the West of Ireland." *Studia Hibernica* 13 (1973): 48–76.

Park, Robert. "Human Migration and the Marginal Man." *The American Journal of Sociology* 33 (1928): 881–93.

Patten, John. *Rural-Urban Migration in Pre-Industrial England*. Oxford: Oxford University Press, 1973.

Perkins, J. A. "The Agricultural Revolution in Germany, 1850–1914." *Journal of European Economic History* 10 (1981): 71–118.

Perlman, Janice. *The Myth of Marginality: Urban Poverty and Politics in Rio de Janeiro*. Berkeley, Calif.: University of California Press, 1976.

Perrot, Jean-Claude. *Genèse d'une ville moderne: Caen au XVIIIe siècle*. 2 vols. Paris: Mouton, 1975.

Perrot, Michelle. *Les ouvriers en grève, France 1870–1890*. 2 vols. Paris: Mouton, 1974.

Petit, Bernard. "Démographie d'une ville en gestion: Versailles sous Louis XIV." *Annales de démographie historique* (1977): 49–84.

Phizacklea, Annie, ed. *One Way Ticket: Migration and Female Labour*. London: Routledge and Kegan Paul, 1983.

Pinchemel, Philippe. *Structures sociales et dépopulation rurale dans les campagnes picardes de 1836 à 1936*. Paris: Colin, 1957.

Piore, Michael. *Birds of Passage: Migrant Labor and Industrial Societies*. Cambridge: Cambridge University Press, 1979.

Plakans, Andrejs. "Peasant Farmsteads and Households in the Baltic Littoral, 1797." *Comparative Studies in Society and History* 17 (1975): 2–35.

———. "Seigneurial Authority and Peasant Family Life." *Journal of Interdisciplinary History* 6 (1975): 620–54.

Poitrineau, Abel. "Aspects de l'émigration temporaire et saisonnière en Auvergne à la fin du XVIIIe siècle et au début du XIXe siècle." *Revue d'histoire moderne et contemporaine* 9 (1962): 5–50.

————. *Les Espagnols de l'Auvergne et du Limousin du XVIIIe au XIXe siècle.* Aurillac: Malroux-Mazel, 1985.

————. *Remues d'hommes: Essai sur les migrations montagnardes en France, aux 17e–18e siècles.* Paris: Aubier Montaigne, 1983.

————. *La vie rurale en Basse Auvergne au XVIIIe siècle.* Paris: Presses Universitaires Françaises, 1966.

Post, John D. *The Last Great Subsistence Crisis in the Western World.* Baltimore: The Johns Hopkins University Press, 1977.

Poussou, Jean-Pierre. *Bordeaux et le sud-ouest au XVIIIe siècle.* Paris: Editions de l'Ecole des Hautes Etudes en Sciences Sociales, 1983.

Rabb, Theodore. "The Effects of the Thirty Years' War on the German Economy." *The Journal of Modern History* 34 (1962): 40–51.

Raman, Michael. "Mésure de la croissance d'un centre textile: Roubaix de 1789 à 1913." *Revue d'histoire économique et sociale* 51 (1973): 470–501.

Ransel, David. *Mothers of Misery.* Princeton: Princeton University Press, 1988.

Rappaport, Steve. *Worlds within Worlds: Structures of Life in Sixteenth-Century London.* Cambridge: Cambridge University Press, 1989.

Ravenstein, Ernest. *The Laws of Migration.* Reprint. New York: Arno Press, 1976.

Razi, Zvi. "The Erosion of the Family-Land Bond in the Late Fourteenth and Fifteenth Centuries: A Methodological Note." In *Land, Kinship and Life-Cycle,* edited by R. M. Smith, 295–304.

Redford, Arthur. *Labour Migration in England, 1800–1850.* Manchester: Manchester University Press, 1976.

Reid, Donald. *The Miners of Decazeville: A Geneology of Deindustrialization.* Cambridge, Mass.: Harvard University Press, 1985.

Rist, Ray C. *Guestworkers in Germany: The Prospects for Pluralism.* New York: Praeger, 1978.

Rogers, Rosemarie, ed. *Guests Come to Stay: The Effects of European Labor Migration on Sending and Receiving Countries.* Boulder, Colo.: Westview Press, 1985.

————. "Post-World War II European Labor Migration: An Introduction to the Issues." In *Guests Come to Stay,* edited by R. Rogers, 1–28.

————. "Western Europe in the 1980s: The End of Immigration?" In *Guests Come to Stay,* edited by R. Rogers, 285–300.

Rosoli, Gianfausto. "Italian Migration to European Countries from Political Unification to World War I." In *Labor Migration in the Atlantic Economies,* edited by D. Hoerder, 95–116. Westport, Conn.: Greenwood, 1985.

Runblom, Harald, and Hans Norman, eds. *From Sweden to America: A History of the Migration.* Minneapolis, Minn.: University of Minnesota Press, 1976.

Sabean, David. "Household Formation and Geographical Mobility: A Family Register Study for a Württemberg Village, 1760–1900." *Annales de démographie historique* (1970): 275–94.

Salaman, Redcliffe. *The History and the Social Influence of the Potato.* Cambridge: Cambridge University Press, 1949.

Salt, John. "A Comparative Overview of International Trends and Types, 1950–1980," *International Migration Review* 23 (1989): 431–56.

————, and Hugh Clout. *Migration in Post-War Europe: Geographical Essays.* London: Oxford University Press, 1976.

Samuel, Raphael. "Comers and Goers." In *The Victorian City: Images and Realities,* 2 vols, edited by H. J. Dyos and M. Wolff, I: 123–60. London: Routledge and Kegan Paul, 1973.

Sarna, Jonathan. "The Myth of No Return: Jewish Return Migration to Eastern Europe, 1880–1914." In *Labor Migration in the Atlantic Economies,* edited by D. Hoerder, 423–34.

Schlumbohm, Jürgen. "Seasonal Fluctuations and Social Division of Labour: Rural Linen Production in the Osnabrück and Bielefeld Regions and the Urban Woolen Industry in the Niederlausitz, c. 1770–c. 1850." In *Manufacture in Town and Country Before the Factory*, edited by M. Berg, P. Hudson, and M. Sonenscher, 92–123. Cambridge: Cambridge University Press, 1983.

Schofield, Roger. "Age-Specific Mobility in an Eighteenth-Century Rural English Parish." *Annales de démographie historique* (1970): 261–74.

Schomerus, Heilwig. "The Family Life-Cycle: A Study of Factory Workers in Nineteenth-Century Württemberg." In *The German Family*, edited by R. J. Evans and W. R. Lee, 175–93.

Schwartz, Robert. *Policing the Poor in Eighteenth-Century France.* Chapel Hill, N. C.: University of North Carolina Press, 1988.

Senior, Carl H. "German Immigrants in Jamaica, 1834–38." *Journal of Caribbean History* 10–11 (1978): 25–53.

———. "Irish Slaves for Jamaica." *Jamaica Journal* 42 (1978): 104–16.

Sewell, William, Jr. *Structure and Mobility: The Men and Women of Marseille, 1820–1870.* Cambridge: Cambridge University Press, 1985.

Sharlin, Allan. "Natural Decrease in Early Modern Cities: A Reconsideration." *Past and Present* 79 (1978): 126–38.

———, and John Sammis. "Migration and Urban Population in Pre-Industrial Europe: Würzburg in the Late Seventeenth and Early Eighteenth Centuries." Paper presented at the annual meetings of the Social Science History Association, Bloomington, Ind., November 1982.

Shaw, R. Paul. *Migration: Theory and Fact.* Philadelphia: Regional Science Research Institute, 1975.

Shorter, Edward. "Illegitimacy, Sexual Revolution, and Social Change in Modern Europe." *Journal of Interdisciplinary History* 2 (1971): 237–72.

———, John Knodel, and Etienne van de Walle. "The Decline of Non-Marital Fertility in Europe, 1880–1914." *Population Studies* 25 (1971): 375–93.

Simon, Rita, and Caroline Brettell, eds. *International Migration: The Female Experience.* Totowa, N.J.: Rowman and Allanheld, 1986.

Smith, Richard M., ed. *Land, Kinship and Life-Cycle.* Cambridge: Cambridge University Press, 1984.

Snell, Keith D. M. *Annals of the Labouring Poor: Social Change and Agrarian England, 1660–1900.* Cambridge: Cambridge University Press, 1985.

Soliday, Gerald. *A Community in Conflict: Frankfurt Society in the Seventeenth and Early Eighteenth Centuries.* Hanover, N.H.: University Press of New England, 1974.

Souden, David. " 'East, West—Home's Best'? Regional Patterns in Migration in Early Modern England." In *Migration and Society in Early Modern England*, edited by P. Clark and D. Souden, 292–332. Totowa, N.J.: Barnes and Noble, 1988.

———. "Movers and Stayers in Family Reconstitution Populations, 1660–1780." *Local Population Studies* 33 (1984): 11–28.

Spufford, Margaret. *Contrasting Communities: English Villagers in the Sixteenth and Seventeenth Centuries.* London: Cambridge University Press, 1974.

Stone, Lawrence. *The Family, Sex and Marriage in England: 1500–1800.* London: Weidenfeld and Nicolson, 1977.

Taylor, Philip. *The Distant Magnet.* New York: Harper and Row, 1971.

Tedebrand, Lars-Göran. "Remigration from America to Sweden." In *Labor Migration in the Atlantic Economies*, edited by D. Hoerder, 357–80.

Terrier, Didier, and Philippe Toutain. "Pression démographique et marché du travail à Comines au XVIIIe siècle." *Revue du Nord* 61 (1979): 19–26.

Terrisse, Michel. "Méthode de recherches démographiques en milieu urbain ancien (XVIIe–XVIIIe)." *Annales de démographie historique* (1974): 249–62.

Thirsk, Joan. *The Rural Economy of England: Collected Essays.* London: Hambledon Press, 1984.

Thomas, Dorothy Swaine. *Social and Economic Aspects of Swedish Population Movements, 1750–1933.* New York: Macmillan, 1941.

Tilly, Charles. *As Sociology Meets History.* New York: Academic Press, 1981.

———. *Coercion, Capital, and European States, AD 990–1990.* Cambridge, Mass.: Basil Blackwell, 1990.

———. "Demographic Origins of the European Proletariat." In *Proletarianization and Family History,* edited by D. Levine, 1–85.

———. "Flows of Capital and Forms of Industry in Europe, 1500–1900." *Theory and Society* 12 (1983): 123–42.

———. "Migration in Modern European History." In *Human Migration: Patterns and Policies,* edited by W. McNeill and R. Adams, 48–74.

———. "Transplanted Networks." In *Immigration Reconsidered,* edited by V. Yans-McLaughlin, 79–95.

———, ed. *Historical Studies of Changing Fertility.* Princeton: Princeton University Press, 1978.

Tilly, Louise. "Lyonnais, Lombardy, and Labor in Industrialization." In *Proletarians and Protest: The Roots of Class Formation in an Industrializing World,* edited by M. Hanagan and C. Stephenson, 127–47. New York: Greenwood Press, 1986.

———. "Occupational Structure, Women's Work and Demographic Change in Two French Industrial Cities, Anzin and Roubaix, 1872–1906." In *Time, Space and Man: Essays in Microdemography,* edited by J. Sundin and E. Soderlund, 107–32. Atlantic Highlands, N.J.: Humanities Press, 1979.

———. and Miriam Cohen. "Does the Family Have a History? A Review of Theory and Practice in Family History." *Social Science History* 6 (1982): 131–79.

———, and Joan Scott. *Women, Work, and Family.* New York: Holt, Rinehart and Winston, 1978.

———, Joan Scott, and Miriam Cohen. "Women's Work and European Fertility Patterns." *Journal of Interdisciplinary History* 6 (1976): 447–76.

Todd, Emmanuel. *The Explanation of Ideology: Family Structures and Social Systems.* London: Basil Blackwell, 1985.

———. "Mobilité géographique et cycle de vie en Artois et en Toscane au XVIIIe siècle." *Annales: E.S.C.* 30 (1975): 726–44.

Tugault, Yves. *La mésure de la mobilité: Cinq études sur les migrations internes.* Paris: INED, 1973.

Turner, Michael. *Enclosures in Britain, 1750–1830.* London: Macmillan, 1984.

Vandervelde, Emile. *L'exode rural et le retour aux champs.* Paris: Alcan, 1903.

van der Woude, A. M. "Population Developments in the Northern Netherlands (1500–1800) and the Validity of the 'Urban Graveyard' Effect." *Annales de démographie historique* (1982): 55–75.

van de Walle, Etienne. "Illegitimacy in France during the Nineteenth Century." In *Bastardy and Its Comparative History,* edited by P. Laslett, K. Oosterveen, and R. M. Smith, 264–77. Cambridge: Cambridge University Press, 1980.

Vecoli, Rudolph, and Suzanne Sinke, eds. *A Century of European Migrations, 1830–1930.* Champaign, Ill.: University of Illinois Press, forthcoming in 1992.

Vidalenc, Jean. *Les émigrés français, 1789–1825.* Caen: Association des Publications de la Faculté des Lettres et Sciences Humaines de l'Université de Caen, 1963.

Wall, Richard. "The Age of Leaving Home." *Journal of Family History* 3 (1978): 181–202.

Wareing, John. "Migration to London and Transatlantic Emigration of Indentured Servants, 1683–1775." *Journal of Historical Geography* 7 (1981): 356–78.

Watkins, Susan Cotts. *From Provinces into Nations: Demographic Integration in Western Europe, 1870–1960*. Princeton: Princeton University Press, 1991.

———, ed. "Special Issue: Spinsterhood." *Journal of Family History* 9, no. 4 (1984): 310–424.

Weber, Adna. *The Growth of Cities in the Nineteenth Century*. 1899. Reprint. Ithaca, N.Y.: Cornell University Press, 1965.

Werner, Heinz. "Migration and Free Movement of Workers in Western Europe." In *Les Travailleurs Etrangers en Europe Occidentale*, edited by Philippe Bernard, 65–85. Paris: Mouton, 1976.

White, Paul E. "Internal Migration in the Nineteenth and Twentieth Centuries." In *Migrants in Modern France*, edited by P. E. Ogden and P. E. White, 13–33.

———. "Migration Loss and the Residual Community: A Study in Rural France, 1962–1975." In *The Geographical Impact of Migration*, edited by P. E. White and R. Woods, 198–222.

———, and Robert Woods, eds. *The Geographical Impact of Migration*. London: Longman, 1980.

Winter, Jay. *The Great War and the British People*. London: Macmillan, 1986.

Wolf, Eric. *Europe and the People without History*. Berkeley, Calif.: University of California Press, 1982.

Wood, Peter. "Inter-Regional Migration in Western Europe: A Reappraisal." In *Migration and Post-War Europe*, edited by J. Salt and H. Clout, 52–79.

Wrigley, E. Anthony. "A Simple Model of London's Importance in Changing English Society and Economy, 1650–1750." In *Towns in Societies: Essays in Economic History and Historical Sociology*, edited by P. Abrams and E. A. Wrigley. Cambridge: Cambridge University Press, 1978.

———. "The Growth of Population in Eighteenth-Century England: A Conundrum Resolved." *Past and Present* 98 (1983): 121–50.

———, and Roger Schofield. *The Population History of England, 1541–1871: A Reconstruction*. Cambridge, Mass.: Harvard University Press, 1981.

Yans-McLaughlin, Virinia, ed. *Immigration Reconsidered*. New York: Oxford University Press, 1990.

Yaşin, Mehmet. "Gather up the Bales, We Are Going Back." In *Turkish Workers in Europe: An Interdisciplinary Study*, edited by İ. Başgöz and N. Furniss, 175–91.

Yücel, A. Ersan. "Turkish Migrant Workers in the Federal Republic of Germany: A Case Study." In *Migrants in Europe: The Role of Family, Labor, and Politics*, edited by H. Buechler and J.-M. Buechler, 117–48. New York: Greenwood Press, 1987.

Zeller, Olivier. *Les recensements lyonnais de 1597 et 1636: Démographie historique et géographie sociale*. Lyon: Presses Universitaires de Lyon, 1983.

Zolberg, Aristide. "International Migration Policies in a Changing World System." In *Human Migration: Patterns and Policies*, edited by W. McNeill and R. Adams, 241–86.

———, Astri Suhrke, and Sergio Aguayo. *Escape from Violence: Conflict and the Refugee Crisis in the Developing World*. New York: Oxford University Press, 1989.

Index

Africans: enslaved, 11, 17, 64, 223n; Sub-saharan in France. 175. *See also* Algerians Moroccans, Tunesians

Agricultural labor: and migration, 38, 111–14; decline after 1945, 172–73. *See also* Circular migration, Seasonal migration, Harvest migration

Agricultural production, changes in 19th c., 108, 111. *See also* Rural crises

Åkerman, Sune, 16, 151

Algeria and decolonization, 175

Algerians: in France, 165–66, 176–77, 182, 185; in Western Europe, 179, 181

Alsace-Lorraine, 165, 167

Alter, George, 19, 134, 145–46

Altun, Kemal, 162–86

Amiens, 47–48, 51–52, 140–42

Amsterdam, 53–55: population, 25, 29, 50, 54; migrants in, 27, 29, 204n. *See also* Dutch Republic

Arbeitshäus of Berlin, 89

Ardèche, 17

Argentina, migration to and labor demand, 152. *See also* Italians, Spanish

Artois, 33

Attitudes toward migrants, 41, 89–90, 92–93. *See also* Hostility to migrants

Auffay, 61, 69, 74, 116

Aurillac, 60, 81, 84. *See also* Auvergne, French in Spain

Austria-Hungary, 108

Austria, lower, 72–73

Auvergnats in Spain, 28–29, 83–88. *See also* French in Spain

Auvergne, 79, 81–82

Bangladesh and decolonization, 175

Bangladeshis in Britain, 182

Barmen, 132

Beauvais, 52–53

Beauvaisis, 45, 53

Beggars and vagrants: preindustrial, 47–48, 50; in 18th c., 80, 88–90. *See also* Marginal migrants

Belgians: in France, 119, 121–22, 133–35, 164, 166–67; in Germany, 164

Belgium: decline of agricultural labor in, 172; Italians in, 181; population increase, 108–109; population registers, 19; urbanization, 102

Berger, John, 176, 182

Berlin, 46, 95

Berlin Wall, 177, 189

Besne, Maturin, 88–89

"Betterment migration," 47

Bicycle, 104

Bordeaux, 95, 97–99

Bouvier, Jeanne, 102–103, 115, 141

Brazil, migration to and labor demand, 152. *See also* Italians, Portuguese

Britain: ethnic minorities in, 175; interregional migration, 173; population increase, 108–109; urbanization, 102, 173. *See also* England, London

British Empire, 11. *See also* Decolonization

British migration: to 18th-c. North America, 64: overseas and World War I, 164. *See also* Migration to the Americas

Cadiz, 83, 84

Caen, 44, 96

Capital and migration, 8

Career migration, 17–18; preindustrial, 31, 50; 19th-c., 105, 142; 20th-c., 163

Castile, migration systems to, 78

Chain migration, 17–18; preindustrial, 31, 50; 18th-c., 76; 19th-c., 105; to the Americas, 153–54; to Europe, 163: and state regulation of foreigners, 162. *See also* Social organization of migration

Champagne, rural industry in, 71

Chevalier, Louis, 143–44

Children: dispossessed, 37, 47–48, 89; migration and the railroad, 12; in rural service, 33–35; Turks in Germany, 188–89. *See also* Beggars and vagrants, Family migration, Dick Whittington

Chinese in France, 165

Circular migration, 17–18; preindustrial, 31, 40–43, 50; 18th-c., 60, 76–88; 19th-c., 104–105, 120–23, 138; to the Americas, 152; to Europe, 163. *See also* Harvest migration, Seasonal migration, Temporary migration

Circular migration to chain migration: 18th-c., 82; 19th-c., 129–30; 20th-c., 163; foreign migrants in postwar Europe, 182–84; and gender, 99; in historical perspective, 183, 190

Clark, Peter, 22–23, 47, 50, 73

Coerced migration in 20th-c. Europe, 161–70. *See also* Displaced persons, Jews, Refugees, World War I, World War II

Cologne, 139–40

Colonies and migration, 11, 108. *See also* British Empire, Decolonization, Dutch Empire

Colonizing migration, 17

Commercial and service city, 139–42

Commuters to 19th-c. Roubaix, 134
Conscription and migration, 11, 80, 134
Construction trades, 2. *See also* Masons, Seasonal contruction workers, Seasonal migration, Temporary migration
Continuity and change in migration patterns, 5–6, 61, 104
Contract labor, 20th-c., 163
Core and periphery regions, 153
Corsica, 78
Counterurbanization, 1970s, 173
Creuse, migrants to Paris, 128–30. *See also* Limousin, Marche, Masons
Crime and migrants, 144–45. *See also* Marginal migrants
Crop failures, 19th-c., 114–15; and migration to the Americas, 150

Dangers of travel, 43, 81, 85
Danish migration to the U.S., 148
Decolonization and migration, 175
Deindustrialization: and gender, 117–18; and migration, 20, 116–18, 151; rural 19th-c., 115–20, 123–24; social effects of, 117–18
Demographic basin, 47, 98, 128, 138
Demographic crises, 25, 45
Demographic patterns: and migration, 8, 25–26; preindustrial, 25–26, 45. *See also* Fertility, Mortality, Population increase
Denmark, 108–109
Dépôts de mendicité, 89–90
de Vries, Jan, 18, 20, 22, 45
Dingler, Carl, 129, 131
Displaced persons, 162, 169
Divorce and migration in Revolutionary France, 87
Domestic servants: Amiens, 140; Duisburg, 138, 141; Nimes, 140; Paris, 140; Roubaix, 133
Domestic service: distinguishing among migrant women in London, 56–57; importance of as migrant female occupation, 140–41, 143, 145; and mobility, 135
Dowry, migration to pay for, 37
Duisburg, 136–39
Dutch East India Company, 54–55
Dutch Empire, 11, 53–55
Dutch: in Germany, 138, 164; in France, 167; population registers, 19

Early industry: definition, 62, 206n; and demographic patterns, 62, 66, 73–74, 94; and migration, 60, 70–76; towns and, 93. *See also* Rural industry
Earnings of migrants, 81–82, 85, 87. *See also* Remittances
East Anglia, 18th-c. migration systems to, 78
East Elbia: deindustrialization in, 123–24; migration to North America, 124–25; migration to western Germany, 124–26; rural crises in, 123–24. *See also* Poles
Eastern Europeans in France, 1920s, 165–66
Economic stagnation, 1650–1750, 24
Elites, migration of, 47–48, 57, 98
Emigration. *See* International migration; Migration to the Americas
Empire and migration, 11, 67. *See also* Decolonization
Enclosures, in England, 67
England: Huguenots in, 28; migration in southern, 30–31, 39; political economy of, 10; rural service in, 33–35
English migration to North America, 148, 156. *See also* British migration, Migration to the Americas
Ensival, 75
Ethnic minorities in 20th-c. Europe, 175, 184, 190. *See also* Circular to chain migration, Hostility to migrants, Muslims
European Economic Community, 174, 188, 190–91
European marriage pattern, 8

Factory towns. *See* Textile city, Heavy industry city
Family and migration, 14–16, 32–40, 86–87
Family economy, 69
Family migration: to textile cities, 135; and the railroad, 130
Family reunification, 182–84, 187
Family strategies, 14, 37
Farmhands. *See* Rural service
Female agricultural labor, 43, 119, 121–23
Female migrants: in Amsterdam, 54; in Bordeaux, 98–99; French Revolution émigrés, 106; in 17th-c. London, 56–57; Muslims, 185; Portuguese in France, 185; and pregnancy, 16, 91–92; and reproduction, 15; Turks in Germany, 186–88; in Verviers, 134. *See also* Gender, Domestic service, Illegitimacy, Marginal migrants
Female migration, 14–15; to the Americas, 153–54; and chain migration, 129–30; to the 19th-c. city, 130–31; and the railroad, 12; and the rural exodus, 171–72; and rural industry, 39; unanswered questions about, 143; visibility of, 80, 105
Fertility decline, 170
Fertility in 19th-c. cities: commercial and administrative, 139–40; heavy industry, 136; textile, 135. *See also* Population increase, Urban populations
Finland, 108–109
Flanders, rural industry in, 70
Flemish in Roubaix, 133. *See also* Belgians
Foreign migrants in postwar Europe, 174–89; and historical patterns, 174–75
Foundling homes, 89

France: decline of agricultural labor, 173; ethnic minorities in, 175; foreign migrants in postwar, 177; interregional migrations in, 173; migration and urban growth, 131; political economy, 10; population, 108–109; recruitment of foreign labor, 164–66; refugees in, 165–67; sedentary preindustrial model, 23; urbanization, 102, 173. *See also* French, French Revolution

François, René, 89, 92

Frankfurt, 27–28, 44–46

French: and migration to the Americas, 149; in North America, 64; in Spain, 28–29, 60, 83–88, 106

French Revolution: émigrés, 105–106, 213; and French in Spain, 88; and fear of vagrants, 90; and migration, 105–106

Friesland, Germans in, 41–43

Fronde, 28

Galicia, Austrian: migration from, 155; migration to Germany, 124–25. *See also* Poles

Galicia, Spanish: migration from, 149; migration to Spain, 78, 128

Gender and marginality, 90–91, 145

Gender and migration, 14–15; to the Americas, 153–54; to Bordeaux, 98–99; to 19th-c. cities, 129–31, 137; preindustrial, 36, 39, 49–50; and return migration, 156; and social organization of migration, 15

Geneva, 28, 95, 176

Germanization policies and migration, 150

German migration: from central and Eastern Europe, 169, 177, 189–90; to North America, 64, 148; to the Netherlands, 29–31, 54; refugees, 169; return from the U.S., 156

Germany: foreign migrants in 20th-c., 177, 181, 184–89; decline of agricultural labor in, 172; migration data, 19; population, 108–109; refugees in, 165; state regulation of foreign labor, 125, 161, 164–66; urbanization, 102, 173; wartime foreign labor in, 164, 168

Gesinde. *See* Rural service

Gleaning, 80

Global labor force, 104, 149–53, 156–57

Global perspective on migration, 7, 155

Gould, J. D., 149, 151

Great Depression and migration, 162, 166, 172

Great Fear, 90

Greece and the EEC, 174

Greeks in Western Europe, 177, 181

Guerre, Martin, 38, 40, 84

Gutmann, Myron, 20, 67–68, 75

Handloom weavers, 116. *See also* Deindustrialization

Harvest migration, 40–43, 119, 122. *See also*

Circular migration, Seasonal migration, Temporary migration

Heavy industry city, 136–39

Hochstadt, Steve, 19, 20, 44, 112

Holland: Germans in, 41–43; migration systems to, 78. *See also* North Sea System, Netherlands

Hollandsgänger, 29, 41–42, 182

Homestead Act of 1862, 152

Hostility to foreign migrants, 183 188–89; Turks in Germany, 188–89

Household structure and migration, 32–37

Huguenots, 27–29, 48

"Hybrid societies," 68–70, 75

Illegitimacy: and deindustrialization, 188; and 18th-c. female migrants, 91–92; and 19th-c. female migrants, 145–46

Immigration. *See* International migration

Impartible inheritance and migration, 36–37

Indentured servants and London, 55, 58

India and decolonization, 175

Indians in Great Britain, 175, 181–82, 189

Indigenous labor force, European, 173–74, 176

Indochinese in France, 165

Industrial cities. *See* Heavy industry city, Textile city

Industrialization: and migration, 20, 126–39; rethinking of, 103–104

Infant mortality, preindustrial, 45

Inheritance: and preindustrial migration, 36–37; and proletarianization, 67

International migrations: from Europe, 64, 104, 147–58; to Western Europe, 161–63; within Europe, 31, 40–43, 54, 104, 127, 164–70

International labor force in 19th-c. cities, 104, 127, 133, 138–39

Interregional migrations, 1960s, 173

Irish migration: to England, 120–21, 181; to the U.S., 147–48; return from the U.S., 156; traditions of, 151–52

Italian migration: interregional, 173; to France, 166–67, 177; to Germany, 128, 138, 177, 181–82; and railroad construction, 121; return from the Americas, 156; traditions of, 152; to South America, 148; to Switzerland, 176, 178, 181; systems in Italy, 78; to the U.S., 148; and urban growth, 131

Italy: in EEC, 174; population increase, 108–109; preindustrial cities, 25; population registers, 19; urbanization, 173

Jackson, James Jr., 19, 137–38

Jewish migration: to Amsterdam, 27, 29; to Palestine, 169; from Spain, 27–28; to the U.S., 148; as refugees in the 1930s, 167; return from the U.S., 156

Jews, persecution of, 27, 150, 168; deaths in World War II, 168–69
Journeymen tramping, 94–95

Kin networks and migration. *See* Chain migration, Circular migration
Kurdistan, 186
Kussmaul, Ann, 33, 112

Labor demand and migration, 7–8, 41, 46, 99, 152, 163–64
Laissez-faire policies and migration, 107
Land ownership and migration, 7, 37–39
Languedoc, 71, 116
Leningrad, 12
Liège, 71
Life cycle and migration, 13, 137–38
Lille, 46
Limousin: rural service in, 33; masons in Paris, 129–30. *See also* Creuse, Masons, Seasonal construction workers
Lippe, 128
Lithuania, 27
Local migration, 16–18, 30–32
Local perspective on migration, 7, 155
Lodève, 116–17
London, 55–58; attraction of, 55–56; population, 25, 50, 102; migrations to, 40, 55–56, 78
Louis XIV, 28–29
Lucassen, Jan, 20, 42, 72
Luxemburg, 167
Lyon, 26–27, 71

Madrid: French in, 29; migration systems to, 78
Male migration: impact on women, 86–87
Marche, Haute: masons from, 49, 80; marriage records and migration, 36
Marginal migrants: 18th-c., 88–93; 19th-c., 143–46; lack of social support, 89–90, 92–93, 145–46; female, and sexuality, 91–92
"Maritime drain," 55
Marriage: patterns of, 66, 73–74; and migration to London, 56–57
Marriage migration, 35–36, 172
Marseille: population turnover, 95; criminals in, 144
Masons in 19th-c. cities, 128. *See also* Auvergne, Marche, Seasonal contruction workers
Mass migrations to the Americas, 152–53
Maszkienice, 155
Mayett, Joseph, 22, 33–35, 70, 112
Measurement of migration. *See* Migration data
Mediterranean plain, migration systems to, 78–79
Middle East, migration to, 190

Migrants: occupations of, 14, 41, 79–80, 84, 142, 176; and urban growth, 94–95, 131, 135–37, 140; and urban economies, 131–42
Migration, 1–2, 5–7, 9; in preindustrial period, 2, 22–59; in age of early industry, 3–4, 60–101; in 19th c., 4, 102–60; in 20th c., 5, 161–91; to the Americas, 147–60, 155, 158, 164; to Australia and New Zealand, 147; definition of, 18; and the family, 32–34; free, 160–61; impact on home society, 86–87; process of, 5; "rules" of, 18–19; to the U.S., 147–48
Migration data and sources, 18–20; apprenticeship registers, 18–20; and the 18th-c. city, 95; censuses, 18–20, 130; church court records, 38; from backward projection technique, 20, 75; citizenship lists, 18–19, 44; and gender, 80, 130–31; German, 19–20, 128, 139; lack of, 23, 44, 47; marriage records, 36, 44; Napoleonic survey, 18, 76–79; Parish records, 18–20, 36, 38; population registers, 19–20, 128, 134
Migration rates, 22–23, 31, 44, 45, 128, 134, 172
Migration streams, 16, 81, 84, 97–99, 133, 134–35, 138, 141, 149, 154–55
Migration systems. *See* Systems of migration
Minden-Ravensberg, 70
Mixed economies, 68–70
Modernization and migration, 5–6
Moen, 33–35
Moors, 28
Moroccans in Europe, 177, 180
Mortality, 45, 66, 108–109, 170
Motives for migration to the Americas, 149–50
Muslims in Europe, 185, 187, 190. *See also* Ethnic minorities

Napoleonic Empire and migration, 11, 88, 105–107
Naumoff, Peter and Anna, 162, 169
Nazi policies, 167–68
Netherlands: foreign migrants in, 181; Germans in, 29–31, 41–43; Huguenots in, 28–29; population, 108–109; urbanization, 102
Net migration rates, 206–209n
Networks among migrants, 16. *See also* Chain migration, Circular migration, Social organization of migration, Systems of migration
New Commonwealth and decolonization, 175
Nîmes, 140–42
Nordic Labor Market, 181
Nordlingen, 45
Normandy, rural industry in, 70–71
North Africans in France, 165. *See also* Algerians, Moroccans, Tunesians

North Sea System, 42. *See also* Germans in the Netherlands
Norwegian migration to North America, 148–49
Norwich, 25, 47–48, 51–52
Nuptiality. *See* Marriage, Single migrants

Occupation. *See* Migrants, occupations of

Pakistanis in Britain, 175, 181, 182
Paris: domestic service in, 140; harvest migrations to feed, 40; illegitimacy and migration to, 146; migrants in, 143–44; population, 102, 139; public works construction, 49
Paris basin, migration systems to, 78
Pays de Caux, 60, 74
Peasantry and migration, 37–39. *See also* Land ownership and migration
Personal contacts and migration to the Americas, 151–52, 154–55
"Personal information field," 16
Plague, 45, 66
Poitrineau, Abel, 83, 86
Poland, Jews in 16th-c., 27
Poles: in France, 166; in Germany, 164, 167–68; return migration from the U.S., 156; sugar beet harvesters, 122; in the U.S., 148; to western Germany, 124–26, 139. *See also* East Elbia
Political economy and migration, 10–11; France and England, 51–52, 68
Poor laws, 48
Poor, migration of, 14, 47–48, 89, 173–74
Population increase: 18th-c., 61, 64–68, 82–83, 88, 94; 19th-c., 108–109; 20th-c., 170; and migration, 110–11, 150
Population pressure and migration to the Americas, 155
Portugal: and the EEC, 174, 184–85; Jews expelled from, 27
Portuguese migration: to France, 165, 184–85; to Germany, 177; return from the U.S., 156; to Latin America, 148; to Madrid, 128; traditions, 149, 151; to northwestern Europe, 178
Potato, 108; famine, 114, 147, 150
Po Valley, migration systems to, 78
Preindustrial: defined, 23, 197–98n; migration, 30–43, 58–59; patterns persisting into the 18th c., 61
Primogeniture and migration, 36–37
Proletarianization, 42, 66–68, 109–10
Proletarians and migration, 7, 20, 82–83, 110–11, 150
Prostitution and migration, 145
Protestants, 28, 48, 141. *See also* Huguenots, Puritans

Protoindustry, 62, 206n. *See also* Early industry, Rural industry
Prussia. *See* East Elbia
Public works construction and migration, 12, 49. *See also* Seasonal construction workers, Railroad
Puritans, 28

Racism, 175–76, 183. *See also* Hostility to migrants
Railroad: construction and migration, 121; impact on migration, 12, 43, 121–22, 130
Ravenstein, Arthur, 18–19
Reconquista, 28, 83, 88
Recruitment of migrants, 124, 152, 154, 225n
Refugees: 17th-c., 48; 20th-c., 162–63, 165–69; and decolonization, 175
Region and migration, 9–10, 127, 133, 143, 150
Rehbein, Franz, 113
Religious persecution and migration, 11–12, 26–28, 149. *See also* Huguenots, Jews, Protestants
Religious wars in France, 23, 26
Remittances from the Americas, 157
Return migration from the Americas, 147, 155–58
Revolt of the Netherlands, 23, 26
Rome, 46, 78. *See also* Italy
Roubaix, 132–36
Rouen, 95–97, 118
Ruhr cities, 133
Rural crises, 19th-c., 103, 111–20
Rural exodus, 163, 171–73
Rural industry, 52, 61–62, 68, 70–72, 119, 208n; and migration, 60–61, 68–69, 72–74; persistence of, 132–34; women workers in, 69–70; vulnerability of workers, 75–76, 100–101. *See also* Early industry
Rural migration, 1–2, 31–43, 94, 110–11. *See also* Circular migration, Harvest migration, Rural service, Seasonal migration
Rural population, 25, 64, 103, 218n
Rural service, 2, 22, 32–35, 111–12, 200n
Rural-urban interdependence, 13, 61, 72, 93, 96, 99
Rural-urban migration, 20th-c., 163–70. *See also* Circular migration, Chain migration, Migrants and urban growth
Russian: migration to the U.S., 147; refugees, 165

Salez, Antoine, 60, 69, 83
Santerre, Mémé, 119, 132, 161, 164, 170
Santiago, 83
Saxony, proletarianization in, 66–67, 109–10
Scandinavian sending areas, 19th-c., 149
Scottish highlands, 149
"Seaborne mortality," 55

Seasonal construction workers, 49, 128
Seasonal migration, 119–22. *See also* Circular migration, Harvest migration
Seasonal urban work, 128–29
Sedentary historical populations, image of, 1, 22–23, 31, 36–38, 44
Selectivity of migration, 13
Sending areas, conditions in, 41–42, 79, 97, 149, 150–51, 185–86, 176–77
Serfdom, end of, 104
Servants in husbandry. *See* Rural service
Settlement laws of 1662, 33–34, 48
Sex ratios, urban, 46–47, 132, 136–37, 139
Sharecropper migration, 38–39
Shepshed, 73–74
Silesia, 73
Silk crisis, 19th-c., 114–15
Single migrants, 32–35, 129, 137
Slavery, abolition of, and migration, 107, 223n, 225n
Slaves. *See* Africans, enslaved
Social mobility, 67, 94, 171
Social organization of migration, 15–18
Société Chinchon, 84–85, 106
Soiron, 75
Souden, David, 20, 56, 73
Spain: and EEC, 174; Empire, 23, 28; expulsion of Jews, 27–28; French in, 28–29, 83–88
Spanish migration: to France, 165–67, 177; to Geneva, 176; interregional, 173; to Latin America, 148; return migration from the Americas, 156; to northwestern Europe, 178
State, 193–94n; German regulation of migrants, 125, 161, 164–66; and migration, 10–12, 107–108; Spanish regulation of migrants, 83; U.S.S.R., 165; 20th-c., 161–65, 175, 183–84
Strasbourg, 67
Subsistence migration, 47, 88
Suburbs, 13, 96–97
Sugar beet: harvest migrations, 112, 119, 122; production, 217n
Sweden: decline of agricultural labor, 172; population registers, 19; urbanization, 173
Swedish migration: to the U.S., 148; return from the U.S., 157
Swiss: in North America, 64; mercenaries, 11
Switzerland, foreign migrants in, 180
Systems of migration, 12, 17, 40, 104; to the Americas, 153; French in Spain, 28–29, 83–88; Germans in the Netherlands, 29–31, 41–43; Portuguese in France, 184–85; Turks in Germany, 185; seasonal, 76–79, 118–20

Taxation and migration, 10–11. *See also* State and migration, Political economy

Temporary migration: to the Americas, 155–57; to cities, 12–13, 98, 103, 127–29, 172. *See also* Circular migration
Textile city: 17th and 18th-c., 24, 51–53, 47–48, 93–95; 19th-c., 132–36
Textile villages, 18th-c., 74–75
Thimister, 75
Thirty Years' War, 2, 23–24, 28, 45
Thresher, 113–14
Tilly, Charles, 7, 16, 20, 82
Transoceanic migration. *See* Migration to the Americas
Transportation and migration, steamship, 152. *See also* Railroad
Travel of migrant groups, 41–43, 80–81. *See also* Dangers of travel
Tunesians in Europe, 177, 180–81
Turkey and the EEC, 188
Turks: in Germany, 177, 181–82, 184–89; in Western Europe, 178–79, 181
Turnover in urban populations: preindustrial, 49–50, 54–55; 18th-c., 95, 96, 99; 19th-c., 127–28, 135, 137, 139, 141–42; 20th-c., 170

Ulster, 70
United States, regulation of foreign migrants, 162. *See also* Migration to the Americas
Urban growth, 8, 12–13; 17th-c., 24, 50; 18th-c., 63–64, 93; 19th-c., 102, 126–27, 132, 136, 139–40
Urbanization, 8, 12–13; 18th-c., 93; 19th-c., 102–103, 126–31; 20th-c., 172–74; and migration, 8, 43–58, 93–99, 127–43
Urban mortality: preindustrial, 44–46, 55–56; 19th-c., 131
Urban-urban migration, preindustrial, 48, 50

Valencia, 84
Valets de ferme. See Rural service
Venice, 46
Versailles, 49
Verviers, 75, 93, 134, 145–46
Vienna, 72

Wages of migrants, 28, 40–41, 83, 134
Walloons, 48, 133
Wars, 23–24, 26–28, 64, 107, 160–61, 167–70; and migration, 11–12, 161, 165; and the preindustrial city, 45
Wartime labor in Germany, 168
Weavers. *See* Handloom weavers
West Indians in Britain, 175, 181
Westphalia: 17th–18th-c., 41–42; 19th-c., 150–51
Westphalians in the Netherlands. *See* Germans in the Netherlands
Whittington, Dick, 57–58

Wine, phylloxera crisis, 115
Women: and deindustrialization, 116–18; impact of male migration on, 86–87; in rural industry, 69–70; in urban populations, 46. *See also* Female migrants, Female migration, Gender and migration
Workhouses, 89
World War I, 5, 160–62, 164–65

World War II, 162, 163, 167–70
Würzburg, 49–50

Yugoslavs in Western Europe, 176–77, 179, 181

Zurich, 46

LESLIE PAGE MOCH is Associate Professor of History at the University of Michigan—Flint, where she teaches European social history. She is author of *Paths to the City: Regional Migration in Nineteenth-Century France* and editor (with Gary Stark) of *Essays on the Family and Historical Change*.